TREASURES OLD AND NEW

TREASURES OLD AND NEW

Interpretations of "Spirit-Baptism"
in the Charismatic Renewal Movement

Henry I. Lederle

HENDRICKSON
PUBLISHERS
PEABODY, MASSACHUSETTS 01961-3473

TABLE OF CONTENTS

PREFACE

Like all good theology, charismatic theology remains contentious. In the following pages the reader will find an attempt to reflect systematically on the central teaching of charismatic theology, the doctrine of "Spirit-baptism" and the differing interpretations given to it.

My interest in the field is of a biographical nature. In January 1980 I had a vivid charismatic experience which caught me unawares theologically. My doctrinal apple-cart was overturned, and I spent a year or two trying to get my bearings again. I had been blessed "right out of my socks" and needed time to digest what God was now doing in my life and in my family. I had found a new dimension to my faith, which I experienced as deeply meaningful, integrative, and transformational. Coming from a Reformed background with both evangelical and ecumenical roots, I sought an acceptable interpretive framework for the fresh upwelling of doxology in my heart. My seminary training seemed to have left me in the lurch. As I started charting my own course I discovered that a variety of contemporary theologians were grappling with the same issue, and I wanted to classify their differing interpretations and develop my own perspective. In time that endeavor led to my completing a doctoral dissertation on "Spirit-baptism" at the University of South Africa in Pretoria – the institution at which I have been teaching for the last decade. This book is based largely on that study.

I came to realize that centuries of Western rationalism, individualism and naturalism had robbed the Christian church of many of its "old treasures." I found that I needed to delve deeper into my heritage as an ecumenical Christian. I rediscovered the "mystical" tradition in Christianity, and in my own Calvinist background. I could identify with Calvin's teaching on the Christian life and was overwhelmed by the beauty of the way in which the Westminster divines described the main purpose of our lives, namely: to glorify God and to enjoy him forever.

In the global spiritual awakening of the sixties and seventies "old treasures" were being rediscoverd; but at the same time many unacceptable and superficial theological theories were being constructed and imposed on the renewal Movement in the churches, leading to experience and event-centered faith, spiritual elitism, and schism. The search for a meaningful interpretation of "Spirit-baptism" had become crucial, and I tried all the various options that were being presented. In a sense I have now come full spiral (rather than full circle!)

in my understanding of the charismatic movement. What I mean by that will become clear from the following chapters in which the neo-Pentecostal position is gradually superseded by attempts at a full integration of the legitimate elements of the renewal into historic Christianity. I believe this entails the recognition of the deeply experiential nature of normal Christian living and an ongoing openness towards an expectancy of the full range of charismatic gifts as a present-day reality which the Holy Spirit freely distributes in the congregations.

It is with deep gratitude that this study is being presented. Thanks be to the triune God–Father, Son and Holy Spirit–for its completion! The enterprise has brought me much joy from beginning to end.

I am also grateful towards Hendrickson Publishers for their unhesitating enthusiasm with this project, and I wish especially to thank Mr. Patrick Alexander for his competent assistance. I also wish to acknowledge with gratitude the financial contributions of the University of South Africa and the Human Sciences' Research Council towards the initial research which I undertook.

In conclusion I wish to *dedicate* this book to two very different South African Pentecostal leaders whom I value and honor for their unusual and unique combination of charismatic spirituality and unrelenting ecumenical fervor.

First I honor the memory of *David du Plessis*, that indomitable Pentecostal pioneer who had the conviction to proclaim the message of forgiveness (70 x 7) worldwide and to venture across so many ecclesiastical barriers and boundaries. He died as this book was being prepared for publication.

Secondly I wish to pay tribute to the youthful and courageous general secretary of the South African Council of Churches, *Frank Chikane*, a saintly radical and an unwaivering advocate of social justice and liberation whose radiant faith shines forth in the midst of political harassment and suffering.

University of South Africa
Pretoria
Pentecost 1988

INTRODUCTION

This study is being written within an ecumenical context. In the sixties and seventies of this century a new religious awakening made its influence felt in Christianity. The charismatic renewal movement spread across the globe in less than a decade reaching all five continents, most Christian denominations of Catholic, Protestant, and Orthodox heritage, and the lives of some sixty million people. This amazing development has been related elsewhere[1] and will not be repeated here. The renewal movement has brought forth a fledgling charismatic theology–especially in the eighties. It is this "renewal theology" that presents its challenges to the broader theological scholarship of the Christian church.

The focus of this study is on one of the aspects of charismatic theology– perhaps the most important distinctive aspect, namely the doctrine of Spirit-baptism. My approach will be to analyze the wide variety of views on this topic critically while at the same time to ask the question: What can be learned from this doctrine in its various forms?

An analysis of this nature is of great importance to systematic theology as an ecumenical enterprise. Only in this century has the challenge of ecumenism made any significant inroads into the life of the Christian church and its theology. Yet two of the major movements in Christianity in the twentieth century, Pentecostalism at the turn of the century and the charismatic movement in the last two and a half decades, have brought forth theological insights which have not been readily integrated into the fabric of Christian theology. Neither the original ecumenical approach of early Pentecostalism, nor its later divisiveness, nor the issue of the ecumenicity of structures are of interest here. I wish to address the challenge presented by the charismatic movement to ecumenical thinking on the level of systematic theology. The major distinctive doctrines of the charismatic movement certainly are Spirit-baptism and the charisms of the Holy Spirit. With the ebbing of the theory of dispensationalism in modern post–World War II theology–mainly due to renewed interest in biblical studies, which questioned the intricate structures imposed on history by fully fledged Scofield dispensationalism–the Christian church became open, at least in theory, to the functioning of the full range of New Testament charismata. Spirit-baptism, however, presents a more serious challenge and raises many questions: Could the church be enriched by this experience or should it be relegated to the "lunatic fringe" on the periphery of Christianity?

How should the biblical argument for this doctrine be evaluated? What is one to say of the experience attested to by so many people? Is this experience correctly termed "baptism in the Holy Spirit"? Are there two groups or classes of Christians: those who have received Spirit-baptism and those who have not? How does Spirit-baptism relate to baptism, conversion, or confirmation? And, especially, does the Christian life have a two-stage pattern? These are the types of questions that an ecumenical analysis of charismatic theology raises and which will be discussed in this book.

In chapter 1 a historical survey will be given. I shall not attempt to write here a history of the charismatic manifestations in the history of the church. It has, in fact, become popular in charismatic circles to heap up analogies from bygone ages in order to justify the charismatic experience. Chapter 1 will mainly survey the basic issue of the two-stage pattern of Christian experience – what has come to be called the theology of subsequence. In reality, this is the major ecumenical stumbling block in charismatic theology. Some forerunners of this Pentecostal view will be discussed, from the seventeenth century onwards.

Chapters 2, 3, and 4 deal with the interpretations of Spirit-baptism given within the writings of the charismatic movement. The neo-Pentecostal interpretation is distinguished from the sacramental interpretation; other theories involving "completed initiation" and the fullness of the Spirit are also discussed.

Chapter 5 presents an alternative interpretation of Spirit-baptism which enables the full integration of the legitimate elements of Spirit-baptism into the evolving enterprise of ecumenical theology.

The limitations of this study should be taken seriously. No attempt is made to analyze and criticize all of charismatic theology. It would be an interesting study to survey and assess e.g. the soteriology, eschatology, anthropology, ecclesiology, even the pneumatology of charismatic theology. It would be fruitful, too, to bring to bear on charismatic theology and charismatic churches the results of psychological, anthropological, and sociological research. Much has already been done along these lines.[2] In this context, however, the approach is that of systematic theology – the major task being the categorizing and assessing of a great variety of contemporary writers who have contributed to the growing structure of charismatic theology's teaching on Spirit-baptism and the developing of an interpretive model for this experience. By taking such a systematic approach a contribution can be made to ecumenical theology.

An initial word needs to be said about terminology, although the meaning of these terms will become clearer when used in their contexts. It is always necessary to try to distinguish the concepts Pentecostal and charismatic. In this study "Pentecostal" refers to the teaching of the classical Pentecostal denominations which historically emanate from the revivals in Appalachia, Topeka, Kansas, and especially, Asuza St., Los Angeles, at the turn of the century. Examples of these denominations are, in America, the Assemblies of God, the various Church of God denominations, the Pentecostal Holiness Church, the International Church of the Foursquare Gospel, the United Pentecostal Church; in Britain, the Elim Pentecostal Church; and in South Africa, the Apostolic Faith Mission Church. Pentecostal theology will refer to the theology of these groups which eventually formed separate denominations and a distinctive kind of theology.

I am aware that "Pentecostal" is sometimes used to denote "not a denomination but an experience." Nevertheless an experience needs to be interpreted, and the Pentecostal interpretation of Spirit-baptism generally correlates with the views of Christians belonging to Pentecostal denominations.

The word "charismatic" refers in this study to the views of those Christians who became part of the renewal movement which started in the late fifties and early sixties in the mainline denominations in the USA. They usually did not form their own new denominations but remained within established Protestant, Catholic, and Orthodox churches. Theologically they represent a variety of reinterpretations of classical Pentecostal positions. The concept charismatic also includes a large number of non-denominational charismatics. In the eighties a new phenomenon is surfacing—some independent and non-denominational charismatics have started developing new charismatic denominations. This underlines the fact that the most useful distinction between Pentecostal and charismatic is whether they have their roots, as it were, in 1906 or 1960, not whether they have formed their own denominational structures. It has become necessary to distinguish between mainline or denominational charismatics (which really include the Catholic and Orthodox) and non-denominational or independent charismatics.

A complicating factor is that theologically speaking some non-denominational charismatics have views which are very close to those of classical Pentecostals. However, because they have not written much theology they will not be referred to often; and since their views are not innovative but close to those of early Pentecostalism, they do not necessarily merit much discussion.

One should furthermore be aware that in the early stages of the charismatic movement, before the word charismatic had become pervasive, some Anglican and, especially, Catholic charismatics used the terminology "Catholic or Anglican Pentecostals." Cashing in on the popularity of the term, some classical Pentecostals also started describing themselves or their churches as charismatic. Hopefully the terms Pentecostal and charismatic will become clearer in the specific usage and context of the following chapters.

It is also necessary to delineate the aims of this study in contrast to some other recent publications. Over against the South African Pentecostal leader, F. P. Möller's book, *Die diskussie oor die charismata soos wat dit in die Pinksterbeweging geleer en beoefen word* [The discussion about the charismata as taught and practiced in the Pentecostal movement], this study focuses on Spirit-baptism rather than the charisms, and on the charismatic movement rather than on Pentecostalism. The same applies to Larry Hart's *A Critique of Ameri-*

can Pentecostal Theology. Although he deals with the charismatic movement, his scope is not limited to Spirit-baptism, and he gives much attention to classical Pentecostalism.

Two Lutheran theologians, Carter Lindberg and Tormod Engelsviken, have produced excellent studies, Lindberg from a Lutheran confessional stance and Engelsviken from a Lutheran charismatic viewpoint.[3] In contrast to these publications, this study wishes to be ecumenical in dealing with charismatic theologians across the denominational board. Engelsviken's work has much the same goal of analyzing differing charismatic approaches but he limits his investigations to Norway. Several studies focusing specifically on the Catholic charismatic renewal exist as well.

That leaves us with the two major contributions specifically on Spirit-baptism, namely Harold Hunter's *Spirit-Baptism. A Pentecostal Alternative*, and Lucida Schmieder's *Geisttaufe. Ein Beitrag zur neueren Glaubensgeschichte* [Spirit-baptism. A contribution to the more recent history of the faith]. The distinctive nature of these studies needs to be clearly delineated. Hunter is from a Pentecostal (Church of God of Prophecy) background but adopts a broader perspective, especially regarding sanctification. His study gives particular attention to biblical exegesis from Pauline, Lucan, and Johannine literature and the history of doctrine from the first century to the beginning of the twentieth century. He then goes on to discuss salvation and sanctification in a manner particularly relevant to Pentecostals from a "three-stage" background. (This concept will be clarified later in 1.2.4.1). He affirms the Pentecostal approach of a distinct work of the Spirit subsequent to one's Christian beginnings. The ultimacy or event-centeredness of this work of the Spirit is not sufficiently clarified so that Hunter's view cannot be clearly contrasted with the findings of this study. This is probably because Hunter does not give detailed attention to all the different charismatic approaches in his systematic section, focusing rather on the more "Pentecostal" issue of sanctification. Schmieder, a German Benedictine sister with years of pastoral experience in Brazil, writes a "Glaubensgeschichte" [history of the faith]. She investigates the concept Spirit-baptism in the sixteenth to twentieth-century revivals, discussing inter alia: Hubmaier, Zwingli, Schwenckfeld, Wesley, John Fletcher, Asa Mahan, Finney, Boardman, Moody, Torrey, the Keswick movement, Jonathan Paul, etc. She also deals with American Pentecostalism, the Welsh revival, and the German "Gemeinschaftsbewegung" [community movement—with a strong focus on evangelism] and experience with early Pentecostalism before coming to the charismatic movement among Protestants and Catholics. Her study seems to peak with the German Catholic approach of Heribert Mühlen and the official recognition that the Roman Catholic bishops gave to the document "Erneuerung der Kirche aus dem Geist Gottes" [Renewal of the church through the Spirit of God]. The concept of renewal in the Spirit as developed here is seen as a correction of the concept Spirit-baptism. This approach is discussed in chapter 4, especially in 4.12.

From this brief analysis of the works of Hunter and Schmieder it will be quite clear that the area of overlapping between these studies and mine is minimal. Hunter, in fact, covers quite different ground and Schmeider, who does discuss the views of various charismatic theologians, does so relatively briefly and only as part of a much broader historical survey, working from a Roman Catholic perspective.

One result of the fact that these two monographs on Spirit-baptism are already in existence was that this present study could shift its focus from the exegetical and historical areas and concentrate on a systematic evaluation of the doctrine of Spirit-baptism. Naturally more work needs to be done in exegesis, and denominational charismatics would generally differ from much of Hunter's analysis – as well as in the history of doctrine. Nevertheless, the historical work of Hunter and Schmieder has laid a firm foundation for further research. When this study was first conceived, a major chapter on historical developments was planned (since I am particularly interested in the history of doctrine), but as the voluminous nature of the writings on Spirit-baptism became apparent, the decision was made to work on a classification and evaluation of the various contributions to a charismatic theology on Spirit-baptism from the vantage point of systematic theology and within an ecumenical setting. The importance of such an undertaking is underscored by the fact that no such critical classification has been attempted up to this point. In the final analysis my Protestant and Reformed roots will be apparent, but the scope and approach of the analysis is ecumenical, as has been explained above.

Chapters 2, 3, and 4 discuss the views on Spirit-baptism of some forty theologians and church leaders. In order to gain some perspective on the charismatic movement as a whole, the rest of this introduction will offer a brief overview of the various groupings found in this movement. This is not a survey of the development of the movement but an update on the various sections of the charismatic renewal with a view to placing the theologians to be discussed in their particular contexts. This outline will deal only with people in the charismatic movement. The pre-charismatic phases, including Pentecostalism, will be dealt with in chapter 1.

Apart from differentiating the various theological views on Spirit-baptism, the only significant ways to group all the various branches of the charismatic movement are according to denomination and geography. One can basically divide the charismatic renewal into three structural groups: (1) those in established church structures, also called the denominational charismatics. They form the overwhelming majority in the charismatic renewal. (2) Those who are involved in sodalities or parachurch structures. Individually they often maintain membership in their particular denominations. (3) Those who have formed new, independent structures, often called the non-denominational charismatics.

The last two groups will be dealt with first because they can be discussed very briefly. The parachurch or transdenominational charismatic groups are bodies like Youth with a Mission, the Christian Broadcasting Network, and Oral Roberts Evangelistic Association. Interestingly enough all three of these have set up their own universities.

The Full Gospel Business Men's Fellowship International is another para-church structure influential in charismatic circles but, as with Teen Challenge International, it is really more classical Pentecostal than charismatic in the theo-logical sense of these words. Melodyland Christian Center also had a School of Theology but is closer to an independent non-denominational structure than to a sodality. The transdenominational groups have not produced much theology. The writings on Spirit-baptism are almost exclusively of a Pentecostal or neo-Pentecostal nature. At CBN University in Virginia Beach, Virginia, the Bible department takes a Pentecostal/neo-Pentecostal line. J. Rodman Williams, a Presbyterian charismatic, now teaches there. He was previously President of Melodyland School of Theology in Anaheim, California. At Oral Roberts University in Tulsa, Oklahoma, there are several competent theolo-gians working within the charismatic tradition. Among those who have written on Spirit-baptism are Howard Ervin, a Baptist who has a neo-Pentecostal approach, and Bob Tuttle, a Methodist, who is discussed in chapter 4. He has a more integrated, Methodist denominational approach. He has since moved from Oral Roberts to Garrett Theological Seminary in Chicago, Illinois.

The independent or non-denominational charismatics present a wide variety theologically. Unfortunately they have not produced much in the way of theological reflection on Spirit-baptism. This grouping includes the many local independent churches as well as the new charismatic denominations such as the Rhema Bible Church, Vineyard Christian Fellowships, Maranatha Ministries, etc. Although these latter groups may not conceive of them-selves as "denominations," they have a translocal church-planting ministry and are, in fact, creating new denominational structures. Theologically there are three main approaches here: the "discipleship," "restoration," and "faith" movements.

The "discipleship-submission" teaching (shepherding) is associated with Fort Lauderdale, Florida, Mobile, Alabama, and leaders such as Charles Simpson, Bob Mumford, Derek Prince, Don Basham, and Ern Baxter. These men used to be organized as the Christian Growth Ministries. In 1975–1976 the Fort Lauderdale discipleship controversy rocked the charismatic world. There were differing views on "shepherding" and discipleship. The issue was later basically resolved after several joint meetings by those from opposing camps. Not much is written specifically on Spirit-baptism, but the view of Don Basham was chosen as being representative of the neo-Pentecostal posi-tion. I don't know of any writings from the whole independent charismatic grouping which do not take the neo-Pentecostal line.

The restoration movement has various expressions. In chapter 1, Arthur Wallis's position on "coming out" of traditional Christian churches will be discussed in an excursus. He represents the so-called British House Church movement. Leaders such as Bryn Jones, Terry Virgo and restoration type covenant communities in the USA, such as Silver Spring Community near Washington, D.C. and its affiliates, all seem to take the neo-Pentecostal line on Spirit-baptism.

This is also the case with the "Faith" movement represented by leaders such as Kenneth Hagin, Tulsa, Oklahoma, and Kenneth Copeland, Fort Worth, Texas. The Rhema Bible Church of Hagin is already an international "denomination." It has a clearly distinctive theology which is described by terms such as "faith-formula" and the "prosperity gospel." Many charismatics – denominational and independent – as well as many Pentecostals are highly critical of this teaching. The theological roots of this view are to be found in E. W. Kenyon.[4] The distinctive approach of the "Faith" groups does not alter their neo-Pentecostal view on Spirit-baptism and so it will not be dealt with in this study.

Just before continuing with the major grouping, the denominational charismatics (and this includes all the churches, even those like Catholic, Orthodox, and Anglican, which do not normally use the word denomination to describe themselves) a brief word needs to be said about covenant communities. Several hundred charismatic communities are found in the world. Especially those in the U.S. have been influential in theological reflection through magazines such as *New Covenant*. Several leaders in these communities have also been active in publishing books and articles on Spirit-baptism. This is particularly true of charismatic Catholics from covenant communities. The views of four of these will be discussed, namely Steve Clark of the Word of God community in Ann Arbor, Michigan; Peter Hocken of the Mother of God community, Gaithersburg, Maryland; and Kevin and Dorothy Ranaghan of the People of Praise community in South Bend, Indiana. The Episcopal theologian, Morton Kelsey, has close ties with the charismatic Catholic monastery, the Benedictine Abbey in Pecos, New Mexico, but is not himself part of the community.

Lastly, attention must be given to the denominational charismatics. Protestants will be dealt with first since the renewal started among them in the late 1950s, then the Catholics (1967) and the Eastern Orthodox (1971) came into the renewal. (There are also Messianic Jews who are charismatic but they have not produced any independent views on Spirit-baptism.) Within the five big communions of Protestantism (Anglican, Baptist, Lutheran, Reformed, and Methodist) denominational organizations have been formed to propagate and coordinate the charismatic renewal activities. The American Parish Renewal Council formed in 1981 represents: the Presbyterian and Reformed Renewal Ministries International, the International Lutheran Renewal Center, the Episcopal Renewal Ministries, the United Methodist Renewal Services Fellowship, and the American Baptist Charismatic Fellowship. The smaller Fellowship of charismatic Christians in the United Church of Christ is also a member. (The international headquarters for Catholic charismatics is in Rome, Italy. The

Lutheran center in St. Paul, Minnesota, the Anglican "Sharing of Ministries Abroad" in London, England, and the Presbyterian and Reformed offices in Oklahoma City, Oklahoma are also international in their outreach).

The Episcopal and Anglican churches are, for the purpose of this study, being considered as Protestant. The charismatic renewal began in Southern California with the events centered around Dennis Bennett at St. Mark's Episcopal Church, Van Nuys. Bennett's views are discussed as are those of another Episcopal leader, Terry Fullam of St. Paul's, Darien, Connecticut. Bennett moved to St. Luke's in Seattle, Washington, soon after the start of the renewal in 1960. Bennett and Fullam represent the original neo-Pentecostal perspective in the Episcopal Church, whereas the sacramental interpretation is given by John Gunstone from England and James Jones from Rutgers University in New Brunswick, New Jersey. Also from the British Anglican tradition like Gunstone, the views of David Watson and Michael Harper are discussed in chapter 4, and in similar vein, those of the South African, Michael Cassidy. These latter three take a more "evangelical" approach. Morton Kelsey, mentioned above in connection with a community, develops his own worldview as a framework for charismatic experiences. He is Episcopalian and taught at Notre Dame University in South Bend, Indiana, before retiring to California.

Lutherans were also involved in the charismatic renewal from the beginning. Their theologians and writers are found in all the various models of interpretation of Spirit-baptism. Larry Christenson in his early writing and Hans-Jacob Frøen from Norway adopt a neo-Pentecostal approach. Christenson later espouses a sacramental interpretation. He has moved from San Pedro, California to the Lutheran Renewal Center in St. Paul, Minnesota. Ted Jungkuntz also gives a sacramental Lutheran interpretation to Spirit-baptism. He is from Valparaiso University in Indiana, but he recently moved to serve as a minister to the Lutheran fellowship of the Word of God community in Ann Arbor, Michigan. Lutherans discussed in chapter 4 are the Norwegian, Tormod Engelsviken, and the German, Arnold Bittlinger. Bittlinger served the renewal in Germany operating from Schloss Craheim, later moving to the Office for Renewal and Congregational Life of the World Council of Churches in Geneva. After serving in the Swiss Reformed Church in Schaffhausen, he has now moved to maintain an international Renewal office in Zürich. He is from a United Church background, which encompasses both Lutheran and Reformed traditions.

The Presbyterian and Reformed world has also been influenced by the charismatic renewal. Several theologians have written on Spirit-baptism from a reformed perspective. Rodman Williams has already been mentioned as being involved in the transdenominational charismatic CBN University. Dutchman John Schep and American Brick Bradford, of the Presbyterian and Reformed Renewal headquarters in Oklahoma City, work from a reformed background. Tom Smail also developed a reformed approach to Spirit-baptism. Upon moving to St. John's, Nottingham, he left the Church of Scotland for the

Church of England. Don Griffioen of Grand Rapids, Michigan, and Barbara Pursey from Ames, Iowa, belong to the Christian Reformed Church and the Presbyterian Church USA respectively. They advocate a full integration of Spirit-baptism into the historic Christian churches.

The charismatic movement has become influential in the mainline of Methodism as well. The only theologian to reflect on Spirit-baptism from this perspective and to come up with something different to neo-Pentecostalism is Bob Tuttle, who has already been mentioned above.

Apart from neo-Pentecostal, Howard Ervin (also from ORU as Tuttle used to be) the following writers and theologians work from a Baptist perspective: Robert Culpepper, Larry Hart (ORU), the British twosome, Donald Bridge and David Phypers, and the Germans, Wilhard Becker and Siegfried Grossmann. They are all dealt with in chapter 4 and present a perspective on Spirit-baptism which can be integrated into Evangelical Free churches.

The largest contingent of charismatic theologians comes from the Roman Catholic Church. In connection with communities, Clark, Hocken, and the Ranaghans have already been referred to. The sacramental interpretation is the dominant model. Heading up the team is Léon Joseph Cardinal Suenens who was primate of Belgium and archbishop of Malines-Brussels, as well as adviser to several popes on the charismatic renewal. The following Catholics also espouse a sacramental approach viewing Spirit-baptism as the experiential "release" of the Spirit granted in the sacraments of initiation: Salvador Carrillo, MSpS (Mexico City), Edward O'Connor, CSC and Josephine Massyngberde Ford (Notre Dame University, Indiana), the Frenchman René Laurentin, Donald Gelpi, SJ, of Berkeley, California, Kilian McDonnell, OSB, of St. John's Abbey and University, Collegeville, Minnesota and Simon Tugwell, OP, of Oxford, England. In chapter 4 two more Catholics are discussed, the German systematic theologian, Heribert Mühlen, and the professor of dogmatic theology at the Gregorian University in Rome, Italy, Francis Sullivan, SJ. They both make unique contributions to the interpretation of Spirit-baptism.

From the Eastern Orthodox churches only the Archimandrite, Eusebius Stephanou and Athanasios Emmert have given an Orthodox perspective on Spirit-baptism. It is similar to the sacramental approach.

With this overview some perspectives on the aims of this study have been provided. In chapter 1 we now proceed with the pre-charismatic interpretations of Spirit-baptism and in chapters 2, 3, and 4 with the variety of charismatic views. (In this context charismatic merely signifies involvement in the contemporary charismatic renewal movement.)

Endnotes

1. For example, M. Harper, *As at the Beginning: The Twentieth Century Pentecostal Revival* (Plainfield, NJ: Logos, 1971); K. and D. Ranaghan, *Catholic Pentecostals Today*

(South Bend: Charismatic Renewal Services, 1983); E. D. O'Connor, *The Pentecostal Movement in the Catholic Church* (Notre Dame: Ave Maria, 1971); V. Synan, *In the Latter Days: The Outpouring of the Holy Spirit in the Twentieth Century* (Ann Arbor: Servant, 1984); and E. W. Gritsch, *Born Againism: Perspectives on a Movement* (Philadelphia: Fortress, 1982) ch. 4.

2. Compare the excellent study of K. McDonnell, *Charismatic Renewal and the Churches* (New York: Seabury, 1976).

3. The titles and particulars of all the recent publications being referred to here can easily be found in the alphabetical list of sources at the back.

4. The forthcoming book by Dan McConnell, *A Different Gospel* (Peabody, MA: Hendrickson Publishers, Inc., 1988) establishes and documents this historical link.

PRE-CHARISMATIC INTERPRETATIONS
OF SPIRIT-BAPTISM

= 1

I have chosen to use the term Spirit-baptism instead of "baptism in/with the Holy Spirit" because it is shorter—no theological decision is hereby implied. One of the most recent Pentecostal dissertations on this topic also favors this term.[1]

It has been suggested that baptism in the Holy Spirit has become as important today as justification by faith (alone) in the time of Luther.[2] This is probably an overstatement, but it does reflect something of the amazing growth of the Pentecostal and charismatic movements in this century.

Church historian Timothy L. Smith insists that the first person to popularize the phrase "the baptism of the Holy Spirit" was John Wesley's appointed successor, John Fletcher.[3] What interests us here are the various theological interpretations given to it in the charismatic movement today. However, it will first be necessary to look at some of the prevailing views held outside the charismatic movement. It will later become apparent that these views have also been influential in shaping the views of charismatics—both negatively and positively. The crucial issue is the question whether the Christian life is characterized by "one or two stages." The meaning of this "loaded" expression will soon become apparent. Those who wish to work within a single encompassing framework identify Spirit-baptism with regeneration or conversion (the evangelical view) or with the sacraments of initiation—either baptism or confirmation—(the sacramental view). Over against these views we find a wide variety of views which accept a basic pattern of two stages: (a) the new life in Christ and then (b) a "second blessing," as it is referred to in its classical Wesleyan form. These categories will now be developed further. It must be kept in mind throughout that we are not yet dealing with the distinguishing views of so-called charismatics but with those of their predecessors and opponents.

1.1 The Unified Pattern of Christian Experience

Strictly speaking, the unified pattern of Christian experience is not part of the pre-charismatic interpretations of Spirit-baptism. These interpretations refer to the different two-stage approaches which follow. In order to contrast them with the regular approach this view is being discussed first.

The unified pattern is the dominant view of the nature of "the Christian life" in Christianity. J. I. Packer calls it "Augustinian Holiness," but he somehow sees fit to limit it to Protestantism.[4] It is a pattern of gradual development within the context of humanity as justified and sinful at the same time (Luther's *simul iustus et peccator*). Packer gives an apt description of the basic attitudes:

> Augustinians affirm without qualification the sovereign power of God's love and accordingly are as optimistic about the transformation that the Holy Spirit can work in a believer's life as they are pessimistic about the possibilities of unregenerate human nature and realistic about the Christian's daily shortcomings when judged by God's standard of perfection.[5]

Within this broad framework we find differing emphases. Those working within the tradition of evangelical Protestantism seem to focus on regeneration and conversion as the start of the Christian life. When the term "baptism with the Holy Spirit" is used, it is seen as another way of expressing the new birth or the new life in Christ. Spirit-baptism is received upon repenting of sin and believing in the Lord Jesus as Savior. Green describes this view by saying that the Spirit's baptism is here considered as identical with conversion.[6] Some representative examples will now be furnished.

Richard Gaffin of Westminster Theological Seminary would basically agree with Green's assessment but somehow seems eager to move away from giving any experiential significance to Spirit-baptism.[7] Indeed, Michael Eaton distinguishes Gaffin's view from the more general one by classifying it as a nonexperiential event, i.e. as occurring below the level of human consciousness.[8]

Gaffin sees the gift or baptism of the Holy Spirit as an encompassing concept which has to do with the salvation revealed in Christ. It is the gift to the church of Christ himself or "the crowning achievement of Christ's work: his coming in exaltation to the church in the power of the Spirit." [9] The "nonrepeatable" (i.e. nontypical, nonmodular) character of Pentecost needs to be stressed.[10] In fact Gaffin asserts:

> The baptism with the Holy Spirit of Pentecost is a unique, epochal event in the history of redemption and is no more capable of being repeated or serving as a model for individual experience than are the death, resurrection, and ascension of Christ with which it is so integrally conjoined as part of a single complex of events.[11]

No one would want to argue for a literal repetition of Pentecost, but one wonders if the symbolic value of the events of salvation history needs to be totally abandoned? In the Reformed tradition the ethical concepts of mortification and vivification have always been developed as analogies of Christ's death and resurrection. Perhaps a "coming" of the Spirit could be seen in the same way.

Whereas Gaffin represents a more reasoned response to the challenge presented by charismatic theology, we find in John F. MacArthur's polemical book, *The Charismatics*, a rather less balanced attempt to discredit those with whom he disagrees. He often seems to confuse Pentecostal and charismatic views and to generalize from a number of particular, unfortunate, personal experiences. He also seems to select a few of the worst spokesmen for the charismatic view available.[12] On the issue of Spirit-baptism he takes the general evangelical line – it is entering into the one body of Christ–1 Corinthians 12:13.[13] He seems to be confusing charismatics with the older Holiness (and sometimes also Pentecostal) groups and their terminology when he levels the following objection:

> When a Charismatic brother approaches and asks, "Have you had the baptism of the Holy Spirit?" our first answer can be, "There is no such thing as the baptism of the Holy Spirit. If you mean the baptism with the Holy Spirit, yes, I have, and so has every other Christian."[14]

James Dunn, who has played an important role in the whole charismatic debate with his exegetical study *Baptism in the Holy Spirit,* sees Spirit-baptism as a crucial part of the event (or process) of becoming a Christian. He is representative of those who would acknowledge this as experiential:

> . . . it [baptism in the Spirit] was the chief element in conversion-initiation so that only those who had thus received the Spirit could be called Christians, the reception of the Spirit was a very definite and often dramatic experience, the decisive and climactic experience in conversion-initiation, to which the Christian was usually recalled when reminded of the beginning of his Christian faith and experience.[15]

As a further example of the evangelical view of Spirit-baptism, the eminent Swiss theologian, Karl Barth, may be cited. He sees Spirit-baptism as the way in which God prepares the individual for the entire Christian life:

> We thus regard it as legitimate to understand by the baptism of the Holy Ghost . . . the divine preparation of man for the Christian life in its totality.[16]

This start of the Christian life lies in an encounter with Christ:

> The beginning of the Christian life takes place in a direct self-attestation and self-impartation of the living Jesus Christ.[17]

Barth is adamant that Spirit-baptism as the liberating work of the Holy Spirit is no different from the reconciling act of God in Christ. The work of the Spirit is not a second or different activity: "It is the one divine work in its movement."[18]

In his discussion of Barth's view, David Olivier points out that Barth deals with the foundation of the Christian life (special Christian ethics) under the headings baptism with the Holy Spirit and baptism with water. Barth sees Spirit-baptism as the *objective* side – God's decisive act in changing and renewing individuals – and water baptism as the *subjective* side of initiation, the individual's response to God, performed in the church.[19] Over against the Pentecostal view of a *subsequent* Spirit-baptism, Olivier describes Barth's view as *synchronous* (with regeneration).

Within traditions that would not readily classify themselves as evangelical, the focus with respect to the start of the Christian life falls, not on conversion, but on infant baptism as a sacrament of Christian initiation. Here Spirit-baptism is seen as closely related to water baptism. Often adherents of this view believe – to varying degrees – in the doctrine of baptismal regeneration. In passing it is important to note that those sacramentalists of the High Church tradition who teach baptismal regeneration seldom, if ever, adhere to the Reformed doctrine of the preservation and perseverance of the saints ("once saved always saved"). The fact that "baptismal regeneration" can be lost does make it somewhat less objectionable.

The identification of Spirit-baptism with water baptism need not necessarily be restricted to the majority of Christian churches that practice infant baptism. It is also theoretically possible to identify adult or believer's baptism with Spirit-baptism. Where this could be done the emphasis falls, however, on the act of conversion, which is then symbolized by the baptismal immersion of professing Christians. I am not aware of any official Baptist groups that would identify Spirit-baptism with the act of water baptism rather than with regeneration/conversion. There are fringe groups in Appalachia which administer immersion baptism and call it the baptism with the Holy Spirit. I have unfortunately not been able to document this unusual view.

These, then, are the main views (outside the charismatic renewal) on Spirit-baptism in a unitary pattern of the Christian life: Spirit-baptism being either conversion or (water) baptism. Before moving on to the two-stage pattern of sanctification it is necessary to mention a view which seems to straddle the one-stage/two-stage distinction. Within the sacramental fold, there are those who refer to infant baptism and confirmation in a way strikingly similar to the two-stage approach of many Pentecostals. I do believe that the similarity is more formal than substantive. In Roman Catholic and Anglican circles the sacrament of confirmation is usually seen as an impartation of the Holy Spirit by the laying on of hands by a bishop.[20]

Mason remarks:

> The difficulty [about the Holy Ghost's presence in the heart] is perhaps lessened by observing that there is a twofold indwelling spoken of in Holy Scripture, of which one is objective and the other is subjective.[21]

The objective indwelling is the gift of confirmation and it ought to be followed by the subjective, also known as the baptism of the Spirit. Mason is hard pressed to define what baptism confers apart from confirmation. To divorce the two is an abnormal situation:

> ... the gift of the new birth is, in God's purpose, to be followed as soon as possible by the gift of the Spirit's indwelling; and therefore all the teaching of the Epistles is concerned with those who have received the completed Baptism, not with those who are in the accidental and momentary position of an inchoate and unfinished initiation.[22]

The term unfinished initiation should be noted as it appears again in charismatic circles.

Green remarks that the phrase "baptism in the Holy Spirit" is not normally used by the baptism-confirmation "two-stagers" (we have seen that Mason does refer to it), but he does think that they clearly advocate a two-stage Christian initiation.[23] Perhaps the difference between these sacramentalists and the various groups teaching a second blessing is that those advocating a high doctrine of confirmation are really just grouping two sacraments together as Christian initiation and expect the regular use of all the sacraments—especially the Eucharist—to be an ongoing pattern of Christian life in a unitary "Augustinian" framework. Pentecostal teaching, however, clearly sees Christians in the second stage as having reached a different "state" in the Christian life which has placed them on a higher level in the eyes of God. For this reason I do not consider this type of "two-stage" initiation, consisting of baptism and confirmation (or, for that matter, in a Reformed setting: of baptism and public profession of faith) as bearing any theological similarity to the two-stage views which we shall now discuss.

1.2 The Two-Stage Patterns of Christian Experience

The four groups advocating a two-stage approach can be dealt with in the order in which they evolved historically. They do, nonetheless, all find a measure of support in contemporary Christianity. What makes them relevant here is that all describe the second experience (after initial regeneration and conversion) as an experience with the Holy Spirit, whether they call it a baptism, a sealing, or an infilling.

The views are (1) the Puritan or Reformed Sealers' view of a sealing of the Spirit as an experience of the assurance of salvation, (2) the Wesleyan and Wesleyan-Holiness movements' views on Spirit-baptism as a sanctifying event of perfecting in love, (3) the Keswick version of an enduement with power for service and, lastly, (4) the classical Pentecostal view of Spirit-baptism as "subsequent," "conditional," and evidenced by glossolalia.

1.2.1 The Reformed Sealers

First, we will examine the view of many seventeenth-century Puritans whom E. H. Andrews has designated as the Reformed Sealers. Prominent representatives are Richard Sibbes, Thomas Goodwin, and John Owen as well as later contributions by Charles Hodge and Charles Simeon.[24] In contemporary scholarship it was J. K. Parratt who focused attention on the sealing of the Holy Spirit with his work, *The Seal of the Holy Spirit in the New Testament Teaching*. From a biblical viewpoint he concludes that the sealing of the Spirit (which he holds to be coterminus with the promise of the Spirit and the phrase "to baptize with the Holy Spirit") is neither water baptism, nor the initial act of faith in Christ, nor does it necessarily involve the laying on of hands.[25] Positively he distinguishes the following aspects: the sealing of the Spirit is profoundly experiential and imparts a faculty to pray and commune with God.[26]

> It is in this Spirit-inspired prayer that he (the Christian) is made conscious of standing in the intimate relationship to God as Father to a son [the inverse order—as a son to a Father—would be more accurate]; thereby the Spirit witnesses to his spirit that he is a child of God (Rom 8:16).

For an understanding of the Reformed Sealers this is the crucial facet. Parratt goes on to distinguish two more facets of the Spirit's sealing: a ratifying to the believer of the validity and veracity of the gospel and the eschatological implication of the gift of the Spirit.[27]

Parratt also points out the extent of the witness of the Spirit regarding assurance of sonship:

> The idea occupied a particularly important place in the theology of the Puritans, and examples of it abound in the voluminous writings of that period.[28]

Thomas Goodwin seems to be the supreme example. He sees the sealing of the Spirit in Ephesians 1:13 as intensely experimental (experiential). It is, "a light that overpowereth man's soul, and assureth him that God is his and he is God's."[29] Interestingly, "sealing" as a further step in sanctification did not seem to evoke the negative criticism that Wesley's views later called forth. Goodwin saw the seal of the Spirit, expressed preeminently in prayer, as an answer of the believer to infant baptism. (This would almost seem to suggest that it be closely connected to conversion.)

Parratt also finds a view quite similar to the Reformed Sealers among certain of the early primitive Baptists. They apparently connected the "sealing" with the laying on of hands subsequent to believer's baptism.[30] He even sees similarities in the position taken by Anglican Jeremy Taylor, who connects this with a strengthening in confirmation. This makes one wonder if the position being discussed here is really correctly classified as a two-stage position! I do feel that the scales are tipped in affirming the classification when one considers that the Sealers teach that sealing or Spirit-baptism is an inner occurrence subsequent to regeneration. It is to be sought as an unsurpassed dramatic experience that changes one permanently. It brings both assurance of salvation and spiritual power for ministry. Andrews describes it in this manner:

> The baptism of the Spirit is, rather, a special visitation or effusion of the Holy Spirit upon the individual believer, in which his apprehension of God is enlarged, his

6

heart melted and his whole being filled with a deep (sometimes almost intolerable) sense of the glory and goodness of God. Many biographical cases are cited in which notable servants of God have recorded such experiences.[31]

In contrast to later developments, the Sealers do not see a necessary connection between this experience and the fruit or the gifts of the Spirit.

In this context it is important to notice the difference between the Reformed Sealers and Calvin. Calvin refers to the sealing with the Spirit as a matter of the heart. The Word of God should not merely "flit(s) about in the top of the brain" but take root in the heart. This deeper action which furnishes the heart with assurance is more difficult:

> The Spirit accordingly serves as a seal, to seal up in our hearts those very promises the certainty of which it has previously impressed upon our minds; and takes the place of a guarantee to confirm and establish them.[32]

Here we still see the immediacy of the relationship between God and humanity. There is a shift in the teaching of the Puritan "Sealers" which we also find among the "Nadere Reformatie" in the Netherlands. A spiritual syllogism is evolved—a system of "signs" whereby the assurance of salvation can be determined. This tends to lead to much agonized "soul searching" and introspection, which later became a characteristic of the "zwaar" (heavy) spirituality of part of the conservative Reformed faith in the Netherlands where many believers consistently refuse to take communion because they still remain uncertain about their assurance of salvation.

J. de Boer describes this in his study, *De Verzegeling met de Heilige Geest volgens de opvatting van de Nadere Reformatie* [The sealing with the Holy Spirit according to the view of the "Nadere Reformatie"–Inner Reformation]. He remarks:

> According to Calvin the assurance of faith is evoked by the Spirit of sonship by which we gain access to the Word of the promise (saving faith). According to the "Nadere Reformatie" (a Dutch post-Reformation movement of a pietist nature) assurance of faith is brought about by a spiritual syllogism. In this process the direct access in our relationship to God is lost.[33]

He later develops this more specifically:

> According to the "Nadere Reformatie" experiential assurance (assurance of feeling) is a separate stage that follows after the assurance of faith and is usually separated from it by considerable space of time. From here a line can be drawn to Pentecostalism and its twofold baptism: water baptism and Spirit-baptism. The experiential assurance must compensate for the loss of religious immediacy experienced in the assurance of faith.[34]

By describing the "Dutch Puritan" position on "gevoelszekerheid" (emotional assurance) as a separate stage following on the assurance of faith, De Boer reveals the "two-stage" nature of this doctrine. It is also salient that he himself notes the theoretical link with Pentecostalism.

In summing up we see that for the Puritan and the subsequent "Sealers" there was a definite second experience of the Holy Spirit after becoming a

Christian. This experience is the assurance of sonship. In modern times this variation of a two-stage Christian life has not become widespread. In fact Dr. Martyn Lloyd-Jones's view of the direct witness of the Spirit is really the only prominent modern representation of the Reformed Sealer's tradition. He expounds it in his book, *God's Ultimate Purpose*,[35] but especially in his sermon series on Ephesians 1:13, Romans 8:15–16, and John 1:26, 33. M. A. Eaton[36] defines Lloyd-Jones's experiential view of Spirit-baptism in this way:

> For Dr. Lloyd-Jones the central characteristic of the baptism with the Spirit was that it was an experience of directly given assurance, bestowed by Christ, surpassing any other form of assurance of salvation, and unmediated by any kind of syllogistic argumentation.[37]

In Lloyd-Jones's view the sealing is a direct and immediate testimony of assurance. Subjectively it is usually accompanied by characteristics such as a sense of God's glorious presence, awe, a sense of humbling, an element of joy, light and understanding, an assurance of God's love, and the desire to glorify him. Objectively Lloyd-Jones speaks of the transformation of facial appearance, a new boldness in speaking, a note of authority, and fearlessness.[38] However, these are just *possible* manifestations. A person may receive Spirit-baptism without any of these phenomena. The assurance of salvation is primary. Power for testimony also comes via this assurance. In line with the Puritan Sealers, Lloyd-Jones also sees no direct connection between the direct witness of the Spirit and the fruit of the Spirit or sanctification. With respect to the gifts or charismata, he rejected the various "cessation of miracles" theories, accepting the possible continuation in the church of charismatic gifts. He emphasized God's sovereign will in distributing his gifts, warning against credulity. Eaton underscores how exceedingly cautious Lloyd-Jones was about accepting the validity of particular claims:

> For him a gift of the Spirit could not be exercised at will. He believed that the gift of tongues could not be initiated by the Christian and that the person who was enabled to speak in tongues, could not do so at will.[39]

This stands in sharp contrast to Pentecostal and charismatic views.

It should be pointed out here that the great American Puritan theologian, Jonathan Edwards, maintained a unified vision on the Christian life. He did not continue in the tradition of the so-called Reformed Sealers. He did not follow, for example, Thomas Goodwin's teaching on Romans 8:16. Edwards repudiated the view which some people were also espousing during the Great Awakening (which actually began in his Northampton Congregational church), namely that God carries on a kind of "revealing" conversation with some Christians leading to extrabiblical knowledge. He also did not have the sealer's interest in introspective self-examination. In his discerning *Treatise on Religious Affections,* he gives a sober evaluation of particular experiences and phenomena associated with the revivals, distinguishing those which afford no

8

decisive evidence such as bodily effects and joy from the true signs such as humility, enlightened minds, and especially holy Christian practice such as deeds of love.[40]

Edwards speaks of men being baptized with the Holy Ghost and with fire at conversion. M. A. Eaton comments:

> Clearly Edwards envisages a gift of the Spirit which is received at conversion and which stirs and rouses the "affectionate" side of man's nature [using the term in Edwards's sense].[41]

The Great Awakening was in a certain sense a monumentally scaled search for assurance of salvation on an emotional as well as on a faith level. Edwards did not consider the awakening experiences as a special second stage in Christian life, but as confirmatory signs of true conversion. Furthermore, he sought evidence for salvation not in introspection but in the active, outward practice of piety. Over against the scholastic tradition of seventeenth-century Calvinism, he emphasized that the essence of true religion was found not so much in doctrinal statements as in religious affections.

Edwards tells of a profound experience in 1737 in which he was filled with "a sense of the excellent fullness of Christ." His thoughts were consumed with the glory of Christ as Mediator, with his love and condescension, and with the ineffable excellency of his person. This brought him to tears for about an hour. This experience was repeated on several other occasions, and these affections confirmed his teaching on the supernatural illumination by the Spirit. The experience did not add anything to what can be found in Scripture, but it brought the truth of God's love home to him in a direct, heartfelt way, almost "empirically."[42]

Edwards's teaching had substantial influence on subsequent American revivalism as well as on the Holiness and Pentecostal traditions. One is tempted to remark with hindsight that if his *Treatise on Religious Affections* had been more closely adhered to, much of the indiscretion of subsequent revivals could have been avoided. It is also important to remember that the debate between Calvinism and Arminianism was very much alive at this time, and Edwards was, in effect, attempting to reconcile the awakenings with orthodox Calvinism.[43]

1.2.2 The Wesleyan Doctrine of Sanctification

In the mid-eighteenth century another two-stage theory of Christian life developed. Where there could still be some debate about the attribute of "two-stageness" in the teaching of the Reformed Sealers, the matter is quite evident in the doctrine of sanctification which developed in Wesleyan circles. This so-called second blessing was seen as an innovation—a distinct second work of grace subsequent to conversion. It is also called entire sanctification, Christian perfection, even sinless perfection of the soul. There has been much debate about this doctrine and Wesley's paper, "A Plain Account of Christian Perfection," seems to add to the lack of clarity. It is clear that John Wesley himself did not explain this concept within a two-stage framework. Towards the end of his life Wesley describes this doctrine as

> the grand depositum which God has lodged with the people called Methodists; and for the sake of propagating this chiefly he appeared to have raised us up.[44]

In the development of his thought Wesley was influenced by Greek patristic thought and the spirituality of Thomas à Kempis, Fénélon, Francke, and William Law, but he is to be held responsible for the novel teaching he developed eclectically. In a tract he gives the following definition:

> Q: What is Christian Perfection?
> A: The loving (of) God with all our heart, mind, soul, and strength. This implies that no wrong temper, none contrary to love, remains in the soul; and that all the thoughts, words, and actions are governed by pure love.
>
> Q: Do you affirm that this perfection excludes all infirmities, ignorance, and mistake?
> A: I continually affirm quite the contrary, and always have done so.[45]

To Wesley a person may be filled with pure love and still liable to actual mistakes. Of course our concept of sin is at stake here. He sees sin merely as "voluntary transgression of a known law," which seems to limit sin to a wrong disposition of the will.

Cox tries to explain:

> This perfect love is not a perfect performance but a pure intention. In entire sanctification the believer's moral likeness to God is fully restored. This perfect love, or Christian perfection, is the only perfection possible in this present life. It is a purity that sets the will free from inclinations to evil. It is freedom from the sinful depravity of the heart or will. It comes in an experience that may be called the fullness of the Spirit, and it is accomplished by the Spirit in response to the faith of the believer. For Wesley it is a Scriptural concept and is attainable here and now by all believers.[46]

Whereas conversion accomplishes an external purification, this second step eradicates indwelling or inbred sin and roots out all sinful motives from the believer's heart instantaneously. Surprisingly, Wesley never claimed this for himself and said it is ordinarily not given till a little before death, but that only because people do not expect it sooner. The work of Christian perfection itself, which would later become known as a "baptism with the Holy Spirit," is accomplished in an instant although, seemingly to guard himself, Wesley adds, "But I believe [in] a dual work, both preceding and following that instant."[47] This distinctive Wesleyan teaching can now hardly be found in the larger Methodist churches. In the last decades of the nineteenth century it became the distinguishing mark of the Wesleyan-Holiness movement and the denominations that eventually developed from that tradition such as the Church of the Nazarene. It needs to be stated that this teaching has had a blessed and transforming influence on thousands of Christians' lives.

This teaching has often been misunderstood as entailing absolute perfection. This is not accurate; but even in its more limited expression as the instantaneous replacement of all evil motives of the heart by perfect love and pure intention, Wesley's teaching is still considered by mainline Protestantism as a grave error. The focus of Reformed criticism has been its view of sin and the inconclusiveness of the arguments from the Bible when compared to "the human condition" and the general teaching on sin in Scripture. For an evaluation of this doctrine Wesley's whole doctrine of grace would have to be considered as well as the classical polarity of Calvinism and Arminianism. This is not part of the aim of this study.[48]

Of primary importance for this study, however, is not the acceptability of Wesley's view of sin and salvation but the fact that a two-tier system evolved as the pattern for the Christian life. One easily sees how Wesley's view of sanctification with its idea of attainable perfection as an instantaneous eradication of sinful intention could be turned into a pattern with concrete, identifiable stages: There are those who have received the new birth and then there are those who are not only saved but also sanctified. Through the experience of this "baptism with the Holy Spirit," as Wesley's contemporaries John and Mary Fletcher began to call it,[49] a new elitist division was struck in Christianity—not connected to function, as the unfortunate dichotomy between clergy and laity which evolved in patristic times, but dependent on a specific spiritual experience. This was not just a growth experience, but effected an ongoing difference in the state of one's soul—a purified heart. (In Wesley's opinion this blessing could still be lost and then regained,[50] but that was not the normal expectation.) On the definite two-stage framework the whole Pentecostal movement would later be built. Donald Dayton sketches the development in terminology from Christian perfection to the baptism of the Holy Spirit via Asa Mahan and Charles Finney.[51] But before that development takes place, a modified version of the Wesleyan view evolved. This is usually called the Higher Life or Keswick movement.

1.2.3 The Keswick Teaching

The Keswick teaching was developed more on the level of piety and sermons than on the level of theological reflection. It has a tremendous popular appeal because it promises: the victorious life, the upward way, the higher or deeper Christian walk. It preserves the Wesleyan two-stage grid, but it rejects the view that believers' hearts may become perfect in love. The second work of grace was not an eradicating of inbred sin but rather living a life of victory in which a perfection of deeds is achieved. The great enthusiasm is for holiness, and this striving is held in common with the Wesleyan-Holiness movement. The underlying theological differences were not always underscored, which has led to a clouding of the issues in much of the literature. With its focus on the way of living rather than the inner purity of heart, the second step or "baptism of the Spirit" was seen as an enduement with power rather than a purification. It would be interesting to trace whether there is any historical connection between this facet of the Keswick teaching and the fact that Puritans in the same country previously taught that the experience of sealing brought new power for ministry.

J. I. Packer has made an analysis of the Keswick teaching. It operates with a passive concept of faith. This view of faith is the secret of holiness. Sanctification is not by works or self-effort. The key is "resting."[52] The sinfulness of the heart is not changed in this world, but one can be free from actual sinning, "From the inner passivity of looking to Christ to do everything will issue a perfection of performance."[53] One must cease striving to be holy and obedient because this is done in the flesh and is a form of spiritual pride. In confessing one's own inability, reckoning oneself dead to sin, and resting in Jesus, one enters the victorious higher life. Although it is said to issue forth into a life of sinless deeds, it is by no means a form of activism or a conscious attempt to heap up good works of merit.

This view contains an inner contradiction. It does not really escape the reproach of self-righteous meritoriousness against which it directs itself so vehemently, but merely succeeds in letting that struggle move underground, as it were. The achieving of this victorious life of happiness and unruffled tranquility is based on an inner struggle to suppress sinful thoughts, to consider oneself dead to sin, to rest in Jesus and let him alone act. In essence this seems to focus on human will—not the will to do good deeds but the will to remain passive. There seems to be something inherently Stoic about it. Romans 6, especially verses 11–14, is widely used to support this theory. As with Wesley's entire sanctification, it occurs as a step or a crisis. The crisis in the Keswick form of Spirit-baptism is followed by a process—indeed a "maintained condition," in which the individual's role is to maintain the consecration and continue to exercise faith in this specific manner. No mean task! The result is complete victory over all known sin. I have to conclude that this doctrine seems to disregard certain elements of the New Testament teaching on human sinfulness. It also seems to harbor a good amount of quietism with its view that all human initiative is the energy of the flesh.

In his book, *So Great Salvation,* Steven Barabas gives a sympathetic overview of the Keswick teaching which basically confirms Packer's analysis. Barabas underscores that the focus is on promoting practical holiness. There is a certain progression of teaching followed at every convention. First the seriousness of sin is unsparingly exposed. Next God's provision for sin is set forth—the Cross and the Spirit. However, knowledge of this truth of salvation is not sufficient in itself, "but is conditional upon our willingness to meet His terms—and His terms, Keswick says, are a complete personal consecration."[54] This consecration is a radical adjustment of one's spiritual condition. It is instantaneous—a crisis with a view to a process. Sanctification is thus a process beginning with such a crisis.[55] E. W. Moore put it rather revealingly: "In consecration there

12

is an adjustment of the will that ensures sanctity."[56] This is seen as life's greatest decision or turning point. Keswick teachers seem to accept two axioms: (1) that such an agonizing crisis of self-denial and consecration is the inescapable condition of progressive sanctification; and (2) once this step has been taken (they acknowledge it should "normally" be at conversion but frequently is not) holiness seems to follow as a matter of course.[57] The simplicity of a "formula" approach makes it very attractive. In fact there is almost an air of Gnosticism—all that one needs is the right knowledge of how sanctification works. Through the Keswick conventions one can be initiated into the group who have this knowledge which then leads to the overcoming life.

Correlating with the act of consecration is God's blessing of the fullness of the Holy Spirit. This is not regeneration (which is also termed being born again or being baptized with the Spirit) but a definite act of faith separable from it, usually experienced by Christians at varying intervals after regeneration.[58] This brings the power of the Holy Spirit for Christian service which is the last theme of the conventions climaxing in a missions-oriented gathering.

G. Campbell Morgan explains the need for ongoing "fullness":

> What is needed for life is the perpetual filling of the Spirit which is the normal condition of those who are living in the way of God, and the specific infillings to overflowing which may always be counted on when special service demands.[59]

It is important to note that the reception of the Spirit's fullness may be lost through sin and is not regarded as a once-for-all experience,[60] although the impression is given that the initial act of consecration does fulfill the role of a decisive, permanent, second crisis experience.

With a large amount of goodwill it may be possible to integrate much of the Keswick perspective within an Augustinian framework—especially because of the lack of theological precision. I suspect that many Keswick supporters effect such an integration unwittingly. The "mood" of the Keswick teaching is, nonetheless, dependent on a two-stage approach—especially the Gnostic elitism and the optimism with regard to human nature after the act of consecration and the reception of the Spirit.

Packer sees the Keswick ideal of "a quiet, sunny, tidy life without agony" as a Christian version of the secular middle-class dream.[61] He spells out the socio-political consequences:

> Why are so many modern Evangelicals slower than other Christians to respond to their neighbors' needs and to weep at the way God is dishonored in today's world? Part of the reason may be that three generations of projecting at each other the Keswick ideal of life have desensitized us at these points.[62]

As previously mentioned, this view has become associated with the Keswick conventions. They have been held in northern England's Lake District since 1875. The gathering was called "The Convention for the Deepening of the Spiritual Life."

C. N. Peckham sets the scene as follows in a study on the "deeper life" teaching:

13

For the last century the annual convention at Keswick . . . has spread the necessity for holy living all over the world. Keswick's emphasis on a second crisis was much more definite in its earlier days but it still stresses this point today. The explanation of what happens at the second crisis is an issue which does not go away. Andrew Murray, probably South Africa's greatest son in the Christian realm, named one of his books, *The Two Covenants: And the Second Blessing.* If someone such as Murray, who is held in the highest esteem and respect everywhere, emphasized this particular aspect of holiness in this way, it should not be lightly dismissed as irrelevant.[63]

Among the leading speakers were F. B. Meyer, Andrew Murray, and R. A. Torrey. The architects of the particular teaching seem to have been Americans such as the couple, Robert Pearsall Smith and Hannah Whitall Smith, William E. Boardman, Asa Mahan of Oberlin College, and Anglicans such as Bishop H. C. G. Moule, who developed a Keswick exegesis in his commentary on Romans.[64] The Smiths were instrumental in establishing Keswick as an ongoing convention and in introducing its emphases into the U.S.[65] The emphasis that Spirit-baptism was not an eradication of sin from the heart but power to live victoriously brought a parting of the ways in Holiness circles. Over against the Wesleyan-Holiness approach, several prominent leaders began to propagate the Keswick version of the second blessing: D. L. Moody, R. A. Torrey, A. J. Gordon, A. B. Simpson and Alexander Dowie.[66] The focus of the Keswick teaching seemed to shift somewhat in America. More and more it was the enduement with power, the anointing for ministry, that was underlined rather than the somewhat uncomfortable teaching of a sinless existence via exercising "resting" faith. The dynamics of this shift have to my knowledge not yet been researched. That it occurred in this manner is merely an assumption which the different reports have led me to make.

Packer sketches the development of the two-stage conceptual grid, pointing out that nineteenth-century Wesleyans conceived of God's salvation as two separate "parcels" of grace: justification and santification. The Holiness movement developed this further with a distinction between "two separable salvations" i.e., deliverance first from the guilt and then from the power of sin.[67]

Whereas the Wesleyan-Holiness movement resulted in several smaller denominations, the Keswick variety did not choose to go this route. Keswick continues to this day as an annual convention, although it has largely lost the original doctrinal emphases of its founders. It receives its support mainly from evangelicals in the Church of England and from some Free churches. It has received only limited recognition within the Wesleyan-Holiness circles, "because of its emphasis on the suppression of evil tendencies."[68] Through its popular devotional literature it remains influential in many evangelical circles today.

The tendency to over-generalize the teaching of Keswick was alluded to above. Among American Pentecostals one finds writers using the term "Keswick Pentecostals" for the Pentecostals who did not have the heritage of the

Wesleyan-Holiness movement.[69] This usage is rather confusing since the basic Keswick teaching of the victorious life through the "formula" of consecration and the fullness of the Spirit has been eclipsed by the single element of such an infilling resulting in an enduement with power for service.

1.2.4 Pentecostalism

The fourth and last of the two-stage approaches is Pentecostalism. Perhaps it is necessary at this stage to underscore the formal nature of the link that is being pursued here. It is the basic element of dividing the Christian life up into distinct stages. To associate the Reformed Sealers or John Wesley with the entire subsequent development of Pentecostalism is like holding Hegel responsible for Stalin just because he developed the tripartite distinction of thesis, antithesis, and synthesis. (This is also meant to be a formal analogy not implying any guilt by association!)

Pentecostalism is a very broad and variegated phenomenon. From the beginning of the century to the present it has become the largest single category in Protestantism, outstripping the traditional groups that date back to the Reformation such as the Lutheran, Reformed, and Anglican communions.[70] To distinguish it from the more recent neo-Pentecostal revival of the 1960s, Pentecostalism is often designated as "classical" Pentecostalism today. The term was coined by the Catholic scholar Kilian McDonnell, well known for his writings on the charismatic renewal.[71]

Classical Pentecostalism is widely viewed as developing out of the Wesleyan-Holiness movement. It is more correct to acknowledge the role of two midwives at the birth of Pentecostalism, the Wesleyan-Holiness movement and the more Reformed evangelical revivalism that was so pervasive in America during the latter half of the nineteenth century. Anderson objects to Synan's overemphasizing the Wesleyan component:

> I find it necessary to reject the central thesis of Synan that "the historical and doctrinal lineage of American Pentecostalism is to be found in the Wesleyan Tradition." To the contrary, that wing of the Pentecostal movement which had earlier connections with Wesleyanism became Pentecostal by accepting Keswick (i.e. Calvinist) teachings on dispensationalism, premillennialism and the Baptism of the Holy Spirit. This acceptance led logically to their ostracism by the "orthodox" Wesleyan Holiness movement, which held them guilty of the "third Blessing heresy.". . . In short, the Pentecostal movement was as much a departure from the Wesleyan tradition as a development from it.[72]

This is a much needed corrective, although it remains true that Wesleyanism did provide the basic two-stage structure for Pentecostalism. The accuracy of Anderson's designation of Keswick teaching as Calvinist is, however, open to serious doubt and needs to be discussed briefly. Although he is probably only referring to the revivalist concept of Spirit-baptism as an enduement with power and not to the Keswick teaching on complete victory over sinful deeds, it is nonetheless not accurate to label this Calvinist. Even if the input from

Presbyterian sources cannot be doubted, one must take into account that in American revivalism many Presbyterians and Congregationalists were by the middle of the nineteenth century already thoroughly Arminian in their views. Among these, Charles Finney is the classic and most influential example.[73] Furthermore the typically Reformed view has always been amillennial; and despite B. B. Warfield's incipient dispensationalism, Reformed theologians have generally been wary of Nelson Darby, Scofield, and others with their facile dividing up of salvation history into different dispensations.

Since the origins and history of the Pentecostal movement have been dealt with in various publications,[74] and the focus of this study is on systematic theology, there is no need for an extended historical analysis here. Doctrinally there are three categories which happen to correlate with the institutional groupings usually employed:[75] (1) the Wesleyan-Holiness, (2) the Baptistic, and (3) the "Oneness" Pentecostals.

1.2.4.1 Wesleyan-Holiness Pentecostals. The Wesleyan-Holiness Pentecostals have a three-stage approach to the Christian life. They developed out of the Holiness movement, which sought to maintain Wesley's doctrine of Christian perfection more strictly when the broader Methodist tradition moved away from it towards the more common Protestant view of sanctification as an ongoing process without any crisis event in which the Adamic nature of indwelling sin is eradicated. At the end of the nineteenth century the Methodist Church denounced the Holiness movement. Especially in the southern U.S. this led to the forming of several new Wesleyan-Holiness denominations. The Wesleyan-Holiness tradition adhered to the two-stage model: first conversion and then sanctification as a subsequent second blessing at a specific moment in time in which carnal human nature is removed and the heart of the person becomes totally pure in love. Those Holiness churches not swept up into the Pentecostal movement still maintain this teaching. The first Pentecostals kept this framework and merely added a third stage for which they reserved the name baptism with the Spirit. This Spirit-baptism is accompanied by speaking in tongues as its initial (physical) evidence. At first it was considered crucial that "the Spirit can only come to a purified heart," i.e. after the second stage! This creates the impression that the Holy Spirit is not involved in the new birth or sanctification. This was sometimes explained by a forced exegesis that tried to distinguish between the Holy Spirit and the Spirit of Jesus as separate entities. This strange view never formed part of mainstream Pentecostalism. It seems to find partial support in an atomistic and literalistic exegesis of John 7:39, "for as yet the Spirit had not been given, because Jesus was not yet glorified"; and Acts 19:2, where disciples are said to remark: "We have never even heard that there is a Holy Spirit" (RSV in both cases).

The third stage of Spirit-baptism could not be seen as a purification or eradication of sin since this had already been taken care of in stage two. Consequently the Wesleyan-Holiness Pentecostals superimposed the Keswick view of an enduement with power on the Wesleyan doctrine of sanctification.

The Fire-Baptized Holiness Church called this third act of grace a baptism of *fire,* by which they also just meant the Keswick concept of an enduement with power.

It was probably at this stage that the Keswick emphasis of the suppressing of sinful tendencies faded into the background since this made no sense to Holiness people who accepted that the heart was already purified, untroubled by any interior "root of sin." The Keswick addition was thus Spirit-baptism as an anointing or enduement with power for service but linked to this was the new distinguishing element—glossolalia.

1.2.4.2 Baptistic Pentecostals. The second doctrinal category of Pentecostals includes the largest denomination: the Assemblies of God. It is difficult to get a proper designation for this group—they are non-Wesleyan in their teaching on sanctification and are trinitarian—as opposed to the "Jesus only" or "Oneness" Pentecostals. Their doctrine of sanctification is basically Reformed and their system of church government is congregational. They practice believer's baptism—like almost all Pentecostals. These three characteristics just mentioned could be covered by the term Baptistic. Many members of this section of Pentecostalism also originally came from Baptist backgrounds. Because of what he perceives to be "historical connections" between the founding of the Keswick conventions and Keswick Pentecostalism, as well as the obvious theological similarities, Harold Hunter prefers the term Keswick Pentecostals.[76]

I do not find his argument at all convincing: first, because the Wesleyan-Holiness Pentecostals already include the Keswick teaching on an enduement of power as their third stage; and second, because of the obvious theological dissimilarities between a more Reformed view of sanctification and the typical Keswick teaching of passive faith and a perfection of deeds by "resting" in Jesus. Granted, on the American continent the term Keswick came, rather inaccurately, to be identified with the views of revivalist preachers such as R. A. Torrey in *The Baptism with the Holy Spirit* (1895). Anderson summarizes Torrey's view:

> Torrey rejected both the extreme Holiness view that the Baptism in the Spirit was an act of grace which "eradicates man's sinful nature," and the more moderate view that it was "primarily for the purpose of cleansing from sin," further, it was "for the purpose of empowering for service." Torrey insisted that "the Baptism in the Holy Spirit is a definite experience of which one may know whether he has it or not."[77]

There also seems to have been a geographical component to the dual source of early Pentecostalism. The evangelical revivalism (which may be called "more Reformed" in a very general sense) was more widespread in the northern U.S. and in Great Britain. This is pointed out by Francis Sullivan. He goes on to describe preachers such as Finney, Robert P. Smith, A. B. Simpson, Moody, and Torrey:

These preachers were masters of the methods of revivalism: emotional preaching, mass meetings where enthusiastic worship was encouraged, the "altar call" when those seeking a crisis experience were invited to come forward for individual ministry. Typical of their preaching was the promotion of a second "crisis experience" (subsequent to conversion), which many of them described as a "baptism in the Holy Spirit," not however for the eradication of the "root of sin," as the Wesleyan tradition would have it, but rather for an "enduement with power" to live the Christian life and to witness to one's faith.[78]

It needs to be noted that such an experience was essentially subjective and there was no external sign by which people could verify that it had taken place. It is my personal opinion that there was a strong psychological desire for external evidence created, especially by the ongoing experiences of Christians who later came to doubt their own Spirit-baptism precisely because they seemed to have lost "the power" or "the purity" (depending on whether they were Keswick or Wesleyan in their understanding). It is in this atmosphere of searching that the Pentecostal gospel of initial (physical) evidence spread like wild-fire.

The major controversy which completed the split of trinitarian Pentecostals into Wesleyan-Holiness and Baptistic camps was the *finished work* debate on the nature of sanctification. William H. Durham of Chicago resisted the second work theory to which the original Apostolic Faith movement of Parham had adhered. Durham, who has been called the only original theologian of the American Pentecostal movement,[79] saw the work of Calvary as sufficient to save and cleanse the individual. Sanctification was not a second work of grace but a gradual process. Durham taught that the words of Jesus, "It is finished," meant that both salvation and sanctification were completed *for* the believer. The work *in* the believer had a progressive character. This was, in fact, no innovation but the general Reformed doctrine of sanctification to which Durham, coming from a Baptist background, had been accustomed. To this only the Keswick notion of an enduement with power through Spirit-baptism could safely be added without any threat to the finished nature of Christ's work. This second experience was not a component part of salvation (viewed broadly) but an equipping with spiritual power to witness and work for the spreading of the gospel and tongues as a sign was the initial evidence. Eventually about 60% of Pentecostals adopted the "finished work" view of sanctification. Anderson has pointed out that finished work Pentecostals tended to be more urban than "second work" Pentecostals. The southern and black Pentecostals held more strongly to the original Wesleyan-Holiness tradition of a "second work" of sanctification.[80] Doctrinal influences and denominational backgrounds also played a role:

> In contrast to the Calvinist-Keswick orientation of Finished Work Pentecostals, Second Work Pentecostals were distinctly Arminian and Wesleyan in religious background. Those who had come into the Pentecostal movement from Methodist, Wesleyan Holiness, and Free Will Baptist fellowships were strongly inclined to resist the Finished Work movement.[81]

18

Reservation about Anderson's facile alignment of Keswick and Calvinist have already been expressed. It also needs to be said that today most Methodists would agree to a finished work view of salvation which implies a progressive sanctification rather than the two-stage approach so characteristic of the Wesleyan-Holiness movement. This does not, however, preclude them from accepting Arminianism.

A further controversy raged about the validity of tongues as the *only* sign of Spirit-baptism. F. F. Bosworth became impressed by the numerous exemplary and successful church leaders who did not speak in tongues. This led him to question the teaching on initial evidence. He felt that other charisms in addition to tongues could be valid signs of Spirit-baptism. Bosworth ultimately joined the Christian and Missionary Alliance of A. B. Simpson, which had the tolerant policy with regard to tongues: "Seek not, forbid not." Eventually most American Pentecostals insisted that *only* tongues as a *sign* (as distinct from tongues as a *gift*) can be regarded as the initial physical evidence of Spirit-baptism. This does not apply to the rest of the world—especially not to groups such as the Mülheim movement in Germany.[82]

1.2.4.3 "Oneness" Pentecostals. The third category of Pentecostals is usually called the "Oneness" Pentecostals. They prefer this designation to Unitarian Pentecostals because the historical Unitarian-Universalist movement grew out of liberal and rationalistic New England congregationalism and actually denies the divinity of Christ. Technically, however, the term Unitarian does apply to their teaching since they hold that there is only one Person in the Godhead—Jesus. For this reason they are also called "Jesus only" Pentecostals. David Reed advocates the term Evangelical Unitarian Pentecostalism.[83] The trinitarian (or triadic) formula "Father, Son, and Holy Spirit" is seen as referring merely to titles or offices of the one God whose name is Jesus.[84] This group accounts for approximately 20% of American Pentecostals and almost half of them are black.[85]

"Oneness" Pentecostals do not substantially differ from the Baptistic Pentecostals on their view of Spirit-baptism. They are being discussed here because their doctrinal positions with respect to the Trinity and salvation are very exceptional and need to be contrasted with the more orthodox views of the rest of Pentecostalism. In this brief discussion a certain amount of historical information is included in order to outline the development of this unusual, doctrinally marginal group of Pentecostalism.

The unorthodox "Oneness" doctrine developed out of a controversy about the correct baptismal formula. Due to an extreme literalism in interpreting the Bible and the romantic restorationist dream of reproducing the New Testament church, the opinion developed that believers should, in accordance with the book of Acts, be baptized in the name of Jesus rather than in the name of the Father, Son, and Holy Spirit. This led to large-scale rebaptisms. Originally the issue of faithfulness to the formula in Acts 2:38 was fundamental, but even though individuals protested, it inevitably led to a denial of the Trinity—a doctrine that cannot easily be defended where a biblicist-fundamentalist framework is employed (as Jehovah's Witnesses are quick to illustrate). Although rebaptism is largely considered unacceptable in both infant-baptizing and Baptist circles, it was fairly common among all Pentecostals in the early years.

New converts often considered their previous baptism as lacking because they questioned the status of the clergy who performed the baptism. Some insisted not only on the conversion of the baptizer as a prerequisite for a valid baptism, but also on his having experienced the baptism in the Spirit. This "Donatist" attitude eroded the New Testament teaching on water baptism as initiation. Some leaders, such as A. J. Tomlinson, even believed that the rite should be performed with each new crisis experience.[86] In such an atmosphere a call to rebaptism in the name of Jesus could reverberate more easily and with more effect. The Oneness Pentecostals came largely out of the finished work or Baptistic category of Pentecostals. After a dramatic showdown for the Oneness leaders at St. Louis in 1916, the Assemblies of God denomination reaffirmed the orthodox doctrine of the Trinity, thereby losing about a quarter of its pastors.

Although the Oneness Pentecostals evolved from the more Reformed finished work section of Pentecostalism, they probably unwittingly canceled this heritage by a very odd view of salvation. From Acts 2:38, which held special significance for them, they constructed a threefold plan of salvation: repentance through faith in Christ, water baptism in the name of Jesus, and the gift of the Holy Spirit (Spirit-baptism with tongues).[87] The innovation was that without all three steps one was not "saved." Some even identified Spirit-baptism with the new birth. Here we have the source of the very suspect doctrine that only people who speak in tongues are really "saved." This misguided view has probably done more harm in relations between "evangelicals" and "Pentecostals" than any other. I suspect that most Pentecostals are probably unaware that this strange view has ever been taught within their ranks.

Before leaving the Oneness Pentecostals, it is interesting to note that there is very little in their faith practice to distinguish them from their trinitarian colleagues. They are typically conservative-fundamentalistic. They reject the rationalism and humanism of the liberal Unitarians and the "additional revelations" of the fanatical Unitarians. It has been said that a Pentecostal believer could join a Unitarian Pentecostal church and be part of their fellowship for a long time before stumbling upon their heretical view of the Godhead. This category of Pentecostals has remained largely concentrated on the American continent. Another rift in Pentecostalism was the racial issue which brought an ongoing division into white and black churches in all the sections of Pentecostalism.[88]

In order to be comprehensive, it is necessary to mention another very small category of Pentecostals. They are ambiguously termed Perfectionist Pentecostals or Deliverance Pentecostals. In 1985 their total community was estimated at 315,300, which includes black membership. David Barrett has classified them as four-crisis-experience-Pentecostals, but it is not clear what the four crises are since he qualifies this by saying that these include "deliverance / ecstatic confession / ascension / perfectionism / prophecy."[89] Personally I would be reticent about incorporating this fringe group as a distinct four-stage group of Pentecostals.

In an article in the collection of essays, *Wiederentdeckung des Heiligen Geistes,* the Swiss-German expert on Pentecostalism, Walter Hollenweger, gives a theological typology of Pentecostalism.[90] He distinguishes between the two-stage and three-stage approaches and the "Jesus only" groups (whom he sees as espousing a modalistic view of the Trinity rather than a Unitarian concept of God). To these three basic categories he adds three more: He sees what could be termed "the charismatics" as a fourth group. Here he refers not to the majority of Protestant neo-Pentecostals (whom he groups with the two-stage Pentecostals) but to the Catholic charismatics and the Protestant charismatics in Germany and France. He calls them Pentecostals with a Reformed, Lutheran, or Catholic doctrine. Also belonging to this group are the Methodist Pentecostals of Chile, the Reformed/Lutheran Pentecostals of Mülheim/Ruhr in Germany and the Quaker Pentecostals in the U.S.

Next Hollenweger mentions the Pentecostal denominations of an Apostolic type. These groups have institutionalized the offices of apostle and prophet. As representative he mentions Apostolic churches in Britain, France, and Germany. It is not all that clear why they are seen as a separate group. In various Pentecostal denominations, even the Assemblies of God in South Africa, there have been attempts to reintroduce the office of apostle.

Hollenweger's final category is important, although some would dispute whether these churches really are Pentecostal. Hollenweger refers to the independent churches in Africa such as the Zionists in South Africa, the Aladura and Seraphim and Cherubim churches in West Africa, and the Kimbanguists in Zaire. Some have historical links with Pentecostal missions, others do not, but all speak in tongues, pray for the sick, or have everybody involved actively in the liturgy.

1.2.4.4 Pentecostal Theology. This rather extensive categorization of Pentecostalism brings us into contact with most of the distinctive features of Pentecostal theology. It would perhaps be useful to summarize them by quoting from two denominational declarations of faith, one from the Wesleyan-Holiness tradition which Anderson calls Second Work, namely from the Church of God (Cleveland, Tennessee) and the other from the Baptistic or finished work category, namely from the U.S. Assemblies of God. Articles 5 to 10 of the Church of God's declaration of faith read as follows:

We believe . . .
5. That justification, regeneration, and the new birth are wrought by faith in the blood of Jesus Christ.

6. In sanctification subsequent to the new birth, through faith in the blood of Christ; through the Word, and by the Holy Ghost.

7. Holiness to be God's standard of living for His people.

8. In the baptism of the Holy Ghost subsequent to a clean heart.

9. In speaking with other tongues as the Spirit gives utterance, and that it is the initial evidence of the baptism of the Holy Ghost.

10. In water baptism by immersion, and all who repent should be baptized in the name of the Father, and of the Son and of the Holy Ghost.[91]

Articles 7 to 9 of the "Statement of Fundamental Truths" of the Assemblies of God, U.S., apply:

7. The Promise of the Father.
All believers are entitled to, and should ardently expect, and earnestly seek, the promise of the Father, the Baptism in the Holy Ghost and fire, according to the command of our Lord Jesus Christ. This was the normal experience of all the early Christian Church. With it comes the enduement of power for life and service the bestowment of the gifts and their uses in the work of the ministry (Luke 24:49, Acts 1:4, 8; 1 Cor 12:1–31). This wonderful experience is distinct from and subsequent to the experience of the new birth (Acts 10:44–6; 11:14–16; 15:7–9).

8. The Evidence of the Baptism in the Holy Ghost
The Baptism of believers in the Holy Ghost is witnessed by the initial physical sign of speaking with other tongues as the Spirit of God gives them utterance (Acts 2:4). The speaking in tongues in this instance is the same in essence as the gift of tongues (1 Cor 12:4–10, 28) but different in purpose and use.

9. Entire Sanctification
The Scriptures teach a life of holiness without which no man shall see the Lord. By the power of the Holy Ghost we are able to obey the command, "Be ye holy for I am holy." Entire sanctification is the will of God for all believers, and should be earnestly pursued by walking in obedience to God's Word (Heb 12:14; 1 Pet 1:15–16; 1 Thess 5:23–4; 1 John 2:6).[92]

The Statement of Truth adopted in 1948 by the Pentecostal Fellowship of North America states very succinctly in Article 5:

(We believe) Sanctification, second baptism with the gift of tongues and the power of healing.[93]

In 1952 the World Pentecostal Conference made the following statement:

Over against all objections, the Pentecostal Movement affirms a baptism in the Holy Spirit accompanied, as at the beginning, with scriptural evidence of speaking with other tongues. . . . Even if very few groups avoid dogmatism on tongues as the initial evidence, the whole Movement is unanimous in affirming that baptism in the Holy Spirit is marked by an immediate, supernatural manifestation of the senses.[94]

Since the main thrust of this study is not on Pentecostalism but on charismatic theology, one could perhaps suffice with the doctrinal statements given above. It should be noted, however, that these documents do not function in the same sense as Reformed or Lutheran confessions. They are more regularly seen as guidelines rather than "legal" documents. Pentecostal theologians do not have the same interest in exegeting and sometimes reinterpreting these classical documents as is found in the more conservative and orthodox schools of the Reformed heritage.

As a representative of Pentecostal theology, Donald Gee (1891–1966), of the British Assemblies of God, deserves examination. He served as principal of the Assemblies of God Bible College at Kenley and was involved in all the Pentecostal World Conferences as a member of the advisory committee till his death. Perhaps his major contribution was as founder and editor of the quarterly international review, *Pentecost*.

Gee declared in 1955 that Spirit-baptism was the central issue in Pentecostalism.[95] He further described what he meant by Spirit-baptism:

> The designation "Pentecostal" arises from its emphasis upon a baptism in the Holy Spirit such as that recorded in Acts 2 . . . as a separate individual experience possible for all Christians . . . subsequent to, and distinct from, regeneration.[96]

Gee is very clear on initial evidence. McNamee points out that he underscores this as early as 1925.[97] Gee believes that the distinctive testimony of the Pentecostal revival is a sacred trust which must never be surrendered. He rejects the temptation to minimize the role of tongues:

> Experience has proved that wherever there has been a weakening on this point fewer and fewer believers have in actual fact been baptized in the Holy Spirit and the Testimony has tended to lose the Fire that gave it birth and keeps it living.[98]

Gee believes that the most profound result of Spirit-baptism as a second experience after conversion is power to witness to Christ. In line with the Baptistic Pentecostal heritage, Gee does not require a crisis experience of sanctification as prerequisite for Spirit-baptism. He accepts the finished work position:

> The baptism in the Spirit does not make a believer sinlessly perfect, and the New Testament does not make spiritual gifts a sign of holiness. They are a sign that the Sanctifier has come; but His work may be proceeding very slowly, especially if the Word is not being obeyed.[99]

In fact Gee's theology could not be more typically Pentecostal, although he presented it with sensitivity. Gee accepted basic evangelical Christianity and played an important "ecumenical" role among the various Pentecostal churches, also becoming as time went on somewhat critical of extreme fundamentalism among Pentecostals. He did not see Pentecostalism as just another denomination, but rather as a renewal. He was not insistent that all Pentecostal outpourings be kept inside the organized forms of the movement.[100] Pentecostalism's contribution to the whole church was, nevertheless, seen in its distinctive elements. Speaking in tongues was the appointed gateway to a life in the Spirit which was seen as being similar to that of the early church. Gee expresses this in his vision of the Pentecostal contribution to all of Christianity:

> We suggest a contribution by the Pentecostal Movement to the whole Church of the greatest value when we testify to the desirability of having His presence made manifest by means of spiritual gifts. We dare to believe that this is one of the supreme purposes of God in sending the Pentecostal Revival in the twentieth century.[101]

It would be inaccurate, even in this very brief discussion of Gee, if some mention were not made of his role as critic of Pentecostalism as well. He expressed his reservations about important failings within the Pentecostal churches such a overcentralized organization, fundamentalism, and lack of social concern. Gee spoke of a new generation of Pentecostal leadership that did not accept the pietistic and individualistic reductions of Christian witness, and urged a move towards impacting human society in a constructive, rather than condemnatory, manner.[102] Next we turn to the critical evaluation of the distinctive doctrines of Pentecostalism.

Pentecostalism was not well received by the historic Christian churches. The initial adherents were more or less forced to leave their churches, and in time they formed a vast number of denominations. It was not merely their "emotional excesses" that drew criticism. Their theology was also criticized, sometimes even caricaturized.

The American fundamentalists officially censured the Pentecostals in 1928. They were rejected by the Wesleyan-Holiness tradition – the Church of the Nazarene dropped the word "Pentecostal" from its official title to distinguish it from the "fanatical glossolalics." Even proponents of the "Deeper life" went to extremes in denouncing the fledgling Pentecostal movement. "In England, Oswald Chambers, a leader in the Keswick Movement, referred to the 'Tongues Movement' as a 'Satanic Counterfeit.'[103] Horace Ward writes a chapter in *Aspects of Pentecostal-Charismatic Origins* on "The Anti-Pentecostal Argument."[104] J. T. Nichol gives both the positive and the negative standard cliches:

> This book [his book *Pentecostalism*] . . . seeks to portray the Pentecostals as they have been and are – sometimes crossly emotional, too often exhibiting, holier-than-thou attitudes, often suspicious of change, anti-intellectual; but, on the other hand, genuinely sincere, vitally enthusiastic, and utterly evangelistic.[105]

Of the standard analyses of Pentecostal theology, several are marred by an obvious hostility towards Pentecostal teaching, e.g., Nils Bloch-Hoell's: *The Pentecostal Movement*[106] and Prudencio Damboriena's *Tongues as of Fire.*[107] Spirit-baptism is undoubtedly the most distinctive doctrine of Pentecostalism. This is underscored by Damboriena:

> Baptism in the Spirit has also become perhaps the cornerstone of the beliefs of Pentecostal denominations. In some of them that experience is required as a *conditio sine qua non* for membership; in others it is at least a prerequisite for holding any responsible position in the church. One may, perhaps, be saved without it, but "one who has not yet had this experience does not have full consecration or full powers for service; hence without Spirit-baptism one's Christian life is incomplete and one's ministry is hampered."[108]

24

There seems to be a consensus that the studies by F. Dale Bruner and James D. G. Dunn are the most important evaluations of Pentecostal theology.[109] Dunn's work deals with both Pentecostal and charismatic views and is much more moderate in its evaluation than that of Bruner, who mainly deals with Pentecostals but doesn't seem to distinguish sufficiently between Pentecostal and charismatic positions, even though his book was published in 1970. This may be due in part to the fact that it is a revision of his Hamburg dissertation of 1963[110] (when the charismatic movement was in its infancy, although the fundamental ecclesiological decision to remain within the historic churches had already been made).

Bruner's critique is sometimes insightful: He directs a three-pronged attack against the Pentecostal doctrine of Spirit-baptism. He rejects (1) the issue of subsequence, (2) tongues as initial evidence, and (3) the teaching that there are pre-conditions for receiving Spirit-baptism.[111] The three main aspects of Bruner's criticism will now be dealt with.

(1) The matter of subsequence was addressed above with reference to Karl Barth's view of Spirit-baptism. The subsequent nature of Spirit-baptism has come in for heavy criticism. The evidence usually cited from the book of Acts is certainly inconclusive. It has been ironically stated that the pattern of Acts is that it has no pattern. Jensen makes this very clear. Of the cases of Spirit-baptism in Acts he remarks:

> It is impossible to make the details of the passages agree with one another. Acts presents no consistent theology of the relationship between baptism, the Holy Spirit, laying on of hands and glossolalia. Luke tells four stories. The details of those stories do not correspond. We must be careful not to find symmetry and meaning where there is none.[112]

Since we have sketched the development of the two-stage theory it is not necessary to elaborate on it. In its primitive form stage one is described as conversion – being saved by the blood of Jesus – and stage two as being purified and filled with the Holy Spirit. John Stott describes the problem very aptly:

> Some Christians give the impression that they hold a kind of "Jesus plus" doctrine, namely, "You have come to Jesus, which is fine; but now you need something extra to complete your initiation."[113]

The unity of the external work of the Trinity is at stake here (cf. Augustine: *Opera trinitatis ad extra indivisa sunt*). In fact the Spirit does not "add" anything to the finished work of Christ on the cross. (Possibly we need to think more comprehensively of what the work of Christ entailed!)

(2) Bruner feels that the heart of the gospel is under attack in Pentecostalism. The Reformation doctrine of justification by faith alone has been impaired. This does not occur consciously. Most Pentecostals believe they are saved by grace. There is, however, a deep longing for "more," which erodes the sola fide. This is more apparent when the idea of "conditions" is surveyed. Bruner sees this as a form of works-righteousness. The evangelical sequence of grace and obedience is reversed, resulting in legalism. This legalism is easily

illustrated in the many things forbidden to Pentecostals in the realm of food and entertainment. Hollenweger entitles his section on ethics in *The Pentecostals*: "Religion is what you must not do."[114]

Bruner supplies an imposing list of "conditions" which various Pentecostal authors advocate as prerequisites to receiving "the Baptism":

Skibstedt	*Conn*
Worship	Separation from sin
Joyous faith	Repentance and baptism
Earnest expectation	Hearing of faith
Praise and thanksgiving	Obedience
Unconditional obedience	Intense desire
Unity	Asking of God
Endurance	
Pearlman	*Baur*
Right attitude	Prayer
Prayer of Christian workers	Faith
United prayers of the church	Separation from sin
Purification by faith	Separation from sinners
Individual prayer	Reparation and restitution
Obedience	
Riggs	*Gee*
Regeneration	Repentance
Obedience	Baptism
Prayer	Faith[115]
Faith	

Although none of these "conditions" are in any way foreign to the gospel, it is the context in which they operate that causes the problem. These conditions are here not seen as operating within the context of loving gratitude towards God for his saving grace, but as steps to achieve a higher level of sanctity and a blessed experience. A more charitable interpretation would be to see the "conditions" merely as possible ways to prepare oneself for what the Lord may have in store. In many cases, however, they seem to be ways to earn what are called "gifts"! Even confession of "all known sin" and restitution are seen as conditions to receive this "subsequent" grace from God. To help people reach this level there was a tradition in early Pentecostalism of "tarrying meetings" at which Spirit-baptism was sought with fervor and tears.

Bruner sums up his basic objection in these remarks:

A principal error of Pentecostalism, shared by some of Pentecostalism's parents and relatives in conservative evangelicalism, is the conviction that the gospel is sufficient for the beginning but not for the continuing of the Christian life, for bringing the Holy Spirit initially but not fully.

Faith suffices for a start but keys, secrets, steps, and conditions must bring the Christian into a higher, deeper, fuller or more victorious life.

It is one of the ironies of nomenclature among those going by the name "full gospel" (and even, at times, "evangelical") that the evangel or gospel itself is not considered full enough to cover and enable the whole of the Christian's life but must be joined with other means, conditions, steps, or laws of the spiritual life in order to be full. The remarkable feature in Paul on the other hand is the dogged insistence of the all-sufficiency of the one gospel for the beginning, for the continuing, and for the fulfilling of the Christian's life.[116]

A word of caution is called for here. Those against whom Bruner is reacting are not writing theological treatises after careful reflection and cautious formulation. Theirs is the language of inspired preaching, a description of experiences and popular revivalistic and inspirational booklets. Their protest is against "cheap grace," against an all too pervasive attitude of spiritual self-righteousness, self-sufficiency and a lack of fervor. Their protest is to be commended. The same "one gospel" which Bruner seeks to defend also calls us to run the race with perseverance, to resist sin to the point of shedding blood, to lift drooping hands and strengthen weak knees (Hebrews 12). Granted there is some pretension in the name Full Gospel, but is it necessarily more offensive than church names which we have become more accustomed to such as Catholic, Reformed, Disciples of Christ, Orthodox Presbyterian?

It seems as if most Pentecostal preachers are, mercifully, inconsistent in that they do not preach a gospel of human achievement. It does, however, appear that these arguments of Bruner are compelling on the abstract, theoretical level. Individuals become the prime movers to reach the second stage. They are the active agents through their "faith." Once again the concept of sin has become superficial, almost "more manageable"; by an act of human will the Christian puts away all known sin. This goes hand in hand with the teaching that the Spirit cannot come to an unsanctified heart or cannot dwell where sin dwells. Certainly the motivation behind such a desire for holiness is to be appreciated, but this cannot excuse such absolute distinctions which inevitably lead to guilt, suppression, and denial. Bruner's critique is actually directed more against the Wesleyan-Holiness Pentecostals than the others.

(3) The doctrine of initial evidence is the innovative and truly distinctive teaching of Pentecostalism. We have seen in the declarations of faith quoted above that tongues is the initial (physical) evidence of the baptism of (or in) the Holy Spirit. The Assemblies of God statement even explicitly distinguishes the "sign" from the "gift" of tongues and explicitly identifies the evidence as "physical." There are some Pentecostal circles, especially in South America and Europe, where there is *no* insistence on glossolalia at all.

The Elim Pentecostal churches in Britain belong to this minority, as well as the Methodist Pentecostals of Chile and the rather Reformational Christlicher Gemeinschaftsverband Mülheim/Ruhr in Germany. The position that rejects tongues as the only sign of Spirit-baptism is also generally espoused in the charismatic movement. The distinction between tongues as a sign–the initial speaking in tongues at the breakthrough experience which is non-repeatable – and tongues as a gift which is then employed in the congregation together with interpretation is very open to exegetical objections from the New Testament exegetes. The distinction actually occurring in 1 Corinthians 14 is rather between a private and a public use of glossolalia. The Pentecostal argument for a differentiation between sign and gift is based on the seeming conflict between 1 Corinthians 12:30, "Do all speak with tongues?" with the implied answer, "No!," and 1 Corinthians 14:5, "Now I want you all to speak in tongues."

Since the whole pericope in 1 Corinthians 12 is explaining the interdependence of the various members of the body, as illustrated by the distribution of gifts – which underscores our need to rely on each other – this can be taken as unambiguous. The verse from 1 Corinthians 14 suggests a wish or desire rather than a blanket statement involving every single one, head for head.

The case for glossolalia as initial evidence is based on the so-called five cases in Acts: Acts 2 – Pentecost, Acts 8 – the Samaritans, Acts 9 – Paul's conversion, Acts 10 – Cornelius and his household, and the twelve disciples who received John's baptism at Ephesus in Acts 19. In three cases (Acts 2, 10 and 19) glossolalia is mentioned, and it can be assumed in the other two for the following reasons: Paul later says in 1 Corinthians 14:18 that "I speak in tongues more than you all," which makes it possible (likely?) that he did so at the "second stage" after his conversion. In the case of the Samaritans, it is asserted, there must have been some perceptible sign which caused Simon to desire the ability that the apostles had (Acts 8:18). New Testament scholars soon dispose of these arguments. They will be dealt with again in the context of the charismatic views.

Bruner, however, seems to be bending over backwards to distance himself from tongues as initial evidence. He goes so far as to practically equate water baptism with the reception of the Spirit.

> Baptism really is the evidence of the Holy Spirit for it evidences the effective work of the gospel and the effected faith of the hearer, and both are due, as we have seen, to the Spirit.[117]

In this context this comes very close to baptismal regeneration since Bruner rejects the doctrine of subsequence. If he is referring only to Acts the "foregoing work of the gospel and the consequent faith of the hearer"[118] can be presupposed. The sentence quoted above, however, is a generalization and seems to disregard the possibility of baptism being performed merely out of habit or superstition as an external rite.

Bruner develops in his rejection of Pentecostal doctrine a caricature of their piety which he calls the Pentecostal passion for "more." He sees this as a "plus" to the gospel of grace.[119] Surely it is necessary to distinguish between a legitimate "thirsting for God" or "hungering after righteousness" and an achievement-oriented desire for unrestrained progress. I believe that few Pentecostals if any would recognize themselves in Bruner's picture. In its overstatement it has become somewhat unbalanced. Nonetheless, even with respect to the characteristic elements of Pentecostal theology there has not always been consensus. In fact one of the main pillars of early Pentecostalism was an emphasis on "freedom," which included the right to disagree on major issues and still be accepted. Hollenweger points out that although many Protestant neo-Pentecostals accepted the Pentecostal teaching on tongues as well as their ethical rigorism and fundamentalism, there were others within Pentecostalism who did not adhere to these views.[120]

In conclusion it is necessary to look briefly at this minority viewpoint within Pentecostalism which does not adhere to the distinctives of Pentecostal theology. It is clearly expressed by Leonhard Steiner in 1960, but according to Christian Krust, who wrote the chapter on Spirit-baptism in the German collection of essays edited by Walter Hollenweger, *Die Pfingstkirchen,*[121] one finds a precursor at the International Pentecostal Conference in Stockholm in July 1955 where a South African Pentecostal, G. R. Wessels, read a paper: "The Baptism with the Holy Spirit—not a Goal, but a Gateway." Krust comments that although Wessels's perspective was not opposed, the majority stuck to the usual teaching of subsequence and initial evidence.[122]

Wessels stated that Spirit-baptism was not indicative of attaining the highest spiritual state. It merely placed one in a new setting for further development. Spirit-baptism is not our goal but just a gateway. The Spirit of God wishes to indwell people and to accomplish things through them. He wants to lead us into a powerful and holy walk with the Lord.[123]

The Mülheim Association of Christian Fellowships, although part of international Pentecostalism, has always been a little exceptional, accepting for instance infant baptism and teaching a theology which is surprisingly close to mainline Reformational doctrine. Christian Krust, one of their leaders, has (according to Hollenweger) started the process (in the 1950s and 1960s) of leading the association even further back to a more Reformational theology.[124] Krust can here appeal to Jonathan Paul, the founder of the German Pentecostal movement, who denied initial evidence from the very beginning and who recognized glossolalia as a natural human gift that the Holy Spirit can use if he wishes.[125] However, Krust goes further than this and denies the two-stage theory so crucial to Pentecostal theology:

> The attempt to present the baptism of the Spirit as a second spiritual experience, to be fundamentally distinguished from rebirth, has no basis in Scripture.... Moreover, the Pentecostal circles which are favorable to this dogmatic pattern also teach the doctrine, equally untenable on a biblical basis, that the baptism of the Spirit must in all circumstances be associated with speaking in tongues as the initial sign. No movement of the Spirit at the present day or in the future, however blessed and however great it is, has the right to call itself a repetition of Pentecost, or the latter rain before the Second coming of Jesus, by comparison with the early rain at the feast of Pentecost. This would be to impair the uniqueness of Pentecost in the history of salvation.[126]

The Mülheim movement has also voiced its opposition to a fundamentalist understanding of Scripture, questioning the normal Pentecostal arguments from Scripture for Spirit-baptism as a second stage. Krust points out that they have the general evangelical interpretation of Spirit-baptism:

> In the Mülheim Association of Christian Fellowships we interpret the concept "Spirit-baptism" to be the same as that which other Christian groups call "coming to a living faith," "conversion," "regeneration," or "an anointing from above."[127]

Christian Krust gave further expression to his ecumenical perspectives when he became the first official Pentecostal pastor to address the World Council of Churches—at the Uppsala Conference in 1968.

Perhaps even more remarkable is the lone protest against the theology of subsequence by pioneer Swiss Pentecostal, Leonhard Steiner. He has been a pastor in the Swiss Pentecostal Mission since 1927, and for twenty-three years he was editor of the periodical *Verheissung des Vaters* [The Promise of the Father]. Steiner was one of the initiators of the first International Pentecostal Conference held in Zürich in 1947.[128]

He not only rejects the doctrine of initial evidence, but from at least 1935 he also spoke out against the doctrine of subsequence, called the "Zweistufentheorie" (two-stage theory) in German. At the European Pentecostal Conference at Stockholm in 1939 we find him questioning the scriptural base for Spirit-baptism in the analogy with the apostles and the cases in Acts.[129] He has also played a role in ecumenical contacts and is an outspoken critic of the extreme practices of some Pentecostal "Faith Healers."[130]

His opposition to the Pentecostal view on Spirit-baptism is unequivocal:

> In our day the testimony of the whole gospel is constantly disturbed and deformed by movements of exaltation and of sectarianism within the Pentecostal Movement. The false doctrine of the Baptism of the Spirit has played a large part in this. . . .The number of those which it has not helped (the number of Pentecostals who have not received the Baptism of the Spirit—Hollenweger) is greater than is supposed. . . .One of the most urgent necessities at the moment is the correction of the doctrine of the baptism.[131]

In a duplicated memorandum which Steiner sent to all important Pentecostal leaders in the world in 1960, he totally rejects the "Zweistufentheorie" —the Pentecostal teaching of stages of salvation. He entitles his appeal: "Sind wir nun keine Pfingstler mehr?"[Are we now no longer Pentecostals?][132]

Hollenweger cites Steiner's conclusion from a personal letter to him and adds that he agrees with this view:

> My conclusion, then, is that one can no longer maintain the doctrine of stages of salvation. This inevitably leads to the rejection of the distinctive doctrines of Pentecostalism. This does not entail the rejection of the Pentecostal movement, that is, the experience of the Spirit which is to be found in it. There are numerous genuine examples of the experience of the Spirit, without there being present a correct understanding of the Spirit.[133]

The radical rejection of Pentecostal distinctives leaves one with the question: Why do Steiner, Krust, cum suis remain Pentecostals? Steiner's appeal in the last quotation to experience is rather vague. It remained the task of some contemporary Pentecostal theologians to define this "experience" factor more clearly and, in fact, redefine the essence of Pentecostalism.

Gordon Fee, in an address to the Fourteenth Annual Meeting of the Society for Pentecostal Studies in 1984, concedes the issue of subsequence. As a Pentecostal New Testament scholar he abandons the attempt to argue subsequence from Scripture. That which is essential to Pentecostalism is neither subsequence nor tongues but, he claims, the dynamic experiential quality of Christian life, the empowering dimension of life in the Spirit which is manifested visibly and phenomenologically in openness to gifts and the miraculous plus obedience to mission.[134]

In an earlier paper before the Second Annual Meeting of the SPS (in 1972) Fee, in fact, follows the same new line of argument. His address, which has been published in *Perspectives on the New Pentecostalism,* is entitled: "Hermeneutics and Historical Precedent–A Major Problem in Pentecostal Hermeneutics."

Fee states that experience generally precedes hermeneutics among Pentecostals:

> In a sense, the Pentecostal tends to exegete his experience. For example, the doctrine of Spirit-baptism as distinct from and subsequent to conversion did not flow naturally out of his reading of Scripture.[135]

He also discounts the normativity of the concept of subsequence as based on historical analogy or the episodes in Acts. To see tongues as the only valid sign of the charismatic quality of life in the Spirit places too much weight on historical precedence.

Fee considers the crucial point to be the experiential, dynamic quality of life in the Spirit:

> Everywhere for Luke it is the presence of the Spirit that signifies the "real thing." . . . Furthermore, in Acts the recurring pattern of the coming (or presence) of the Spirit has a dramatic, or dynamic, element to it. It was experienced, or to use contemporary parlance, it was very often charismatic in nature.

> If in his attempt to recapture this New Testament pattern, the Pentecostal saw the dynamic element as "distinct from and subsequent to," he should not thereby be faulted. The fault perhaps lay with the church which no longer normally expected or experienced life in the Spirit in a dynamic way.[136]

It would certainly be legitimate to ask how this remarkable development within present-day Pentecostalism took place. I am not aware of any appeal to the "lone pioneers" from Pentecostal tradition like Steiner by Pentecostal theologians such as Fee or Spittler.

It is probably fair to assume that Fee's view is not dominant in his denomination, especially not among the denominational leaders, but that it is through dialogue in academic circles such as the SPS and evangelical schools such as Gordon-Conwell and Fuller that Pentecostal theologians have broadened their outlook and have come to redefine what the distinctive element of Pentecostalism is. In Fee's case, the influence of the Reformed New Testament scholar, James Dunn, who is a sympathetic critic with participant-observer experience in charismatic groups in England, is marked. This development within classical Pentecostal circles has a substantial potential for ecumenical discussion and the developing of a truly ecumenical systematic theology–both in what it denies and in what it affirms.

Interestingly, some Catholic charismatics point in the same direction. Abdalazis de Moura, Helder Câdmara's theological research secretary, agreeing with Brazilian Lutheran theologian Harding Meyer, calls for a theology "that does not begin with theory but with Pentecostal practice."[137] In effect this is the same route that Fee wishes to follow: the realization that the Pentecostals "have something," although they may explain what it is very ineptly, and believe what they believe for all the wrong reasons!

It seems fitting to conclude the discussion on classical Pentecostalism here since many would agree that by this approach the doctrinal demarcation line between Pentecostal and charismatic has been crossed. It is to the wide variety of views within the charismatic movement that we now turn.

Endnotes 1

1. H. D. Hunter, *Spirit-Baptism: A Pentecostal Alternative* (Lanham, MD: University Press of America, 1983).

2. B. Bradford, *Releasing the Power of the Holy Spirit* (Oklahoma City: Presbyterian Charismatic Communion, 1983) 5.

3. I have this on the authority of Prof. R. Tuttle. See his *Help is on the Way: Overcoming Barriers to Spirit-Assisted Prayer* (Nashville: The Upper Room, 1983) 76. See also G. H. Williams and E. Waldvogel (Blumhofer), "A History of Speaking in Tongues and Related Gifts," in *The Charismatic Movement*, ed. M. P. Hamilton (Grand Rapids: Eerdmans, 1975) 81; and J. I. Packer, "Theological Reflections on the Charismatic Movement, Part 1," in *The Churchman* 94 (1, 1980): 21 n. 10.

4. J. I. Packer, *Keep in Step with the Spirit* (Old Tappan, NJ: Revell, 1984) 122.

5. Ibid. 126.

6. M. Green, *I Believe in the Holy Spirit* (London: Hodder and Stoughton, 1975) 124.

7. R. B. Gaffin, *Perspectives on Pentecost: Studies in New Testament Teaching on the Gifts of the Holy Spirit* (Phillipsburg, NJ: Presbyterian and Reformed, 1979) 27–28.

8. M. A. Eaton, "The Direct Witness of the Spirit in the Theology of David Martyn Lloyd-Jones (1899–1981)" (M.Th. thesis, University of South Africa, Pretoria, 1984) 3.

9. R. B. Gaffin, "The Holy Spirit and Charismatic Gifts," in *The Holy Spirit Down to Earth* (Grand Rapids: Reformed Ecumenical Synod, 1977) 5, 8.

10. Gaffin, *Perspectives on Pentecost,* 24.

11. Gaffin, *The Holy Spirit,* 6.

12. J. F. MacArthur, *The Charismatics: A Doctrinal Perspective* (Grand Rapids: Zondervan, 1978) 31, 58, 59, 64, etc.

13. Ibid., 120–22.

14. Ibid., 123.

15. J. D. G. Dunn, *Baptism in The Holy Spirit: A Reexamination of the New Testament Teaching on the Gift of the Spirit in Relation to Pentecostalism Today* (London: SCM, 1970) 4. See also Dunn's later study, *Jesus and the Spirit: A Study of the Religious and Charismatic Experience of Jesus and the First Christians as Reflected in the New Testament* (London: SCM, 1975).

16. K. Barth, *Die Kirchliche Dogmatik* IV.4 (Zürich: EVZ-Verlag, 1967) 34 (English translation by G. W. Bromiley, *Church Dogmatics* IV,4 [Edinburgh: T. & T. Clark, 1969] 31).

17. Ibid., 35.

18. Ibid., 32.

19. D. F. Olivier, "The Baptism With the Holy Spirit: An Exposition, Comparison and Evaluation of the Subsequent and Synchronous Concepts of the Baptism with the Holy Spirit with Reference to the Relation Christ-Spirit as Foundation of Man's Experience of God" (Ph.D. diss., Free University of Amsterdam, 1980) 48.

20. See, e.g., A. J. Mason, *The Relation of Confirmation to Baptism as Taught in Holy Scripture and the Fathers* (London: Longmans, Green & Co., 1891).

21. Ibid., 448.

22. Ibid., 456.

23. Green, *Holy Spirit,* 125.

24. E. H. Andrews, *The Promise of the Spirit* (Welwyn, England: Evangelical Press, 1982) 29.

25. J. K. Parratt, "The Seal of the Holy Spirit in the New Testament Teaching" (Ph.D. diss., University of London, 1965) 301–3.

26. Ibid., 304.

27. Ibid., 304–5.

28. J. K. Parratt, "The Witness of the Holy Spirit: Calvin, the Puritans and St. Paul," *EvQ* (July, 1969): 163.

29. Ibid.

30. Ibid. See also J. K. Parratt, "An Early Baptist on the Laying on of Hands," *Baptist Quarterly* 21 (7, 1966): 325ff.

31. Andrews, *Promise of the Spirit,* 29.

32. J. Calvin, *Institutes of the Christian Religion* (LCC: XX, XXI), tr. F. L. Battles (Philadelphia: Westminster, 1960) 584.

33. J. de Boer, *De Verzegeling met de Heilige Geest volgens de opvatting van de Nadere Reformatie* (Rotterdam: Bronder, 1968) 166.

34. Ibid., 166–67.

35. D. M. Lloyd-Jones, *God's Ultimate Purpose: An Exposition of Ephesians 1:1–23* (Edinburgh: Banner of Truth, 1978) esp., 243–311.

36. For an intensive exposition of Lloyd-Jones's views, see Eaton, "Direct Witness."

37. Ibid., 107–8.

38. Ibid., 108, 115.

39. Ibid., 121.

40. J. Edwards, *A Treatise on Religious Affections* (repr., Grand Rapids: Baker, 1982) esp., 302–45.

41. Eaton, "Direct Witness," 59.

42. Ibid., 62–63.

43. T. A. Askew and P. W. Spellman, *The Churches and the American Experience: Ideals and Institutions* (Grand Rapids: Baker, 1984) 44.

44. Quoted by H. K. La Rondelle, *Perfection and Perfectionism: A Dogmatic-Ethical Study of Biblical Perfection and Phenomenal Perfection* (Kampen: Kok, 1971) 309–10. It comes from the *Letters of the Rev. John Wesley,* American Standard ed. 8:238.

45. J. Wesley and C. Wesley, "A Plain Account of Christian Perfection," in *Selected Prayers, Hymns, Journal Notes, Sermons, Letters and Treatises,* ed. F. Whaling (London: SPCK, 1981) 327.

46. L. G. Cox, "John Wesley's Concept of Perfection" (Ph.D. diss., Iowa State University, 1959) 344.

47. Quoted from R. N. Flew, *The Idea of Perfection in Christian Theology: An Historical Study of the Christian Ideal for the Present Life* (Oxford: Clarendon, 1934) 327–28.

48. Cf. Packer, *Keep in Step,* 145, for a Reformed criticism of this aspect of Wesleyan theology.

49. Williams and Waldvogel, "Speaking in Tongues," 81.

50. Wesley, *A Plain Account,* 359.

51. D. W. Dayton, "From Christian Perfection to the 'Baptism of the Holy Ghost'," in *Aspects of Pentecostal-Charismatic Origins,* ed. V. Synan (Plainfield, NJ: Logos, 1975) 39–54.

52. Packer, *Keep in Step,* 147.

53. Ibid.

54. S. Barabas, *So Great Salvation: The History and Message of the Keswick Convention* (London: Marshall, Morgan & Scott, 1952) 109–10.

55. Ibid., 110.

56. Ibid., 121.

57. Ibid., 127.

58. Ibid., 134–35.

59. Ibid., 133–34.

60. Ibid., 135.

61. Packer, *Keep in Step,* 153.

62. Ibid.

63. C. N. Peckam, "An Investigation into Some of the Terms and Texts Used by Exponents of the 'Deeper Life' teaching" (M.Th. thesis, University of South Africa, Pretoria, 1984) 155.

64. Packer, *Keep in Step,* 161.

65. W. M. Menzies, "The Non-Wesleyan Origins of the Pentecostal Movement," in *Aspects of Pentecostal-Charismatic Origins,* ed. V. Synan (Plainfield, NJ: Logos, 1975) 86.

66. Ibid.

67. Packer, *Keep in Step,* 151.

68. C. E. Jones, *A Guide to the Study of the Holiness Movement* (Metuchen, NJ: Scarecrow Press, 1974) 485.

69. See next section on Pentecostalism.

70. D. B. Barrett, *World Christian Encyclopedia: A Comparative Study of Churches and Religions in the Modern World A.D. 1900–2000* (Nairobi: Oxford University Press, 1982) 838.

71. R. Quebedeaux, *The New Charismatics II* (San Francisco: Harper and Row, 1983) 198.

72. R. M. Anderson, *Vision of the Disinherited: The Making of American Pentecostalism* (New York: Oxford University Press, 1979) 43.

73. R. F. Lovelace, *Dynamics of Spiritual Life: An Evangelical Theology of Renewal* (Downers Grove, IL: Inter-Varsity, 1979) 120, 234, 252. Cf. J. Gresham, *Charles G. Finney's Doctrine of the Baptism of the Holy Spirit* (Peabody, MA: Hendrickson, 1987).

74. V. Synan, ed. *Aspects of Pentecostal-Charismatic Origins,* (Plainfield, NJ: Logos, 1975); and *The Holiness-Pentecostal Movement in the United States* (Grand Rapids: Eerdmans, 1971); Anderson, *Vision of the Disinherited;* and works by C. Brumback and C. W. Conn.

75. L. D. Hart, "A Critique of American Pentecostal Theology" (Ph.D. diss., Southern Baptist Theological Seminary, Louisville, 1978) 109. The division was suggested by Vinson Synan.

76. Hunter, *Spirit-Baptism,* 12.

77. Anderson, *Vision of the Disinherited,* 42.

78. F. A. Sullivan, "Pentecostalism 2." This article has been published in *Dictionnaire*

de Spiritualité (Paris: Beauchesne, 1984) Tome XII Première Partie, 1036–37. The author supplied me with the English original which has not yet been published.

79. W. J. Hollenweger, *The Pentecostals* (London: SCM, 1972) 25.

80. Anderson, *Vision of the Disinherited,* 168–71.

81. D. Reed, "Aspects of the Origins of Oneness Pentecostalism," in *Aspects of Pentecostal-Charismatic Origins,* ed. V. Synan (Plainfield, NJ: Logos, 1975) 143.

82. Anderson, *Vision of the Disinherited,* 180.

83. Ibid., 187.

84. Ibid., 176–77.

85. Ibid., 180.

86. Ibid., 176–77.

87. Ibid., 180.

88. Ibid., 188.

89. Barrett, *World Christian Encyclopedia,* 838.

90. W. J. Hollenweger, "Charismatische und pfingstlerische Bewegungen als Frage an die Kirchen heute," in *Wiederentdeckung des heiligen Geistes. Der Heilige Geist in der charismatischen Erfahrung und theologischen Reflexion,* Oekumenische Perspektiven 6, ed. M. Lienhard and H. Meyer (Frankfurt: Otto Lembeck, 1974) 55–57.

91. Hollenweger, *The Pentecostals,* 517.

92. Ibid., 515.

93. P. Damboriena, SJ, *Tongues as of Fire: Pentecostalism in Contemporary Christianity* (Washington, DC: Corpus, 1969) 66.

94. Ibid., 103.

95. J. J. McNamee, "The Role of the Spirit in Pentecostalism. A Comparative Study" (Ph.D. diss., Eberhard Karls University, Tübingen, 1974) 46. In the following section section on Gee, extensive use is made of this source.

96. Ibid., 48.

97. Ibid.

98. Ibid., 50–51.

99. Ibid., 71.

100. Ibid., 50.

101. Ibid., 77.

102. Quoted by K. McDonnell in his article "Classical Pentecostal/Roman Catholic Dialogue: Hopes and Possibilities," in *Perspectives on the New Pentecostalism,* ed. R. P. Spittler (Grand Rapids: Baker, 1976) 256.

103. J. T. Nichol, *Pentecostalism* (New York: Harper and Row, 1966) 208.

104. Synan, *Aspects of Pentecostal-Charismatic Origins,* 99–122.

105. Nichol, *Pentecostalism,* xiii.

106. N. Bloch-Hoell, *The Pentecostal Movement: Its Origin, Development and Distinctive Character* (New York: Humanities Press, 1964).

107. Damboriena, *Tongues as of Fire.*

108. Ibid., 93. The citation in the latter part of this quotation is from C. W. Conn, *Like A Mighty Army Moves the Church of God* (Cleveland, TN: Church of God Publishing House, 1955) 136.

109. Dunn has been referred to in 1.1 (see n. 15). F. D. Bruner, *A Theology of the Holy Spirit: The Pentecostal Experience and the New Testament Witness* (Grand Rapids: Eerdmans, 1970). Harold Hunter refers to Bruner and Dunn in *Spirit-Baptism,* xi, as the most notable who have called Classical Pentecostal Pneumatology into question. Hart, "American Pentecostal Theology," 129, sees them as "perhaps the two most significant evaluations of Classical Pentecostal Theology."

110. Hart, "American Pentecostal Theology," 129.

111. See ch. 3, 56–117.

112. R. A. Jensen, *Touched by the Spirit: One Man's Struggle to Understand his Experience of the Holy Spirit* (Minneapolis: Augsburg, 1975) 122.

113. J. R. W. Stott, *Baptism and Fullness: The Work of the Holy Spirit Today* (Leicester: Inter-Varsity, 1975) 10.

114. Hollenweger, *The Pentecostals*, 399.

115. Bruner, *A Theology of the Holy Spirit*, 92.

116. Ibid., 240.

117. Ibid., 205.

118. Ibid.

119. Ibid., 129.

120. W. J. Hollenweger, *New Wine in Old Wineskins: Protestant and Catholic Neo-Pentecostalism* (Gloucester, England: Fellowship, 1973) 42.

121. W. J. Hollenweger, ed. *Die Pfingstkirchen Selbstdarstellungen, Dokumente, Kommentare* (Stuttgart: Evangelisches Verlagswerk, 1971). Krust's article "Geistestaufe" is on 176–82.

122. Ibid., 178.

123. Ibid., 177–78.

124. Hollenweger, *The Pentecostals*, 341.

125. Ibid., 236.

126. Ibid.

127. Hollenweger, *Die Pfingstkirchen*, 181.

128. Ibid., 206.

129. Hollenweger, *The Pentecostals*, 552.

130. Compare his article "Glaube und Heilung" in Hollenweger, *Die Pfingstkirchen*, 207–19.

131. Hollenweger, *The Pentecostals*, 335.

132. Hollenweger, *Die Pfingstkirchen*, 552.

133. Hollenweger, *The Pentecostals*, 335.

134. G. D. Fee, "Baptism in the Holy Spirit: The Issue of Separability and Sequence," a paper read at the Society for Pentecostal Studies' Fourteenth Annual Meeting, 15–17 November 1984, at Gordon-Conwell Theological Seminary. The theme was "Toward a Pentecostal/Charismatic Theology: 'Baptism in the Holy Spirit.'" Fee's presentation later appeared in *Pneuma. The Journal of the Society for Pentecostal Studies.* 7 (Fall, 1985): 87–99.

135. G. D. Fee, "Hermeneutics and Historical Precedent. A Major Problem in Pentecostal Hermeneutics," in *Perspectives on the New Pentecostalism*, ed. R. P. Spittler (Grand Rapids: Baker, 1976) 122.

136. Ibid., 131.

137. Hollenweger, *New Wine in Old Wineskins*, 40.

NEO-PENTECOSTAL INTERPRETATIONS
OF SPIRIT-BAPTISM

$=$ **2**

2.1 The Search for Categories

Charismatic theology is still in its infancy; and yet when one surveys the literature of the last decade it is impossible not to be impressed by the way in which several theologians have tackled the problem of giving a comprehensive theological interpretation of that central renewal experience, the so-called baptism in the Holy Spirit.[1] The Roman Catholic scholars have led the way.[2]

In many of the early attempts at constructing a theology of Spirit-baptism, however, we do not find much coherent theology but rather a reflection on personal experience and a generalizing from that. As time went on this changed and we now find the first serious analyses on Spirit-baptism.

The charismatic renewal movement is unashamedly experiential in its nature. It is this "experience" of Spirit-baptism that usually takes people by surprise. Several theologians have started to attend charismatic gatherings as observers, ending up as participants. Due to the strong influence of a Western rationalistic mind-set very few modern Christians have the theological resources and historical insight to be able to interpret "what has happened to them" immediately. Their "theological apple cart" has, as it were, been overturned and the new charismatics are left scurrying in all directions to try and retrieve and maintain something of their religious tradition. This state of theological imbalance only seems to occur in contexts where religious experience is either frowned on as something "primitive" or else resolutely ignored in theological training.

Since this point is crucial in arriving at a satisfactory classification of charismatic viewpoints the pervasiveness and the results of this initial period of theological imbalance will be illustrated by quoting from several authors on the renewal. It is the aim to construct a new, more comprehensive categorization of charismatic views.

Larry Christenson quotes Clarence Finaas on the difficulties that arise when one tries to import another tradition (Pentecostalism) into the church. Finaas calls for a strategy of tolerance and restraint:

> Much caution and discretion is needed if we wish to share our new and fuller experience of Christ with our fellow-men, . . .

> In the flush of your new spiritual experience you are carried off your feet and your judgment may be temporarily unreliable. You feel that everything is so wonderful and therefore everything that you do must be right.

> Certainly what you do at such times may not be the wrong action, but it may not be the wisest thing.[3]

Richard Jensen, a Lutheran scholar, deals with the same issue in a more profound manner:

> . . . few Protestant churches have offered theological help for interpreting spiritual experience. Lutheran neo-Pentecostals, for example, seldom know how to interpret their experiences in the light of their own tradition. The same is true of other denominations.

> In the absence of good interpretive data a phenomenon like speaking in tongues often happens to people in a theological vacuum. They don't know how to interpret that experience. They look for help in the interpretive process.[4]

He goes on to express his view that they usually find this help in books, pamphlets, and tapes of questionable orthodoxy. To put it bluntly: although charismatics generally opted to remain in their respective denominations—a very significant ecclesiological decision—their denominations could not help them to understand these experiences (which to them were beyond question in their legitimacy but usually suspect in the eyes of the denominational leaders); so they took over the only interpretive framework which was readily available in popular form, namely, that of classical Pentecostalism.

It was the Roman Catholic scholar, Father Kilian McDonnell, who with profound insight immediately recognized the grave dangers of such a predicament. He sounded a clarion call warning of the polarization which Pentecostal theology would cause within the respective churches between the charismatics and non-charismatics.

Carter Lindberg (another Lutheran) also mentions Fr. McDonnell's role:

> Of those alert to this problem, one of the most consistent and cogent has been the Roman Catholic scholar of charismatic movements, Fr. Kilian McDonnell. In 1972 he wrote: "I know a Lutheran charismatic who is no longer theologically identifiable as a Lutheran. He has borrowed from the classical Pentecostals in the areas of their greatest weakness: exegesis and systematic theology. . . . But if the Lutheran charismatic is to be of service to those who need a theology of the charismatic spirituality within a Lutheran framework it will not do to take over uncritically the Wesleyan or the classical Pentecostal categories. The Lutheran neo-Pentecostals must set the charismatic spirituality within the authentic Lutheran theological tradition."[5]

McDonnell even gives certain suggestions about how this can be done.[6] Although some Catholics, McDonnell himself included, were busy at this very task of constructing a new Catholic framework for the renewal, there were other Catholics who were not heeding this timely warning. Even David du Plessis, who was given the title "Mr. Pentecost" by the American press and consistently expounded classical Pentecostal theology in all his international addresses in Catholic and World Council of Churches' circles, consistently pointed out to denominational charismatics that they did not need to become burdened by "Pentecostal baggage." They should appropriate the message of Pentecost for themselves and distinguish it from the incidental trappings which have become traditional in classical Pentecostal denominations. These trappings are seldom specifically mentioned but I would suspect that a list could include such issues as a two or three-stage view of the nature of the Christian life, believer's baptism by immersion, fundamentalistic usage of Scripture, premillennialism, dispensationalism, anti-intellectualism, lack of ecumenism and social involvement, cultural alienation, more demonstrative and louder style of worship, and legalistic moralism. Naturally this list of "sins" does not apply to all Pentecostals, but it includes those views which have traditionally been held against Pentecostalism by the established churches. In general one could possibly say it seems to apply less and less as time goes by and Pentecostal denominations move closer to mainstream Christianity.

Arnold Bittlinger attempts to contrast the European and American charismatic movements on precisely the point of Pentecostal influence:

> I am disturbed at the development in the USA, where the Pentecostal vocabulary is simply transferred to the new charismatic revival.[7]

Heribert Mühlen, Bittlinger's Catholic colleague in Germany, has also focused on differences between the American and European (or German) approaches to parish renewal in the charismatic movement.[8] This contrasting seems more familiar than accurate. Too often observers from outside the U.S. focus on the less acceptable religious phenomena they observe, and then they generalize, describing those elements as the typically American viewpoint. Of course Bittlinger does not go that far, but I am convinced that influential circles in the U.S. hold exactly the same views as Bittlinger and Mühlen with respect to the use of Pentecostal vocabulary and the need for the renewal of parishes.

Let us conclude this discussion of the unsettled nature of charismatic theology by a quotation from outside the movement. The British evangelical, John Stott, sums it up in this way:

> The Pentecostal churches, which have come into being since the turn of the century, do have published confessions of faith to which their pastors must adhere. But the charismatic movement is still very fluid, and its leaders and members are not all in full theological accord with one another. Some, it seems, hold a full "Pentecostal" position, virtually indistinguishable from that of Pentecostal churches. Others claim to have had what they are happy to call a "Pentecostal"

experience, but do not formulate it in terms of classical "Pentecostal theology." Yet others are in a state of flux in their own understanding, and are still seeking the right way to express their experience theologically.[9]

We now need to face the issue of categorizing the different emphases within the charismatic movement. This can be done in a number of ways. There are the possibilities of adopting denominational or general doctrinal approaches. One certainly could make an analysis of the Catholic, Lutheran, Anglican (or Episcopal), Presbyterian and Reformed, Baptist, Methodist, and non-denominational or independent charismatic views. All the denominations mentioned have organizations seeking to foster the charismatic renewal within their own churches. Some of them even work on an international level. However, I have chosen not to adopt this kind of approach as sole criterion for two reasons: (1) Some of the leading figures are hard to classify, e.g., Arnold Bittlinger comes from a German United Church background which includes Lutheran and Reformed traditions. He has served as a pastor of the Swiss Reformed Church, but he is usually referred to as a Lutheran theologian. Tom Smail, one of the leading British charismatic scholars, moved from the Church of Scotland (Presbyterian) to the Church of England (Anglican). It remains to be seen if this is going to amount to any doctrinal shift in his thinking. The basic issue is, of course, that a theological category such as Reformed or Wesleyan runs through several denominational barriers; e.g., apart from the (Dutch) Reformed and (Scottish) Presbyterian churches, Reformed doctrine is also accepted to varying degrees within Congregational, Baptist, and even Anglican denominations. (2) Furthermore there seems to be an unconscious "relativizing" influence at work in Christian churches–at least in mainline Protestant denominations. I wish to call this the Christian "genetic pool" theory. It is often quite baffling how, after a church schism ostensibly based on doctrinal issues, there seems to reappear within three or four generations with remarkable regularity the theological viewpoints of the church from which the new group seceded. This is not merely a matter of doctrine, but it is also observable within the realm of worship style, spirituality, and social ethics. A few personal examples may make this clearer. During a visit to the U.S. in 1984 I came across a strongly liturgical and sacramental thrust within some Reformed churches that even included elements such as vestments with bells, weekly communion with children included, candles, footwashing ceremonies, and Gregorian chants.

Within a Catholic context I found the Reformed transformational approach to culture as taught in H. Richard Niebuhr's classic, *Christ and Culture*,[10] being advocated as the Roman Catholic answer to societal issues. More general examples are the pervasiveness of Arminian attitudes in many Presbyterian churches and Brethren theories of dispensationalism and premillennialism among church members of traditionally amillennialist groups such as the mainline Lutheran and Calvinist denominations. It seems as if traits from the common genetic pool regularly reappear. Undoubtedly ecumenical dialogue and the broad availability of religious literature play a role in these processes.

Another possible grid for classification purposes could be the viewpoints taken on church structures. The denominational charismatics would then be contrasted with the independent, non-denominational groups. There is much merit in such an approach. It does nonetheless leave us with too substantial an overlap. There are many within the denominations whose views on Spirit-baptism are exactly the same as those who have opted to move out into local non-denominational structures. Such a classification has the added disadvantage that all non-denominational groups would be lumped together, whereas there seems to be marked differences between those who moved out of so-called dead denominations to form local and unrelated non-denominational Christian centers in the early years of the charismatic movement and the new charismatic denominations developing in the eighties and spreading across America and the world through aggressive church-planting strategies.

The use of denominational categories and standard doctrinal groupings has thus been found lacking, as well as the "stay in" or "come out" classification principle. The only apparent path is to categorize charismatic views on Spirit-baptism according to their content or distinctive characteristics (denominational perspectives can then be incorporated within this framework). There have been at least three minor attempts to do this. In his article in *The Church is Charismatic,* Arnold Bittlinger (previously of the Renewal and Congregational Life Department of the World Council of Churches in Geneva) distinguishes three main streams:

(1) classical Pentecostalism (2) so-called neo-Pentecostalism and (3) the charismatic congregational renewal. It is the distinction between (2) and (3) that is relevant to our purposes. He uses the term "neo-Pentecostal" innovatively–usually it is viewed as being synonymous with charismatic. The neo-Pentecostals are according to Bittlinger, those who largely adopt the theology of classical Pentecostals and attend regular interconfessional prayer meetings. The representatives of charismatic congregational renewal do not take over Pentecostal theology

> but interpret their spiritual awakening in the light of and within the context of their own theological tradition. Nor do they establish prayer groups independent of their congregations; rather, they seek to renew their own churches charismatically.[11]

Bittlinger is regarded by Kilian McDonnell, himself certainly one of the foremost Catholic authorities on the charismatic renewal, as "perhaps the most competent theologian within the charismatic movement."[12] (I would prefer to qualify this by adding the word Protestant before "charismatic movement" in this statement.) Unfortunately Bittlinger does not develop these categories mentioned above any further. They are, in fact, rather close to the three groups that Stott mentioned except for the third category.

Richard Jensen also makes some kind of a classification. After pointing out that charismatics are often faced with a theological vacuum because they receive no help in interpreting their experiences from their own denominations, he mentions two schemes of interpretation as dominating the horizon—both of which he considers to be highly problematic.[13] One is classical Pentecostal theology, which he describes as supplying evidence of the Spirit while Paul calls us to walk by faith, not by sight (2 Corinthians 5:7). The other interpretive framework Jensen describes as "the Kingdom within." He associates this with a general cultural shift in the Western world from intellectualism to romanticism expressed in trends like the "Jesus movement," Eastern mysticism, drugs, and the occult. This has also influenced theology: "In the early '70s theology has experienced some movement from an emphasis on intellect and will to an emphasis on experience and feeling."[14] The attempt to explain charismatic phenomena along these lines was led by the Episcopal scholar, Morton T. Kelsey, who argues for direct experiences of God and distinguishes two equally real worlds: (1) the visible space-time box of the empirical world and (2) the spiritual world. Jensen also sees a strong connection here with the Chinese Christian writer, Watchman Nee.[15]

Another brief but interesting distinction appears in Vinson Synan's book *In the Latter Days*. He writes as a classical Pentecostal and mentions that charismatic scholars soon developed their own position of "subsequence" and "initial evidence." This gave them "new theological respectability," avoided the idea of "two baptisms" and the dividing up of churches into the "Spirit-filled" and "second-class" members who had not received "the baptism."[16] Synan points out that they nevertheless "bordered" on initial evidence, seeing tongues as one of several authenticating gifts of the Spirit. He is of the opinion that "most charismatics felt that their experience was somehow incomplete if they failed to speak in tongues."[17]

Synan summarizes the new charismatic theology (which he sees as basically unified) as follows:

> Essentially, the "organic view" [Synan's term for the distinctive charismatic view] saw the Pentecostal experience as an essential part of the "rites of initiation," i.e., baptism, confirmation, and the Eucharist. Being "baptized in the Holy Spirit" was thus identical with water baptism, while the later experience of tongues and other gifts of the Spirit constituted a "release" or "actualization" of the grace given and received at baptism.[18]

As advocates of this view he mentions Kilian McDonnell, Larry Christenson, and Arnold Bittlinger. It is perhaps necessary to point out that most sacramental charismatics would be reticent to see Spirit-baptism as identical with water baptism and prefer the term "baptized in the Holy Spirit" (if at all acceptable) for what Synan calls "the later experience of tongues," which does then constitute for them a flowering of baptismal grace.

A very useful categorization was made by the German scholar, Siegfried Grossmann. He sees the need for developing clearer distinctions:

We must look for a screen which will make it easier to see finer differentiations than the broad categories of "classical Pentecostalism" and "new charismatic movement" allow.[19]

The only unambiguous distinction that he finds between Pentecostalism and the charismatic movement is that of structures—the Pentecostals formed their own denominations and the charismatics did not. (I would add that the historical distinction—1906 over against 1960—is also unambiguous, and in actual fact the structural dividing line no longer holds true since some independent charismatics have recently started forming separate denominational structures of their own.) Grossmann's classification is as follows:

1.1 Classical Pentecostalism.
1.2 Neo-Pentecostalism. These are charismatics who belong theologically to Pentecostalism but have not left the traditional churches. As examples he mentions the greater part of the Protestant charismatic movement in the U.S. and the United Kingdom, especially those associated with Dennis Bennett, Merlin Carothers, and the Full Gospel Business Men's Fellowship International.
2.1 Churches of the Charismatic Renewal.

By this designation Grossmann does not mean the new charismatic denominations but certain exceptional Pentecostal churches that do not really espouse classical Pentecostal theology. He makes reference to American Pentecostal churches with a Quaker tradition, to the Chilean Pentecostals influenced by a Methodist tradition, and to the Christlicher Gemeinschaftsverband Mülheim/Ruhr which is a loose Pentecostal group with a basically Reformational theology.

2.2 The movement towards the charismatic renewal of the churches. This is elsewhere less cumbersomely referred to as Parish renewal.

These groups are concerned to integrate the renewal into the life of the original denominations. Grossmann speaks of the aim to develop "eine kirchlich integrierte Theologie"[20] [a church-integrated theology]. This applies especially to the Roman Catholic Church and Protestant groups influenced by Larry Christenson and Arnold Bittlinger.

With these four attempts by Bittlinger, Jensen, Synan, and Grossmann as the interpretive tools to classify the theology of charismatics, one is aware that much "trail blazing" remains to be done. Of course there have also been some controversies in the renewal movement which have led to a polarization into opposing camps. Three come to mind immediately: (1) the Discipleship-Shepherding-Submission controversy, which arose in 1975 over the teaching of Bob Mumford and Derek Prince of the Christian Growth Ministries then centered in Fort Lauderdale, Florida; (2) the stir caused by the criticism of ecumenical covenant communities by J. Massyngberde Ford of Notre Dame University, South Bend, Indiana in 1978; and (3) the polarization since 1982 among the Catholic leadership of covenant communities over the role of Chris tians in the world, which has resulted in two parallel networks of Christian communities centered in Ann Arbor and South Bend. None of these, however, directly touched on the interpretation of Spirit-baptism or charismatic gifts and are thus not relevant to our present task.

In a University of South Africa study guide published in 1983 and reflecting research done in 1982, I myself made a threefold distinction of charismatic views on Spirit-baptism: (1) the Pentecostal-oriented approach, (2) the sacramentalistic view, and (3) the Reformational approach. The sacramentalistic view was that expanded by Cardinal Suenens and the first Malines Document compiled largely by Kilian McDonnell. It is also adhered to in some Lutheran and Anglican circles. This view of Spirit-baptism can best be summarized by the words: "release of the Spirit." On an experiential level the grace of infant baptism and confirmation is actualized and revitalized.

The Reformational view (which can also be dubbed evangelical) reserves the term "baptism in the Spirit" for the unique salvation-historical event of Pentecost. The reality that the term refers to is better described by the term "infilling" or "fullness" of the Spirit, which is an ethical category employed in the ongoing process of sanctification.[21] We come now, finally, to a new classification of charismatic views on Spirit-baptism. The rest of this study will be devoted to a development and exploration of these categories.

I am of the opinion that several different models of interpretation for Spirit-baptism have evolved over the last twenty-five years—at least four:

(1) A view which I wish to call *neo-Pentecostal* in the sense that Arnold Bittlinger has used the term. This view largely approximates to the classical Pentecostal doctrine of Spirit-baptism as a second stage in Christian life subsequent to conversion and generally resulting in the gift of speaking in tongues. Some minor modifications have been made to the original Pentecostal view.

(2) Second, the *sacramental* interpretation of Spirit-baptism as an experiential flowering of baptismal grace through the *release* of the Spirit. This seems to have been the earliest Catholic response to the charismatic renewal and has also become influential in some Anglican and Lutheran charismatic circles.

(3) A third, more evangelical, interpretive framework has been provided by those who see Spirit-baptism as the *final stage of Christian initiation* completing an otherwise incomplete initiation. Here there is substantial overlap with our second category. Akin to this are the views which substitute the biblical category of the *fullness* or *infilling* of the Spirit for Spirit-baptism and the position where Spirit-baptism is seen as an experience of the opening up of an individual's spirit to direct encounters with God in the realm of Spiritual reality. There are also other variations on this theme.

(4) The final category interprets Spirit-baptism as a spiritual growth experience, a highlight or milestone encounter, sovereignly granted by God but strongly influenced by personal and communal expectations. It is sometimes associated with the term "fullness" of the Spirit, but I prefer to see that as an ethical concept. As an experience "Spirit-baptism" is "loseable" and repeat-

able and does not necessarily lead to charismatic gifts. This category advocates the full integration of charismatic insights into the whole congregation trying to avoid two classes of Christians.

2.2 Introduction to Neo-Pentecostalism: The Representative Views of Don Basham

Estimating with any degree of accuracy the relative numerical strengths of the adherents of the four models which are now to be discussed is virtually impossible. The neo-Pentecostal model was certainly dominant in the early stages of the charismatic awakening and is still adhered to by millions of charismatics—especially those who belong to independent and non-denominational churches. There are, however, also leading exponents of the neo-Pentecostal interpretation within the established churches.[22] Most of these leaders came into the renewal movement in the sixties. From the seventies onwards we find that there has been a concerted effort in various circles to interpret Spirit-baptism within more traditional theological categories. The emergence of the other models begins to take place.

The standard study on Pentecostalism by Hollenweger reported in 1972:

> In contrast to the Catholic Pentecostals, the greater part of the Pentecostal movement within the Protestant churches seems to have taken over the Pentecostal doctrine of the two sorts of Christians, those who have been baptized in the Spirit and those who have not. The former are qualified by speaking in tongues.[23]

This doctrine of subsequence is found among both Catholic and Protestant charismatics, and the move away from it can be found not only in Catholic but in Protestant circles as well. Nonetheless, Hollenweger's assessment is largely accurate of the early phase of the charismatic movement. He also remarks that the adopting of the thought categories of Pentecostal doctrine exposes charismatics to all the misunderstandings of Pentecostal doctrine.[24] This is especially the case in America. Hollenweger concludes:

> It will become harder and harder to make a clear-cut distinction between American Pentecostals and American non-Pentecostals in the future, now that the experience and message of the baptism of the Spirit have found a way into all the American denominations.[25]

From his whole assessment it becomes clear that Hollenweger is not referring to the fact that the "renewal" has moved into mainline America, but to the fact that the response there (in contrast to Germany for example) has been an uncritical, virtually wholesale acceptance of the classical Pentecostal teaching on Spirit-baptism. I would venture that in 1988 not the neo-Pentecostal, but the sacramental model is adhered to by the majority of denominational charismatics, probably even by the majority of all charismatics, but there certainly has not been any survey done along these lines.

How would one define the neo-Pentecostal view of Spirit-baptism? A plethora of popular material exists. Rodman Williams probably presents the most detailed, biblical case in his work, *The Gift of the Holy Spirit Today*.[26] But for an orientation we should rather turn to Don Basham's little classic, *A Handbook on Holy Spirit Baptism*.[27] Don Basham is representative of the non-denominational charismatic movement which really is the most authentic form of neo-Pentecostalism. He was editor of *New Wine*[28] and part of the Christian Growth Ministries of Fort Lauderdale, Florida. He describes the baptism in the Holy Spirit in these words: "[It] is a second encounter with God in which the Christian begins to receive the supernatural power of the Holy Spirit into his life," and further: "[It] is given for the purpose of equipping the Christian with God's power for service."[29] He then goes on to contrast conversion, which he tends to associate closely with baptism by immersion in water, and Spirit-baptism:

> According to Scripture, these two baptisms are indicative of two separate, major experiences of the power of God. The first is conversion; the sinner's acceptance of Jesus Christ as Lord and Savior which brings salvation. He (the repentant sinner) gives testimony to his response to the gospel and his acceptance of Christ by receiving baptism in water for the remission of sins. Here, we see the new believer as the *object* of God's redemption. But the Lord is not satisfied with our conversion alone; He has promised us power to be His witnesses. So, a second time we are confronted with the power of God, this time in the baptism in the Holy Spirit through which the Christian is brought into a deeper relationship with Christ and the Holy Spirit for the purpose of making him—not an *object*—but an *instrument* of redemption.[30]

A few more elements in Basham's presentation need to be noted. Spirit-baptism has Jesus Christ as the baptizer (the baptizing agent) and the Holy Spirit as the baptismal element.[31] Note that in expressing the purpose of Spirit-baptism—namely an enduement with power—a conscious choice has been made for the Keswick rather than the Wesleyan tradition. Spirit-baptism is not seen as essential for salvation, but every Christian is meant to have this experience. In explaining the importance of Spirit-baptism, Basham lists a number of reasons from a pamphlet by Rufus Moseley. Here the impression is given that Spirit-baptism is the only (or main?) channel to experience the power of the Holy Spirit. Moseley's first point is:

> It is only through this Heavenly gift empowering us, guiding us and transforming us that we have immediate union with the glorified Jesus and are given power to do His work and His will and to grow up into His likeness.[32]

This does, of course, place those who claim that they have not (yet?) had the experience in a rather dubious position. It is apparent why Spirit-baptism is considered so vital, and even more apparent why those outside the Pentecostal/charismatic fold receive the impression that they are being downgraded to "second-class" Christians! In his further explication Moseley states that Jesus' redemptive work on the cross and his resurrection were merely preparatory to his role as Spirit-baptizer to impart believers with power. If the word "preparatory" has more than chronological significance in this context serious problems arise. Surely the work of Christ is a unity, and value judgments on the significance of the various elements involved are irrelevant (even irreverent) or erroneous if they are somehow intended to elevate the Third Person of the Trinity above the Second. It would, however, not be fair to implicate Basham in these consequences of the remarks even if he does quote them in agreement. Moseley was probably not trying to formulate doctrine.

How is Basham's view to be appraised? From this brief presentation it is plain that the typical two-stage Pentecostal grid is faithfully adhered to. This "theology of subsequence" leads one to classify this view as neo-Pentecostal rather than charismatic, if one wishes to use the word neo-Pentecostal in the sense that Grossmann and Bittlinger use it, namely in strong continuity with classical Pentecostalism. With respect to the "conditions" for receiving Spirit-baptism we find the clearest deviation from classical Pentecostalism. Basham is careful to underscore that one can never become worthy to receive "the baptism." It is an unmerited gift "immediately available to all who humbly and sincerely ask in faith."[33] This is a far cry from the introspection and anguish of the old-time "tarrying meetings" (note the words "immediately available"). Although Basham sees ignorance of Scripture and fear of public opinion as common hindrances,[34] they never take on the shape of the "conditions" which made Bruner despair of the sola fide in Pentecostalism.[35]

With respect to the doctrine of initial evidence, Basham, like all neo-Pentecostals, stays rather close to the classical Pentecostal view. The gift of tongues is the only certain scriptural evidence of Spirit-baptism. Nevertheless Basham is not dogmatic about this. One can receive Spirit-baptism without speaking in tongues because (and here Basham quotes from Matthew 19:26) "with God all things are possible."[36] One does get the impression that this is a concession which he tries to downplay. He refers to David du Plessis's comment "You don't have to, but you will."[37] Basham sums it up in words mirroring the neo-Pentecostal view on the relationship between Spirit-baptism and tongues:

> While there may be, and frequently are, other spiritual manifestations which accompany the experience of receiving the Holy Spirit, speaking in tongues remains the primary initial evidence.[38]

Here one notices the subtle identification of "receiving the Spirit" with Spirit-baptism. Although the work of the Spirit in conversion is recognized, the word "receiving" the Spirit gets an added connotation, namely to receive the Spirit in Spirit-baptism.

The more guarded tone that Basham employs with respect to tongues as initial evidence is actually not an innovation or development among charismatics. It represents faithfully the minority view taken by some Pentecostals—especially outside the U.S. Nils Bloch-Hoell refers to Swiss and English Pentecostals who are not dogmatic on tongues as the only form of initial evidence:

Even Pentecostals such as Barrett and Pethrus [leaders in Scandinavian Pentecostalism] admitted the exceptional possibility of Spirit-baptism without the accompanying glossolalia. The dominant opinion of the Pentecostal Movement is that the Spirit-baptism is accompanied by the speaking of tongues, but, at the same time, it allows, theoretically, the possibility of Spirit-baptism without glossolalia. Small opposing groups exist within the Pentecostal Movement which either deny the validity of a Spirit-baptism without the speaking with tongues, or oppose the doctrine of glossolalia as proof of Spirit-baptism.[39]

In contrast, the other views on Spirit-baptism move even further from classical Pentecostalism than the so-called neo-Pentecostals on the issue of tongues as initial evidence. The following quotation from Father O'Connor is fairly representative:

Besides the inner experience just described, the baptism in the Spirit is often manifested by the reception of some charism, especially the gift of tongues. Some people begin speaking in tongues at the moment of the baptism. Others do not begin until hours, days, or even weeks later, and some never do.[40]

2.3 The Dilemma of Neo-Pentecostalism and Denominational Structures (Excursus)

A very significant fact in the neo-Pentecostal view is the attitude towards denominational structures. Here, too, there is some ambivalence. It has been mentioned that the decision of the charismatic pioneer Dennis Bennett to stay in the Episcopal Church was an ecclesiologically significant step. This is—besides the historical differences—the major distinction between the Pentecostal movement and the first phase of the charismatic movement.[41]

Basham addresses the issue in answer to the question, If I receive the baptism in the Holy Spirit will it lead me away from my own church?[42] His answer, published in 1969, is succinct: "No, not unless you let it." He goes on to describe that even ten years prior to his writing, the chances that people would have felt compelled to change churches was much greater. He describes the establishment of the Pentecostal denominations and suggests that there is much more openness among denominations; they exert less pressure on charismatics to leave.[43] This situation has subsequently changed radically in many neo-Pentecostal circles. In the models to be discussed later, the view and attitude of Basham are still very much accepted as the norm and are probably emphasized even more strongly. In the neo-Pentecostal approach however, there is much ambiguity and difference of opinion. Those neo-Pentecostals still remaining (often only nominally) in their respective mainline denominations may adhere to Basham's view; however, practically all neo-Pentecostals who belong to independent and non-denominational churches disagree (as one would generally expect, since fellow members from mainline denominations chose to leave) and form or join independent and non-denominational churches often with a purely local character. Besides these (largely local) non-denominational groups there are also the new independent "church planting" groups which are actually forming new denominations—a phenomenon evolving especially in the eighties. These latter groups are often more Pentecostal than charismatic, both in their willingness to set up new denominations and in their theology. They are often led by pastors with a classical Pentecostal background. Their views on established church structures, together with the more locally based independent and non-denominational churches, encourages followers to separate rather than to remain.

Apart from the well-known view of David du Plessis, that Christians who receive the baptism in the Spirit should be encouraged to remain in their own churches and denominations, we find that classical Pentecostals did not all agree that charismatics should stay. Even someone like David Wilkerson who played a facilitating role in the Catholic Renewal movement (through his book *The Cross and the Switchblade*) caused a stir with his "one-man prophecy" on leaving the denominations. Fichter reports:

> He (Wilkerson) predicted that the warm reception Catholic Charismatics are receiving in the Catholic Church will not continue and that both Catholic and Protestant charismatics will be forced to leave their churches and form a "supernatural church of true believers."[44]

This prediction was rejected by Ralph Martin and David du Plessis. After an initial period of uneasiness (well attested to by Vinson Synan in his booklet *Charismatic Bridges*),[45] most classical Pentecostals have now accepted that the charismatic movement is not destined to result in a large-scale swelling of their ranks, and they accept the legitimacy of denominational charismatics remaining "to be a witness" to the others in their traditions. Often it is less the doctrinal issues and more the concerns of lifestyle, culture, and ethics that form barriers between Pentecostals and charismatics. This is succinctly illustrated by the original title of Douglas Wead's book: *Father McCarthy Smokes a Pipe and Speaks in Tongues.*[46]

Ronald Knox, a Roman Catholic scholar, has written a history of "Enthusiasm," a significant and polemical interpretation of the so-called marginal or sectarian groups in the history of the church.[47] His book is often used in critiques of the charismatic movement. A Catholic charismatic scholar, Alan Schreck, wrote his thesis on "Ronald Knox's Theory of Enthusiasm and Its Application to the Catholic Charismatic Renewal" in 1979.[48] What concerns us here is Knox's view of the development of a sect. In this he represents a rather one-sided tradition which almost always sees the "church" as *real* Christianity while the enthusiasts are deterministically destined to form an elitist cult group on the periphery of Christendom. Although this is an invalid generalization, Knox's argument is very convincing and certainly applies to the development of some of the independent charismatic groups:

> There is, I would say, a recurrent situation in the Church history—using the word "church" in the widest sense—where an excess of charity threatens unity. You have a clique, an elite, of Christian men and (more importantly) women, who are trying

to live a less worldly life than their neighbors, to be more attentive to the guidance (directly felt, they would tell you) of the Holy Spirit. More and more, by a kind of fatality, you see them draw apart from their co-religionists, a hive ready to swarm. There is provocation on both sides, on the one part, cheap jokes at the expense of overgodliness, acts of stupid repression by unsympathetic authorities, on the other contempt of the half-Christian, ominous references to old wine and new bottles, to the kernel and the husk. Then, while you hold your breath and turn your eyes in fear, the break comes; condemnation or secession, what difference does it make? A fresh name has been added to the list of Christianities.[49]

My basic objection to this interpretation of history is the deterministic element. I believe a careful study of the history of the church will also reveal pockets of "enthusiasm" that opted to remain within the established structures and eventually had a renewing influence on them, as well as the re-uniting of groups after schisms.

Due to the importance of this particular facet of the neo-Pentecostal view it will be dealt with in greater detail in the following pages before further attention is given to the neo-Pentecostal doctrine of Spirit-baptism. The attitude towards church structures is rather important to the understanding of the neo-Pentecostal view on Spirit-baptism. The facile rejection of established denominations as being "spiritually dead" correlates with the incipient elitism of a two-stage view of Christian life. To those who see themselves as "first-class Christians" because they have been Spirit-baptized it is much more acceptable to leave the "second-class Christians" and the nominal Christians behind in the traditional churches, while they attempt to form new structures that would be only for "born again" and "Spirit-baptized" believers.

The alternatives "come out" or "stay in" have almost a classical ring to them. The traditional debate has often centered on the scriptural admonition: "Therefore come out from them, and be separate from them, says the Lord" (2 Corinthians 6:17). It would seem that the "dead denominations" are here viewed as tantamount to consisting of non-believers, since that surely is the context of these words. The come out/stay in debate has certainly been relevant from the time of the historic Protestant reformation where the magisterial Reformation of Luther and Calvin was questioned by the more radical Anabaptist Reformers. A few decades ago the same debate surfaced in British evangelicalism when Martyn Lloyd-Jones advocated "coming out" and John Stott "staying in." More recently (1974) Arthur Wallis and David Watson defended the respective positions again. This time it happened within the context of the charismatic renewal. Their positions will now be discussed.

Arthur Wallis, who is associated with the British House Church movement, (a misnomer but the only one available at present) develops his view in *The Radical Christian*.[50] He explains that in the early seventies many Christians from the historic churches left to form new groups due to ostracization and opposition to their receiving Spirit-baptism. In reaction to this

the charismatic renewal has issued an uncompromising call to all church waverers, dissidents or potential deserters–"stay in your church," at least as much as in you

50

lies. If you get thrown out join some other established church but do not form a new church. That would be to miss God's best. . . . As one quite deeply involved in the charismatic movement from the start I sounded a different note.[51]

His solution sounds perfectly reasonable – reject "blanket" calls. It is the prerogative of the Holy Spirit to guide the individual in each particular instance. However, as one continues through the chapter it becomes increasingly apparent that Wallis cannot conceal the ax he has to grind:

> I see no future for denominations because I don't find them in the heavenly blueprint. They are contrary to God's declared purpose for his church in this age. But I do see a glorious future for the people of God, many of whom are currently in denominations. There are some reading these pages who should leave the churches with which they are associated, and need to seek God earnestly as to where he would have them planted. Equally, there are others who may want move but should be counselled to stay where they are.[52]

The last sentence with its reservation may come as a surprise. Wallis mentions three reasons for staying put: (1) when the motivation for leaving is a spirit of rebellion against leaders, (2) when it is simply boredom with the old or a yearning for "some new thing," and (3) when there is no biblical conviction and church affiliation is merely a matter of convenience or expedience. Certainly these seem to be legitimate reasons for staying, but one wonders if they are the only ones that could be mentioned.

The basic thrust of Wallis's argument is, nonetheless, to question "denominational loyalty," to present a radical restoration movement over against the ideals of reformation and renewal and to give the concept of tradition a thoroughly negative content by viewing it as designating only an unscriptural accommodation to the ways of the "world." The charismatic movement is seen as having compromised with the "world" and being unmistakably on the decline: "We must continue to move because the cloud is still moving. If we stop we stagnate. If we crystallize we shall soon fossilize."[53] There is a stirring romantic enthusiasm here which has a strong appeal, but to the student of history it looks unmistakably like the yearning after the "restoration" of the golden age, or in lighter vein, seeking the pot of gold beyond the rainbow! Countless restorationist attempts to reestablish the authentic "New Testament church" have occurred. Generally they took no account of biblical perspectives such as found in Christ's parable of the kingdom being like the wheat that grew together with the tares (Matthew 13:24–30).

Wallis's exposition will have to suffice as representing this perspective since the neo-Pentecostals who advocate "coming out" are not given to much documentation of their view. A facile identification of other Christian churches as being "spiritually dead" or the loaded question, Shouldn't you join the church where you see things happening and the Spirit of God moving? is generally the approach in conference addresses and sermons.

David Watson, who was a leader in the Anglican renewal movement in England, took the other side in this debate and argued for staying in. He discusses the issue in the light of various parts of Scripture. He points out that in the Old Testament God frequently worked through a remnant. There were times of spiritual decline and apostasy:

> Yet, although God frequently chastened and judged His people, He did not finally overthrow them. . . . It was in fact because of the remnant that Israel itself could be saved. Nothing is beyond the sovereign grace God. Even Ezekiel's dry bones rattled and came to life.[54]

The same principle continues in the New Testament. Watson points out how Paul stresses the vital importance of maintaining unity of the Spirit in the bond of peace:

> He called the motley, worldly sinful, divisive Christians at Corinth "the church of God.". . . He urged them to act as one body, to heal all divisions, to bring together all splinter groups.[55]

In his call to keep the unity Watson is just as radical as Wallis:

> Any attempt to split off into separate groups, whether on grounds of relative spirituality or different personality, was acting "in the flesh." Rather they (the Corinthians) were to submit to one another in love, to see themselves as members one of another, and to find their freedom in Christ, not just in their situation. Yet here, in this particular church, were some Christians who were denying the resurrection, or getting drunk at the Lord's supper, or living with prostitutes! Still, even they had to keep united in Christ![56]

Watson continues with perspectives from 1 Thessalonians, the Pastorals, and Galatians:

> [Paul] made it clear that there was to be no spiritual élite, creamed off from the other weaker, worldly Christians. Rather, the more mature Christians had to "admonish the idle, encourage the faint-hearted, help the weak, be patient with them all." And this was to a church that had a very lively expectation of Christ's return. Instead of the mature splitting off from the weak to prepare a "pure bride" for the coming of Christ (as some have often advocated), they were to stay together, not quenching the Spirit but increasing and abounding in love. And to the Galatians Paul wrote that only by bearing one another's burdens, and by restoring those who had gone astray, could they fulfill the law of Christ.[57]

Turning to church history Watson criticizes the restorationist view, now resorting to a rather one-sided presentation:

> Countless Christian groups have split away from some traditional denomination, with every intention of forming a "pure" church. For a time all is well. Certainly God may bless them. After all, His word is always powerful among those who believe. But before long the same pattern emerges: purity becomes impurity, vitality becomes formality, orthodoxy becomes hypocrisy. And the Christian landscape is further polluted with yet another "denomination" to confuse the world.[58]

This brief presentation of denominational development in church history is open to question. One almost senses a deterministic downward trend. Watson does mention that God often brings new life within the mainstream churches. Once again he oversimplifies when he asks:

Can the Spirit really lead Christians away from the less spiritual brethren to form a more spiritual church, when that same Spirit has already commanded in Scripture that we should do our utmost to maintain unity? And isn't it dangerously akin to spiritual pride to assume that this new fellowship is more spiritual or more pure than the old one? By whose standards? "Every way of a man is right in his own eyes, but the Lord weighs the heart." Indeed, if we have the mind of Christ, we are in humility to count others better than ourselves.[59]

To those who have come into the charismatic renewal Watson seems to direct this reminder:

In most places we should be able to find some signs of spiritual life before long. And where there is life, we may well be called by God to strengthen that life.

God forbid that we shall split off simply to form a fellowship to our own liking, however biblical that fellowship may seem to be. We come to church primarily to give, not to get; and the more we give the more we shall receive. Indeed we all need one another.[60]

Having presented some of the arguments in this perennial debate it is necessary to weigh them briefly. Watson's position has perhaps been argued more soundly and yet Wallis's pathos for uncompromising discipleship is laudable. I believe we are presented with a dilemma. We should not try to play "unity" and "purity" against one another. They are both essential biblical challenges which need to be presented to the church. It is true that many people have seceded too rapidly and too easily from historic Christianity. It is also correct that there are circumstances when this is truly unavoidable and therefore necessary. This general principle seems obvious. The real problems lie in the interpretation of the situation and circumstances. If any generalization is permissible with respect to the charismatic movement I would think that there is an overly limited view on maintaining unity.

The issue of the relationship to established church structures is very important to the charismatic movement as a whole. It is being discussed under the neo-Pentecostal position because this is the only model of interpretation where there is some ambiguity and difference of opinion regarding the legitimacy of established church structures. To conclude with this issue reference will be be made to the views of Richard Lovelace of Gordon-Conwell Seminary. He is well-known as a historian of church revivals. He discusses the issue of unity and revival in chapter 10: "Unitive Evangelicalism" in his classic, *Dynamics of Spiritual Life. An Evangelical Theology of Renewal.* He portrays the contemporary scene in America:

Currently our denominations seem to break down into two categories: the smaller, conservative separatist bodies maintaining the pure church ideal with an antiseptic discipline so strong that it occasionally sterilized their own creativity; and the large historical descendants of earlier separations, now so indiscriminately inclusive that to Evangelicals they resemble mission fields.[61]

Lovelace is quick to point out that the evangelical awakenings do not arise in the separatist Anabaptist circles, but rather in the mainstream flowing from the unitive Protestantism of the magisterial Reformers, which was transformationist in its strategy and ecumenist in its goal.[62]

He maintains that historic evangelicalism has a unitive thrust.[63] Lovelace also presents a biblical model of recovery from backsliding and decay.[64] To divide the church in order to renew it is, according to Lovelace, like severing the parts of a body to improve its health. Nevertheless, there are situations when separation is necessary, to extend the metaphor: gangrenous limbs must be amputated if possible. This happens when consciences are violated and the practice of Christians in essential areas is restrained. Lovelace is aware that the ascertaining of guidance from Scripture in such cases is not unproblematic:

> . . . in fact the Scriptures simply give us accurate criteria concerning the apostasy of individuals, not groups, and even then it is not assumed that every apostasy is terminal.[65]

Lovelace clearly advocates a *unitive* evangelicalism. In this inclusive stance much of the power and influence of the church in society seems to lie. The separatist idea of "coming out" has been a contributing factor towards the decline of Christian influence in the Western world—especially in the English-speaking part of it. One's attitude towards church structures consequently has far-reaching repercussions. The divisiveness that has run rampant in Protestant circles in the last few centuries has aided the inroads of secularism. I am in full agreement with the basic thrust of Lovelace's argument which he develops in the following manner.

Lovelace laments the loss of evangelical influence in American Protestantism. He states that evangelical churchmen were still in control by the middle of the nineteenth century. The subsequent loss of ground is due in part to weaknesses within the evangelical movement, such as loss of faith and the divisiveness of twentieth-century fundamentalism. Persuaded that the end of history was near and that the institutional church was damaged beyond repair by secularism, fundamentalists withdrew much of their influence.[66]

In conclusion we need to look at the connection between the separatist, restorationist ideal and the neo-Pentecostal variety of charismatic thinking. One could say that Lovelace here represents the views of the denominational charismatic movement. The "pure church" ideal which he rejects is seen more distinctly in the early development of Pentecostalism. In fact the two-stage grid for the pattern of Christian life which is typical of both Pentecostalism and neo-Pentecostalism often tends to favor the separatist ideal. The theological position of dividing Christians into two qualitatively distinguished groups does, of course, not necessarily lead to a splintering off of the "more spiritual" Christians. The Roman Catholic Church has managed to distinguish lay people from the ordained ministry, or even the "religious" (monastic structures) from the "secular" (parish structures), and have demanded differing levels of spiritual discipline from the respective groups. These distinctions are, however, largely based on office, differing vocations and function, and the tensions which arise can usually be contained or solved within the framework of authority of the Catholic episcopal structures.

It is also true that Protestantism has always harbored a separatist ideal and a restorationist spirit in some form or degree. This suggests that, given the potential of a natural tendency to polarize unity and purity in the church, and given the tradition of Western individualism, the two-stage pattern of Pentecostalism tends to facilitate divisiveness rather than to counter it. This can be easily illustrated by looking at the broad field of the charismatic movement. It is precisely within those groups adhering to the neo-Pentecostal teaching that the independent and non-denominational churches have come into being. Where the other interpretations of Spirit-baptism are adhered to a more unitive thrust is apparent, and the possibility of splitting off to form a new group seems more remote. Only history will show if this continues to hold true. The hidden elitism of the doctrine of subsequence which partitions Christians off into the "haves" and "have nots" often leads to divisiveness in a local congregation and the same holds true for a denomination. In a fair number of cases this same spiritual pride seemingly leads pastors and their followers to break their existing denominational ties and form independent, separatist congregations. Here, again, one should be careful not to generalize.

2.4 The Neo-Pentecostal Position on Spirit-Baptism

After presenting Basham's views as an introduction to the neo-Pentecostal position and discussing the issue of remaining within established church structures, it is now necessary to deal with neo-Pentecostal doctrine in greater detail, especially the teaching on Spirit-baptism. This task presents us with a problem. Unfortunately, there is no detailed or systematic presentation of the neo-Pentecostal argument, and to discuss the views of various writers will still not present a balanced overview. Very often the sections on Spirit-baptism in neo-Pentecostal writings are not much more than the mentioning of the scriptural passages where the expression occurs and then a discussion on the role of tongues as the sign of one's having received the baptism. Two prominent critics of the movement help in defining the neo-Pentecostal view of Spirit-baptism.

Anthony Hoekema gives a traditional Reformed critique of neo-Pentecostal teaching on baptism in the Spirit. He summarizes:

> The central doctrine of neo-Pentecostalism is its teaching on the baptism in the Holy Spirit. So basic is this teaching to the neo-Pentecostal movement that if you take this doctrine away from it, what you have left is no longer neo-Pentecostalism.[67]

He defines Spirit-baptism as commonly viewed by neo-Pentecostals as follows:

The baptism in the Holy Spirit is an experience distinct from and usually subsequent to conversion in which a person receives the totality of the Spirit into his life and is thereby fully empowered for witness and service.[68]

He continues:

though the Spirit touches a person's life at the time of conversion, He does not come into one's life in His totality until the time of the Spirit-baptism. In neo-Pentecostal circles, therefore, one is not considered to have available to him the full power of the Holy Spirit until he has experienced Spirit-baptism; hence all Christians are urged to seek such a Spirit-baptism.[69]

This is, indeed, a good summary. Hoekema's point that without Spirit-baptism there would be no neo-Pentecostalism should be noted. In a later chapter it will be argued that the essence of the charismatic movement actually lies elsewhere, although this is not often realized or conceded by neo-Pentecostals. The similarity of neo-Pentecostal Spirit-baptism to the Pentecostal view can be seen from Bruner's definition of the Pentecostal concept of Spirit-baptism:

...the baptism in the Holy Spirit is a critical experience subsequent to and/or distinct from conversion granting the believer the benefits of a permanent, personal, and full indwelling of the Holy Spirit and so providing power for Christian service, particularly evangelistic service, with the equipment of the spiritual gifts.[70]

Instead of first discussing a number of neo-Pentecostals and their sketchy views on Spirit-baptism, an attempt will now be made to present the entire argument in outline form. The similarity of neo-Pentecostalism to the finished work Baptistic Pentecostals will become apparent.

Neo-Pentecostals see Spirit-baptism as a distinct crisis experience subsequent to conversion-regeneration. It is not essential for "salvation," but it is necessary for every Christian and is available to all believers through faith. It results in an enduement with power for witnessing and service. It has no direct connection with the sacraments of water baptism or holy communion. Neither does it necessarily guarantee greater holiness, but the general expectation is that it should lead to growing in grace and a prospering of the fruit of the Spirit. "Spirit-filled" or "Spirit-baptized" believers are seen as existing on a higher level of grace since they have been converted or born again as well as having "received" the Holy Spirit as a second experience. This experience of Spirit-baptism has changed their lives permanently and placed them in a new state in the eyes of God. This is evidenced by the outflow of the gifts of the Spirit. Tongues usually occupies the first position with respect to these gifts, often occurring at the time of the experience of Spirit-baptism itself. It is probably the gift found most frequently among neo-Pentecostals, but few would dogmatically insist on tongues as the *only* acceptable form of "initial evidence." Spirit-baptism opens the door to a whole range of charismata and spiritual experiences and a new awareness of the "supernatural" dimension of reality.

After the initial Spirit-baptism which brings one into the higher spiritual level there may be occasional further "infillings" of the Spirit.

The biblical "evidence" for this neo-Pentecostal teaching is found mainly in the book of Acts but is not limited to it. There are seven references to one "being baptized in the Holy Spirit" in the New Testament, namely Matthew 3:11; Mark 1:8; Luke 3:16; John 1:33; Acts 1:5; 11:16; and 1 Corinthians 12:13. Jesus is seen as the baptizer in or with the Holy Spirit. Jesus is the agent and the Holy Spirit the element into which the believer is immersed as in water.

The Pauline reference in 1 Corinthians 12:13 presents a problem to neo-Pentecostals. It reads: "For by one Spirit we were all baptized into one body— Jews or Greeks, slaves or free—and all were made to drink of one Spirit" (RSV). Several exegetical options are available, and they will be discussed more fully when we try to establish the New Testament usage of being baptized in the Spirit. Some neo-Pentecostals see the whole verse as referring to the equipping and empowering activity of the Spirit—the crucial second experience, and consider the "all" as merely referring to all the Corinthian believers. Others view the first half of verse 13 as denoting regeneration/conversion and the second half Spirit-baptism. A third rather shaky neo-Pentecostal interpretation is to let the *eis* (into) have the meaning of "for the sake of": "For in one Spirit we were all baptized for the sake of one body." This gives the sense of receiving Spirit-baptism while already in the body. Another important issue is whether the *en* should be translated *in* or, instrumentally, *by*—the latter yielding a baptism *by* the Spirit rather than *by* Jesus *in* the Spirit.

The main neo-Pentecostal argument is usually presented with a three-pronged approach. The two-stage nature of Christian life is defended analogically. The experience of Jesus, the apostles and several "cases" in Acts are seen as following the same twofold structure.

2.4.1 The Analogy Based on the Life of Jesus

The main thrust of the first part of the argument is as follows: Jesus is born, conceived of the Holy Spirit, through the Virgin Mary. This correlates with our supernatural rebirth or regeneration. It appears, however, that this was insufficient for the public ministry of Jesus. Before embarking on this he receives water baptism and the anointing of the Holy Spirit from on high: "And when he came up out of the water, immediately he saw the heavens opened and the Spirit descending upon him like a dove" (Mark 1:10). This is seen as Jesus' Spirit-baptism, which brought an enduement with power and initiated his period of public ministry which included signs and wonders. It is then concluded that if the Son of God needed this extra experience how much more do we, his disciples.

This argument fails to take sufficient cognizance of the uniqueness of Jesus and his unrepeatable role in salvation history. The "Jesus as example," which was a common model in the liberal ethical tradition of the nineteenth century, is inevitably very selective. Neo-Pentecostals use it within a different framework but still take some elements in Jesus' life as normative for his followers while others are passed by, e.g., the fact that he remained unmarried, was circumcised, or that he waited until his thirtieth year before starting his ministry! Surely Jesus' virgin birth is a very specific and unique event, just as his "only begotten" sonship is different from the fact that all believers are sons and daughters of the Father too. The baptism of John is also quite different from Christian baptism. This becomes apparent when those who had received the baptism of John are rebaptized in Acts 19:5. The special sign of God's pleasure in his Son–the voice from heaven proclaiming "thou art my beloved Son; with thee I am well pleased"–speaks of a singular relationship with the Father and bears connotations of the divine enthronement ceremonies of Israel. It is repeated at the Mount of Transfiguration (Mark 9:7). These elements do not feature in the analogy of the neo-Pentecostals.

The imagery of the dove descending on Jesus could have evoked at least three associations. In Song of Solomon 2:12, "the voice of the turtledove is heard in our land," the dove is seen as the herald of spring. This may seem a far-fetched analogy, but the Jewish Targum identified this singing as "the voice of the Holy Spirit of salvation."[71] The dove also features after the flood as the sign of new life–the freshly plucked olive leaf–and the sign that the waters had subsided and a new age could commence (Genesis 8:10–12).

There is also the possibility of a creation motif–the Spirit of God hovering over the waters like a bird brooding over her nest. This interpretation given to Genesis 1:2 may not be considered all that authoritative today, but in rabbinic tradition this bird was expressly identified as a dove.[72] Montague relates all of this to the baptism of Jesus.[73] Such application makes it clear that we have here the dawning of a new age or era and that the baptism of Jesus in the Jordan certainly cannot be directly applied to any specific experience in the life of every Christian. Jesus is assuming his ministry as the Messiah, the long-expected anointed one, not setting an example for his followers but proclaiming the kingdom and inaugurating the salvation in which they will all share.

2.4.2 The Analogy Based on the Lives of the Apostles

The case of the apostles is also seen by neo-Pentecostals as a twofold or "two-stage" experience. The "Johannine Pentecost" of John 20:22 is seen as the regeneration-conversion of the apostles. Yet they are told to tarry in Jerusalem. Their experience of God's Spirit in coming to faith is still incomplete. On the day of Pentecost they receive their Spirit-baptism, which is an enduement with power to witness (Acts 1:4–8).

However, I would submit that the position of the apostles/disciples as living between the ages–the old and the new–places them in an unrepeatable position. It is really futile to ask exactly when they were "born again" or even baptized in water since the New Testament does not tell us. The Gospels are written from the post-resurrection perspective. If John 20:22 does speak of conversion, as neo-Pentecostals suggest, does this also mean that they set the example for the way of conversion? Few Christians today would advocate the following as a method of evangelizing:

> he breathed on them, and said to them, "receive the Holy Spirit. If you forgive the sins of any, they are forgiven; if you retain the sins of any, they are retained" (John 20:22, 23).

The writer of John is connecting the mission of the disciples to the enduement of the Spirit's power, which brings new creative life. The act of breathing on the disciples would surely have evoked associations of Genesis 2:7 (when God breathed the breath of life into man's nostrils in the second creation account) and Ezekiel 37:9 (the valley of dry bones that come alive through breath or wind from God). In other words, the symbolism is that of a new creation. Montague comments:

> John joins the moment of giving of the Spirit to the moment of the missioning word of Jesus, thus showing the theological inter-relationship once more of word and Spirit.[74]

The absence of the article before Holy Spirit probably reinforces the connection with creation. John is also concerned to associate the power of the Spirit to the forgiveness of sins.

It may be concluded that the "Johannine Pentecost" does speak of newness of life, the Spirit creating life anew, but this is, perhaps, focused more on the new life or regeneration of others that will follow from their mission and witnessing than on their own regeneration. It certainly does not do justice to the context to suggest that we find evidence here for the first stage (conversion) of a two-stage grid.

The idea that it is still necessary to "tarry in Jerusalem" has been given up by neo-Pentecostals. One could say that the older Pentecostals who advocated such a period of preparation were more consistent in their application of the analogy of the apostles. Neo-Pentecostals are wary of it because it smacks of adding some form of human merit to God's grace. The period of "tarrying" sometimes fulfilled the role of anguished searching and emotional repentance and restitution for past sins. It is furthermore not possible to place a one-to-one correlation between present-day Spirit-baptisms and the day of Pentecost. Although tongues form an easy part of the analogy, there is seldom mention of the other elements such as "a sound from heaven like the rush of a mighty wind" or "tongues as of fire resting on each one." Like the crucifixion and resurrection, Pentecost as the outpouring of the Spirit on the church is a unique event of momentous salvation-historical significance. In a strict sense it is logically unrepeatable, although this fact should not be allowed to blind us to the symbolic value of these events. Reference has already been made to the use of the cross and the resurrection as the ongoing symbols of sanctification— dying to self and sin and the rising up of the new life in Christ. In a similar vein Pentecost can be a symbol of a fresh coming of the Spirit, of greater commitment, of a spiritual breakthrough. That does not mean, however, that the two-stage experience of the apostles (if one can speak of this at all in their case) forms a paradigm for contemporary experience.

This conclusion is further underscored by the fact that the apostles began believing in Jesus (in some or other form at least) before the Spirit was poured out on the church on the day of Pentecost. This places them in a situation different to every Christian living after Pentecost. It was thus necessary that the apostles experience the new freedom and life in the Spirit which came with Pentecost in a unique way because they could not experience it before it had come (prior to Acts 2).

2.4.3 The Cases from Acts—Particularly Acts 8 and 19

The third basic argument of the neo-Pentecostals hinges on the five cases in Acts. These are Pentecost (Acts 2), the Samaritans (Acts 8), Paul (Acts 9), Cornelius (Acts 10), and the disciples in Ephesus (Acts 19). The neo-Pentecostal position here is the same as that of the classical Pentecostals who build their doctrine of initial evidence on the fact that tongues is explicitly mentioned in three of these instances and may be presumed in the other two (Acts 8 and 9). The case for a two-stage grid for Christian experience is most clearly illustrated from Acts 8 and Acts 19. In both cases we seem to have a situation where there are Christian believers who experience some or other lack. This is then taken care of through a further experience which is accompanied by the Holy Spirit coming upon them. There has been a great deal of exegetical debate on these passages within charismatic and anti-charismatic circles, and it would not be helpful to try to repeat all the argumentation in this context. Reference can be made to Bruner, Culpepper, Dunn, Ervin, Hoekema, Hummel, Hunter, Smail, and Williams.[75] There seems to be a growing consensus that there was a great fluidity with respect to the initiation rites at this early stage in the development of the Christian church. This should prevent us from making doctrinal conclusions from the chronology and the form in which the Spirit worked in the particular instances.

The most puzzling case of all—that of the Samaritans—also seems to be the case which could have given the strongest backing to the Pentecostal and neo-Pentecostal position. Acts 8:16 refers to a receiving of the Spirit a period of time after the Samaritans had been baptized in the name of the Lord Jesus (and had thus been converted?). Montague summarizes the arguments:

> There are two possible explanations for this exception. The first is that something was missing in the dispositions of the Samaritans which impeded the full normal effect of baptism.[76]

> The other explanation is that Philip's mission to Samaria was not officially commissioned by the Jerusalem church and the apostles (Philip simply left Jerusalem because of persecution), and that this event was a sign of unity with the apostles in Jerusalem.[77]

With respect to the first argument—that there was something wrong with the faith of the Samaritans—it can be argued that these people had been under the spell of Simon the magician. It may be that they had just switched their allegiance to another "cult personality" who seemed more powerful—Philip. Luke writes in Acts 8:12 that the Samaritans "believed Philip." this expression differs from the more usual—"believed God," "believed in (or) on the Lord" and is unique in Acts.[78]

There appears to be more evidence for the second possibility. The Samaritans were not recognized by the Jews as part of the chosen race. They were of mixed stock which had resulted from intermarriage at the time of the Assyrian conquest of Palestine. This could potentially have caused tensions with the church in Jerusalem; therefore, Philip's mission needed the official backing of the apostles, illustrating the order of Acts 1:8, "and you shall be my witnesses in Jerusalem and in all Judea and Samaria and to the end of the earth."

Montague concludes:

> Perhaps the combination of both these explanations is best. Luke, aware of the Samaritans' fascination with magic and magicians, used the story at one level to distinguish authentic faith and the Holy Spirit from any possible confusion with the occult or with personalities. At another level he found the story an excellent example of how the order of the mission given by the risen Lord was in fact confirmed by the events. At any rate, as far as the relation of the Holy Spirit to baptism is concerned Luke narrates the Samaritan episode as an exception, and one cannot draw from it any kind of doctrine about an essential separation of the gift of the Spirit from baptism.[79]

Of course much more can be said about the issue. For the sake of brevity I have given first the line of thought of one particular Catholic exegete with whom I happen to agree. The positions of Dunn and Bruner also need to be noted.

Bruner acknowledges that Acts 8:14–17 is the only recorded case in the New Testament of people who received Christian baptism without receiving the Holy Spirit. Yet by the very exceptional nature of this case he sees it as illustrating the union of baptism and the gift of the Spirit:

> In this text, as we have seen, Christian baptism and the gift of the Holy Spirit are taught not as contrasted or separated realities but as the correlates of the one reception of Christian salvation. The doctrinal constructs which have been raised on the frail and isolated foundations of Acts 8:14–17 (with the illegitimate help, often, of the John-baptized of Acts 19:1–7; see the exposition below) from positions as seemingly disparate as the spiritual baptisms of Pentecostalism and Markus Barth to the sacrament of confirmation episcopally administered in some Anglo and Roman Catholicism—are enough to make one ask with the Psalmist, "Lord, if (this) foundation be removed, what will the righteous do?"[80]

Bruner seeks to illustrate the uniqueness of this case by underscoring the "racial-religious" cleft between the Samaritans and the Jews. He, in effect, sees the action of the apostles coming down to Samaria as a way of preventing the start of a separate Samaritan "denomination":

The reason behind the absolutely unique division of what everywhere else since Pentecost is one–Christian baptism and the gift of the Spirit–may most satisfactorily be found in the divine will to establish unequivocally for the apostles, for the despised Samaritans, and for the whole church present and future that for God no barriers existed for his gift of the Spirit. . . that the gift of God's Holy Spirit was free and for all.[81]

The legitimacy of this argument is accepted by Montague as cited above. He further points out that the order of the evangelizing commission given by the risen Lord specifically mentions the role of Samaria. However, the point of Bruner that the nature of the Samaritans' faith in Christ is above question I do not find to be clearly established. It also happens to be the main thrust of Dunn's argument to try and refute this. He believes that God's giving of the Spirit is what makes a person a Christian. Consequently he questions the so-called conversion of the Samaritans. His contention is not only that their response and commitment was defective, but that Luke intended his readers to know this.[82] Dunn's argument involves inter alia pointing out the superstitious nature of the Samaritans, their concept of the long-awaited second kingdom which they mistakenly thought Philip was ushering in, the negative example of Simon's faith, and the linguistic argument that *pisteuein* when governing "a dative object (except perhaps *kyrios* or *theos*) signifies intellectual assent to a statement or proposition, rather than commitment to God."[83] This theory of a merely nominal assent of the mind was previously expressed by Donald Bloesch:

> Upon closer examination we find that the people had believed only on the basis of the signs and wonders which Philip had performed. They did not have the faith that brought forth fruits of repentance. Simon, the magician, had believed (v. 13) and yet he had not repented (vv. 20–22). The Samaritans had been baptized, but their new birth was aborted because they had not forsaken their old way of thinking and living. They had believed with their minds (credentia) but not with their hearts (fiducia). The Spirit was consequently given to them not after their conversion but at the time of their conversion.[84]

Personally I find this a little overstated. To draw such a definite conclusion from the singular usage of *pisteuein* is perhaps possible but not altogether convincing. This point of the anti-Pentecostal exegesis seems to have just as "frail and isolated" a foundation as the Pentecostal exegesis of establishing Spirit-baptism as a second stage on Acts 8 about which Bruner waxed so eloquent above, asking, "Lord if (this) foundation be removed, what will the righteous do?"!

The modern German exegete Ernst Haenchen is of the opinion that Luke combined two traditions in this pericope which were originally separate–the story of Simon and the story of Philip. The issue of the postponed reception of the Spirit was developed for a particular purpose:

> In doing so Luke did nothing but divide up the combination of water baptism, laying on of hands and reception of the Spirit which formed a unity according to

the belief and usage of his time in such a way as to accord to Philip the beginning and to the apostles the end.[85]

The reason for introducing Simon the magician was to illustrate the superiority of Christian miracles over the magical powers of contemporary sorcerers. Haenchen sees the coming of the Spirit in Acts as unmistakably related to glossolalia and visible ecstatic manifestations. The interesting point is that he sees the unity of Christian initiation as primary. The purpose of this pericope in which baptism and the reception of the Spirit appear to be separated is actually to show how strongly connected they are.

B. A. du Toit wrote a dissertation on this topic: "Die ontvangs van die Heilige Gees in Samaria. 'n Eksegetiese studie van Handelinge 8:14–17" [The reception of the Holy Spirit in Samaria. An exegetical study of Acts 8:14–17], and in fact distinguishes ten different interpretations, some of the views being: that the gift of the Spirit is only given by the laying on of hands (Jackson, Lake, de Ru); that this pericope provides the justification for the sacrament of confirmation (N. Adler); that the Samaritans were not truly converted (James Dunn, A. A. Hoekema); that the Holy Spirit is given at water baptism (F. D. Bruner). A rather unique view of F. W. Grosheide is also discussed – that Acts 8 is a "repetition" of Pentecost. The schema of Acts 1:8 is taken as the key to the development of the church's missionary activity.

Du Toit's own conclusion is:

> with reference to Acts 8:14–17 it needs to be stated in conclusion that there in fact was, historically speaking, a lapse of time between coming to faith and being filled with the Spirit and that this phenomenon is related to the unique character of God's mode of operation in the first phase of the early church after Pentecost.
>
> What happened in Samaria may consequently not be viewed as being normative for the church of all times. The key to the understanding of the events lies in the uniqueness of the phase of salvation history in which they occurred.[86]

Although some of the Samaritans may have had a defective faith, especially due to their background of occultic practices and a fascination with personalities, this does not constitute a convincing argument for the delayed reception of the Spirit. Clearly the Samaritan experience is exceptional, and the unique nature of the situation precludes generalizations of method. Samaria was a milestone of missionary endeavor fulfilling a specific role in the history of salvation, as du Toit stated above. It cannot illustrate for modern believers *how* the Spirit should be received, but it does indicate that charismatic manifestations are an authentic accompaniment to receiving the Spirit. Acts 8 seems to indicate that Acts does not prescribe any fixed order for Christian initiation and that, at most, we can legitimately conclude that it cannot function as a foundation on which to erect the neo-Pentecostal structure of a two-stage pattern for Christian life.

Acts 9 and 10 (the conversion of Paul and the household of Cornelius) are also sometimes used to try and bolster a theology of subsequence. The argument is, however, very weak. To find two stages, Paul's three-day experience (with a case of the healing of his blinded eyes thrown in) needs to be divided up in a rather forced way. Even more unconvincing is the classical Pentecostal argument that claims that Cornelius was already saved before his encounter with Peter. Both these cases should rather be seen as unified experiences. I do not think that they warrant serious discussion where the focus of attention is the theology of subsequence.

Acts 19:1–7 is the other case which seems to supply evidence for the Pentecostal and neo-Pentecostal positions. Here Paul meets some disciples who had received the baptism of John. He soon perceives something amiss for he inquires whether they have received the Holy Spirit. They indicate ignorance of the Holy Spirit, and Paul also finds it necessary to instruct them about the differences between John's baptism and the baptism of the One who was to come after John, namely Jesus. They are then baptized in the name of Jesus and receive the Holy Spirit at the laying on of hands, with tongues and prophecy as manifestations. Very few modern exegetes would deny the exceptional nature of this occurrence. Once the nature of the discipleship of these twelve Ephesians has been established any analogy for a two-stage doctrine of Christian life falls away.

Dunn deals with this most effectively. He argues that the twelve at Ephesus were not already Christians before their encounter with Paul. Acts 19:1 is the only time that *mathētai* (disciples) is used without the definite article. Dunn explains further:

> Luke's description of the twelve as *tines mathētai* therefore probably implies that the twelve did not belong to "the disciples" in Ephesus—a fact confirmed by their ignorance of basic Christian matters. Indeed, I would suggest that Luke deliberately describes them in this way in order to indicate their relation, or rather, lack of relation to the church at Ephesus.[87]

Dunn is, nevertheless, careful not to call this group simply "disciples of John the Baptist." He is of the opinion that the use of *mathētai* requires some connection with Christianity, even though it might be an incomplete relationship. The mere fact that they received John's baptism does not prove that they were his disciples. Dunn concludes and I concur: "In short, they are disciples, but do not yet belong to the disciples; that is, they are not yet Christians."[88]

And if they were not yet Christians there can be no question of their forming an example or pattern for a two-stage Christian life. Bruner makes the same point:

> . . .on learning of their ignorance of the Holy Spirit Paul's subject, surprisingly, was *not* the Holy Spirit, it was Jesus Christ. This is significant. The remedy for those who knew little or nothing of the Holy Spirit is not special instruction or knowledge on access to the Spirit, or a new set of conditions, a new regimen of emptying, added obediences, deeper commitment, or ardent prayer, but instead simply the great fact: the gospel of faith in the Lord Jesus Christ and baptism in his name.[89]

In a recent study by Harold Hunter, a Pentecostal scholar from the Church of God of Prophecy, we find support for viewing Acts 19:1–6 as describing a *unified experience* of the Ephesians rather than a two-stage account. He criticizes Ervin, who also concedes that the Ephesian disciples were not previously Christians but then goes on to argue for a time lapse between their conversion at water baptism and a *later* Spirit-baptism.[90] Hunter argues that the "rebaptism" indicates that the previous baptism could not have been Christian. He also doubts that a Christian group could have been ignorant of the work of the Holy Spirit in the new age.[91]

Haenchen relativizes the whole issue by his theory that Luke is using this story against a sect which was influential at the time Luke wrote Acts. This sect venerated John the Baptist, and Luke is, in fact, portraying Paul as the focal point in this whole scene and as the one who sets those who received John's baptism straight.[92] What this exegesis has in common with the previously cited approaches is that it precludes the use of Acts 19 as an example for modern approaches to the Christian life.

Looking back on the discussion of Acts 8 and 19–the best possible examples for a theology of subsequence–I have to agree with Bruner that there is no record in Acts of a "second blessing" pattern. There certainly are incidental further infillings with the Spirit (e.g., Acts 4:31) but these do not function as a prescribed second stage. Bruner states:

> The fundamental, basic gift of the Spirit in Acts comes but once, in Jesus Christ, and does not need fillings or improvement or "more." In neither Acts 2, 8, 10 or 19–the standard Pentecostal texts for the doctrine of the believer's subsequent baptism in the Holy Spirit–is there a record of the Spirit's first and partial entry followed then by his second and finally personal reception. It is worth noting, then, that Pentecostalism builds its doctrine of a necessary second entry of the Holy Spirit on texts that teach his one entry.[93]

While I am in agreement with the basic contention of this quotation, I must mention that it will become clear in a later context that I am not against speaking of various "entries" or "comings" of the Spirit once the two-stage grid has been disposed of.

It is interesting to note, having attempted to do justice to the Pentecostal argument, that there are today leading Pentecostal theologians–especially from the American Assemblies of God–who readily concede that the Pentecostal and neo-Pentecostal case as based on historical precedent is actually irrelevant. Gordon Fee writes:

> Likewise the analogies of Jesus and the apostles as having been "born" of the Spirit and later "baptized" in the Spirit may be interesting as analogies, but they are of such different kind from succeeding Christian experience that they can scarcely have normative value. The Day of Pentecost is a great line of demarcation, it marks the beginning of the age of the Spirit. Surely valid patterns of *Christian* experience must follow that Day, not precede it.[94]

Fee, in fact, also maintains that the whole theology of subsequence is exegetically indefensible. What is of consequence is the charismatic dimension, the dynamic experiential quality of the Christian life.[95]

This brings us to the end of the portrayal of the three-pronged approach of neo-Pentecostals to distinguish Spirit-baptism from regeneration-conversion and thereby continue the classical Pentecostal position of a theology of subsequence. If we cannot deduce two stages from the life of Jesus or the apostles, if the Samaritans and the twelve Ephesians do not guide us to such a conclusion either, one question clearly remains: What, then, is the baptism with the Holy Spirit? To answer this question a clear distinction must be made between what this term refers to in the New Testament and the experience that it has come to designate in Pentecostal and charismatic circles. My basic contention is that the term is being incorrectly applied and used today, but the experience it refers to is a perfectly valid experience. The nature of this experience will be discussed in a later context. What the New Testament means by Spirit-baptism must now be briefly explored.

2.5 Some Perspectives on the New Testament's Usage of Spirit-Baptism (Excursus)

Even a superficial reading of the six references to "being baptized in the Holy Spirit" in the Gospels and Acts (Matthew 3:11; Mark 1:8; Luke 3:16; John 1:33; Acts 1:5; 11:16) brings one to the conclusion that they all refer ultimately to what happened in Acts 2 on the day of Pentecost. The references in the Gospels occur in a particular context – the contrasting of the work of John the Baptist with the work of Jesus. John baptized people in water – Jesus will baptize them in the Holy Spirit and fire. Jesus is superior to John and will baptize with a superior baptism. His baptism will not just be preparatory. He will confer the Holy Spirit; this is what Jesus did in Acts 2. Matthew and Luke add the words "and with fire" to "He (Jesus) will baptize you with the Holy Spirit." Since these words are not found in Mark, New Testament exegetes conclude that they probably came from Q – the other common source of Matthew and Luke. The association seems to be that of judgment. The image of the winnowing fork is used – in connection with wind and fire – the chaff will be burned after it has been blown away by the wind (Matthew 3:12; Luke 3:17). John preaches repentance preparing the way, but it will be in relationship to Jesus Christ that the ultimate decisions will be made. The same concept of eschatological judgment is found in John 15:6: "If a man does not abide in me, he is cast forth as a branch and withers; and the branches are gathered, thrown into the fire and burned." It can surely not be coincidental that this same image of wind and purifying fire is taken up again in Acts 2. These elements are frequently used in the Old Testament as the signs of God's presence: Isaiah 4:4; 2 Samuel 22:16; Psalm 50:3; Isaiah 66:15; and Jeremiah 30:23.[96]

The baptism in the Holy Spirit and fire should, according to Dunn, not be seen as two baptisms but as "only one baptism in Spirit-and-fire,"[97] which initiates the messianic role. It would bring blessing to the repentant and destruction to the unrepentant—a dual result of a single baptism. Dunn sums it up in these words:

> . . .the baptism in Spirit-and-fire was not to be something gentle and gracious, but something which burned and consumed, not something experienced by only Jew or only Gentile, only repentant or only unrepentant, but by all. It was the fiery *pneuma* in which all must be immersed, as it were, and which like a smelting furnace would burn up all impurity. For the unrepentant it would mean total destruction. For the repentant it would mean a refining and purging away of all evil and sin which would result in salvation and qualify to enjoy the blessings of the messianic kingdom. These were the sufferings which would bring in the messianic kingdom; it was through them that the repentant would be initiated into that kingdom.[98]

Dunn is probably overstating his case here somewhat since the fire on the day of Pentecost (fiery tongues) apparently loses the elements of judgment and destruction. Even in Malachi 3:2, 3, for example, the metaphor of fire operates simply as an instrument of refining and purifying. This whole analysis, nevertheless, makes it patently clear that in its primary sense New Testament Spirit-baptism had a unique function. The outpouring of the Spirit at Pentecost heralded the new age—affecting everybody. There are a wealth of Old Testament allusions behind Acts 2, and yet Pentecost should not be limited to them. Luke broadens the context of the strong wind and the destroying and purifying fire and introduces a new element—the speaking of "languages" under the inspiration of the Spirit:

> And suddenly a sound came from heaven like the rush of a mighty wind, and it filled all the house where they were sitting. And there appeared to them tongues as of fire, distributed and resting on each one of them. And they were all filled with the Holy Spirit and began to speak in other tongues, as the Spirit gave them utterance (Acts 2:2–4).

It is to this milestone in salvation history—the outpouring of the Holy Spirit by Jesus on the church that the term "baptism in the Holy Spirit" ultimately refers. This is underscored in Peter's sermon:

> This Jesus God raised up, and of that we all are witnesses. Being therefore exalted at the right hand of God, and having received from the Father the promise of the Holy Spirit, he has poured out this which you see and hear (Acts 2:32, 33).

The "case" of Acts 2 in the framework of Pentecostal and neo-Pentecostal theology was not dealt with above because a "better case" could potentially be developed from Acts 8 and 19. Acts 2 only makes sense as an argument for a theology of subsequence if one concedes an analogy between the "conversion experience" of the apostles in John 20:22 and our conversion, concluding then that we also need another stage—a "Pentecost" as they did. By this time it will be clear that I do not consider this analogy at all convincing but some brief attention should still be given to the significance of the day of Pentecost. There is a sense in which Pentecost is the climax of Jesus' ministry.[99]

Pentecost has a depth of theological meaning which certainly cannot be adequately dealt with here. It occurs within the context of the Jewish feast of the weeks which lies between the feast of the unleavened bread and the harvest festival. It was the time for the offering of the first fruits and in later Judaism in addition to the agrarian elements new historical meaning was given to the festival as the feast of covenant renewal and the giving of the law. The designated Torah readings introduced elements such as the tower of Babel and the theophany at Sinai.[100] There has also been much debate about whether the "tongues" which the apostles spoke constituted a miracle of speech or hearing. Montague concludes

> It may never be possible to sort out whether on the historical level Luke intended to describe a miracle of speaking or of hearing. It was in any case a marvel, and there can be no doubt as to how he interpreted the event on a literary and theological level: the first Christian Pentecost was the eschatological Sinai event where the promised covenant of the Spirit was given. But this event was also symbolic for all the nations of the earth, for it is a reversal of the curse of Babel. (We remember that the Babel story in Genesis 11 was one of the prescribed readings in the triennial cycle for the Jewish feast of Pentecost.) The divisive nature of languages, Genesis' climactic symbol of man's social disintegration due to his hubris, is now overcome by the one Spirit.[101]

Many elements remain and cannot be discussed. But they all seem to underscore that Pentecost was a pivotal turning point in history. Peter's sermon introduces the element of the fulfillment of Joel's prophecy; this designates the bestowal of the Spirit as a decisive mark of the coming age. Dunn develops the concept of Pentecost as the beginning of the new covenant for the disciples—cf. Ezekiel 36:27 and Jeremiah 31:33—the law that will be written in the hearts.[102] Pentecost also inaugurates the age of the church: "For Luke Pentecost constitutes the disciples as the new covenant people of God, and is 'the beginning of the period of the Church.'"[103]

The Holy Spirit is the constitutive life principle of the church and the manifestations of the Spirit's presence and power were a normal part of her life as portrayed in the book of Acts. This acknowledgement of the "charismatic" dimension of the Spirit is the element of truth in the neo-Pentecostal position. Dunn suggests

> The epochal significance of Pentecost raises the whole course of salvation-history to a new plane. As the beginning of the new age of the Spirit, the new covenant, the Church, it is what happened at Pentecost and not before which is normative for those who would enter that age, covenant and Church.[104]

It is in this inaugural and initiatory sense that Christians today can participate in Pentecost. The baptism in the Holy Spirit is primarily a metaphor for becoming a Christian—for entering the new age and the church as Christ's body. This is to be so near (and yet so far!) from the oft quoted words of Ernest Williams, one of the pioneering systematic theologians of classical Pentecostalism:

> To be Pentecostal is to identify oneself with the experience that came to Christ's followers on the Day of Pentecost; that is, to be filled with the Holy Spirit in the same manner as those who were filled with the Holy Spirit on that occasion.[105]

That which Pentecostalism and neo-Pentecostalism after it has made into a distinctive Pentecostal trait is actually the hallmark of all Christians, namely regeneration, the new life in Christ, entering God's kingdom or the new age, conversion, being born from above or any of the other New Testament metaphors for becoming a believer. It is through Christian initiation that we as individuals become "Pentecostal." This, I believe, is an important element of the New Testament understanding of Spirit-baptism.

The four references in the Gospels to "being baptized in the Spirit" point towards this occurrence in Acts 2. The fifth reference in Acts 1:5 is also predictive. The sixth reference—Acts 11:16—actually points back to the historic day of Pentecost within the context of Peter relating the events at the house of Cornelius to the Christians in Jerusalem. Yet another reference—1 Corinthians 12:13—needs to be discussed more fully. In a sense it is the odd verse out since the seventh reference does not point directly to the day of Pentecost; but, if the interpretation of Pentecost as the corporate inauguration of a new era which then correlates on the individual level with the believer's initiation into the new life of Christ is correct, it merely serves to confirm this position from a Pauline perspective.

In defending this position, which interprets Spirit-baptism as Christian initiation, it is essential to keep in mind that this does not imply that that is all there is to the Christian life. Although the neo-Pentecostal position of Spirit-baptism as a second stage cannot be exegetically defended, it must be acknowledged that Luke consistently emphasizes the "charismatic" dimension of the Spirit's work—the manifestation of gifts, the empowerment for service and witness. These elements do not indicate a "further stage" of development but are the natural accompaniments of life in the Spirit, i.e. the Christian life.

Before examining the single Pauline reference to "being baptized in the Spirit" it is good to keep in mind the differences between the approaches of Luke and Paul. Hummel warns that it has become common for theologians such as Bruner and Dunn to "harmonize" Paul and Luke.[106] This leads invariably to Luke getting painted with Paul's brush when the picture is portrayed by a theologian from the historic churches. Pentecostals attempt the reverse—painting Paul with Luke's brush; 1 Corinthians 12:13 is a case in point. However, I am not totally convinced by this argument. The differences in perspective need to be acknowledged, but when this leads Hummel to speak of "the two meanings of baptize in the Spirit"[107] I think he has gone too far.

Luke's context in Acts is the unfolding of salvation history and the mission activity of the church. This leads him to focus on the enduement with power for service and mission, and yet the element of the inauguration of the new age that is so central to his teaching in Acts is, in my opinion, closely related to what Hummel instead sees as the typically Pauline perspective, namely, the believer's incorporation into the body of Christ. The experience of the rebirth of the individual believer is, in fact, his or her personal entry into the new age. Where Luke is sketching structural, cosmic, and historic dimensions in Acts 2, Paul is referring in 1 Corinthians 12:13 to the individual aspects of the same reality. When Christ baptizes the church with the Spirit on the day of Pentecost he inaugurates the new age. When he saves repentant sinners and brings them into the church he initiates new life on the personal level. This is not a harmonizing of Luke and Paul but an acknowledgement that they are using the term "being baptized in the Spirit" from two different vantage points but with essentially the same meaning. New age and new life are metaphors of Christ's work on earth and in us, both through the Holy Spirit. Paul also employs structural and cosmic terminology in his letter, but in the case in point, 1 Corinthians 12, he is dealing with the unity and interrelatedness of the individual members of the church. He states:

> For just as the body is one and has many members, and all the members of the body, though many, are one body, so it is with Christ. For by one Spirit we were all baptized into one body—Jews or Greeks, slaves or free—and all were made to drink of one Spirit (1 Corinthians 12:12, 13).

From the above discussion it is already obvious that I have chosen to interpret this text as referring to Christian initiation. Brief reference has also been made to this text previously. I will, however, go to some lengths to present the variety of views which exegetes hold with respect to 1 Corinthians 12:13. Ronald Cottle distinguishes four positions: (1) Paul is referring to water baptism. (2) The baptism into one body is spiritual, referring to conversion. (3) It should be translated: "For in one Spirit we were all baptized for the sake of one body" giving *eis* the force of "for the sake of" instead of "into." This supports the Pentecostal position since it then refers to a Spirit-baptism of those already in the body. (4) The first part of the text refers to conversion and the second part to Spirit-baptism as a "second blessing" experience.[108]

Still other possibilities exist: (5) Many neo-Pentecostals insist that the Greek preposition *en*, which they translate as "in" in the other six cases, should here be translated as "by," i.e., instrumentally. The text then refers to conversion, because Spirit-baptism according to their view is a baptism by Christ, while conversion is a baptism by the Spirit. This view is similar to (4) above, but it does not give the other part of the text a different twist. In fact this approach to 1 Corinthians 12:13 seems to be a concession to the traditional evangelical viewpoint which pointed out that the "all" precludes any division into those who are Spirit-baptized (in the neo-Pentecostal sense) and those who are not. (6) Other neo-Pentecostals argue that the "all" refers specifically to the Corinthians, who would all have received a "Pentecostal" Spirit-baptism, and see the whole text as referring not to conversion but to the empowering activity of the Spirit as a second work of grace.[109]

Although Cottle does not go into detail, there is wide support for the first position that Paul is referring to baptism in water in the first part of the verse and to holy communion in the second part. The Dutch exegete Herman Ridderbos writes:

> There is every reason therefore to understand the pronouncement of 1 Corinthians 12:13b: "and were all made to drink of one Spirit" after the reference to baptism in verse 13a, as referring to the Lord's Supper. However much the Supper is communion with the body and blood of the Lord, i.e., with his self-surrender on the cross, it also makes the church share in the gift of the Spirit of the exalted Lord. One cannot here separate the one from the other.[110]

This view is also supported by Schlatter, Käsemann, Wendland, and Goppelt.[111] Whether the second part refers to communion or not is not crucial in this context. It does seem possible, but I prefer to see the two parts of the text as an example of *parallelismus membrorum*, expressing the same basic idea in both parts.

Perhaps the most satisfactory discussion of this "problem text" is that given by Tom Smail.[112] He reviews the warfare between evangelicals and charismatics exemplified in the books of John Stott and John Baker[113] in the sixties. Smail comments:

> In that basic conflict many others joined till the terrain around the verse became so soft and soggy, after being trodden by the hooves of so many war horses, that many of us despaired of ever being sure precisely what it meant.[114]

Smail's new position is that 1 Corinthians 12:13 refers to baptism in water by which believers are initiated into Christ. The emphasis on experiences—either conversion (Stott) or neo-Pentecostal Spirit-baptism (Baker)—is here replaced by an encompassing concept of Christian initiation. Smail acknowledges that Stott was closer to the truth than Baker by recognizing the initiatory *context* of this verse, but underscores that Baker was right in insisting that the actual *content* was the charismatic empowering and engifting by the Spirit of the baptized members of Christ's body.[115] Smail is seemingly right but needs to reverse the words "context" and "content" (which he underlined). The context of 1 Corinthians 12:13 is certainly the variety and unity of spiritual gifts.

Of crucial significance is Smail's conclusion about the integral nature of the baptismal experience as Christian initiation:

> Baptism as the New Testament understands it includes within itself a pentecostal element, the very thing in fact the Pentecostals have called baptism in the Spirit. To be initiated into Christ is to be vested with the outpoured Holy Spirit and to be set free to exercise his gifts in the Church and for the world. On our interpre-

tation, 1 Corinthians 12:13 stands witness that the empowering of the Spirit does not stand apart from initiation into Christ as a postponed appendix or an optional extra but is integrally connected with it, as part of what it means to be a normal Christian[116]

To speak of baptism in this encompassing sense often leads to the misunderstanding of baptismal regeneration, and yet this seems to be the way in which Paul speaks of baptism—with faith and repentance included as an integral element. Perhaps misunderstanding can be avoided by rather using the term Christian initiation.

Summing up then, the term "baptism in the Spirit" refers ultimately to the unique and historic events of the day of Pentecost, but this inauguration of the new age has its individual correlation in Christian initiation. The outpouring of the Spirit at Pentecost symbolizes this personal incorporation into Christ's body. This ongoing symbolic significance of Pentecost ought not to surprise one. It holds no threat to the unique salvation-historical importance of Acts 2.

The unique events of Christ's crucifixion, resurrection and Pentecost—his outpouring of the Spirit—can all be employed in various ways as symbols of receiving the new birth or becoming a believer.

Dunn expresses it in the following manner:

> I hope to show that for the writers of the New Testament the baptism in or gift of the Spirit was part of the event (or process) of becoming a Christian, together with the effective proclamation of the Gospel, belief in (*eis*) Jesus as Lord, and water-baptism in the name of the Lord Jesus; that it was the chief element in conversion-initiation so that only those who had thus received the Spirit could be called Christians; that the reception of the Spirit was a very definite and often dramatic *experience*, the decisive and climactic experience in conversion-initiation, to which the Christian was usually recalled when reminded of the beginning of his Christian faith and experience.[117]

Alfred Kuen, the astute French observer of the charismatic movement, dismisses the two-stage theory with four arguments which he backs up exegetically in his analysis.

1. All believers receive the Holy Spirit at their regeneration.

2. The expression "baptized with the Holy Spirit" always refers to the initial Christian experience—conversion or regeneration.

3. The New Testament knows no "second experience" or "second blessing."

4. Glossolalia is not the sign of a second experience.[118]

To the actual *experience* that has come to be called Spirit-baptism by millions of Pentecostals and charismatics and to my own interpretation of what the term as they use it refers to, we will return in the last chapter. It now remains to take a look at a variety of neo-Pentecostal writers, none of whom have developed the argumentation for a theology of subsequence quite as fully as presented above but who usually have added some perspectives of their own to the neo-Pentecostal apologetic–often influenced by their own development and background.

2.6 A Survey of the Views on Spirit-Baptism of Some Leading Neo-Pentecostals

Neo-Pentecostal leaders from various denominational backgrounds will be dealt with–Anglican, Lutheran, Roman Catholic, Presbyterian and Reformed, and Baptist. It should be noted that the views discussed here are neo-Pentecostal in their theology regardless of their denominational setting. In some cases the individual scholars underwent a change in perspective, and in their later writings they no longer qualify to be grouped under the heading neo-Pentecostal.

2.6.1 Dennis Bennett and Terry Fullam (Episcopal)

The pioneering leader in the charismatic movement, Dennis Bennett, is a good representative of the neo-Pentecostal view. This holds true for most of the early leaders as one would perhaps expect. His book *Nine O'Clock in the Morning*[119] is a personal account of his renewal experience. In the follow up, *The Holy Spirit and You*,[120] he and his wife come closer to defining Spirit-baptism theologically:

> Let us sum up, then, by saying that the first experience of the Christian life, salvation, is the incoming of the Holy Spirit, through Jesus Christ, to give us new life, God's life, eternal life. The second experience, is the receiving, or making welcome of the Holy Spirit, so that Jesus can cause Him to pour out this new life from our spirits, to baptize our souls and bodies, and then the world around, with His refreshing and renewing power.[121]

To explain the problem: How can one receive the Spirit who is already living in one? Bennett uses a simple analogy. He likens it to receiving guests–they may have already entered the house; perhaps they are being provisionally entertained in the lounge by the children, but only when the hosts have completed their preparations do they come downstairs and receive their guests.[122] A further facet of Bennett's teaching is that there are actually three "baptisms" in the Christian life. He sees 1 Corinthians 12:13, "In one Spirit we were all baptized into one Body. . .and were all made to drink of one Spirit," as referring to "the spiritual baptism into Christ which takes place as soon as Jesus is received as Savior."[123] Bennett continues:

> This was followed by the baptism with the Holy Spirit, in which the now indwelling Holy Spirit poured forth to manifest Jesus to the world through the life of the believer. Either before or after the baptism with the Holy Spirit there was the outward sign of baptism with water–symbolic of the inner cleansing by the Blood of Jesus, the death of the "old man," and the resurrection to new life in Christ.[124]

With respect to tongues Bennett also underscores the "necessity" of this gift in the typical guarded neo-Pentecostal way. To the question if one can receive the Spirit without speaking in tongues he replies that it comes with the package:

> Speaking in tongues is not the baptism in the Holy Spirit, but it is what happens when and as you are baptized in the Spirit. . . .You don't have to speak in tongues to have times of feeling filled with the Holy Spirit, but if you want the free and full outpouring that is the baptism in the Holy Spirit, you must expect it to happen as in the Scripture.[125]

The impact of Bennett's doctrine of Spirit-baptism is clearly neo-Pentecostal. There is certainly nothing which could lead one to suspect that he is operating within the Episcopal tradition. On the contrary, he describes the first experience of the Christian life as salvation or God giving us eternal life through Jesus Christ. He seems to be using the word salvation as referring to the new birth rather than the whole process of God's sacramental grace working in us. The reception of the Spirit is clearly a second step in a two-stage approach. The analogy of receiving guests seems to underline the necessity of the second experience. It is quite unthinkable to have those guests in your home and still keep them waiting for any extended time period. One can feel the anomaly of there being any true Christians who have not yet "received" the Spirit. The standard Episcopal practice of infant baptism also seems like an alien element. Apart from considering conversion as "the first experience of the Christian life,"[126] infant baptism just doesn't seem to fit into the three-fold baptismal concept, since receiving Jesus as Savior is normally "followed by" Spirit-baptism, and water baptism is either before or after Spirit-baptism. It may be that the order here is regarded as logical rather than chronological. But apparently the framework in which Bennett theologizes is more compatible with Holiness, Baptist, and evangelical categories flavored with Pentecostalism than with a sacramental structure.

Bennett's "threefold baptism" concept is open to serious questioning. Even an allusion to the Trinity of God and humanity (body, soul, and spirit!) cannot really resolve the conflict between three different baptisms—referring to different events—and the refrain of Ephesians 4:5, "one Lord, one faith, one baptism." Bennett also refers to Hebrews 6:2 where the plural "baptisms" is used; but modern translations like the RSV favor translating this as "ceremonial washings" or "ablutions" rather than interpreting it as a reference to water and Spirit-baptism or even conversion. It may be that Bennett was accommodating himself to as broad a group of readers as possible. He nevertheless leaves himself open to attack. An elitist approach over against Christians who are not Spirit-baptized seems unavoidable if his teaching is taken to its logical conclusions. Interestingly German author Siegfried Grossmann makes special reference to Dennis Bennett in his book, *Haushalter der Gnade Gottes. Von der charismatischen Bewegung zur charismatischen Erneuerung der Gemeinde.*

(*Stewards of God's Grace* is the English translation. Literally the full German title can be translated: Householders of God's grace. From the charismatic movement to the charismatic renewal of the congregation.) In the context he is referring to the fact that the only unambiguous distinction between classical Pentecostalism and the charismatic movement lies in the distinction that the former created its own denominational structures while the latter has remained within its churches and has so far been allowed to remain there. This distinction does not, however, necessarily correlate with theological positions. As an example he mentions the Mülheim Pentecostals, who are basically Reformational but are classified as Pentecostal since they have their own structures. He continues:

> On the other hand great parts of the Protestant charismatic movement in the USA, e.g., the groups influenced by Bennett, ought to be reckoned as belonging theologically to Pentecostalism. They are however regarded as part of the charismatic movement because they have not formed themselves into a separate denomination.[127]

Grossmann is obviously writing from a particular perspective not sympathetic towards the neo-Pentecostal position. The subtitle of his book (which is not used in the English translation)[128] suggests that the charismatic movement was an initial phase that has been (or should?) be superseded by the ideal of parish renewal. (This ideal is not as exclusively European or Catholic as is sometimes suggested. The influential Parish Renewal Council, which unites the charismatics of almost all the mainline Protestant churches, is effectively furthering this very ideal in the USA. Another good example is found in the Catholic Renewal in Southern California.) In 1977 Grossmann gave the following description of those he classifies as neo-Pentecostal rather than as belonging to the charismatic renewal:

> I categorize as neo-Pentecostal the greater part of the Protestant charismatic movement in the U.S., e.g., the groups associated with the names of Dennis Bennett and Merlin Carothers; the Full Gospel Businessmen's Fellowship International; the greater part of the charismatic movement in the United Kingdom (although Michael Harper disagrees with the Pentecostals on some points); and a considerable proportion of the Jesus People both in the U.S. and in Europe, where they claim definite charismatic experiences. Many smaller groups might be mentioned as well, but it is safe to say that a substantial part of the charismatic movement in Germany, France and Holland is more properly classified under the heading of "charismatic renewal."[129]

In the mid-eighties Dennis Bennett (Episcopal) and Merlin Carothers (Methodist) no longer speak for the majority of Protestant charismatics. Within the Anglican communion the majority view would probably be the sacramental model, although besides Bennett another one of the leading Episcopal spokesmen in American, Everett Fullam, still holds to a neo-Pentecostal view. This can be illustrated by a cassette tape address given on Spirit-baptism at Nairobi. In this he uses the typical analogies between Christ's life, the lives of the apostles, and the present-day Christian. His interpretation of Acts 8 and 10 also follows the neo-Pentecostal approach, although the bottom line seems to be a convincing argument that there is more to Christian life than the impoverished spiritual life of traditional Christianity–in other words, he argues for the charismatic dimension but still ties this to an event-centered view of Christian experience. The gift of the Holy Spirit is seen as something distinct from and subsequent to regeneration-conversion.[130]

In conclusion, while Bennett is consistently neo-Pentecostal in his theology, he does use the term "release of the Spirit," which later came to function as a key concept in the sacramental model of Spirit-baptism. This is in his testimony *Nine O'Clock in the Morning*. Bennett uses it within the two-stage framework. In the context he answers the question: Where are Christians going to get the power to show the rescuing love of God in the world outside?

> By the accepting of Jesus the Savior and by the release of the Holy Spirit in and through our lives–by a renewal of the experience of Pentecost![131]

Bennett remarks that he came to realize that one of his main tasks (on his trip to England) was to help "unhook" some of the "hang-ups" which hamper theologians in their understanding of Spirit-baptism.[132] While there are those like Grossmann who probably think Bennett did more than his fair share of causing these "hang-ups" for theologians, his use of "the release of the Spirit" may eventually lead to some "unhooking," despite the fact that Bennett seems to be unaware that this could unravel the problem of the two-stage pattern. It may, of course, be that it was Watchman Nee's *Release of the Spirit*[133] that suggested this usage, both to Bennett and to those of the sacramental model. Nee's concept of releasing has to be understood in terms of his trichotomist anthropology, which Bennett also uses in his volume, *Trinity of Man*.[134] From the Anglican or Episcopal Communion we now turn to another sacramental tradition, Lutheranism.

2.6.2 Larry Christenson and Hans-Jacob Frøen (Lutheran)

One of the very first Lutheran pastors to become involved in the charismatic movement was Larry Christenson. Today, working from the international Lutheran Renewal Offices in the twin cities, Minnesota, he plays a leading role in Lutheran Renewal internationally. In his early phase his views can be classified as neo-Pentecostal. He later went on to develop a more distinctly Lutheran position. His later views will be discussed under the following model. Carter Lindberg gives a general appraisal of the situation in the early stages of renewal among Lutherans in America:

> In the beginning of the charismatic renewal during the early 1960's, Lutheran as well as other charismatics depended upon classical Pentecostalism as a framework for understanding and expressing their new experience. This imported two basic Pentecostal perspectives that by the next decade were recognized as sources of major tension with the Lutheran tradition. One was fundamentalism . . . the second

76

was a two- or three-stage scheme for receiving the Holy Spirit that was in opposition to the Lutheran understanding of baptism as a sacrament and that separated the reception of the Holy Spirit from baptism.[135]

It seems as if Christenson was wary, from the very beginning, of a theology of subsequence, and yet he does not manage to avoid it in his early booklet, *Speaking in Tongues and Its Significance for the Church*. He struggles with the typical problem of a neo-Pentecostal approach: How to justify the need for something extra—for Spirit-baptism. He voices the objections of an evangelical Christian very clearly:

> All right: I'm saved and I'll go to heaven and I have the Holy Spirit. What more do I need? Isn't it just a matter of buckling down and being the kind of Christian the Lord wants me to be?[136]

His solution is that there is no rational, understandable reason to argue for more but there is an analogy from Scripture which doesn't make much logical sense either:

> Beyond conversion, beyond the assurance of salvation, beyond having the Holy Spirit, there is a baptism with the Holy Spirit. It might not make sense to our human understanding any more than it made sense for Jesus to be baptized by John. But when John would have prevented Him, Jesus said, "Let it be so now. For thus it is fitting for us to fulfill all righteousness." There is a Divinely Appointed Pattern. It is fitting for us to fulfill it. It "fits into" God's purpose for us. We are not called to understand it, or justify it, or explain it, but simply to enter into it in humble obedience and with expectant faith.[137]

It is tempting to try and rise to the occasion and "make sense" of Jesus' baptism by John. Clearly it was a source of embarrassment to the early Christian congregations as can be ascertained from the slightly different renderings in the Gospels. Some see the reason in Jesus' identification with sinful humanity or, more accurately, with the repentant Jews who heeded John the Baptist's call, others in the fact that he wished his identity as Messiah to remain hidden and only be revealed little by little. But such a discussion is not really relevant here. Christenson has taken refuge in an authoritarian view which overrules questioning. It simply is so. The same anti-intellectual attitude seems apparent from his refusal to discuss or analyze the theology of Spirit-baptism:

> There is a sound biblical theology for the baptism with the Holy Spirit. But the baptism with the Holy Spirit is not a theology to be discussed and analyzed. It is an experience one enters into.[138]

One wonders why it cannot be both at the same time!

When developing the concept of Spirit-baptism in Acts Christenson unmistakably expresses the neo-Pentecostal view. He uses an acrostic, PILOT: *P*ower, *I*nstantaneous, *L*ink, *O*bjective, and *T*ongues. Under Instantaneous he says, "both Scripture and experience testify to the reality of this initiatory, instantaneous event where Jesus baptizes you with the Holy Spirit,"[139] using the term "baptism" with the Holy Spirit as something distinct from conversion, which he terms "repentance and faith." The five cases in Acts are seen as recording Spirit-baptisms as subsequent to conversion:

> In each of these the experience is dealt with in the aorist tense, which describes an action taking place at a definite point in time. Paul's question to the disciples in Ephesus, Acts 19:2, is pointedly phrased with a time-reference: "did you receive the Holy Spirit when you believed?"[140]

Christenson thus operates, perhaps unwittingly, with a theology of subsequence. He also comes very close to a Pentecostal view on initial evidence. He claims that Spirit-baptism is objective—it has an outward manifestation. Wherever this outward manifestation is mentioned, it is speaking in tongues.[141] He admits that Scripture does not see tongues as the only valid objective manifestation: "But in showing us the pattern Scripture gives us no consistent suggestion of any other."[142] He claims that asking, Do you have to speak in tongues? is a little like a child asking, Do we have to have presents in order to celebrate my birthday?[143]

From a broader (less detailed) vantage point, the neo-Pentecostal nature of Christenson's early view is also demonstrated by his choosing to introduce his teaching on Spirit-baptism in a booklet entitled *Speaking in Tongues* and even more so by his chapter divisions: "Speaking in Tongues as 'Sign'" and "Speaking in Tongues as 'Gift.'" This distinction between tongues as sign (initial evidence) and gift (as it operates in the life of individual believers in an ongoing sense as they live and serve within a congregation) was, in fact, one of the first classical Pentecostal "trappings" that neo-Pentecostals usually shed —replacing it by a distinction between tongues as an individual prayer language and tongues as operating in the assembled congregation. Christenson has a further chapter entitled "Speaking in Tongues as Ministry," but this is really a misnomer since he uses the chapter to discuss the other charismatic gifts and ministries besides tongues. In his later writings Christenson switches to a sacramental understanding of Spirit-baptism.

Another Lutheran, Reverend Hans-Jacob Frøen, is a more consistent representative of the neo-Pentecostal position. He is from the Seaman's Church, Oslo, Norway and the editor of the magazine *Dypere Liv* (Deeper Life) and founder of the Norwegian Agape Foundation, established in 1971. Although Frøen works within the Lutheran Church of Norway, his theology can be described as "non-confessional Lutheran."[144] Frøen openly advocates a theological revision of the Lutheran confessions.

From the analysis by the Norwegian charismatic theologian, Tormod Engelsviken, a few of Frøen's basic perspectives will be dealt with. He distinguishes and separates regeneration and Spirit-baptism. Spirit-baptism is both logically and temporally subsequent to regeneration.[145] Furthermore Frøen actually teaches a threefold experience of the Spirit. This encompasses regeneration, Spirit-baptism, and the infilling with the Spirit. Engelsviken states:

This distinction between the baptism in the Spirit and the fullness of the Spirit as two "separate experiences" is a peculiar trait of Frøen's theology which has certain important ramifications.[146]

Interestingly, Frøen sees the fullness of the Spirit as related to sanctification – a holy life – but places it third in the normal sequence of these three separate experiences. This is different from the Wesleyan-Holiness Pentecostals who added Spirit-baptism with signs following to their two-stage system of conversion and sanctification. The argument was used that the Spirit cannot come to an unsanctified heart. Frøen, however, believes that Spirit-baptized Christians may fall and live in sin while simultaneously retaining charismatic gifts and doing great works in the kingdom of God. Once one is filled by the Spirit one cannot live in open sin.[147] Engelsviken points out that Frøen differs from the three-stage Pentecostals when he sees sanctification partly as continuous and repeatable, and partly as subsequent to Spirit-baptism.[148]

A touch of "Spirit-Christology" is seen where Jesus is described as the ideal of a Spirit-filled man, inspiring Christians to seek the same power which Jesus used in his humanity.[149] (This perspective will be referred to again in the context of Tom Smail who operates with an Irvingite Christology.) Frøen even comes close to developing a set of "conditions" for the subjective appropriation of Spirit-baptism. Although the charisms are not exclusively tied to the experience of Spirit-baptism, this is the case with two of them: tongues and interpretation. Tongues is allotted a special place and is meant for all Christians. It should be distinguished from the gift of presenting a message in a congregation.[150] This exposition has illustrated how close Frøen's view is to neo-Pentecostalism despite his "novel" position on "fullness" as a third experience of the Spirit.

At the first International Lutheran Conference on the Holy Spirit, held in Minneapolis, Frøen spoke on the topic: What is the baptism in the Holy Spirit? Since this was on a very popular level only brief reference will be made to this talk. His two-stage stance is apparent:

> Today there are many who confuse the spiritual rebirth and the baptism in the Holy Spirit. These are two separate manifestations of the working of the Holy Spirit. I want to underline this: rebirth and the baptism in the Holy Spirit are two different and separate manifestations of the Holy Spirit.[151]

Frøen also emphasizes the purpose of Spirit-baptism as an enduement with power in order to witness:

> . . . if I am to give it (Spirit-baptism) its true description, I can do so in one word – and that word Jesus Himself uses in Acts 1:8 and that word is power. "You shall receive power." The baptism of the Holy Spirit is to receive power.[152]

2.6.3 Stephen Clark and the Life in the Spirit Seminars (Catholic)

Next we turn to the Roman Catholic Church. Here two neo-Pentecostals' views will be dealt with: those of Stephen Clark, a leader of the large ecumenical covenant community, the Word of God in Ann Arbor, Michigan, as well as those of Peter Hocken, a leader of the Catholic Mother of God community in Gaithersburg, Maryland.

Although no particular significance can be attached to it, it is rather exceptional that both these Catholic leaders should be converts to Catholicism. This is also the case with the leading woman theologian of charismatic Catholicism, Josephine Massyngberde Ford, whose views will be dealt with under the sacramental model.

Before dealing with individual Catholic views, indeed before discussing Steve Clark's views as an individual Catholic scholar in the renewal, we need to look at the standard handbook used in Catholic charismatic circles across the globe.

The Life in the Spirit Seminars were developed by the Word of God, an ecumenical community in Ann Arbor, Michigan. Ralph Martin and, especially, Steve Clark were mainly responsible for writing the manuals. The seminars are designed to help Christians to be baptized in the Spirit. They have been instrumental in bringing thousands of Christians, especially Catholics into the charismatic renewal. A special edition is used for Catholics and another for people from other backgrounds, but it is suggested that the Orthodox and some Episcopalian and Lutheran groups may find the Catholic edition suitable with some adaptation.[153] Since I am dealing with the neo-Pentecostal approach in the Roman Catholic Church I shall be using the Catholic edition which contains the traditional episcopal Imprimatur. (The other edition, as may be expected, is more clearly neo-Pentecostal in its teaching.) The seminars consider their goal to be very limited. They are designed to present "only the first step in a completely new way of life."[154] They do not address serious theological issues and believe that

> the basic teaching about what the Lord is willing to do for all who come to him can be stated in a simple enough way to by-pass all dogmatic and theological questions and reach directly to a person's heart.[155]

The seminars run for seven weeks. The first four weeks are devoted to presenting central gospel concepts such as God's love, salvation, and the gift of new life in Christ. The fifth week is the crucial turning point. It deals with Spirit-baptism and experiencing the power and gifts of the Holy Spirit. The last two weeks deal with spiritual growth and the need to be part of a community or prayer group.

The goal of the fifth seminar is: "To help people make an authentic commitment to Christ, to help them be baptized in the Spirit and speak in tongues."[156] Because of the brief nature of the manual and the express desire to avoid all theological questions (which is, in fact, not really possible) there is very little "evidence" to prove that the position is neo-Pentecostal. The clearest references seem to be to the role of tongues. Care is taken to sound the warning: "Don't make the mistake of identifying 'being baptized in the

Spirit' with 'getting the gift of tongues.' "[157] Nevertheless what "being baptized in the Spirit" really is, in distinction from tongues, is never explained. The Pentecostal view of tongues as "a necessary sign" is rejected and yet categorical statements such as, "Everyone should want to have tongues,"[158] are made. But even more significantly, tongues usually turns out to be the gateway to the charismatic dimension.[159] We also read, "Tongues comes when a person is baptized in the Holy Spirit."[160] These statements show that the "theology" operating at "low profile" behind the Life in the Spirit Seminars is more neo-Pentecostal than charismatic. The expectation is that every believer can speak in tongues which certainly goes against the principle of distribution found in 1 Corinthians 12. The only explanation must be the classical Pentecostal distinction between tongues as a sign and tongues as a gift or the neo-Pentecostal distinction between tongues in the assembly and tongues as an individual prayer language.

The attitude of the Life in the Spirit Seminars towards church structures is explained in the following words:

> Church life as it exists in most parishes is not enough. To grow in the life of the Spirit we need to get together with Christians who have experienced the same thing we have.

> The Lord does not want us to leave the Church, but to become more active, better members of it.[161]

One can empathize with the agonizing tension and ambivalence expressed in these last sentences. The revised (Protestant) edition states more bluntly, "Normal church life is not enough."[162] This tension between the fundamentalist, Free church background of Pentecostalism and the loyalty to the established Catholic tradition later leads to a flowering of charismatic theology among Catholic charismatic theologians. The Life in the Spirit Seminars Team Manual (Catholic edition) represents the earliest phase of Catholic reflection on the renewal experience which has not broken out of the neo-Pentecostal framework of the earliest leaders.

In her controversial book, *Which Way for Catholic Pentecostals?*, Dr. Josephine Massyngberde Ford devotes a chapter to reflections on the Life in the Spirit Seminars.[163] She faults them for religious indifference, being based on group dynamics rather than the free working of the Spirit, and constructing para-ecclesial structures. Her basic criticism is that it is not Roman Catholic enough. The teaching on tongues and the exorcism of evil spirits should be moderated and deemphasized and reference made to the Holy Eucharist. More freedom should be accorded to the individual conscience. The prayer for tongues could rather include such a phrase as "if You wish" or "if it be Your will."[164] Throughout the chapter it is apparent that Dr. Ford is objecting to the neo-Pentecostal nature of the Life in the Spirit Seminars and advocating an approach which could be better integrated into the Catholic theological tradition.

Steve Clark has expressed his own personal position more clearly in a book, *Baptized in the Spirit and Spiritual Gifts*. His view is described by Robert Culpepper:

> For Catholic charismatic interpretations that are nearer typical Protestant neo-Pentecostal ones, see Ralph Martin...and Stephen B. Clark....Clark discusses baptism in the Spirit largely as a second stage of Christian experience, but he says that normally "a person should be joined to Christ and baptized in the Spirit at the same time" (p. 58).[165]

There is actually a lot more to Clark's view than this remark by Culpepper would lead one to expect. From the discussion below it will become clear that Clark should still be categorized as neo-Pentecostal, although it must be noted that Culpepper was not using this term in the same specified sense as it is being used in this present study. Clark defines Spirit-baptism as meaning:

> that we have a change in our relationship with God such that we can begin to experience in our lives all the things which God promised that the Holy Spirit would do for believers.[166]

He also uses the more typically sacramental language and describes it "as the release of the Spirit in us or as our being opened in the Spirit."[167] Apparently Clark does not see the dichotomy between a theology of subsequence and a "release of the Spirit" clearly. Perhaps this is part of the dilemma of being a leader in an ecumenical community. When he discusses Acts 8 and 19 he can conclude with the typical neo-Pentecostal position:

> In other words, in both passages, receiving the Holy Spirit came subsequently to believing and being baptized. The difference between being joined to Christ and receiving the Spirit is confirmed in passages in the New Testament which mention the two in a parallel but separate way.[168]

Clark also sees this illustrated in Titus 3:5–6 and John 3:5. Even if one were to concede that the parallel expressions in these texts refer to different and separate works of God, there is no indication of subsequence here. In fact it is much more acceptable to see "the washing of regeneration" and "renewal in the Holy Spirit" (Titus 3:5) as both referring to the new life in Christ—just from different perspectives. The context is plainly Christian initiation and water baptism. One could possibly distinguish between regeneration as the initial entrance into the Christian life and renewal as an ongoing process beginning at baptism, but that is not the same as the two-stage Christian life hypothesis.

The reference in John 3:5 is to being "born of water and the Spirit." If Clark is suggesting that one cannot enter the kingdom of God without both water baptism and Spirit-baptism (and Spirit-baptism is not seen as a metaphor for regeneration-conversion by Clark), this implies that Spirit-baptism is essential for salvation—a position not even taught by most classical Pentecostals. The basic problem is really that there are not two births involved but one—a being born of water-and-Spirit. The article does not appear before either of these words, and that they are grammatically governed by the same preposition indicates close unity.[169]

True, Clark concedes that the normal pattern is that "a person should be joined to Christ and baptized in the Spirit at the same time"[170] (as Culpepper mentioned above). However, Clark adds that this still needs to be applied in a present-day situation, which is quite different from the early church. Clark also makes the astute observation that our experiences usually go according to our expectations. We often won't allow them to happen in other ways.[171]

He distinguishes three main categories of Spirit-baptism, since the people who have this experience are at different places in their relationship with God. The first group includes non-Christians, nominal Christians, and fallen-away Christians. This category experiences: "a complete coming into the full life of Christ (the full life of the Spirit) – from nothing to everything,"[172] i.e. both conversion and Spirit-baptism together. The second group are those: "who believe in Christ and are trying to live the Christian life (with some degree of devotion), but who have no direct experience of the working of the Spirit in them."[173]

In the third category we find people "who have had some formation in spirituality and have experienced the presence and working of the Spirit in some kind of way."[174] They experience a charismatic release – a freeing of their faith – or "a freeing of the Spirit in them in such a way that they can experience all the normal workings of the Spirit."[175]

In this context Clark mentions tongues, prophecy, healing. He also adds that there is one last group – those who have experienced these workings of the Spirit without having realized it. Although he does not say so, I would presume that Clark believes that these people must have actually experienced Spirit-baptism itself as well but not have realized that either, since Clark seems to see Spirit-baptism as the door to experiencing the charismata.

Clark's is certainly more refined than the general neo-Pentecostal view. He also explains briefly what Spirit-baptism is not: It is not conversion, not "a new realization of the doctrine of the Holy Spirit in us," not a greater devotion to the Spirit or a sign of spiritual maturity or holiness. It is also not a panacea – everything we need.[176]

His use of Acts 8 and 19, as well as his definition of Spirit-baptism as a change in people's relationship to God, makes one still want to classify his view as neo-Pentecostal. He sees Spirit-baptism as distinctly separate from conversion and yet essential for a full life in the Spirit. It also seems to be a prerequisite for the functioning of the charismata. Although much more sophisticated, this still is a doctrine of subsequence. The fact that conversion and Spirit-baptism may sometimes occur simultaneously is acknowledged by classical Pentecostals as well, but this does not alter the basic pattern.

If Clark were to write another book on Spirit-baptism he would probably rethink the issue of the two-stage model of Christian life. He has already given indications of a broader perspective by acknowledging the singular role of those who are "spiritually experienced."[177] His Catholic tradition has stood him in good stead here. He uses the sacramental view of the "release of the Spirit" together with the neo-Pentecostal view but appears to limit it to those people, often the "religious," who have had some formation in spirituality.

Another more "Catholic" perspective in Clark's theology which he does not develop in his book is the role of confirmation. Rodman Williams comments:

> For some Catholic Pentecostals there is a serious attempt to bring together a unity of sacramental action and inward experience by speaking of "baptism with the Spirit" as "experiencing the effect of confirmation."[178]

Williams refers especially to Clark here but this same tendency is found in the teaching of the German Catholic theologian, Heribert Mühlen, and the Lutheran, Theodore Jungkuntz. Reference will be made to them later. These perspectives of Clark make it likely that he may choose to shift to the sacramental interpretation in subsequent publications.

In a 1969 article, "Confirmation and Baptism of the Holy Spirit," Steve Clark relates Spirit-baptism directly to the Catholic sacrament of confirmation. He mentions that there is a new interest in "renewing" sacraments in the Catholic Church because many people, although truly baptized, do not live as if they have been baptized. Then he asks the question:

> If a real conversion to Christ can renew the sacrament of baptism in a person's life so that the effect of the sacrament is realized, should there not be a similar renewal of the sacrament of confirmation? Is there no way in which a person can "receive" the grace of the sacrament (the new presence of the Holy Spirit conferred by confirmation), so that he can experience the presence and operation of the Holy Spirit in his life? Can not all the things which happened to the early Christians as a result of the presence of the Holy Spirit among them, also happen today?[179]

Clark answers yes. This happens when one receives the "baptism of the Holy Spirit." He points out that the many Catholics who are experiencing this are not being given the Spirit for the first time. They are, rather, experiencing the power of the Spirit which is being *released* in their lives as the effects of confirmation.

Always sensitive to the position of non-Catholics Clark explains that those who have not been sacramentally confirmed can, by their desire and example, be said to have received "a confirmation by desire." He explains:

> In other words, they so much desired the power of the Holy Spirit, that God conferred it upon them without their being officially confirmed. We might even say, then, that Cornelius and his household received a confirmation by desire.[180]

To project the sacrament of confirmation back into Acts 10 is surely questionable exegesis and was probably not meant in any strict sense. It is, however, significant that Clark is seen to be striving towards the integration of the charismatic renewal and his Catholic beliefs. Although he uses the idea of the "release of the Spirit" at this stage, this is not really operating within a sacramental framework. The basic two-stage structure of neo-Pentecostalism still seems intact, with conversion as a renewal of baptism and Spirit-baptism as a subsequent renewal of confirmation.

2.6.4 Peter Hocken (Catholic)

The other Catholic neo-Pentecostal thinker whose view I wish to discuss is Father Peter Hocken. His recent thoughts on Spirit-baptism are in "The Meaning and Purpose of Baptism in the Spirit," a paper read before The Society for Pentecostal Studies (1984).[181] He argues that Spirit-baptism changes the believer's relationship to the Persons of the Trinity. The Pentecostal statements of faith commonly describe the purpose of Spirit-baptism as an enduement of power for ministry and service. Hocken sees this as a very limited perspective. Revelation is a more basic category than power. Revelation is not to be restricted to special or new messages. Spirit-baptism brings an indwelling and inward revelation which is broader in its scope. The Spirit-baptized person hears the Lord speaking today. He points out that something like power belongs only to the period of the church, whereas seeking the meaning of Spirit-baptism in changed relationships with the Trinity expressed in revelation, brings one into the realm of the eternal. These changes initiated at Spirit-baptism last for ever. Hocken clearly wishes to preserve the doctrine of subsequence. It would seem as if the permanent effects of Spirit-baptism, which cannot be had any other way, make a two-stage theory essential. A change in relationship to the Triune God also seems to give Spirit-baptism as momentous an impact as regeneration-conversion has. Although every grace of God changes us, Spirit-baptism resulting in revelation is the greatest qualitative change possible in our relationship to God. The word "change" could be understood as operating within a two-stage framework.

Perhaps the viewpoint of Hocken will become clearer in future publications. With the present state of available articles it already appears that Hocken represents a position in the Catholic charismatic renewal which is decidedly neo-Pentecostal. He speaks of experiencing a double loyalty:

> This double loyalty is not to the Roman Catholic Church and to the Catholic charismatic renewal, but to the Roman Catholic Church and the worldwide Pentecostal movement (which has its origins and its lengthiest experience in the Pentecostal Churches).[182]

Hocken also seems to believe that Pentecostalism is more compatible with Catholicism than one would expect from a superficial acquaintance or from the limited self-understanding of Pentecostals. He quotes from Hollenweger:

> Catholics have rightly seen that the Pentecostals are—in contrast to their self-interpretation—not a typically Protestant church.[183]

To define adequately what Hocken's position and all its consequences are is not possible. He wishes to preserve a doctrine of subsequence and, together with Simon Tugwell, a British Dominican who is discussed under the sacramental position, he seems to see interesting theological possibilities in further work on sacramental elements in the Pentecostal understanding of glossolalia. Hocken writes:

> Simon Tugwell, OP, makes an interesting comparison between the Catholic understanding of sacraments as efficacious signs and the classical Pentecostal understanding of tongues as the initial evidence of Spirit-baptism.[184]

On the other hand, Hocken does not fall prey to the elitism inherent in the Pentecostal doctrine of subsequence. He rejects the idea of two sorts of Christians:

> For those Christians who determine faith primarily by appeal to experience, it may be possible to accept the classical Pentecostal division of believers into the "filled" and the not yet "filled." But for those [like himself] who believe that the Holy Spirit is given in the sacraments of initiation, there is difficulty in marking out any category of baptized person qualitatively different and distinctively endowed. Hence arise problems of a theological nature about baptism in the Holy Spirit, being "Spirit-filled" and the meaning of the term "charismatic."[185]

To come to grips with Hocken's perspective a series of articles in *The Clergy Review, The Heythrop Journal, The Way,* and *One in Christ* need to be surveyed.[186] A complicating factor is that Hocken is attempting in these articles to give a survey of key questions rather than to develop his own position. He points out that charismatics have both accepted and modified Pentecostal views on Spirit-baptism. According to Hocken there seem to be three positions:[187]

(1) Protestants who have simply taken over the Pentecostal doctrine of Spirit-baptism. (In this study they have been dubbed neo-Pentecostals and I would maintain that Hocken himself—although a Catholic—really belongs here.)

(2) Those who keep the Pentecostal terminology but qualify the nature of the doctrine. Hocken here refers specifically to Michael Harper, but he goes on to refer to Catholic charismatic authors as well. He says they usually relate the Spirit-baptism experience to the sacraments of baptism and confirmation. (Several of these writers will be discussed in the next section on the sacramental model of Spirit-baptism.) Personally I don't find Hocken's criterion of "keeping the Pentecostal terminology but qualifying the doctrine" helpful here since many charismatic authors keep the term "baptism in the Spirit" merely out of convenience or because no better one has presented itself. Furthermore several of them advocate a term such as "the release of the Spirit" to describe their doctrinal position, while at the same time still using Spirit-baptism or baptism in the Holy Spirit because they are realistic enough to accept that this terminology has become so common that it is here to stay. Hocken finds this position (2) unacceptable because it leads to a watering down of the Pentecostal position. The definitions of Spirit-baptism by these theo-

logians become so vague, according to Hocken, as to apply to almost any form of spiritual growth,[188] and people on this position don't seem to be able to define the role of glossolalia adequately. Hocken states that they either worry about canonized saints who have not had an identifiable Spirit-baptism or the fact that they know people who speak in tongues but have never had a crisis-point experience.

(3) Hocken's third category consists of those who abandon Spirit-baptism terminology but still maintain the validity of "the Pentecostal experience"[189] (note the definite article). Here Hocken refers to Simon Tugwell and J. Massyngberde Ford.

So much for Hocken's categorization. In the following sections I shall be developing another system of models. What I find particularly important in Hocken's perspective is that he is resolutely resisting the general move among charismatic Catholics to both reinterpret Spirit-baptism within a Catholic framework and to play down any similarities with classical Pentecostalism. He states:

> I am suggesting then that any Catholic attempt to formulate a doctrine of "Spirit-baptism" that can be harmonized with Catholic teaching on the sacraments of baptism and confirmation is a misguided enterprise.[190]

He wishes to accord a different status from that of doctrine to Spirit-baptism and is afraid that the tendency to widen the meaning of Spirit-baptism in the reinterpretation attempts by Catholics "may reduce the chances of our learning important spiritual lessons from the Pentecostals."[191] Elsewhere Hocken warns that this tendency to include other types of experience under the concept of Spirit-baptism "can end up by emasculating the impact of the Pentecostal 'filling.'"[192] He makes this more explicit by referring to Kilian McDonnell's *Statements of the Theological Basis of the Catholic Charismatic Renewal* which was presented to the first International Conference of Catholic Charismatic leaders at Grottaferrata, 1973. Hocken objects to the following statement in McDonnell's document:

> But there is a problem in the use of the phrase (baptism in the Holy Spirit), as it could be taken to mean that only those who have had a particular kind of experience of the Spirit have really been baptized in the Spirit. This is not the case, since every valid and fruitful Christian initiation confers "the gift of the Holy Spirit" (Acts 2:38), and "to be baptized in the Holy Spirit" is simply another scriptural way of saying "to receive the Holy Spirit."[193]

This is a very crucial point and it will be developed further as we continue to analyze various positions. Why Hocken should still be classified as neo-Pentecostal despite the reservations that he has introduced in his analysis becomes clear from his sympathy with "initial evidence" rather than from a clear statement about the theology of subsequence.

Countering this "widening tendency" to "depentecostalize" Spirit-baptism and to reinterpret it in sacramental (or other) categories, Hocken sees another tendency "undoubtedly found throughout the Pentecostal movement [which for him includes the charismatics] which correlates the experience of Baptism in the Spirit with reception (*sic*) of yielding to the gift of tongues."[194]

Hocken underscores the role of glossolalia and is convinced that however much charismatics admit in theory that one may receive Spirit-baptism without tongues, they do readily assume that in practice the two go together.[195] This is clearly the neo-Pentecostal teaching on the issue.

Yet another important facet to Hocken's unique position is evident. He is against the "total denominational integration of charismatic renewal."[196] He is not afraid that the charismatic renewal will develop a sectarian or schismatic mentality (which seems to be the main fear of many church leaders – borne out by myriad examples in practice, I might add). Hocken declares:

> I believe, on the contrary, that the greatest dangers facing charismatic renewal come from the opposite direction, namely from too hasty and superficial an integration of the charismatic and the denominational in a manner that anesthetizes God's challenge to the Churches through charismatic renewal.[197]

The reason for Hocken's rejection of such uncritical integration is that he finds it incompatible with the ecumenical character of the charismatic renewal. At the beginning of the movement in the sixties and seventies there was a groundswell of grassroots ecumenism expressed in ecumenical prayer groups and large ecumenical conferences. Later this enthusiasm seemed to dissipate, leading to much disappointment and causing some observers to interpret the change as an uncritical return to denominational traditions. Perhaps the real difference between Hocken and the other position – exemplified by McDonnell – is a different concept of what ecumenism entails, McDonnell cum suis seeing the variety of theological traditions as positive and Hocken viewing the variety as something which should eventually be overcome.

McDonnell's position can be easily illustrated by two quotations. Outlining the relationship of the charismatic renewal to the established denominations, he writes:

> . . . the goal of the ecumenical movement is not one culture. The goal rather is the coming together of a plurality of theological cultures in one faith allegiance, under one Lordship, confessing one baptism, each theological culture standing under judgment, each retaining its own integrity and identity. The formation of a number of denominational charismatic fellowships is not, therefore, in opposition to the goals of ecumenism. Quite the opposite, ecumenism presupposes oneness of faith but a plurality of theologies and a plurality of cultures and ecclesial types.[198]

In his booklet, *Spirit-baptism as an Ecumenical Problem,* McDonnell states in a similar vein:

> I would not want to suggest that all the elements in each of these ecclesiastical traditions is sacred, nor that we can mix elements from each tradition to come up with a viable theology. Rather I want to suggest that the variety of theological traditions is a thing to be treasured. No one tradition has managed to exploit to the full the richness of God's gift in Jesus Christ and his Holy Spirit. We can learn from the strengths of the various ecclesiastical traditions.[199]

This is the concept of ecumenicity which Hocken finds unacceptable and I would suspect that his disagreement with this vision is the basic reason why he has not followed so many other charismatics in the endeavor to develop a new model to reinterpret Spirit-baptism within a denominational framework or theological ecclesial culture (to use McDonnell's terminology).

Of course Hocken's position is not the average neo-Pentecostal one. He is aware of the many drawbacks and problems in this position but apparently still finds it more convincing than the alternatives which will be developed in the next chapters of this study. An insightful example of his critique against Pentecostalism is what he terms the shadow-side of Pentecostalism. He explains:

> This is the fate of those who have been wrongly encouraged to seek a dramatic break-through but have experienced nothing, and those so encouraged who have had an inauthentic humanly-induced substitute with no spiritual substance; such people, left damaged and disillusioned, are the price paid for the mistakes of the undiscerning, and their voices are not heard when the testimonies to God's mighty works among others are announced.[200]

This quotation makes it quite clear that though Hocken comes very close to the original Pentecostal teaching of claiming glossolalia to be the sign of Spirit-baptism, he is, at least, patently aware of some of the pastoral problems caused by a dogmatic insistence on this teaching.

It is to be hoped that Hocken will in time develop his unique perspectives more fully in a monograph so that his ideas (which have here been gleaned from various articles) can be elaborated on, systematized and presented to a broader audience. He seems equipped and poised to play a pivotal role in dialogue between classical Pentecostals and charismatics who are not of a neo-Pentecostal persuasion. As we experience a new upsurge of Pentecostal scholarship (e.g. the latest publications of Hendrickson Publishers, Peabody, Massachusetts)[201] the theological importance of this mediating role of Peter Hocken cannot be overestimated for the ongoing development of Pentecostal and charismatic studies.

Although one has the sensation of having had to try to "freeze a flowing river" in order to analyze the present position of these neo-Pentecostal Catholics, and it is plain that more thinking and research needs to be done, it is apparent that the Catholic representatives of neo-Pentecostalism are more nuanced and theologically sophisticated than the Protestant and non-denominational neo-Pentecostals. It also seems likely that further development in their thinking will not necessarily lead all of them to move over to one of the other models which will be discussed next. In the case of Hocken, rather than Clark (whom I would expect to move in the direction of the sacramental position), further expression and development of this thinking may lead to an even more vivid and dynamic presentation of the same neo-Pentecostal model. If this conjecture proves to be correct, it could give a new lease on life to the neo-Pentecostal approach to Spirit-baptism, which is becoming more and more suspect in theologically aware Protestant circles and which has always been unacceptable to many from liturgical and sacramental churches because it was experienced as part of the "cultural baggage" of classical Pentecostalism. Next our attention moves to the Presbyterian and Reformed expression of neo-Pentecostalism.

2.6.5 J. Rodman Williams and John Schep (Presbyterian/Reformed)

J. Rodman Williams is a charismatic with a Presbyterian background whose latest views can be seen as unavoidably neo-Pentecostal. He has written a book of 150 pages on *The Gift of the Holy Spirit Today*.[202] This is probably the most extensive monograph on Spirit-baptism to date – not counting dissertations. Like most of the early Protestant charismatics, he adheres to a basic two-stage schema. His book deals with the background, dimensions, response, purpose, reception, means, context, and effects of the gift of the Spirit – his term for Spirit-baptism. However, in *The Gift of the Holy Spirit Today* he never directly states what Spirit-baptism actually is; neither does he address the typical issue of the theology of subsequence directly.

Despite further developments in Williams's theology of Spirit-baptism (prior to his monograph) it is important to note that in a recent article included at the back of the papers from the Fourteenth Annual SPS meeting in 1984, Williams adds nothing substantial to his perspective given in *The Gift of the Holy Spirit Today*. His paper is entitled "Baptism in the Holy Spirit – A Biblical Study." In this paper he says it is clear in Acts that there can be those who believe but have not yet received the Spirit. This smacks of the typical two-stage theory built on Acts 8. At the same time Williams sees Spirit-baptism as one of the foundations of Christian faith and practice.

With respect to initial evidence Williams seems to take the neo-Pentecostal line, but with some sophistication:

> So tongues are not constitutive of the gift of the Spirit (as if it were not possible to have one without the other), but are declarative, namely, that the gift has been received. Tongues are – and remain – a peculiar sign.[203]

In a footnote on tongues he declares "A helpful discussion of this matter is to be found in the chapter, 'Speaking in Tongues as Sign,' by Larry Christenson in his book, *Speaking in Tongues*."[204] As was indicated above, it was precisely this discussion by Christenson which was indicative of the neo-Pentecostal nature of his early thinking on the renewal experience.

In the epilogue Williams clearly teaches that new life in Christ and the gift of the Spirit are two distinct and distinguishable elements of God's work in us. He states:

> But the all-important point is that the gift of eternal life is not the gift of the Holy Spirit, though the latter presupposes the former and both are mediated by Christ.

> If we have experienced through Him the life-changing wonder of forgiveness of sins and eternal life, have we also received the empowering miracle of the gift of the Holy Spirit?[205]

In a review of Williams's book the editor of *Renewal News* and general secretary of the Presbyterian Charismatic Communion (later renamed Presbyterian and Reformed Renewal Ministries International), Dr. Bradford, sees this distinction made in the quotation above as appearing "to be a departure from the writer's Reformed theological roots."[206]

Williams points out that he is fully aware of working in a seldom charted theological area and trusts that he has helped set the stage for further theological reflection.[207] Bradford is certainly correct in considering Williams's failure to identify the gift of the Spirit with regeneration-conversion as being "unreformed." What is of interest here is that it also presupposes a two-stage view of the Christian life. This does not, however, represent the comprehensive thinking of Williams on the subject. He sometimes advocates Spirit-baptism as part of Christian initiation and rejects tenets of the neo-Pentecostal view. Why he did not include these perspectives in *The Gift of the Holy Spirit Today* is puzzling. The only conjecture I can make is that he did not wish to focus specifically on controversial issues there and he chose rather to write "largely a biblical study."[208]

In contradistinction to Christenson, who moved further and further away from his original, more Pentecostal, view of Spirit-baptism, Williams seems to have moved in the opposite direction, later becoming closer to the classical Pentecostal or at least neo-Pentecostal view than he was in his two earliest books.

Another characteristic of his earlier work is its intense creativity. He also seems to be grappling to find an acceptable theology of Spirit-baptism. In three contributions in the early seventies he discusses Spirit-baptism in quite different ways. We need to look first at *The Era of the Spirit,* published in 1971.[209] In the section entitled "Theological Implications" he develops a line of thought showing that none of the traditional theological categories such as regeneration, sanctification, or confirmation can in fact adequately accommodate the contemporary renewal in the Spirit. Rather these categories become operational in a new way through this renewal. Williams speaks of a movement of the Spirit beyond redemption.[210] It is, in fact, the major activity of the Spirit and can be called effusion (externally) and pervasion (internally).[211] Williams seems to fear a subordination of the Spirit to the Son in Western theology. This almost leads him to seek the characteristic activity of the Spirit beyond redemption which is so closely associated with Christ. I personally think a more fruitful approach would be to say that there are elements of Christ's work which have been neglected. The church has not fully realized the full scope of this work of God in Christ. We do not need a "particular" or "special" activity of the Spirit beyond Christ's work.[212] We need to appropriate the fullness of Christ's work which is indivisible from the Spirit's work. Augustine has already warned us that the work of the Trinity *ad extra* is indivisible. This is furthermore supported by the realization that it is Jesus who pours out his Spirit on the church or, as the Pentecostals point out, Jesus is the Baptizer.

Williams also uses the language of Spirit-baptism as a release–the dynamic movement of the Spirit as explosive in nature. Latently the Christian has the fullness, but it must come to manifestation:

> To be "filled" with the Spirit of God is not so much to have something "more" as it is to be in the new, wonderful, and at times fearful situation of having the Spirit of God break into the whole round of existence and pervade it all. As a result of this–yes, explosion–what may be violent at the beginning can become the steady and driving power of a mighty dynamo–the Spirit of the living God.[213]

Two articles in *The Pentecostal Reality* focus on Spirit-baptism: "The Event of the Spirit" and "Pentecostal Spirituality."[214] In the first of these Williams underscores Spirit-baptism as a door into the new fullness of life in the Spirit.[215] The person is penetrated by the Spirit in his or her conscious and subconscious existence, resulting in an energizing which fulfills new possibilities. Spirit-baptism as such has nothing to do with sanctification: "The effect is not a certain quality of existence but a way of life in which one is open to the Spirit's activity."[216]

Aware of the debate about the expression "baptism with the Holy Spirit," Williams chooses to adhere to it until some better way comes along of saying what has happened.[217] The models of Spirit-baptism in the following chapters would see themselves as presenting such a way. For Williams the issue remains deeply existential:

> The person of Pentecostal experience does not begin with a theology about the Holy Spirit, not even a biblical teaching as such, but with something that has happened in his life.[218]

What is tantalizing about Williams is that he wants the best of both worlds. In a footnote he comes very close to the sacramental position on Spirit-baptism:

> For there is a sense in which the whole Pentecostal reality, or event of the Spirit, is anticipated in the third part of the baptismal formula [being baptized in the name of the Holy Spirit]. From this perspective "baptism with the Spirit" could be understood not as the wholly new but as the appropriation of what was given in baptism.[219]

The interpretation of Spirit-baptism becomes relatively unimportant, for with a touch of American pragmatism Williams can conclude:

> Whether one follows the line of "baptism with the Spirit" as representing a totally new dimension of Christian living, or an appropriation of what has already been given, the same result may follow.[220]

In the second article Williams deals more systematically with the "Pentecostal" approach to Spirit-baptism. (Today, it is my guess, he would probably use the word charismatic here. I am, however, not quite sure about this.) He points out that Spirit-baptism is seen as distinct from and subsequent to conversion. Even when they occur simultaneously they are clearly not identical.[221] Williams does not explicitly show his own personal perspective in this article on Pentecostal spirituality, presumably since he was presenting the paper for the first Roman Catholic/Pentecostal dialogue.

He points to some differences among "Pentecostals." There are three ways of expressing the different nature of the work of Spirit-baptizing from the Spirit's work in conversion/regeneration. Harold Horton (classical Pentecostal) and Derek Prince (neo-Pentecostal) are seen as distinguishing between the Spirit dwelling with the believer in conversion and abiding within or indwelling the believer after Spirit-baptism. The second way of expressing this is by distinguishing between indwelling and Spirit-baptism. R. M. Riggs (classical Pentecostal) and Dennis Bennett (neo-Pentecostal) accept that all Christians are indwelt by the Spirit but not all are Spirit-baptized Christians. The third way is to speak of the "second experience" as a "release" of the Spirit.[222]

With respect to initial evidence Williams points out that neo-Pentecostals (and he could, in fact, just as well be using the term in the way it has been defined in this study) often prefer the expression "normal accompaniment" to initial evidence and allow for the possibility that tongues may occur later.[223]

In the collection of essays from the Society for Pentecostal Studies Second Annual Meeting (1972) Williams has reached a further stage in his development of understanding Spirit-baptism.[224] He makes an interesting division between Pentecostal, evangelical, and sacramental perspectives, arriving in the end at a "synthesis" which in my opinion attempts to place the best of the neo-Pentecostal and the sacramental positions unintegrated alongside one another. Apparently Williams does not recognize that "two distinct experiences" backed up by Acts 8 cannot logically be reconciled with seeing Spirit-baptism as "an aspect of Christian initiation" and the refusal "to speak of Christians and Spirit-baptized Christians."[225]

Williams's "constructive proposal" is:

(1) To criticize evangelicalism for not recognizing that there is non-identity between conversion and Spirit-baptism. (This, of course, goes against the thrust of many exegetical studies in this area, cf. Dunn.)

(2) To criticize sacramentalism for "binding" regeneration and Spirit-baptism to particular sacramental actions.

(3) To criticize Pentecostalism for teaching two kinds or levels of Christians and for failing to recognize that sacraments are means of grace.[226]

The suggested synthesis is understanding Spirit-baptism as the climactic moment of entrance into Christian life. Although the elements of regeneration/conversion and Spirit-baptism are not to be identified and are often separated in actual occurrence (sometimes by decades), one should speak only of persons in process of Christian initiation not using words such as Spirit-baptized Christians.[227]

This certainly is a valiant attempt to achieve the impossible—to maintain the distinctives of both views and yet integrate the views. Perhaps it is symptomatic of this unsuccessful harmonization that Williams returns in his later works to one of the alternatives—the neo-Pentecostal position. When writing to Presbyterian ministers in 1970 he gives the clearest expression of the sacramental viewpoint:

> In receiving baptism long ago, I was not only baptized in water but also in the Holy Spirit. I have been led within the past few years into such an appropriation of my early baptism in the Holy Spirit that it was actually a receiving of this baptism.[228]

This brings us to the conclusion of the contribution of J. Rodman Williams. Apart from inconsistencies and a measure of confusion, his position represents a protest against the separation and evolving of the neo-Pentecostal and the sacramental views. With remarkable tenacity he tried to bridge the gap by accepting the validity of both positions. In my opinion he could not maintain this dichotomy; in his most recent writings he either evades the issue or gives basic support to the neo-Pentecostal interpretation of Spirit-baptism.

Another Reformed neo-Pentecostal to whom I do not wish to devote a separate section is the Dutch theologian, John A. Schep. The following quotation will suffice to summarize his approach. He uses prepositions to clarify his position as he focuses on the distinction between the first stage: regeneration-conversion and the second stage: Spirit-baptism:

> In the light of all that we have found we draw the conclusion that there is a baptism *by* the Spirit and a baptism *with* the Spirit.

> The former denotes the Spirit's work in conversion and regeneration, by which He makes sinners members of Christ and His church under the seal of water baptism.

> The baptism *with* the Spirit is somewhat different. It is a blessing given by Christ to those who by the Spirit have been incorporated into Christ's Body, the Church. Our Lord baptizes them with His Spirit, pouring the Spirit out upon them. He fills them with the Spirit, thus granting them power from on high for witness and Christian service.[229]

Schep also appeals to Reformed tradition to legitimate his neo-Pentecostal theology. As one could deduce from the pre-charismatic two-stage views of the Christian life discussed in chapter 1, the only strictly Reformed heritage is that of the Reformed Sealers. Schep accordingly appeals to the exegesis of Ephesians 1:13, 14 by Puritan Thomas Goodwin, born 1600. Goodwin teaches a sealing of the Spirit which is distinct from being justified by faith. It is experiential, causing great joy. It is a sealing which makes believers sure of their salvation and should be earnestly sought by all. In his commentary on Ephesians Goodwin writes:

> This is the great fruit of your baptism. . . .You have not that great fruit of your baptism till you have this. . . .Therefore you shall find it called: baptized with the Holy Ghost. . . .Therefore Peter bids them to be baptized and they should receive this promise, Acts 2:38. You that believe are to wait for this promise of the Holy Ghost to come and fill your heart with joy unspeakable and glorious.[230]

Schep waxes eloquent about this apparent support for his position:

> Meantime, it is comforting to hear an undoubted Calvinist, of a time shortly after the Synod of Dordt, preach a specific, personal baptism with the Holy Spirit as available for all believers and to be recommended to all.[231]

Further on he continues, "And it is a great pity that the Reformed tradition has nearly completely ignored this voice."[232] The fact that Goodwin's Spirit-baptism was an experience primarily of the assurance of salvation and that this cannot just be identified with two-stage Pentecostalism does not seem to have made any impact on Schep.

2.6.6 Howard Ervin (Baptist)

In *These Are Not Drunken, As Ye Suppose*[233] Howard Ervin presents a defense of the neo-Pentecostal position – one of the earliest scholarly accounts available. His background is Baptist, but his theology is Pentecostal. He states:

> The baptism in the Holy Spirit is not synonymous with conversion and the "new birth." Rather, it is subsequent to conversion and regeneration.[234]

His views on tongues are equally clear and unequivocal:

> And whether stated, or implied, it is a fair conclusion from the Biblical evidence, that tongues are the "external and indubitable proof" of the baptism in/filling (*sic*) with the Holy Spirit.

> In the author's opinion, a baptism in the Spirit without the charismatic evidence is not a Biblical datum. It is a theological improvisation dictated by sub-apostolic experience to extenuate the impotence of the Church's life and ministry in the face of secularism, humanism, and atheistic materialism. So it is that other "evidences" of the Spirit-empowered life have been advanced.[235]

He rejects other evidences such as prophecy, discerning of spirits, or healings since they were manifested among the disciples before Pentecost and have other biblical parallels too. Only glossolalia will suffice as evidence of Spirit-baptism because it appeared with the first instance of the baptism in the Spirit at Pentecost. The other gifts cannot be a substitute for tongues. They are rather a consequence of Spirit-baptism.[236]

In a chapter entitled "The Pattern of Pentecost" Ervin develops the classical argument for a theology of subsequence. An interesting feature is that he not only works with the usual 5 cases (Acts 2, 8, 9, 10, 19) but adds Acts 4 – the second Jerusalem "Pentecost" and the Ethiopian Eunuch's "Pentecost" (Acts 8:38).[237]

In 1984 Ervin published an apologetic for this same neo-Pentecostal perspective: *Conversion-Initiation and the Baptism in the Holy Spirit*. In this study he presents a critique of James D. G. Dunn's book, *Baptism in the Holy Spirit*. His interest seems to be largely exegetical. In his preface Ervin states:

No attempt has been made to present a systematic and comprehensive theological synthesis of the conclusions reached. Rather, I have limited myself to an examination of the inadequacies and errors in the exegesis offered in support of the conversion-initiation thesis. I have simply accepted the gauntlet wherever Dr. Dunn has thrown it down.[238]

One can only hope that Ervin will, in due time, formulate "a systematic and comprehensive theological synthesis" of his perspective. Without that his attempt to revitalize the Pentecostal position on Spirit-baptism will probably flounder as readers struggle to see the forest for the trees. One gets the impression that this new dialogue between "Pentecostals" and "Evangelicals" also needs to get out of the rut of detailed exegetical debate which seems to call for statement and rebuttal ad infinitum. To me a more constructive approach seems to be the position of Gordon Fee and Russ Spittler, discussed previously, in which the essential "charismatic element" of the New Testament church is emphasized rather than the traditional line of a theology of subsequence with tongues as initial physical evidence of the "second state." Ervin's latest book seems, nevertheless, to be one of the best presentations of the neo-Pentecostal case supported by detailed exegesis and merits further discussion.[239]

In conclusion one can say that the neo-Pentecostal position is one of the most pervasive interpretations of Spirit-baptism. It dominated the early phases of the charismatic renewal penetrating the major denominational and non-denominational traditions. In many circles it is still accepted as the authoritative position and in at least one line of Catholic charismatic thought it is being refined and continues to hold its own against the newer interpretations. A new attempt to defend this position exegetically is also found in Howard Ervin's latest book.

Endnotes 2

1. For a thorough review of all recent Pentecostal and charismatic literature, see C. M. Robeck's article "The Decade (1973–1982) in Pentecostal-Charismatic Literature: A Bibliographic Essay," in *Theology, News and Notes* 30 (1, 1983): 24–29. A revised edition of this was published as brochure R22 by the Zadock Centre Dickson ACT in 1984 under the title *Pentecostal/Charismatic Literature: A Survey of the Last Ten Years.*

2. E.g., the works of K. McDonnell: *Charismatic Renewal and the Churches*; K. McDonnell, ed., *Presence, Power, Praise: Documents on the Charismatic Renewal* 3 vols. (Collegeville, MN: Liturgical Press, 1980); F. A. Sullivan, *Charisms and the Charismatic Renewal* (Ann Arbor: Servant, 1982); R. Laurentin, *Catholic Pentecostalism* (New York: Doubleday, 1977). To this list can be added the works of Cardinal Suenens, Edward O'Connor, Donald Gelpi, Simon Tugwell, Alan Schreck, Peter Hocken, Steve Clark, Josephine Ford, and the Malines Documents.

3. L. Christenson, *Speaking in Tongues and Its Significance for the Church* (Minneapolis: Bethany, 1968) 99–100.

4. Jensen, *Touched by the Spirit*, 87.

5. C. Lindberg, *The Third Reformation? Charismatic Movements and the Lutheran Tradition* (Macon, GA: Mercer University Press, 1983) 224.

6. See his article, "The Relationship of the Charismatic Renewal to the Established Denominations," *Dialog* 13 (3, 1974): 223–29.

7. Hollenweger, *The Pentecostals*, 245.

8. In a taped address at a Lutheran Renewal conference at the Dominican Convent Frankfurt in 1980.

9. Stott, *Baptism and Fullness*, 8.

10. H. R. Niebuhr, *Christ and Culture* (New York: Harper and Row, 1951) 190–206, esp., 217–18.

11. A. Bittlinger, "Charismatic Renewal–An Opportunity for the Church?" in *The Church is Charismatic* (Geneva: World Council of Churches, 1981) 10.

12. Lindberg, *The Third Reformation?* 233.

13. Jensen, *Touched by the Spirit*, 87–88.

14. Ibid., 90.

15. For Jensen's discussion of "The Kingdom Within" see ch. 6, and ch. 7 for his critique of Pentecostal theology.

16. V. Synan, *In the Latter Days*, 121.

17. Ibid.

18. Ibid., 120.

19. S. Grossmann, *Haushalter der Gnade Gottes. Von der charismatischen Bewegung zur charismatischen Erneuerung der Gemeinde* (Wuppertal: Oncken, 1977) 54. The English translation is *Stewards of God's Grace* (Exeter, Devon: Paternoster, 1981), 50.

20. Ibid., 60.

21. This is developed in an unpublished study guide for students: "Systematic Theology STH408–Y (The charismatic movement)" (Pretoria: University of South Africa, 1983) 137–54.

22. Among the better known are Dennis Bennett and Terry Fullam (Episcopal), J. Rodman Williams (Presbyterian), in his earlier thinking Larry Christenson (Lutheran), Howard Ervin (Baptist), and Steve Clark and Peter Hocken (Roman Catholic).

23. Hollenweger, *The Pentecostals*, 9.

24. Ibid., 16.

25. Ibid., 15.

26. J. R. Williams, *The Gift of the Holy Spirit Today: The Greatest Reality of the Twentieth Century* (Plainfield, NJ: Logos, 1980).

27. D. Basham, *A Handbook on Holy Spirit Baptism* (Springdale, PA: Whitaker, 1969).

28. *New Wine* was a well-known periodical in charismatic circles. It represented the non-denominational restorationist perspective. The editorship was overseen by the Christian Growth Ministries until the publication's demise in 1986.

29. Basham, *Holy Spirit Baptism*, 21.

30. Ibid., 22–23.

31. Ibid., 23.

32. Ibid., 24.

33. Ibid., 123.

34. Ibid., 124–25.

35. Bruner, *A Theology of the Holy Spirit*, 190.

36. Basham, *Holy Spirit Baptism*, 83.

37. Ibid., 85.

38. Ibid., 82.

39. Bloch-Hoell, *Pentecostal Movement*, 131–32.

40. O'Connor, *The Pentecostal Movement*, 134.

41. Cf. the similar observations attributed to Jaroslav Pelikan in a document of the LCA: "The Charismatic Movement in the Lutheran Church in America. A Pastoral

Perspective," from Appendix B in *The Holy Spirit in the Life of the Church, from Biblical Times to the Present,* ed. P. D. Opsahl (Minneapolis: Augsburg, 1978) 269. Unfortunately no bibliographical reference is given to the original statement of Pelikan.

42. Basham, *Holy Spirit Baptism,* 113–14.

43. Ibid., 113.

44. J. H. Fichter, *The Catholic Cult of the Paraclete* (New York: Sheed and Ward, 1975) 126.

45. V. Synan, *Charismatic Bridges* (Ann Arbor: Word of Life, 1974).

46. R. D. Wead, *Father McCarthy Smokes a Pipe and Speaks in Tongues* (Wisdom House, 1972). Reprinted as *Catholic Charismatics: Are They for Real?* (Carol Stream, IL: Creation House, 1973).

47. R. A. Knox, *Enthusiasm: A Chapter in the History of Religion with Special Reference to the XVII and XVIII Centuries* (London: Oxford University Press, 1950).

48. A. Schreck, "Ronald Knox's Theory of Enthusiasm and its Application to the Catholic Charismatic Renewal" (Ph.D. diss., University of St. Michael's College, Toronto, 1979).

49. Knox, *Enthusiasm,* 1.

50. A. Wallis, *The Radical Christian* (Eastbourne: Kingsway, 1981) esp., ch. 11: "Denominational Dilemma," 122–36.

51. Ibid., 122.

52. Ibid., 133.

53. Ibid., 136.

54. D. Watson, "Stay In or Come Out? New Life from Inside," *Renewal* 52 (August/September, 1974): 10.

55. Ibid., 11.

56. Ibid.

57. Ibid.

58. Ibid., 12.

59. Ibid.

60. Ibid., 13.

61. Lovelace, *Dynamics of Spiritual Life,* 291.

62. Ibid., 295.

63. Ibid., 294.

64. Ibid., 302.

65. Ibid., 310.

66. Ibid., 315.

67. A. A. Hoekema, *Holy Spirit Baptism* (Grand Rapids: Eerdmans, 1972) 10.

68. Ibid.

69. Ibid., 10–11.

70. Bruner, *A Theology of the Holy Spirit,* 75.

71. G. T. Montague, S.M. *The Holy Spirit: Growth of a Biblical Tradition* (New York: Paulist, 1976) 240.

72. Ibid.

73. Ibid., 241.

74. Ibid., 363.

75. Bruner, *A Theology of the Holy Spirit;* R. H. Culpepper, *Evaluating the Charismatic Movement* (Valley Forge, PA: Judson, 1977); Dunn, *Baptism in the Holy Spirit;* H. M. Ervin, *These Are Not Drunken, As Ye Suppose* (Plainfield, NJ: Logos, 1968); Hoekema, *Holy Spirit Baptism;* C. E. Hummel, *Fire in the Fireplace* (Downers Grove, IL: Inter-Varsity, 1978); Hunter, *Spirit-Baptism;* T. A. Smail, *Reflected Glory* (London: Hodder and Stoughton, 1975); Williams, *Gift of the Holy Spirit.*

76. Montague, *The Holy Spirit,* 293.

77. Ibid., 294.
78. Ibid.
79. Ibid.
80. Bruner, *A Theology of the Holy Spirit*, 180.
81. Ibid., 175.
82. Dunn, *Baptism in the Holy Spirit*, 63.
83. Ibid., 65.
84. D. G. Bloesch, "The Charismatic Revival: A Theological Critique," in *Religion in Life* 35 (1966): 370.
85. E. Haenchen, *Die Apostelgeschichte* (Göttingen: Vandenhoeck & Ruprecht, 7. Auslegung, 16. Auflage, 1977) 298. Cf., English translation: *The Acts of the Apostles* (Oxford: Blackwell, 1971), 308.
86. B. A. du Toit, "Die ontvangs van die Heilige Gees in Samaria. 'n Eksegetiese studie van Handelinge 8:14–17" (D.Th. diss., University of South Africa, Pretoria, 1977) 355–56.
87. Dunn, *Baptism in the Holy Spirit*, 84.
88. Ibid., 85.
89. Bruner, *A Theology of the Holy Spirit*, 209.
90. Hunter, *Spirit-Baptism*, 89.
91. Ibid.
92. Haenchen, *Die Apostelgeschichte*, 529–34, esp., 534. Cf., English translation: *Acts*, 552-57.
93. Bruner, *A Theology of the Holy Spirit*, 214.
94. Fee, "Hermeneutics and Historical Precedent," 128.
95. Ibid., 130–31.
96. Montague, *The Holy Spirit*, 277.
97. Dunn, *Baptism in the Holy Spirit*, 11.
98. Ibid., 13–14.
99. Ibid., 44.
100. Montague, *The Holy Spirit*, 276.
101. Ibid., 282.
102. Dunn, *Baptism in the Holy Spirit*, 47–48.
103. Ibid., 49.
104. Ibid., 53.
105. Ibid., 38.
106. Hummel, *Fire in the Fireplace*, 262.
107. Ibid., 182.
108. R. E. Cottle, "All Were Baptized," *JETS* 17 (1974): 75–80.
109. For more detailed analysis, refer to Hunter, *Spirit-Baptism*, 39–42; J. Rea, ed. *The Layman's Commentary on the Holy Spirit* (rev. edition, Plainfield, NJ: Logos, 1974) 146–51, 256; Ervin, *These Are Not Drunken*, 40–50.
110. H. Ridderbos, *Paulus. Ontwerp van zijn theologie* (Kok: Kampen, 1966) 469 (English translation by John R. de Witt, *Paul: An Outline of His Theology* [Grand Rapids: Eerdmans, 1975] 420).
111. Ibid., 416 n. 46.
112. T. A. Smail, "1 Corinthians 12, 13 Revisited," *Theological Renewal* 9 (June/July, 1978): 2–6.
113. J. Stott, *Baptism and Fullness,* and J. P. Baker, *Baptized in One Spirit. The Meaning of 1 Cor. 12:13* (London: Fountain Trust, 1967).
114. Smail, "1 Corinthians 12, 13," 2.
115. Ibid., 4.
116. Ibid., 5.

117. Dunn, *Baptism in the Holy Spirit,* 4.

118. A. Kuen, *Die charismatische Bewegung. Versuch einer Beurteilung* (Wuppertal: Brockhaus, 1976) 77–81.

119. D. J. Bennett, *Nine O'Clock in the Morning* (Plainfield, NJ: Logos, 1970).

120. D. Bennett and R. Bennett, *The Holy Spirit and You* (Plainfield, NJ: Logos, 1971).

121. Ibid., 20.

122. Ibid.

123. Ibid., 34.

124. Ibid.

125. Ibid., 64–65.

126. Ibid., 20.

127. S. Grossmann, *Stewards of God's Grace,* 50 (Original German edition, p. 55).

128. Ibid. See note 127.

129. Ibid., 52–53 (Original German edition, pp. 57, 58).

130. I have not yet been successful in procuring a copy of this tape for myself but the view is corroborated by other taped sermons supplied by the St. Paul's, Darien, CT Tape Ministry.

131. Bennett, *Nine O'Clock,* 136.

132. Ibid.

133. W. Nee, *Release of the Spirit* (Bromley, Kent: Send the Light, 1965). See also J. R. Williams' reference to the terminology in *The Pentecostal Reality* (Plainfield, NJ: Logos, 1972) 68.

134. D. Bennett and R. Bennett, *Trinity of Man* (Plainfield, NJ: Logos, 1979).

135. Lindberg, *Third Reformation?* 223.

136. L. Christenson, *Speaking in Tongues,* 37.

137. Ibid.

138. Ibid., 40.

139. Ibid., 48.

140. Ibid., 47.

141. Ibid., 53.

142. Ibid., 54.

143. Ibid.

144. T. Engelsviken, "The Gift of the Spirit: An Analysis and Evaluation of the Charismatic Movement from a Lutheran Theological Perspective" (Part 1 and 2) (Ph.D. diss., Aquinas Institute of Theology, Dubuque, IA, 1981) (University Microfilms International, Ann Arbor, 1982) 206.

145. Ibid., 216.

146. Ibid., 217.

147. Ibid., 219.

148. Ibid., 233.

149. Ibid., 226.

150. Ibid., 235.

151. H. J. Frøen, "What is the Baptism in the Holy Spirit?" in *Jesus, Where Are You Taking Us? Messages from the First International Lutheran Conference on the Holy Spirit,* ed. N. L. Wogen (Carol Stream, IL: Creation House, 1973) 117.

152. Ibid., 123.

153. *The Life in the Spirit Seminars Team Manual,* Catholic Edition (Ann Arbor: Servant, 1978) 2.

154. Ibid., 10.

155. Ibid., 3.

156. Ibid., 138.

157. Ibid., 149.

158. Ibid., 143.

159. Ibid.

160. Ibid., 147.

161. Ibid., 158.

162. *The Life in the Spirit Seminars Team Manual,* Rev. Edition (Ann Arbor: Servant, 1979) 65.

163. J. M. Ford, *Which Way for Catholic Pentecostals?* (New York: Harper and Row, 1976) 102–34.

164. Ibid., 102–9.

165. Culpepper, *Evaluating the Charismatic Movement,* 177 n. 13. In the 1976 edition of Clark's book, which I will be using, the quotation mentioned by Culpepper is on p. 79.

166. S. Clark, *Baptized in the Spirit and Spiritual Gifts* (Ann Arbor: Servant, 1976) 65.

167. Ibid., 117.

168. Ibid., 72.

169. Montague, *The Holy Spirit,* 342–43.

170. Clark, *Baptized in the Spirit,* 79.

171. Ibid., 93.

172. Ibid., 96.

173. Ibid., 97.

174. Ibid., 97–98.

175. Ibid., 98.

176. Ibid., 40–49.

177. Ibid., 87–96.

178. Williams, *Pentecostal Reality,* 27 n. 7.

179. S. B. Clark, *Confirmation and the Baptism of the Holy Spirit* (Pecos, NM: Dove, 1969) 11.

180. Ibid., 16.

181. Unfortunately direct quotations from this paper may not yet be given until the material is published elsewhere.

182. P. Hocken, "The Significance and Potential of Pentecostalism," in *New Heaven? New Earth?* ed. S. Tugwell, P. Hocken, G. Every, and J. O. Mills (Springfield, IL: Templegate, 1976) 48.

183. Ibid., 37. Hollenweger originally made the statement in *New Wine in Old Wineskins,* 48.

184. Ibid., 32.

185. Ibid., 44.

186. "Pentecostals on Paper I: Character and History," *The Clergy Review* 59 (11, 1974): 750–67; "Pentecostals on Paper II: Baptism in the Spirit and Speaking in Tongues," *The Clergy Review* 60 (3, 1975): 161–83; "Pentecostals on Paper III: The Gifts of the Spirit and Distinctive Catholic Features," *The Clergy Review* 60 (6, 1975): 344–68; "Catholic Pentecostalism: Some Key Questions, I and II," *HeyJ* 15 (2, 1974): 131–43 and (3, 1974): 271–84; "The Charismatic Experience," *The Way* 18 (1978): 44–55; and "Charismatic Renewal, the Churches and Unity," *One in Christ* 15 (1979): 310–21.

187. Hocken, "Catholic Pentecostalism I," 134–38.

188. Ibid., 137.

189. Ibid., 135.

190. Ibid., 140.

191. Ibid., 142.

192. Hocken, "Baptism in the Spirit," 165.

193. The Statement is reproduced in T. Flynn, *The Charismatic Renewal and the Irish Experience* (London: Hodder and Stoughton, 1974) 141–55; the quotation given is from 150–51.

194. Hocken, "Baptism in the Spirit," 166.

195. Ibid.

196. Hocken, "Charismatic Renewal," 314.

197. Ibid.

198. K. McDonnell, "The Relationship of the Charismatic Renewal to the Established Denominations," *Dialog* 13 (3, 1974): 228.

199. K. McDonnell, "The Baptism in the Holy Spirit as an Ecumenical Problem," in *The Baptism in the Holy Spirit as an Ecumenical Problem*, ed. K. McDonnell and A. Bittlinger (Notre Dame: Charismatic Renewal Services, 1972) 31.

200. Hocken, "Catholic Pentecostalism I," 143.

201. Examples would be: R. Stronstad, *The Charismatic Theology of St. Luke* (Peabody, MA: Hendrickson, 1984); H. M. Ervin, *Conversion-Initiation and the Baptism in the Holy Spirit: A Critique of James D. G. Dunn, Baptism in the Holy Spirit* (Peabody, MA: Hendrickson, 1984); R. Kydd, *Charismatic Gifts in the Early Church* (Peabody, MA: Hendrickson, 1984); P.A. Pomerville, *The Third Force in Missions* (Peabody, MA: Hendrickson, 1985); S.S. Schatzmann, *A Pauline Theology of Charismata* (Peabody, MA: Hendrickson, 1987); J.L. Gresham, *Charles G. Finney's Doctrine of the Baptism of the Spirit* (Peabody, MA: Hendrickson, 1987). In the same context one could mention the following dissertation: Hunter, *Spirit-Baptism;* and the *Journal of the Society for Pentecostal Studies, Pneuma.*

202. Williams, *Gift of the Holy Spirit.*

203. Ibid., 37.

204. Ibid. See n. 21.

205. Ibid., 152.

206. Book review in *Renewal News for Presbyterian and Reformed Churches* 64 (Jan./Feb., 1981): 14.

207. Williams, *Gift of the Holy Spirit,* 153–54.

208. Ibid., 553.

209. J. R. Williams, *The Era of the Spirit* (Plainfield, NJ: Logos, 1971).

210. Ibid., 51.

211. Ibid., 52.

212. See Williams, *The Pentecostal Reality,* 19–21.

213. Williams, *Era of the Spirit,* 55.

214. Williams, *The Pentecostal Reality,* 11–27 and 57–84.

215. Ibid., 12.

216. Ibid., 13.

217. Ibid., 18.

218. Ibid., 17

219. Ibid., 24 n. 6.

220. Ibid.

221. Ibid., 61–62.

222. Ibid., 65–68.

223. Ibid., 75.

224. J. R. Williams, "Pentecostal Theology: A Neo-Pentecostal Viewpoint," in *Perspectives on the New Pentecostalism,* ed. R. P. Spittler (Grand Rapids: Baker, 1976) 76–85.

225. Ibid., 81–82.

226. Ibid., 80–82.

227. Ibid., 82–84.

228. Quoted from J. R. Williams, "An Open Letter to the Editor," Newsletters of the Charismatic Communion of Presbyterian Ministers, in L. Christenson, *A Message to the Charismatic Movement* (Minneapolis: Bethany, 1972) 61–62.

229. J. A. Schep, *Geestesdoop en Tongentaal* (Franeker: T. Wever, n.d.) 117. The English translation, *Baptism in the Spirit According to Scripture* (Plainfield, NJ: Logos, 1972), gives the date of the first edition as 1969.

230. Ibid., 54. Schep gives the reference to Goodwin only as p. 248 of his "very elaborate commentary (in the form of sermons) on the first two chapters of this epistle."

231. Ibid., 52.

232. Ibid., 54.

233. Ervin, *These Are Not Drunken*.

234. Ibid., 57.

235. Ibid., 105.

236. Ibid., 106.

237. Ibid., 88–104.

238. H. M. Ervin, *Conversion-Initiation*, v.

239. Unfortunately I was only able to procure a copy of Ervin's book as this manuscript was undergoing its final revision. Moreover, a revision of *These Are Not Drunken*, retitled *Spirit Baptism: A Biblical Investigation* has been published (Peabody, MA: Hendrickson, 1987).

SACRAMENTAL INTERPRETATIONS
OF SPIRIT-BAPTISM

═ **3** ═══════════════════════════════

3.1 Introduction

As the impact of the charismatic renewal on the established churches became more pronounced, a need emerged to interpret the "Pentecostal experience" within the theological framework of other ecclesiastical traditions. From the beginning of the charismatic movement it was apparent that the liturgical or sacramental High Church traditions were more open to the renewal than the more conservative evangelical denominations. One of the reasons for this is that the latter groups were more concerned with doctrinal orthodoxy than the more "liberal" mainline Protestant churches. Another factor was the influence of dispensationalism. Although the renewal started in the Episcopal, Lutheran, and Presbyterian churches it really was the Roman Catholic Church that pioneered the process of in-depth theological interpretation of Pentecostal and neo-Pentecostal categories.

Very soon it became apparent that different models of interpretation were developing in charismatic circles. One of the earliest indications of theological distinctions is given by J-P Dietlé. Alfred Kuen gives the following quotation from Dietlé describing two groups of charismatics:

> The first group takes over the Pentecostal theology of the "Baptism in the Holy Spirit" and its "sign," speaking in tongues, with hardly any changes. (They are the charismatic movements in the Protestant churches in the U.S.A. and in the French Protestant Churches.) The second group purposefully distinguishes itself from Pentecostalism in its quest for its own identity. (This includes the Catholic charismatic movement and the charismatic movement in the Protestant churches in Germany.)[1]

It is clear that the first group is that section of the charismatic movement which is designated neo-Pentecostal in this study. The second group includes

104

the Catholics and German Protestants. As we continue it will become necessary to introduce further distinctions—both within Catholicism and between the sacramental Catholic position and the one shared by Catholics and Protestants in Germany.

The Catholic theologian of St. John's Abbey and University, Kilian McDonnell, played the major role in evolving a sacramental interpretation of Spirit-baptism and in sounding the call to the various Protestant denominations that a similar task lies ahead of them. He presented this to Reformed charismatics, and in an article he even quoted from some Lutheran theologians giving a brief outline of how a Lutheran charismatic theology might possibly be developed.[2]

McDonnell argued persuasively that a "theological ecclesial culture" is essential to the life of the church and to theology. Under this term he refers to a shared heritage of belief, confessional statements, liturgy, forms of piety, systems of church polity, etc. Such a theological culture cannot be dispensed with in order to achieve ecumenical goals. McDonnell states:

> It is not possible for a group of like-minded believers to live in community over an extended period of time without developing this kind of theological culture. It is imposed by necessities which are inherent in the manner in which men gather together over a long period of time for a common purpose.[3]

In terms of this description the ecumenical ideal is not forming one "culture," but "the coming together of a plurality of theological cultures in one faith allegiance, under one Lordship. . . ."[4]

Within this framework the specific task of "charismatic" theologians is to work within their theological ecclesial cultures to integrate the charismatic dimension (or Pentecostal reality if that term is preferred) into a Lutheran, Reformed, Catholic, etc., culture. The most serious problem of the early charismatic movement was, in effect, the uncritical absorption into their different ecclesial cultures not only the foundational charismatic experience with Spirit-baptism and charisms but also the revivalist and holiness tradition in much of Pentecostalism. Moreover, many in the early stages absorbed their approach to morals and societal issues and their fundamentalist usage of Scripture. In warning against this in the early seventies McDonnell was way ahead of his time. Seemingly this challenge is only now really being grappled with by the leadership in the charismatic community, fifteen years later. Various options are also possible within one theological ecclesial culture.

The Catholic contribution to charismatic theology has been substantial. Russell Spittler of Fuller, himself from a classical Pentecostal background, writes:

> Roman Catholics, although the latest of the charismatics (they're 15 years old now), have produced a more substantial theological literature in a half-generation than have their Pentecostal forbears over the past three generations.[5]

The original Catholic interpretation of Spirit-baptism is that it is a "release" of the Spirit—a revitalization or flowering of the sacramental grace received in Christian initiation, breaking through into the personal conscious experience of the believer. Later voices within the same Catholic tradition asserted that there are also other ways to interpret Spirit-baptism within a Catholic framework. The sacramental interpretation, however, comes close to being the official Catholic position and has also received support from Lutheran, Anglican, and Presbyterian circles.

Several of the leading exponents of the sacramental position will be discussed below. An analysis of this nature has, to the best of my knowledge, not yet been attempted. This study wishes to be a contribution towards the task of categorizing the variety of views found on Spirit-baptism within the charismatic movement. Although the treatment is not exhaustive, I have attempted to represent all the major theological figures, especially where we find differing emphases. In the process of selection an important factor was that the respective charismatic church leader or theologian had published specifically on Spirit-baptism, although this publication need not necessarily be a monograph.

3.2 The Malines Document I

The development of this view is closely connected with two people – the above-mentioned theologian, Kilian McDonnell, and Léon Joseph Cardinal Suenens, who was archbishop of Malines-Brussels and primate of the Catholic Church in Belgium. Cardinal Suenens was also moderator of the Second Vatican Council and played a major role in the affirming reception which the charismatic renewal has received in the Roman Catholic Church. In a series of official documents called the Malines Documents, guidelines are provided for the international Catholic charismatic renewal. Two works develop the sacramental interpretation of Spirit-baptism: *Theological and Pastoral Orientations on the Catholic Charismatic Renewal*,[6] and Cardinal Suenens's *Une Nouvelle Pentecôte?* [7]

In the theological activity of charismatic Catholics the role of the Second Vatican Council is more important than is generally realized. Apart from the successful attempt by Cardinal Suenens, who featured prominently at the Council, to get the assembly to reject the dispensational view of differentiating between the extraordinary and temporary charisms of the Spirit and the more ordinary, permanent ones, Vatican II also influenced the mood of the whole Catholic Church.[8]

In a new ecumenical climate of openness and tolerance it was possible for the Catholic charismatic movement to find sympathy from prominent theologians such as Karl Rahner, Gregory Baum, Heribert Mühlen and others who will be discussed in this chapter. Support was also received from the Vatican, but especially from bishops such as McKinney and Vath; Cardinal Suenens played the most crucial role.

The semi-official and international character of Malines Document I is due in part to the comprehensive manner in which it was initiated and compiled. Cardinal Suenens was instrumental in bringing together an international team of Catholic theologians and lay leaders in Malines during May 1974. Theological consultants not involved in the renewal also contributed to the final document, which was written by Kilian McDonnell. In his introductory words to the text of the document in *Presence, Power, Praise. Documents on the Charismatic Renewal. Vol. III, International Documents* McDonnell summarizes the theological aspects of Malines I as follows:

> Although there was an attempt to place the renewal in a trinitarian and ecclesial context, the center of attention was on the meaning of baptism in the Spirit, the role of experience in a life of faith, and the function of the charisms in the community. Baptism in the Spirit was seen to be related to the celebration of initiation (baptism, confirmation, Eucharist) in that it brings to conscious awareness the graces received during that introduction to the Christian life. In treating of the charisms they were explained in such a way as to open the church to the full spectrum of the gifts, not just from A–P, but also from P–Z. While it was recognized that the Spirit is sovereign and free and is in no way bound by the subjective dispositions of individuals or communities, there was a parallel recognition that awareness, expectancy, and openness to the full spectrum of the gifts can affect the life and experience of individuals and groups.[9]

The Malines Document I points out that terminology from classical Pentecostalism and Protestant neo-Pentecostalism have meanings within their "theological cultures." Catholics have a different "theological culture":

> These differences are extremely important for our discussion. For instance, many classical Pentecostals and Protestant neo-Pentecostals [as well as some Catholic neo-Pentecostals!] have a two-level doctrine of sanctification. This doctrine speaks of a conversion experience and the experience of the "baptism in the Holy Spirit.". . .These precise distinctions are, however, generally foreign to the Catholic culture. Receiving the fullness of the Spirit does not belong to a later stage of Christian life, but theologically belongs to its beginnings.[10]

Malines Document I warns that by taking over terms current in the renewal outside the Catholic Church, it is possible that foreign theological content may also be imported. From the above quotation it is already patently clear that the sacramental position distinguished itself from the two-stage interpretation of neo-Pentecostalism. Part of the concern with the neo-Pentecostal view is the "event-centeredness" of their view of the Christian life. The Malines Document acknowledges the legitimacy of both the peak or crisis experience and the gradual unfolding of a growth pattern. Both ways are authentic and can also be experiential.[11] The point seems to be that the gradual growth pattern is not acceptable in many non-Catholic approaches to the experience of the Holy Spirit.

The most important section of the Malines Document I for the purposes of this present study is the paragraph entitled: The Meaning of "Baptism in the Holy Spirit" among Catholics.[12] Here McDonnell evolves his "solution" to the problem of the apparent incompatibility of Spirit-baptism with sacramental theology. He makes a distinction between the theological and experiential senses of Spirit-baptism. In the theological sense every member of the

107

church is Spirit-baptized having received the sacrament(s) of Christian initiation. The experiential sense refers to the conscious experience of the grace received at infant baptism. This grace has, as it were, lain dormant, and at a particular moment in time or over a longer period it breaks through into the awareness of the individual. It is this conscious experience which is generally called "the baptism in the Holy Spirit" in charismatic circles.

I would here like to question the wisdom of introducing a chronological distinction between the theological and the experiential dimensions of Spirit-baptism. It seems to be the case in millions of Christian's lives that twenty, thirty or more years go by between the sacrament of infant baptism and the "experiential dimension" associated with it. Surely there is an experiential aspect to infant baptism even if the child does not have conscious memory of the event. In like manner there must be a theological dimension (not only an experiential one) to the experience of renewal and this is apparent from the way in which the Malines Document describes this experience:

> When the Spirit given at initiation emerges into consciousness, there is frequently a perception of concrete presence. This sense of concrete, factual presence is the perception of the nearness of Jesus as Lord, the realization at the personal level that Jesus is real and is a person. . .with great frequency this sense of presence is accompanied with an awareness of power, more specifically, the power of the Holy Spirit. . . .This power is experienced in direct relation to mission. . . .Another characteristic response to presence and power is an intensification of the whole prayer life, with a special love for the prayer of praise. For many this is a new event in their spiritual life. The experience has a resurrection quality about it that is joyous and triumphant. . . .The experience of the Spirit is also the experience of the cross. It expresses itself in a continuing metanoia and in the acceptance of redemptive suffering.[13]

The above description of the renewal experience not only interprets it theologically but also clarifies the title that Kilian McDonnell chose to typify the documents on the charismatic renewal, namely *Presence, Power, Praise.*

Catholic renewal leaders who espouse a neo-Pentecostal position generally wish to retain the phrase "baptism in the Holy Spirit," but those who see the need for a reinterpretation of the renewal experience are aware that to Catholic ears this terminology may cause some confusion with respect to the sacrament of baptism. This has led to the search for a better term. There are a variety of suggestions, but none is without an objection or two. In France the expression "l'effusion de l'Esprit" is generally used while in German Catholic circles "Firmerneuerung" is popular—the renewal of the sacrament of confirmation.

In English-speaking countries "baptism in the Holy Spirit" still seems to dominate because no acceptable alternative has been offered. Actually the formulations "the release of the Spirit" or "renewal of the sacraments of initiation" are really more accurate as a description of this perspective. The Malines Document cautions:

> Whatever the terminological decisions of each country it is important that all be saying the same thing, namely that the power of the Holy Spirit, given in Christian

initiation but hitherto unexperienced, becomes a matter of personal conscious experience.[14]

Where another term is not chosen the solution is often to define its meaning with care. Balthasar Fischer seems to express the authentic Roman Catholic view in his short article: "The Meaning of the Expression 'Baptism of the Spirit' in the Light of Catholic Baptismal Liturgy and Spirituality."[15] (The fact that he speaks of "baptism of the Spirit" instead of the more usual and acceptable "with or in the Spirit" raises the question of Fischer's familiarity with charismatic theology. The expression "baptism of the Spirit" was current at the time of and in the context of the Holiness movements and early Pentecostalism.)

Fischer maintains that baptism with water is the only "true and irrevocable baptism of the Spirit."[16] Consequently any further experience of the Spirit can only be a "becoming aware" or "deepening" of a presence already active. The use of the term "baptism of the Spirit" can lead to an undervaluing of baptism, the mistaken idea of a new sacrament and the false conviction that every Christian needs a conscious experience or "precise happening." Nevertheless if used in the sense of "realizing" or "fulfilling" the gift of the Spirit conferred by baptism and confirmation, Spirit-baptism is found to be acceptable.[17]

Obviously in the Malines Document Spirit-baptism is thoroughly integrated into a sacramental framework; a decisive break with the two-stage heritage of Pentecostalism has been effected. In order to discard the "cultural baggage" of Pentecostalism, Catholic reflection on the experience of Spirit-baptism has evolved a new theological theory which is acceptable in mainstream Catholic thinking. Since Catholicism sees the grace of God as being dispensed mainly through the sacraments, it follows that the renewal experience should be linked to the sacraments of Christian initiation.

The major disadvantage of this interpretation is that the renewal experience cannot be seen as something new or something that God is doing in people's lives at the time at which they experience it. As a "release of the Spirit" it is not a coming or a receiving of the Spirit but simply the activation of what has been received at a previous sacramental rite. The change that takes place in a Christian's life is not interpreted as the result of any new or direct action of God. It is merely a change in the believer's subjective awareness. Inevitably associations such as delayed action timers or a "time-bomb" set to go off later are evoked. This standard Catholic approach has also been criticized from within Catholic charismatic circles. Francis Sullivan of the Gregorianum suggests an alternative to this view. Simon Tugwell expresses Sullivan's objection rather succinctly: "Francis Sullivan has argued well against such a view of the Spirit, that it treats him as a kind of commodity that can be stored away."[18]

Apart from the Malines Documents there are no other official or rather semi-official interpretations of the Catholic charismatic viewpoint. On the level of the Life in the Spirit Seminars, written largely by Steve Clark and discussed under the neo-Pentecostal position, there is Abbot David Parry's *This Promise Is for You*.[19] Although by no means as popular or widely disseminated as the Life in the Spirit Seminars, this book is written for a fifty-day retreat "in order to introduce ordinary Christians to the charismatic renewal movement and he (Parry) has attempted to do so by providing a scheme of fifty days of meditation, prayer and spiritual renewal."[20]

Parry admits the difficulty of an exact definition of Spirit-baptism on account of the great variety of its effects.[21] He nonetheless defines it as

> an experienced spiritual renewal, worked by the Holy Spirit within a person. In the case of Christians, it is an actualization, a bringing to blossom and to fruit of the divine life conferred originally at baptism, and carried forward by confirmation and the eucharist.[22]

He underscores that one should not so much seek after a spiritual summit experience. The "release of the Spirit" should not be an end in itself but rather a fresh start.[23]

This clearly is the sacramental position. In a rather unsatisfactory review article Simon Tugwell discusses Parry's book.[24] The major part of the review concentrates on one (certainly unfortunate) phrase of Parry's, namely "the release of the Spirit within us enables us to turn to God with an undivided heart."[25] The basic problem that the Dominican, Tugwell, seems to have with the book is that it is not "Pentecostal" enough! He decries Parry's attempt to reassure the reader that the charismatic movement is very much in line with traditional Catholic piety. Something which Kilian McDonnell, I suspect, would have commended.

Tugwell makes his point in this manner:

> . . . there is something rather disingenuous about the way in which some "charismatics" (like Abbot Parry) try both to reassure us that they are not in any way criticizing people who prefer not to be "charismatic" and at the same time to present their particular spirituality as if it were, in some way, a necessary consequence of basic Christian beliefs.[26]

Tugwell's point is well taken but he seems to exhibit a limited understanding of the complexity and difficulty of the task of balancing the authentic elements of continuity with one's heritage with the necessary perspectives of discontinuity brought about by any form of renewal. Parry has attempted to do this—not in a systematic treatise—but in a more devotionally oriented retreat handbook and his book should be evaluated within that context.

3.3 A Survey of the Views on the Sacramental Approach to Spirit-Baptism of Some Leading Catholic Charismatics

The sacramental view of Spirit-baptism as described in the Malines Document I (and, for that matter, also in *This Promise Is for You*) has received broad approval in the Roman Catholic Church and has influenced some Protestant renewal authors as well. Some of the views of Catholic representatives of this sacramental position will now be discussed. No attempt to be comprehensive will be made.

3.3.1 Cardinal Suenens

First place should be given to the "leading" Catholic charismatic–Léon Joseph Cardinal Suenens. In *A New Pentecost?* he grapples with the problem of analyzing Spirit-baptism. He is adamant that there is but one baptism–not a duality of baptisms, and for that reason he rejects classical Pentecostal theology and states that in order to avoid ambiguity it would be better not to speak of "baptism in the Spirit," but rather to look for another expression.[27] He also points out that the action of the Spirit necessarily eludes our categories. There is a newness to the charismatic experience apart from our having received the Spirit in sacramental baptism:

> The "newness" then is of a particular quantity: we are concerned here with a new coming of the Spirit already present, of an "outpouring" which does not come from outside, but springs up from within.[28]

That Cardinal Suenens is giving classic expression to the sacramental position on Spirit-baptism can be illustrated by the following longer quotation:

> Different expressions are being used to define this experience of baptism in the Spirit: the grace of actualizing gifts already received, a release of the Spirit, a manifestation of baptism, a coming to life of the gift of the Spirit received at confirmation, profound receptivity or docility to the Holy Spirit. By whatever name we call it, those who have had this experience speak of it as a very special grace, as a renewal of their spiritual life accompanied by a feeling of peace and joy of a kind hitherto unknown. They esteem this grace as a revitalizing of the sacramental graces they have already received, conferred at baptism, then at confirmation, as well as at the reception of the other sacraments. . . .This Renewal is experienced as a release of the latent potentials of the Spirit whose desire is to lead each one of us to the full realization of his own vocation, be this lay or religious. It is a new and more developed awareness of our true Christian identity which only faith can reveal to us; and which brings alive this faith, giving it a new reality and an awakened eagerness to spread the Gospel.[29]

3.3.2 Kilian McDonnell

The Benedictine theologian, Kilian McDonnell, who played such a prominent role in the formulation of the first Malines Document, also expresses the sacramental view in various articles which he has published. However, he does not wish to be seen as a "charismatic" himself–rather as a sympathetic observer. In the booklet that he wrote together with Arnold Bittlinger in 1972 we already find his recommendation that charismatic theologians should work out a theology of charismatic experience within the categories of their own denominational traditions as referred to above. For Catholics he mentions the option of relating Spirit-baptism to the mystical heritage of St. John of the Cross and Teresa of Avila. (To my knowledge this line has not yet been seriously developed except by Edward O'Connor, who has done some rudimentary "trail blazing").[30] McDonnell's main proposal is, however, to relate Spirit-baptism to the whole rite of Christian initiation:

> In sacramental terms I would say that baptism in the Holy Spirit belongs together with water baptism to the rite of initiation, the making of a Christian. Baptism in the Spirit as to its theological locus is the same as Christian initiation, though the full potentiality may be actualized only later.[31]

He points out that in the New Testament the whole initiation process is sometimes simply called baptism. To be baptized in water is to be baptized in the Holy Spirit. Spirit-baptism is also another name for initiation/conversion.

From patristic documents McDonnell illustrates how the elements of the water-bath and the imparting of the Spirit through the laying on of hands developed into two sacraments: baptism and confirmation. Essentially, however, they are one—forming a complete baptism. In time the specific charismatic dimensions of the initiation process ceased to manifest themselves, due, according to McDonnell, to the institutionalization of charisms, the formalization of religion, and the over-reaction of the church to Montanism.[32]

In his article "Holy Spirit and Christian Initiation" McDonnell again relates Spirit-baptism to becoming a believer:

> If these early Christians were asked to locate "the baptism in the Holy Spirit," they would point to the celebration of initiation (baptism, confirmation, Eucharist) by virtue of which the Spirit is imparted and received in his fullness. What the contemporary charismatic renewal calls "baptism in the Holy Spirit" belongs to the making of a Christian and does not belong to a later, more mature stage of the Christian life.[33]

The relating of Spirit-baptism to Christian initiation is an important aspect. Even though the experiential side of Spirit-baptism may follow decades after first receiving the sacraments of initiation, it is still considered part of the beginnings, the initiation. The Pentecostal doctrine of Spirit-baptism as the reaching of a "plateau," an elitist second-stage for "first-class" Christians here receives its strongest critique. The "event-centeredness" of Pentecostal and neo-Pentecostal interpretations is also questioned. The Christian life is not a glorious progression from one mountain-top experience to another. The believer needs to walk by faith in the valleys when he loses sight of God's face. Drawing on the rich spirituality of Catholic mysticism, McDonnell points out that Spirit-baptism and traditional gifts such as infused contemplation are not of the same order:

> These experiences [of Christian initiation, i.e. Spirit-baptism] belong to a different order of religious reality than the great gifts of infused contemplation, raptures and visions. Here [at Spirit-baptism] experience is spelled with a small "e."[34]

Within the framework of the sacramental position Spirit-baptism receives a thorough relativizing which would have been unthinkable in a neo-Pentecostal context. McDonnell emphasizes that it is not the experience itself but the ongoing relationship that is important:

> There are warnings that the baptism in the Holy Spirit is not an end in itself, an isolated experience. What is important is not whether or not one has had "it" but whether one is "living and walking in the Spirit." The on-going relationship is what is important, not an isolated experience. Rather than seeing the baptism in the Holy Spirit as the moment when one gets something, the tendency now is to see it as a manner of entering into a new relationship with the Holy Spirit so that one can hear the Gospel with a new sensitivity and orient one's life more clearly toward Christ.[35]

With this idea of Spirit-baptism as a possibility to develop a new relationship with the Holy Spirit (in fact with Father, Son, and Spirit) we find McDonnell is not only expanding the concept of Spirit-baptism somewhat but is also relating it to the ongoing development of the Christian life.

3.3.3 Salvador Carrillo

At the First International Catholic Charismatic Leaders conference, held in Rome in 1973, Father Salvador Carrillo Alday M.Sp.S. read a paper on Spirit-baptism. Carrillo studied at the École Biblique in Jerusalem and received a doctorate in Sacred Scripture from the Vatican's Pontifical Biblical Commission, later teaching New Testament in Mexico City. His status as biblical scholar may have contributed to his perspectives having become so influential in the Catholic renewal. Differing from several other Catholic theologians, he considers the expression "baptism in the Holy Spirit" worthy of being retained.[36] It is, however, the content that he gives to this concept that is important.

Carrillo sees Spirit-baptism as a prayer by a Christian community to Jesus to pour out his Spirit "in a new way and in greater abundance" upon the person seeking Spirit-baptism.[37] He defines the experience as

> neither the sacrament of baptism nor that of confirmation, [it] . . . is another effusion of the Holy Spirit that activates the rich potential of grace that God has given everyone, according to his own vocation and according to the personal charism of his own state of life (cf. 1 Cor 7:7).[38]

In his paper we find sacramental expressions such as the reviving of the graces of baptism and confirmation, the vitalizing of graces, a new giving of the Spirit to set the potential of grace received in motion.[39] To the question, Is Spirit-baptism for all? Carrillo answers circumspectly.

> The baptism in the Holy Spirit in its profound truth, though not necessarily in its outward forms nor in its sensible manifestations, can be an invitation to all, since it is nothing else but another effusion of the Holy Spirit, which deeply renews the inner self of the Christian and sets in motion and enriches all its wealth of graces.[40]

It should be noted that Carrillo does not really emphasize the link of

Spirit-baptism and the sacraments in the sense of a "release" of the Spirit given in the sacraments of initiation. He focuses more on the aspect of a new effusion of the Spirit. It may be that his position is quite close to that of Francis Sullivan of the Gregorian University, who later developed an alternative Catholic interpretation to the sacramental, "release of the Spirit" view. This position will be discussed later.

3.3.4 Edward O'Connor

Next we shall look at some other Catholic theologians who were not as directly connected with the Malines Document as Suenens and McDonnell. Father Edward O'Connor, CSC, was involved with the charismatic renewal at Notre Dame University from the very beginning. His book, *The Pentecostal Movement in the Catholic Church*,[41] was one of the first serious theological reflections on the renewal by a Roman Catholic theologian. In her analysis of Spirit-baptism Lucida Schmieder states that O'Connor's view is very close to that of the Malines Document.[42] O'Connor relates the renewal experience to traditional Catholic spirituality, comparing the role of the "inspirations" of the Spirit for personal guidance and infused contemplation with Spirit-baptism. He states:

> As I see it, there is nothing substantially new in what is called the baptism in the Spirit, but there is something new in the circumstances and mode of its occurrence. Substantially, it is an experience of the presence and action of the Holy Spirit. Such an experience is the normal flowering of the life of grace, a fulfillment of our status as sons of God; it is called for by the very nature of grace, the theological virtues, and the gifts of the Holy Spirit.[43]

O'Connor clarifies his position further by explaining that this does not imply that any religious experience can be identified with Spirit-baptism:

> It is a turning point in one's spiritual development; it is the beginning of, the entry into, a new regime of life in which one is led and strengthened and enlightened by the Holy Spirit much more effectively and manifestly than before.[44]

He also distinguishes between two main types of renewal experiences: the manifest and hidden forms. The first type experiences a definite, conscious sense of God's presence while the other type leads to a response such as: "Well, nothing happened to me!" The people "baptized" in this hidden form only begin to realize a change gradually.[45]

In O'Connor's discussion of Spirit-baptism we see the ease with which the broad tradition of Catholic spirituality can encompass and integrate the charismatic experience – it is seen as the blessing of the presence of the Holy Spirit, which can in some cases manifest itself only very gradually over a period of time. Although O'Connor sees this experience as a turning point which should lead to a new "regime" of life, this should not be interpreted as the second-stage of neo-Pentecostalism. As a Catholic theologian O'Connor will immediately concede that this grace of Spirit-baptism can be lost. Catholics believe that one can also lose the grace that flowers into eternal life, whereas the Reformed teaching accepts the doctrine of the perseverance of the saints. (Only the character which the sacraments of baptism, confirmation, and holy orders confer is seen by Catholics as being indelible.)

3.3.5 Josephine Massyngberde Ford

Like O'Connor, Notre Dame University's Josephine Massyngberde Ford was involved in the Catholic renewal in its earliest stages. Despite its title, her book *Baptism of the Spirit* offers no discussion of Spirit-baptism as such. That she follows the Catholic charismatic position can be deduced from the following quotation. She is here discussing the answers to a questionnaire sent out to Catholic charismatic prayer groups:

> Perhaps the most encouraging discovery was the response to the question requesting the recipient to state how he would explain the "baptism of the Spirit" to a non-Pentecostal. Not one paper confused this with the Sacrament of Baptism or mentioned tongues but most saw it as a release of the Spirit who was already given in the Sacraments of Baptism and Confirmation, a closer life with Jesus and the development of the fruits of the Spirit. There was no sign of elitism.[46]

She defines baptism or release in the Spirit as

> the essence of an experiential or experimental sense of the presence of God of such strength that one knows with the deepest sense of certainty that one not only believes in God but "knows" Him—in the Hebrew sense of the word, "know" as experience.[47]

In a footnote Ford says that her definition would be consonant with, but not identical to those given by O'Connor and Simon Tugwell. Under the heading release of the Spirit she describes several personal experiences of "release in the Spirit."[48]

3.3.6 Kevin and Dorothy Ranaghan

Kevin and Dorothy Ranaghan, also from South Bend, Indiana, where the University of Notre Dame is situated, played a leading role in the Catholic charismatic movement from the outset. They are still very much involved, with Kevin being one of the most prominent leaders in the network of charismatic communities grouped around the People of Praise community in South Bend. The Ranaghans' book, *Catholic Pentecostals* (1969), was translated into at least six languages and served as a very popular introduction to the Catholic renewal movement. A self-awareness of their Catholic heritage causes the Ranaghans to distinguish their position from that of classical Pentecostals. The title of their book, however, is still reminiscent of the early stage of the Catholic renewal when the words "Catholic Pentecostals" were used—later to be superseded by "charismatic Catholics."

The line taken on Spirit-baptism is expressly sacramental. In the revised edition, *Catholic Pentecostals Today*, the Ranaghans stress that

...the baptism in the Holy Spirit is essentially a part of our Christian initiation – the sacrament of baptism and its ongoing actualization in our celebration of the eucharist and living the Christian life.[49]

Spirit-baptism is compared to the renewal of baptismal vows – it is a renewal in faith of the desire to be everything that Christ wants us to be.[50] In this sense it is often an experience of reaffirmation rather than initiation. We find the typically Catholic concern that Spirit-baptism not be seen as a new sacrament. If a radical distinction is called for the Ranaghans wish to see Spirit-baptism as a prayer rather than a sacrament.[51] Although it is not developed in detail, they also are sensitive to a communal aspect in Spirit-baptism:

> Prayer for baptism in the Holy Spirit is, most simply, a prayer in expectant faith that an individual's or community's baptismal initiation be existentially renewed and actualized.[52]

3.3.7 René Laurentin

René Laurentin is a French Catholic theologian and journalist. His book, *Catholic Pentecostalism,* provides a valuable overview of the charismatic movement in the Catholic Church. Inevitably he also discusses Spirit-baptism. After dealing with the biblical material he outlines three different theological interpretations of the renewal experience. He also sounds a relevant note of caution:

> ...the attempt has been made to justify Catholic Pentecostalism by systematically contrasting it with classical Pentecostalism; in the process, the latter becomes a scapegoat on whose back all errors are laid.[53]

The sensitivity which this warning expresses is further illustrated by the three interpretations of Spirit-baptism. In Laurentin's analysis we find the first conscious indication that there could be a variety of possibilities for interpreting Spirit-baptism within the Catholic tradition.

The first position is that of Francis A. Sullivan of the Gregorian University in Rome. Sullivan's view is connected with Thomas Aquinas's theology of the divine missions. Sullivan sees Spirit-baptism as a new sending or outpouring of the Spirit which can be repeated in a person's lifetime. It involves a real innovation of the person's relationship with the indwelling Spirit.

Because this position will be more fully developed in the next chapter it will not be dealt with here. Laurentin faults this interpretation for not being sufficiently related to the theology of the sacraments. He sees "baptism in the Spirit" as implicitly sacramental.[54]

The other two interpretations are very explicitly sacramental. The second position relates Spirit-baptism to the scholastic distinction between *opus operatum* (the work done) and *opus operantis* (the action of the doer). Spirit-baptism is connected with the latter since it deals with the becoming effective of the sacrament of baptism. Laurentin warns against contrasting the two elements and laments the apparent ambiguities. The third position is related to the three moments or aspects found in every sacrament: *sacramentum* (the sacramental sign or external rite), the *res et sacramentum* (the effect which is also a sign and is independent of the recipient's disposition) and the *res* (the ultimate effect, namely the sharing in the divine life). Spirit-baptism is seen as belonging to the *res*. However, this too is ambiguous. Perhaps Laurentin's own view is best expressed when he leaves these distinctions behind and simply states:

> We may say, therefore, with greater accuracy, that the function and purpose of baptism in the Spirit is the effective accomplishment in a Christian's life of what baptism called for but to some extent did not accomplish.[55]

The bottom line is once more the flowering of baptismal grace or the release of the Spirit previously given in Christian initiation.

3.3.8 Donald Gelpi

A rather unique role among Catholic charismatic theologians is played by a Jesuit from San Francisco, Donald L. Gelpi. He does his theologizing on the renewal experience within the framework of contemporary science of religion and against the backdrop of modern American philosophy. The originality of his approach has caused Russ Spittler of Fuller Theological Seminary to herald Gelpi as the initiator of "published charismatic theology."[56] He states that with Gelpi's *Experiencing God* published charismatic theology was born—a judgment which I personally would seriously call into question since Gelpi's theology and/or philosophy seems to me to be singularly unsuited for the advancement of the mainstream of present-day charismatic theological endeavor: I refer particularly to his most recent publications: *Experiencing God. A Theology of Human Emergence* and *The Divine Mother. A Trinitarian Theology of the Holy Spirit*,[57] in which Gelpi employs such a wide range of philosophical approaches that he undercuts basic communication with most of those interested in a theology of the charismatic renewal.

In this context it is necessary to refer to his earlier works, *Pentecostalism. A Theological Viewpoint* and *Charism and Sacrament. A Theology of Christian Conversion*.[58] In *Pentecostalism* he does not define the term "charismatic experience" but relates it to a full docility to the grace given in baptism and confirmation. Once more it is clear that Gelpi also operates within the sacramental position on Spirit-baptism. He emphasizes that Spirit-baptism itself is not a sacrament. From a human standpoint it is essentially a prayer of petition and from God's standpoint the divine response to such a prayer.[59] He gives the following description:

> Spirit-baptism is in effect a prayer to the Father in the name of Jesus that the Spirit will come to a given individual who has decided to break with sin and seek the light of Christ and that the Spirit will transform him by leading him from whatever state of spiritual development he might be to full docility to the inspirations of the Spirit and to complete openness to whatever charismatic gifts the Spirit may wish to give him. Spirit-baptism presupposes, then, that the one who seeks it has indeed determined to break with sin and does indeed desire full docility to the Spirit.[60]

Gelpi sees Spirit-baptism as requiring different interpretations according to the level of initiation of the candidate. For those both validly baptized and confirmed it expresses the desire to break with sin and cooperate more fully with the sacramental grace of confirmation. For those baptized but not yet confirmed Spirit-baptism is a request for transformation at the present state of spiritual development and implicitly a prayer to be led eventually to full participation of sacramental life. To someone neither baptized nor confirmed the prayer for Spirit-baptism in effect is a prayer to be led to the fullness of Christian faith and the participation of the Christian church.[61]

One can question the accuracy of formulation in Gelpi's approach. Is Spirit-baptism the prayer itself or the reaction to the prayer? Is it the request for transformation or the transformation that follows the request? I ask this quite apart from the distinction between "the standpoint of God" and "the standpoint of man." Surely both these aspects (divine and human) can be found in the prayer as well as in the resulting change or experience – the prayer or request need not be solely human, since the Spirit could be guiding, prompting, and inspiring the prayer; the transformation effected is probably best seen as God's work in a person which can involve a whole series of divine initiatives and human responses. I suspect, however, that Gelpi would not disagree with this. Perhaps he wished to reserve his final formulation for a later publication.

In *Charism and Sacrament* Gelpi admits to previously deliberately avoiding the defining of Spirit-baptism since a host of technical considerations needed to be explained first. He writes:

> A charismatic experience is a faith experience whose evaluative form and concrete satisfactions are shaped by habitual and prayerful docility to the call of the Spirit of Jesus.[62]

This charismatic faith experience is initially effected by docility to the Spirit but is intensified and enhanced through the reception of one or more of the Pauline gifts. After a long discussion of baptism in water and the problems surrounding rebaptism, Gelpi attempts to clarify his position further. His main objection to the popular expression "the baptism in the Holy Spirit" is the article *the,* which implicitly ties Spirit-baptism to a single moment in human experience: "In point of fact, Spirit-baptism is a lifetime process."[63] This is why it cannot be equated with the reception of a single gift like glossolalia. There can be a decisive charismatic breakthrough as Jesus is considered to have received in his messianic anointing at the Jordan. For Gelpi this breakthrough consists, in the initial reception, of one or more of the charismata. The baptismal faith of the believer is intensified and personalized. Gelpi acknowledges the legitimacy of phrases such as "a baptism in the Holy Spirit," "a deeper plunging into the Spirit received in baptism," "an experience of Spirit-baptism," and "a fuller release of the gifts of the Spirit"– the latter with the proviso that one does not imagine that all of the gifts of the Spirit lie latent in each believer waiting to be triggered.[64]

By recognizing the legitimate role of a charismatic breakthrough experience as well as a lifelong process of Spirit-baptism, Gelpi has developed and enriched the sacramental interpretation of Spirit-baptism. I still find it necessary to classify Gelpi's view as sacramental since his concept of docility is basically a receptiveness to the sacramental grace of baptism and confirmation as mentioned above. It does, however, seem as if he does not underscore this as much in his later works as he did in *Pentecostalism*.

In his article "American Pentecostalism" Gelpi points out that the Catholic charismatic movement "is historically significant as the first popular revival of religion in the American mode in which the American Roman Catholic community has participated."[65] He is of the opinion that Protestant neo-Pentecostal piety has a tradition of individualism, subjectivism in worship, and what he calls an antinomian tendency towards church leaders (a disregard for authority). For this reason the Catholic charismatic needs to be fully integrated into the sacramental and hierarchical dimensions of the church. Gelpi outlines the parameters within which the Catholic renewal operates:

> The official Catholic stance towards the charismatic dimension of the faith experience is indicated in Lumen Gentium, 12. The Catholic position presupposes that in the Pentecostal era, conversion and the gifts of the Spirit are mediated to the individual by the presence of the sacramental community. And the sacramental system grounds the community's hierarchical structure.[66]

Here we see how the sacramental and hierarchical elements form the foundation and framework for the functioning of the charisms of the Spirit. Elsewhere Gelpi illustrated the obverse side of the coin: charismatic presuppositions are also necessary to both the sacramental and hierarchical aspects of Catholic thought and practice.[67] Gelpi supports his stance that the charismatic element is crucial by reference to the documents of Vatican II. The council teaches that the Spirit distributes his gifts and often inspires lay members as well. Gelpi states that legal and bureaucratic structures which stifle charismatic growth are usurping the role of the Holy Spirit.[68]

3.3.9 Simon Tugwell

The last Catholic theologian to be dealt with is the British Dominican, Simon Tugwell. Apart from his book *Did You Receive the Spirit?* he has written several articles in the area of charismatic theology.[69] Although Tugwell rejects outrightly the Pentecostal and neo-Pentecostal doctrine of Spirit-baptism, he accepts the reality of a variety of spiritual experiences. It is with some hesitation that I have grouped him in this sacramental model since he is not convinced that new terminology for the experience of Spirit-baptism such as "the release of the Spirit" is really appropriate. He is highly critical of the attempt by some Catholic theologians to reinterpret Spirit-baptism within their own traditional categories. Tugwell's position is really *sui generis* and will be referred to again later in the context of his debate with Sullivan.

119

Tugwell dismisses the Pentecostal arguments for a doctrine of subsequence. He sees Christian baptism as "the appointed locus, the appointed 'visibility,' of the reception of the Spirit."[70] He also rejects the Pentecostal devaluation of baptism as mere "water baptism." He suggests that the Holy Spirit is received in conversion and that this is evidenced sacramentally in baptism. The Pentecostal exegesis arguing for a "second stage" is found to be faulty. There is not "something more" subsequent to conversion and baptism which gives us the fullness of the Spirit in some special, absolute way:

> We should not aim at "Christianity plus"; that is the royal road to heresy, as St. Paul already has to warn some of his churches (the Colossians, for instance).[71]

Up to this stage Tugwell's view probably has the full approval of evangelical critics such as Bruner. His rejection of the doctrine of subsequence, however, opens up a discussion of spiritual experiences. He advocates a recognition of the diversity of experience. That is why new terminology is not in itself enough, although Tugwell does suggest two alternatives with an Eastern Orthodox background, namely "discovery of the Spirit" and "manifestation of baptism."[72] Tugwell maintains:

> So we cannot, for scriptural, theological and pastoral reasons, accept the Pentecostal doctrine of "baptism in the Spirit," and we should avoid the term. Nor should we simply substitute some other term; we must recognize that there is a diversity of experiences of the Spirit, and we should be more precise and subtle in our teaching.[73]

This implies at least two things: Firstly, we should acknowledge a variety of experiences of the Spirit and not generalize from one particular kind of experience. In this regard Tugwell refers to Wesley who pointed out that spiritual experience should never become a "shibboleth" by which we judge everybody else who has not had the same experience. Secondly Spirit-baptism is not the final "fullness" of the Spirit, but rather of an initiatory nature and still quite compatible with considerable spiritual immaturity. There is, in this sense, always more ahead! Here Tugwell quotes St. Bernard: there is no proof of the presence of the Spirit which is more certain than a desire for ever greater grace.[74] Put differently it is the reification of a particular kind of experience to which Tugwell objects.

With regard to the issue of "initial evidence" Tugwell is, *mirabile dictu,* much more appreciative of the Pentecostal position. He finds the physical sign of tongues much more satisfactory than subjective inward feelings as a form of evidence.[75] He comments:

> Now I am sure that there is very good reason indeed for insisting on some kind of evidence, and this is fully borne out by almost all traditions of spirituality in the church; on that, I am at one with the classic Pentecostals against most of the neo-Pentecostals.[76]

In another article Tugwell is even more explicit:

> By taking the theological weight off the central experience of Pentecostalism, what
> they call the "baptism in the Spirit," we can accept their spiritual practice with
> considerably less reserve. Neo-Pentecostals have tended to play down the Pentecostal
> insistence on tongues, while keeping to their doctrine of "baptism in the Spirit."
> It seems to me preferable *to keep their insistence on tongues,* but to take the theological
> weight off[77] (my [Emmanuel Sullivan] emphasis).

Tugwell's use of "neo-Pentecostal" is not in line with its meaning in this
study. He probably means what would here be called charismatic—in a general
sense—with less emphasis on the "neo-Pentecostals" and more on the other
charismatics who reinterpret Spirit-baptism in a non-Pentecostal sense. On the
point of tongues as "initial evidence" Tugwell comes very close to Peter
Hocken who was discussed under the neo-Pentecostal position.

The above quotation of Tugwell, which is presented in that exact form in a
paper, "Can the Pentecostal Movement Renew the Churches?" by Emmanuel
Sullivan, is, however, really quite misleading. The very next sentences read:

> As they (the Pentecostals) present it, tongues becomes the criterion of reception of
> the Spirit, a position clearly untenable in Catholic or Protestant circles. But if we
> see it as one way of giving body to our Christian desire to surrender ourselves
> completely to the power of Christ, then the problem disappears.[78]

It is very muddling to speak of keeping the Pentecostal insistence on
tongues and then to add that doesn't mean that tongues are the criterion for
the reception of the Spirit. What else has the Pentecostal insistence on tongues
ever meant? Perhaps this is symptomatic of an attempt to keep the best of both
worlds. Whether it was responsible for Sullivan to end his quote where he did
is also questionable. Furthermore, it is interesting to note that whereas Tugwell
to a high degree kept to his text from the articles first appearing in *New Blackfriars* when they were reproduced in *Did You Receive the Spirit?* this particular
section has been changed and rewritten in the book.

Tugwell apparently wishes to steer a course between the Pentecostal position on tongues and the charismatic attempt to relinquish initial evidence and
tone down the focus on glossolalia. I am not convinced that there is sufficient
space for such a new position. Possibly an answer can be found in the fact that
Tugwell reflects on glossolalia in a very novel way. He seems to appreciate the
bodiliness of it and sees parallels between the Pentecostal insistence on physical
evidence and the role played by the sacraments in Catholic theology. Tugwell
sees the human capacity for speech as something marvelous—the human
animal talks.[79] He states:

> There is good reason to think, both from scriptural evidence and from the witness
> of patristic tradition, that the Pentecostals are on to something in picking out
> inspired utterance as being in some way symptomatic of the whole working of the
> Holy Spirit in our lives, a typical fruit of the Incarnation.[80]

Tugwell seeks to uncover an area for fruitful ecumenical dialogue beneath
the surface (which we might not have expected to find) between Catholics and

Pentecostals. This aspect naturally requires further research. There certainly are points of similarity between Catholicism and Pentecostalism which cause one to question the general classification of Pentecostals as a branch of Protestantism.

O'Connor has pointed out that although they derive from Protestant backgrounds, Pentecostals are not typically Protestant in their beliefs, attitudes or practices.[81] Hollenweger agrees:

> Catholics have rightly seen that the Pentecostals are—in contrast to their self-interpretation—not a typically Protestant church.[82]

Perhaps more than anyone else, Tugwell is aware of this affinity between the deepest intentions of Catholic and Pentecostal theology. (It is also significant that evangelical Protestant critiques of the charismatic movement sometimes denounce it as a "Romeward" trend.) Tugwell expresses something of this "Catholic" element in Pentecostalism with respect to glossolalia:

> And in a very special way the Pentecostals believe in the sacramentality of speaking in tongues. I think it would not be too far wrong to suggest that for them speaking in tongues is a sacrament in the fullest Catholic sense of that word, in that it is a human act given to men to do, in which however, according to their belief, we may unequivocally and without reserve identify an act of God himself.[83]

One hopes that Tugwell will continue to explore along these lines and perhaps further develop his concept of the wide variety of spiritual experiences, especially since he calls us all to be more precise and subtle in this regard. His writings are seasoned by interesting references to patristic and medieval spirituality, such as the experience of "a baptism of tears" taught by Symeon the New Theologian and the so-called "second baptism" related to joining a religious order. In his article "Reflections on Baptism in the Holy Spirit," Tugwell closes with an interesting list of nine testimonies to experiences of spiritual breakthrough from the history of the church. He states that tradition is adamant about the need for spiritual experience and on the possibility of there being a decisive initial experience.[84]

The sincerity of Tugwell's ecumenical endeavor is superbly illustrated in these words:

> Rather than close on this somewhat negative note, let me say that I think "baptism in the Holy Spirit" is the wobbliest part of Pentecostalism. Their actual living experience of the Holy Spirit, and their analysis of the passions of the human soul striving towards purity of heart, are at times closely parallel to the best ascetic and spiritual traditions of the undivided Church. Their insistence on praise is extremely salutary. I think their teaching on tongues is far more important than some neo-Pentecostals seem to allow, both because of its relationship to prophecy, and because of its bodiliness. Their witness to the charisms in the life of the Church is very important. Although I think their doctrine of the "baptism in the Holy Spirit" is erroneous and even dangerous, I think Pentecostalism presents a challenge to the Church, which we ignore at our peril.[85]

It is already apparent that Tugwell presents a perspective which differs from the other representatives of the sacramental position. To some extent his perspective is shared by Peter Hocken who was seen in this study to be a rather innovative representative of neo-Pentecostalism. Hocken is discussed there because he accepts the basic viewpoint of subsequence (which Tugwell rejects). What Tugwell and Hocken have in common can, perhaps, best be explained by referring to a remark by Hollenweger, who is generally acknowledged to be an important authority on Pentecostalism. In his preface to *New Heaven? New Earth?* Hollenweger refers to the fact that in the conclusion of his definitive book *The Pentecostals* he presented this challenge:

> A genuine dialogue with the Pentecostal movement will lead the traditional churches not to imitate the Pentecostal movement, but to make a critical examination of their own tradition.[86]

Hollenweger later laments that this did not happen. Instead most Protestant and Catholic charismatics either imitated the Pentecostals (in terms of this study: developed a neo-Pentecostal position) or returned to affirm their denominational traditions. Hollenweger comments with reference to Anglican charismatics:

> . . .they said: Pentecostalism has made us better Anglicans. We believe and teach and celebrate everything traditional Anglicanism stands for. There is no need for a critical review of our theological position. Neo-Pentecostalism does not change any of our melodies, but it changes the rhythm and sometimes the key.[87]

I do not agree with this assessment. I think that Hollenweger is right in warning against imitation of Pentecostalism – numerous examples of this have been given. From Hollenweger's viewpoint, however, it may seem that those theologians who have reinterpreted Spirit-baptism in sacramental terms – as well as the other options still to be dealt with in this study – have merely returned uncritically to their denominational traditions. I do not find this to be an accurate assessment of the situation. However, the point that Hollenweger is making is that a few Catholic charismatics did take up the challenge he presented and are critically reviewing their own tradition. The four British Catholic theologians who wrote *New Heaven? New Earth?* (Hocken, Mills, Tugwell, and Every) are regarded by Hollenweger as belonging to the few who understand that charismatic theology is more than an additional "chapter on 'charismata' in an otherwise unchanged theological system."[88]

It may be that in his criticism of charismatics who glibly return to their traditions Hollenweger is not referring to the endeavors of theologians such as McDonnell, Gelpi, Ford, Laurentin, and O'Connor. Perhaps he merely means some individual priests who have uncritically "fled back" to their mother churches afraid of Pentecostal excesses. However a remark by Peter Hocken about this issue leads me to suspect otherwise. In his reflection on Spirit-baptism in *The Clergy Review* Hocken notices a concern by many Christians to relate their Pentecostal experience to the teachings of great spiritual writers of their own denomination. The experiences of such "spiritual giants" of the past are then included in a broader definition of being charismatic. Hocken states:

> This tendency to widen the concept of Baptism in the Spirit can end up by emasculating the impact of the Pentecostal "filling," a process most evident in the more apologetic writings.[89]

Hocken then proceeds to refer to McDonnell's "Statement of the Theological Basis of the Catholic Charismatic Renewal," which served as a basis for the first Malines Document.

Tugwell and Hocken, perhaps stimulated by Hollenweger, represent a perspective that is critical of the work being done by the major reinterpreters of Spirit-baptism along "traditional denominational lines." Perhaps this divergence is at present more one of mood than of content. Hocken and Tugwell view attempts to establish a Catholic charismatic identity as a threat to the earlier ecumenical nature of the charismatic renewal. They are more sensitive to acknowledging the work of classical Pentecostals. Peter Hocken alone of all the Catholic charismatic leaders in the U.S. has regularly and resolutely participated in the Society for Pentecostal Studies. A recent recognition of his unique role is that he became (for 1985) the first Roman Catholic president of this overwhelmingly classical Pentecostal body! When Hocken speaks of a double loyalty it is not, as I have pointed out previously, to Catholicism and the Catholic charismatic renewal (as one might expect) but to Catholicism "and the worldwide Pentecostal movement (which has its origins and it lengthiest experience in the Pentecostal Churches)."[90]

In closing this discussion I still need to justify my classification of Tugwell within the sacramental position. Despite his rather unique approach, he clearly rejects the neo-Pentecostal position of subsequence and any elitist mentality. He calls for a more nuanced treatment of spiritual experiences emphasizing the necessity of spiritual experience for the church. "What it is all about, surely, is the bringing to conscious effectiveness of the sacramental grace received in baptism."[91] This statement tipped the scales for me and legitimizes the grouping of Tugwell with those who describe Spirit-baptism as "a release of the Spirit" and "the flowering of baptismal grace."

3.4 A Survey of the Views on the Sacramental Approach to Spirit-Baptism of Some Leading Protestant and Eastern Orthodox Charismatics

3.4.1 Introduction

The sacramental position is also found in some Protestant charismatic circles, especially in the Lutheran tradition. Charismatics from Reformed, Baptist, and Methodist backgrounds (who have not remained neo-Pentecostal) have mainly chosen other options which will be discussed in the next chapter.

The Lutheran renewal movement, however, has led to several publications and a major study–the result of work by an international team of Lutheran theologians–appeared in 1987. Research on the Lutheran charismatic perspective has also been facilitated by a critical study in this area, *The Third Reformation? Charismatic Movements and the Lutheran Tradition* by Carter Lindberg.[92] His work is done from a typically confessional Lutheran standpoint rather than from a Lutheran charismatic perspective.

In the process of reinterpreting Pentecostal and neo-Pentecostal doctrines from a particular denominational perspective charismatic theologians are often led to the rediscovery of "charismatic" elements in their own heritage–especially in the most prominent figures or founders of that tradition. This should not be automatically dismissed as prejudiced research. It is a recurring theme in theology that contemporary perspectives play an indisputable role in our constant reinterpretation of historical figures.

Just as the history of New Testament research produced a liberal Jesus, a kerygmatic Christ, an eschatological Son of man, a revolutionary Jesus, etc., so we find that prominent theologians like Thomas Aquinas and John Calvin are also continually being "rediscovered" and consequently play a certain role as authoritative legitimators of "new" ideas. Bengt Hoffman produced a study on Luther in which he attempts to validate contemporary charismatic renewal by referring to the mystical and spiritual elements in Luther. He is not merely operating with a "vested interest" but contends that Western rationalism has obscured or eclipsed much of this mystical dimension of faith which played a crucial role in Luther's theology. At the conclusion of his study Hoffman writes:

> The charismatic renewal is in essence a recovery of the New Testament experience that the Holy Spirit bestows new forms of life on the Christian. In this sense it can also be termed mystical.[93]

Further on he develops this more specifically:

> "Baptism of the Holy Spirit" refers to no one single individual spiritual gift–which especially the glossolalists tend to overlook. "Baptism of the Holy Spirit" is experience of "the births" of Christ in the soul, as Luther expressed it. This view of the work of the Holy Spirit embraces the presence of Christ as dynamic force and loving support.

> The mystical dimension of faith is the essence of the charismatic renewal. Unbiblical and unspiritual aberrations in this "movement" provide no adequate reason for Christian believers not to take it seriously. Martin Luther's mystical-charismatic consciousness and his practice of the presence is a reminder of the Third Article of the Creed which many of us have intellectualized and institutionalized. Luther would no doubt have recognized and greeted with joy the current evidences of the power of the Holy Spirit, both in Protestant and Roman Catholic circles.[94]

As representatives of the sacramental position on Spirit-baptism from a Lutheran perspective, the views of Americans Larry Christenson and Theodore Jungkuntz will be discussed. Arnold Bittlinger of West Germany will be referred to, but discussed more fully later, since (together with Heribert Mühlen) he represents a further development of the sacramental view. Bittlinger is also not exclusively Lutheran–coming from a united (Lutheran and Reformed) background–and has served as a minister in the Swiss Reformed Church.

The process of formulating a specifically Lutheran interpretation of the charismatic renewal was, paradoxically, stimulated by Roman Catholics. Larry Christenson refers to a challenge presented to him by Steve Clark and Ralph Martin from the Word of God community,[95] while Kilian McDonnell sounded the following warning:

> A renewal which is presented to the Lutheran Churches worked out in categories of another culture, however admirable, can never be integrated into the life of the Lutheran culture. A Lutheran charismatic renewal which is essentially revivalist and classical Pentecostal in thought and style can exist only on the periphery of the Lutheran Churches. Such a renewal, whatever the validity of its insights and whatever the authenticity of its life, will never affect the total life of Lutheran Churches.[96]

McDonnell, whose perspective in this regard has been repeatedly referred to above, even attempted a rudimentary outline of how the charismatic renewal could be theologically integrated in a Lutheran context using suggestions by Tormod Engelsviken, a Norwegian Lutheran charismatic.[97] McDonnell's challenge seemed to have fallen on deaf ears. At the time he presented it (1974) the general atmosphere of the renewal was that of the joyous discovery of ecumenical contact, and a call to reemphasize denominational distinctives could make no headway. Proof of the prophetic nature of McDonnell's insight was the move consciously to start theologizing within a Lutheran framework some years later. In 1983 Lindberg wrote that this process only started within about the last five years.[98] It is also significant that the charismatic Lutheran theologians did not take the line of underscoring traditional Lutheran distinctives such as justification by faith alone or "Christ in us," but rather opted for the sacramental position along with Catholic and Anglican charismatics.

3.4.2 Larry Christenson (Lutheran)

Mention has already been made of Larry Christenson's neo-Pentecostal phase. By 1976 when his book, *The Charismatic Renewal among Lutherans,* was published, it was evident that a shift in his theologizing has started. A recent statement is found in the newsletter *International Lutheran Renewal.*[99] Lindberg is quite frank about comparing Christenson's 1968 book *Speaking in Tongues* with his 1976 book *The Charismatic Renewal among Lutherans.* He says "the earlier book appears to be much more influenced by Pentecostal theology."[100]

In *The Charismatic Renewal among Lutherans* Christenson consciously chooses to break with a theology of subsequence:

> The two-stage view of classical Pentecostalism (conversion and baptism with the Holy Spirit) was widely used as a theological model in the charismatic renewal

during the early 1960's. By the end of the decade, however, another view, more akin to the historic view, was emerging. This could be characterized as an "organic view" of the Spirit's work.

Among churches with more of a sacramental tradition (primarily Lutheran and Roman Catholic) charismatic experience has come to be seen as an outgrowth or actualization of the Spirit's work, which began when one was first grafted into Christ. This organic view is being used more and more widely as a theological model in the charismatic renewal.[101]

Christenson also seems to take over McDonnell's view in the first Malines Document that one can distinguish between the theological and experiential aspects of Spirit-baptism.[102] Nevertheless one is still left a little puzzled as to where Christenson really stands in *The Charismatic Renewal among Lutherans*. After explaining the organic view and rejecting the division of Christians into those who "only have salvation" and those who "have the Spirit," he goes on to say that the Wesleyan-Holiness-Pentecostal tradition remains a vital part of the charismatic renewal and a direct experience of personal renewal "continues to be a normal occurrence in the renewal."[103] Surely it is not the occurrence which is to be questioned but the interpretation of the occurrence, and here a clear choice is called for.

The ambiguity in Chrisenson's "second stage" theology (after moving from a neo-Pentecostal position) is further underscored by the fact that one cannot readily determine whether he is opting for the sacramental approach or what might be called a further development of the sacrament approach.

It (the organic view) understands the kind of experience which people are having in the charismatic renewal as a manifestation of Christian growth. Lutheran theologian William Lazareth described a charismatic's experience as "a particularly dramatic form of sanctification." It marks a progression in one's life as a Christian, not an event by which one becomes a Christian. Understood in this way it does not present us with any great theological innovation; it accords with categories of historic Christianity.[104]

This is a very significant statement since it opens perspectives for the full integration of Spirit-baptism into historic Christianity. One has the impression, however, that Christenson does not really develop his thoughts along these lines, and it may be more accurate to say that he is basically just reflecting Lazareth's view which was presented in an open forum at the National Leaders Conference for Lutheran Charismatic Renewal in Ann Arbor, Michigan, February 12, 1974.

Christenson's view is largely sacramental. Appealing to Martin Luther, he points out that the sacrament of baptism is the start of a lifelong "spiritual baptism."

Baptism, however, is not understood as a one-time bestowal of the Holy Spirit, but as an event which initiates an ongoing work of the Spirit. Luther calls this ongoing work of the Spirit a "Spiritual baptism" which continues throughout life.[105]

In his recent article "Baptism with the Holy Spirit" in *International Lutheran Renewal* (January 1985) Christenson basically repeats the view he expressed in *The Charismatic Renewal among Lutherans*. He points out that there is only one baptism and that Spirit-baptism is not separate from Christian baptism but is integrally united with it. He again uses typical sacramental terminology when he sees the charismatic experience as "a flowering or actualization of baptismal grace" and concurs with the statement:

> . . . the efficacy of baptism is not tied to the moment of time wherein it is administered. What is given in baptism may become active or realized at other moments in the life of the believer.

These are quotations from a Roman Catholic bishop and Arnold Bittlinger respectively.[106] The clearest sacramental expression in Christenson's own words seems to be:

> In this sense (i.e., experientially) baptism with the Holy Spirit is the Spirit being actualized, or coming to more conscious manifestation, in one's life.[107]

In her dissertation Lucida Schmieder deals briefly with Christenson's views.[108] Her assessment is that although he was touched by the typically Pentecostal teaching, he came to reject the "Stufenlehre" (two-stage view) and initial evidence.[109] She makes no reference to Christenson's earlier book *Speaking in Tongues,* which probably explains why she does not document any clear shift in his theological position with respect to Spirit-baptism.

3.4.3 Theodore Jungkuntz (Lutheran)

Next, attention will be given to the views of Theodore Jungkuntz from the generally more conservative Missouri-Synod Lutheran Church. Lindberg's assessment is that, unlike Christenson, Jungkuntz definitely sets out to relate charismatic experience to Lutheran theology.[110] Jungkuntz writes, "I have labored to articulate a Lutheran theology of charismatic renewal,"[111] and refers in this regard to his response to "The Lutheran Church and the Charismatic Movement: Guidelines for Congregations and Pastors—a Report of the Commission on Theology and Church Relations of the Lutheran Church—Missouri-Synod."[112]

In this response Jungkuntz explains the relationship between Spirit-baptism and the sacrament of baptism:

> Baptism in the Holy Spirit is understood not as an event "beyond" sacramental baptism in the sense of "separate from," but as an event "within" sacramental baptism and yet an event to be "distinguished" from its initial expression with water. Such a view in no way diminishes the significance of sacramental baptism, but merely speaks of the manner by which, according to God's promise, the benefits of sacramental baptism might be more fully released and manifested in the life of the believers.[113]

Once again we recognize the terminology akin to the sacramental interpretation: "more fully released and manifested." Jungkuntz also describes

Spirit-baptism. . .as the coming to awareness of one's subjectivity as a child of God, with the experiential knowledge that one can depend on the Father-son relationship sacramentally established through water-baptism.[114]

These two statements reflect an intensity of commitment to sacramental theology that even surpasses similar references in the writings of some Roman Catholic charismatics. The following quotation will remove any doubt about this. Jungkuntz writes in 1976:

Any experience designated "Baptism in the Spirit" which called into question the bestowal of the Holy Spirit through sacramental baptism, even when administered to an infant, could not be harmonized with Holy Scripture and the Lutheran Confessions and would be tantamount to selling one's birthright for a mess of pottage.[115]

Jungkuntz also develops a rather startling analogy to describe the relationship between the Word, baptism, and charismatic manifestations. He compares these three elements with engagement, marriage, and sexual intercourse. Charismatic gifts without baptism and commitment to the Word are like premarital intimacy. What interests us is the relationship between baptism and Spirit-baptism in this analogy. Jungkuntz explains:

Such a situation (engagement and marriage) invites intimacy and a confident giving a yielding of self in the loving consummation of the marriage expressed in sexual union, an experience sometimes leading to conception and comparable to the way in which faith-intimacy with Jesus (prayer) produces the experience of being filled with the Holy Spirit and the consequent conception of charismatic gifts.[116]

Lindberg wonders if this means that Christians without charismatic gifts are like marriage without sexual intercourse[117] Perhaps the analogy could rather lead to the question, Are those who have not yet experienced Spirit-baptism like unconsummated marriages, and those without "gifts" like barren marriages? Obviously the analogy has not helped understanding without simultaneously hindering it! To compare the charismatic element with something so central to marriage as intercourse and conception tends to militate against the other statement above about the mess of pottage, which completely rejects any Spirit-baptism outside a sacramental framework.

The most valuable contribution of Jungkuntz to charismatic theology is undoubtedly his study, *Confirmation and the Charismata*.[118] Because it only relates to Spirit-baptism indirectly, reference to it will have to be somewhat brief. Jungkuntz points out that in his sermons Luther deals with charismatic gifts as Pentecostal expressions still to be expected and experienced as "confirmation" of the gospel.[119]

Jungkuntz laments the fact that so few within the charismatic renewal have worked out a theology and practice of confirmation which would integrate their new insights with the traditional doctrine of confirmation.[120] He mentions some work by Roman Catholics (Steve Clark, Vandagriff, Tydings, Donald Gelpi, and Heribert Mühlen) but he views Lutheran and Episcopalian charismatics as having been slow to articulate such a "theology of 'confirmation' in terms of prayer for a baptism in the Holy Spirit with a consequent manifestation of charismata."[121]

Jungkuntz develops such a theology seeking a "holistic" concept of confirmation which encompasses three different types of confirmation corresponding roughly to the central concerns of liturgical renewal, pedagogical renewal, and charismatic renewal. The first of his concluding theses will explain this briefly:

> 1. The word "confirmation" may legitimately describe the following situations in the church:
>
> (a) God's "confirmation" of our new birth and identity through baptismal faith by a reaffirmation of his promises to us through his Word (and sacraments).
>
> (b) Our own "confirmation" of our new birth and identity through baptismal faith by (increasingly mature) reaffirmations of that faith.
>
> (c) God's "confirmation" of our new birth and identity through baptismal faith by his own fulfilling of his baptismally based promises to us in our experience (specifically, the manifestations of "charismata") as we respond to these promises in faithful obedience and prayer.[122]

Unfortunately Jungkuntz does not address the specific relationship between Spirit-baptism and the charismata in his theology of confirmation. It would seem, however, as if he holds to the general charismatic view that Spirit-baptism is the gateway to the charisms. Of Jungkuntz's charismatic theology one can surely maintain that it operates within a sacramental framework and also within the bounds of the Lutheran Confessions.

Not all Protestants wishing to reinterpret their theology of Spirit-baptism have come up with a conformity to the sacramental model. One Lutheran theologian from Norway, Tormod Engelsviken, for example will not be discussed here but in the next chapter.

3.4.4 Brick Bradford (Reformed)

From the Reformed world there are some charismatics who explain Spirit-baptism in terms of the release of the Spirit's power and in a loose sense can be classified as espousing the sacramental position. Brick Bradford, general secretary of the Presbyterian and Reformed Renewal Ministries International, has written a booklet entitled: *Releasing the Power of the Holy Spirit.*[123] In this he gives a guarded defense of the sacramental perspective; but as one would expect from someone from a Reformed background, the focus is not as predominantly sacramental as in Jungkuntz or some of the Catholic writers.

Bradford states his position quite simply:

> We of the Reformed perspective believe we were "baptized with the Holy Spirit" when we became Christians, but we find ourselves wanting to more fully experience the release of the power of the Holy Spirit in our lives in order to become more effectual Christians.[124]

130

He undeniably associates Spirit-baptism with being "born of the Spirit" or conversion, whereas the breaking forth of the charismatic element he would rather call an *appropriation* or *release* of the power of the Holy Spirit.[125] There is a sacramental element to Christian initiation, but Bradford is not prepared to say that the Holy Spirit *always* enters one's life at the moment of infant baptism. He acknowledges the sovereignty of God to come even before the person is born or years after baptism.

Bradford quotes from the study of the Theological Commission of the Reformed Church in America. This document was approved in 1975 and gives the general Reformed view:

> The Spirit-baptism should not be seen as a second work of the Holy Spirit which brings with it certain of the gifts.

> . . .in short "baptism in the Holy Spirit" is a metaphor describing the initial activity of the Holy Spirit among Christ's people, resulting in his continuing dynamic work in their midst. Every believer in Jesus Christ has been "baptized in the Holy Spirit." Every Christian is eligible for every work and gifts of the Spirit.[126]

Bradford advocates a "balanced view" of Spirit-baptism which brings both the presence and the power of the Spirit into one's life. He associates presence more with the traditional Reformed view and power with the Pentecostal teaching. In a technical sense Bradford's formulations are a little ambivalent since he identifies Spirit-baptism with becoming a Christian, while in expounding the "balanced view" he uses the expression "baptized with the Holy Spirit" to refer to both becoming a Christian and experiencing the release of the power of the Spirit in gifts and ministries. This probably is just a way of emphasizing the relatedness of the two and that moving in the charismatic dimension should be the natural consequence of Christian growth.

In a very real sense Bradford's view, which is not really extrapolated in any theological detail, forms a bridge to the next chapter, which deals with charismatic theologians who are neither sacramental nor neo-Pentecostal. Bradford stands in a mediating position. He still employs the typically sacramental language of "a release" but prefers to speak of a release of the Spirit's power rather than a release of the Spirit himself. It is difficult to determine if this is a conscious significant shift. To my mind there is no substantial difference here. Bradford also states:

> An increasing number of those in the Reformed tradition believe that water baptism and the baptism with the Holy Spirit occur simultaneously.[127]

However, he does not commit himself personally with regard to this view.

On the other hand, Bradford couples Spirit-baptism rather closely with conversion or becoming a Christian; this is not typical of the sacramental position. The sacramental interpretation could accommodate becoming a Christian or "being born of the Spirit," as Bradford phrases it, very easily with the doctrine of baptismal regeneration. Nevertheless, Bradford does not accept baptismal regeneration. Were he to publish further it could well be necessary to reclassify Bradford's position.

3.4.5 Eusebius Stephanou and Athanasios Emmert (Greek Orthodox)

Something needs to be said about the Eastern Orthodox perspective on Spirit-baptism. The Eastern Orthodox churches, the Roman Catholic Church, and Protestantism make up the three main divisions of Christianity. The charismatic movement first started in the American branch of the Greek Orthodox Church in 1971. The interest of this study is, however, not to describe the historical development of the charismatic movement in this or any other branch of Christianity. Consequently brief attention will now be given to the views of the Archimandrite, Father Eusebius A. Stephanou, a prominent leader in Orthodox renewal and editor of the journal *The Logos,* which explicitly sees itself as "Serving the Charismatic Renewal in the Orthodox Church." Then another leader in the same context, Athanasios Emmert, will be examined. It will also be necessary to reflect some of the criticism against the Orthodox renewal movement.

Stephanou underscores the charismatic nature of the Greek Church fathers and writes extensively on the charisms of the Spirit as reflected in their writings. Stephanou urges those charismatic Christians seeking a theology for Spirit-baptism to return to the Fathers.[128]

Of St. Symeon, the "New Theologian" (AD 949–1022) Stephanou states:

> The baptism of the Holy Spirit is a basic presupposition running throughout his works. It is surprising how timely his message is for our own day of Pentecostal resurgence. The misunderstanding he endured is reminiscent of the experience of many modern-day charismatics.[129]

Note the inaccurate reference to baptism *of* the Spirit, which is unusual among contemporary Protestant charismatics. Even more startling is a quotation from St. Symeon's *Catechesis:*

> He that lacks awareness of his baptism and was baptized in infancy, accepting it only by faith and having effaced it by sins, but refuses the second one–I mean the baptism of the Spirit, given by God in His love to those who seek it in repentance–how can he ever be saved? Not in the least![130]

One should, of course, be very wary of giving a modern Pentecostal interpretation to these words from the eleventh century. The Orthodox practice of chrismation and the "baptism of tears" form part of the context. Also note the unusual concept of an effacing of baptism by sins. The phrase "lacks awareness of his baptism" underlies the basic sacramental structure of Orthodox theology. In this sacramental context Stephanou describes his own personal experience as "The existential renewal of my baptism in the Holy Spirit."[131] Unfortunately I could find no specific exposition on Spirit-baptism by a charismatic Orthodox theologian (it may be that this does not yet exist). Nevertheless, from the above quotations from Stephanou, coupled with the following statement by Plowman on Stephanou, one can safely conclude that the Orthodox charismatic position would be that of the experiential breakthrough of baptismal grace—the sacramental view.

Morton Kelsey has pointed out that the gift of glossolalia never died out in the Orthodox monasteries throughout the history of Christendom.[132] Plowman comments on the Orthodox charismatic position on the role of tongues:

> Stephanou sides with Catholic charismatics in opposition to the classic Pentecostal doctrine that tongues is the universal sign or evidence of Spirit-baptism. Tongues is but one of the spiritual gifts, he says, explaining that it may be a norm—but not a mandate—for those who have the baptism.[133]

At a conference on "Church and Charism" in Germany in 1966 the Orthodox bishop Johannes (Eugraph Kovalevski) presented two papers—one on charisms in the history of the Orthodox Church and one on charisms in the Orthodox Church today.[134] He reflects on the one hand the view that charisms are extraordinary exceptions that are no longer necessary while on the other hand maintaining that taken as a whole the history of the Orthodox Church is filled with charisms:

> However, when one surveys the history of the Orthodox churches over the last 2,000 years one sees that it is a stream of charisma, a great flux.
>
> If one takes time to study the history it appears that there was never a time, a people, nor a local church which did not always also exhibit the manifestations of the Holy Spirit, and one can maintain that the Orthodox church is not to be understood without recognizing the charismatic dimension.[135]

In his paper on charisms in the modern era of the church, the bishop refers only to charisms of "saints" canonized in the nineteenth and twentieth centuries. This was to be expected of the sixties. For lay (unordained) Christians and ordinary priests (not saints who may later be canonized) in the Orthodox tradition to receive charisms was not at all common until the inroads of the charismatic renewal in the seventies.

J. W. Morris writes a stringent critique of the charismatic movement in the Orthodox Church. He refers to neo-Pentecostal influences in parishes of Greek, Antiochian, and Russian Synod Abroad jurisdictions even before the work of Eusebius Stephanou. His assessment is that the movement is essentially Protestant emphasizing personal experiences and individualized spirituality.[136] It is foreign to Orthodoxy, has been condemned, and should be avoided.[137]

Morris's evaluation of tongues differs from the claim mentioned above that glossolalia continued in Orthodox monasteries throughout history.

> It is highly probable that the glossolalia, so treasured by Neo-Pentecostals, is not a manifestation of the Holy Spirit, but is merely learned behavior. It is also highly likely that tongues, as practiced by charismatics, only bear a superficial resemblance to the gift of tongues found in Holy Scriptures. The disappearance of glossolalia from the Church as an individual experience for almost 2000 years, only to be

"rediscovered" by persons outside of Orthodoxy, is reason alone to question the validity of the phenomenon for Orthodox Christians.[138]

Morris rejects the notion of receiving the Spirit in a separate experience in addition to becoming a Christian. He gives a novel source for neo-Pentecostal teaching:

> Indeed, the charismatic division between Christ and the Holy Spirit is a reflection of the influence of the filioque clause on Western Christendom. Due to the influence of the Roman addition to the Symbol of Faith, Western Christians have neglected the Holy Spirit and have even at times implied a subordination of the Holy Spirit to the Father and the Son. This has led to an artificial separation between Christ and the Holy Spirit that is the basis for the charismatic insistence on the necessity of two separate spiritual experiences, one becoming a Christian, justification; and the other, the reception of the Holy Spirit, baptism of the Holy Spirit.[139]

Among Protestant charismatics there is also, interestingly enough, some stirring with respect to the Filioque. In the Anglican communion there is a move to make the addition "and from the Son" optional, while Rodman Williams states that it would seem improper to speak of the Spirit proceeding from the Father and the Son.[140] Personally I am not convinced that the abstract distinction between the Western Filioque and the Eastern per Filium has any theological implications for a charismatic approach to the Spirit's work.

Morris gives further content to Stephanou's view when he observes that Stephanou is careful not to stray too far from the Orthodox concept that one receives the Spirit through the rite of chrismation immediately after baptism. Stephanou adds (according to Morris), ". . . one must awaken one's chrismation through a 'new Holy Spirit experience' that comes through involvement in the charismatic movement."[141] Morris acknowledges that there is constant need for personal spiritual renewal but continues, "However, the Orthodox Church itself needs no renewal, for 'it always remains new' through the grace of the Holy Spirit."[142]

Although this has been a very rudimentary treatment of the charismatic movement in the Orthodox tradition, one is left with a very different impression from the situation in Catholicism. A church that defines itself as not needing renewal as Morris stated above would scarcely be open to it to any large degree when renewal comes. Possibly, pre–Vatican II Catholicism may have reacted in much the same way as the critique of Morris. Elements of Protestantism reacted in a similar vein in the sixties. The Orthodox approach to Spirit-baptism will probably remain ambiguous for the near future. Certain more positive signs are also forthcoming from Orthodox hierarchy, but the issue is far from resolved. For this study it is important to note that Stephanou's view is basically that of Spirit-baptism as a release of the Spirit given in Christian initiation–specifically the awakening of one's chrismation. The Orthodox are proud of the fact that in the East baptism and chrismation remained united while in the West baptism and confirmation evolved into two rituals with a long separation of time in between. Before closing this discussion on the Orthodox views we need to take a look at the other major figure among Orthodox charismatics.

Athanasios Emmert of St. George's Orthodox Church, Danbury, Connecticut, another leader in the charismatic renewal in the Greek Orthodox Church, seems to say the opposite of Morris regarding the need for renewal in the Orthodox churches: "Orthodoxy itself desperately needs renewal and an awakening in the lives of its faithful if it is to survive in this age."[143]

Brief attention will now be given to Emmert's views. He affirms the basic stance of Stephanou and Bishop Johannes when he claims that the spirituality of the Orthodox Church is theoretically and practically charismatic, supplying many historical examples. The basic difference from the experience of the charismatic movement seems to be that the Orthodox have always associated the charisms with persons of a high degree of faith, devotion, and personal holiness. The Orthodox view of salvation does not conceive of separate stages; even redemption and sanctification are not seen apart but as one process.[144]

Emmert does not give a detailed doctrine of Spirit-baptism but states that it takes place primarily in the sacraments of baptism and chrismation, but a certain "stirring up," "filling," or "coming down upon" those already baptized can occur since, although the Spirit is in all Christians, he is not active in all.[145]

Emmert quotes a contemporary Orthodox theologian, Archimandrite Lev Gillet, who speaks of baptism with water being completed by Spirit-baptism. He states that receiving the mystery or sacrament of the Spirit in chrismation is not enough. "The question is whether and how this seed of the Spirit has been afterwards developed within the soul."[146] Gillet even acknowledges a non-sacramental Spirit-baptism.[147]

Once again there is some ambiguity about tongues. F. P. Möller points out that Emmert (who participated in the Vatican-Pentecostal International dialogue in June 1972) maintains that glossolalia has continuously occurred through the ages among Greek Orthodox monks.[148] In his article for the Society for Pentecostal Studies, Emmert says the charisms of 1 Corinthians 12, with the possible exception of tongues, have always been considered normative by nearly all in the Orthodox Church. He goes on to say that tongues appeared to die out rather rapidly. Glossolalia at Corinth was not comprehensible to the later fathers of the church (and the role of expectancy was in Emmert's opinion crucial):

As a result, the significance of glossolalia was minimized by the later fathers or limited only to local situations for the apostolic period. And, of course, when a gift is not anticipated or expected, however much it may be of the Holy Spirit, it is not received.[149]

Emmert clearly takes a denominational approach to the renewal (although the Orthodox would not themselves refer to their churches as denominations).

He serves on the staff of *The Logos*–a magazine for Orthodox renewal. Perhaps the following statement most clearly reflects the Orthodox charismatic approach:

> As for those Orthodox who have experienced this new encounter in religious experience [in the charismatic movement], it has caused them to discover nothing really new but rather to re-examine within the Orthodox tradition and spirituality that which has always been there.[150]

This perspective can be seen as viewing the charismatic renewal as a key to the storehouse from which one can bring forth treasures old and new.

3.4.6 John Gunstone and James Jones (Anglican/Episcopal)

Although the Church of England forms a remarkable "bridge" between Catholicism and Protestantism, it is here considered to be a Protestant church. The sacramental interpretation would most naturally appeal to Anglican charismatics. Interestingly enough quite a few charismatic Anglican writers represent, to some extent, an evangelical or "Low Church" wing of Anglicanism. John Gunstone, however, comes from the "High Church" or Anglo-Catholic wing of the Church of England.

In his foreword to Gunstone's book, *Greater Things Than These. A Personal Account of the Charismatic Movement,* the archbishop of Canterbury (1974) writes:

> I welcome this book as an account of charismatic revival as experienced by an Anglican priest who sees such revival not apart from but within the sacramental life of the Church.[151]

That sums up Gunstone's perspective rather well. He is clearly critical of the concept of a "second blessing," stating that it is difficult to accommodate to most theological traditions.[152] He does not find the division of Christians into two types–the Spirit-filled and those who are not–to be supported by the witness of the New Testament as a whole. He maintains:

> Christian initiation is our baptism with the Holy Spirit. But the totality of the saving act of God in Jesus Christ is so vast that Christian expectation and Christian practice have failed to contain the whole in view.[153]

Gunstone considers the development in the West in which infant baptism and confirmation became separated as the disintegration of the rites of initiation. This caused the church to lose sight of the implications of Spirit-baptism. Gunstone uses the language of the sacramental interpretation. He notes that if theology and experience went hand-in-hand one would expect to experience Spirit-baptism at the time of receiving the sacrament of initiation. He sees the later experience as a fulfillment:

> The phrase "the baptism with the Holy Spirit" is, therefore, full of meaning when it is applied to a Pentecostal experience by the person concerned. For it describes a fulfillment in his life of what the sacrament of baptism promised, namely, a new encounter with God through the power of the Spirit which opens the Christian's

136

eyes to the truth of what Christ meant when he said to his disciples, "You shall see greater things than these" (John 1:50).[154]

In a certain sense Gunstone's descriptions of what Spirit-baptism implies forms a bridge to the next chapter. He does incorporate it within a sacramental framework, and yet also refers to it in terms of a spiritual breakthrough or moment of growth. He speaks of a moment when the presence of God becomes more real or an opening up to God through a conscious decision for him which exposes us more to his influence than before.

Gunstone sees this as an ongoing process:

> . . .although all that God desires to give us is present in Christian initiation, his gift is only gradually appropriated by us through the years of our life, with many backslidings and failures. We have to "take up our cross daily," to "die daily," to be "renewed every day"–the New Testament has a variety of expressions–and in this sense baptism is also a sign of what God will continue to do in us for the rest of our lives. We progress towards the kingdom of heaven among toils and tribulations; but they cannot divert us as long as we are in the Spirit. . . . If we are to be true to our Christian vocation, we must always be "baptized with the Holy Spirit." To be immersed in him is, as we have seen, the mark of being one with Jesus Christ in his Church. When we cease to live and move and think and talk outside the realm of the Spirit, we cease to be Christian.[155]

This line will be developed more fully in the next chapter. With the content that he gives to Spirit-baptism Gunstone is already reaching beyond a particular "release" of the Spirit. Would this metaphor be able to endure several, even daily, "releases"? I have the impression that the "release" of the Spirit is limited by a certain event-centeredness. Attempts to break out of this will be explored in the next chapter.

Apart from John Gunstone of Britain, the sacramental position is also defended by the Episcopal theologian of Rutgers University in New Brunswick, New Jersey, James W. Jones. He explains his approach in *Filled with the New Wine. The Charismatic Renewal of the Church.*[156]

Jones sees the Christian life as a matter of evolutionary growth. That which has gone before, needs to be affirmed and appropriated. He is rather sharp in his criticism of a "sectarian" spirit that he sees as predominating on the American scene. This implies a view of church history that functions as a repetitive schism. Jones describes the process as the "sectarians" view it:

> . . .when the church of Rome got too corrupt, the church of England broke off from it, and then, when the church of England fell into ruins, Wesley had to leave it in order to gather a true fellowship. None of this is historically true, but it is the American sectarian version of English church history.[157]

Jones's point is that in churches where this is taught (e.g., in the Methodist and Baptist traditions) those who experience a charismatic renewal tend to become sectarian, splitting off to form their own groups. In Catholic, Anglican, and Lutheran traditions, where such "sectarianism" is not part of the heritage, there is no need for the charismatic renewal to lead to schism.

Jones sees openness as a precondition for experience. To be truly responsive to God's Spirit is very hard for us because we are used to putting ourselves and our sense of logic and priorities first. Significant experiences of a religious nature can be missed because we are not open to them.[158]

Jones conceives of Christian life as a continual series of experiences that deepen the potential received in baptism. This happens when we take communion, read the Bible, hear the preaching of the Word, etc. This also applies to the gifts of the Spirit. They are part of the potential which we received in Christian initiation. In this context Jones is explicit about Spirit-baptism:

> ... I am uncomfortable at basing too much theology on the term "baptism in the Holy Spirit." It implies that the Spirit was not present earlier. I prefer "release of the Spirit." For what spiritual gifts do is to release the Spirit present since baptism and give the person a new openness to it. Baptism in the Spirit does not demand that one suddenly condemn as unspiritual everything that has gone before. Rather, it is one more event by which a Christian life is further deepened and renewed.[159]

Jones is clearly advocating the sacramental position of the "release of the Spirit." He is very careful to acknowledge that the Spirit is not absent from the lives of non-charismatic churchgoers, but he does see the renewal movement as an opportunity to receive further deepening of the faith: "Baptism in the Holy Spirit is one more stage in that long, slow process of incorporating God's love which begins at original baptism and will not end until the Last day."[160]

Jones is developing a charismatic theology which can be readily integrated into the High Church tradition. In the following chapter several other attempts to formulate such a theology of Spirit-baptism will be discussed. To varying degrees they are all seeking a fuller integration into Christianity at large. In chapter 5 a model for full integration into standard Christian doctrine and practice will be proposed. Jones's ultimate aim, as one would expect, is the renewal of the (whole) church. He considers the present structures of the charismatic movement as scaffolding to renew the building of the church. When this has been achieved the scaffolding should be dismantled. Jones sounds a timely warning to the charismatic movement: "the Spirit cannot be released by techniques but only by humble openness and responsiveness."[161]

This representative of the Anglican renewal shows that theologizing within the sacramental framework has reached a high level of maturity. This is further enhanced by Jones's next book, *The Spirit and the World,* in which he explores an area which will certainly become more important as the charismatic movement matures.[162]

Endnotes 3

1. Kuen, *Die charismatische Bewegung,* 23.
2. McDonnell, "Relationship of the Charismatic Renewal," 223–29, esp., 228.
3. Ibid., 226.
4. Ibid., 228.

5. R. P. Spittler, "Suggested Areas for Further Research in Pentecostal Studies," *Pneuma* 5 (2, 1983): 41.

6. McDonnell, *Presence, Power, Praise,* Malines Document I:13–70.

7. English translation in L. J. Cardinal Suenens, *A New Pentecost?* (Glasgow: Collins, 1977).

8. J. Moore, "The Catholic Pentecostal Movement," in *A Sociological Yearbook of Religion in Britain* 6 (London: SCM, 1973): 78.

9. McDonnell, *Presence, Power, Praise,* III:13.

10. Ibid., 38–39.

11. Ibid., 34.

12. Ibid., 39–40.

13. Ibid., 32–33. The emphasis on the words presence, power, and praise in this quotation is my own.

14. Ibid., 42.

15. B. Fischer, "'Baptism of the Spirit.' The Meaning of the Expression 'Baptism of the Spirit' in the Light of Catholic Baptismal Liturgy and Spirituality," *One in Christ* 10 (1974): 172–73.

16. Ibid., 172.

17. Ibid.

18. S. Tugwell, OP, "Faith and Experience I: The Problems of Catholic Pentecostalism," *New Blackfriars* 59 (699, 1978): 363.

19. D. Parry, OSB, *This Promise is for You: Spiritual Renewal and the Charismatic Movement* (London: Darton, Longman and Todd, 1977).

20. Ibid., back cover.

21. Ibid., 56.

22. Ibid., 57.

23. Ibid., 60.

24. Tugwell, "Faith and Experience I," 359–69 and "Faith and Experience II. Charisms and Ecclesiology," in *New Blackfriars* 59 (700, 1978): 417–30.

25. Parry, *This Promise Is for You,* 103.

26. Tugwell, "Faith and Experience II," 420.

27. Suenens, *A New Pentecost?* 80.

28. Ibid.

29. Ibid., 81.

30. Apart from ch. 7, "Pentecost and Traditional Spirituality," in E. D. O'Connor, *The Pentecostal Movement,* 179–219, see his "The Holy Spirit, Christian Love, and Mysticism," in *Perspectives on Charismatic Renewal,* ed. E. D. O'Connor (Notre Dame: University of Notre Dame Press, 1975) 133–53.

31. McDonnell, "Ecumenical Problem," 33.

32. Ibid., 44.

33. K. McDonnell, "The Holy Spirit and Christian Initiation," in *The Holy Spirit and Power: The Catholic Charismatic Renewal,* ed. K. McDonnell (New York: Doubleday, 1975) 81.

34. K. McDonnell, "The Experience of the Holy Spirit in the Catholic Charismatic Renewal," in *Concilium: Conflicts about the Holy Spirit,* ed. H. Küng and J. Moltmann (New York: Seabury, 1979) 99.

35. K. McDonnell, "Die charismatische Bewegung in der katholischen Kirche," in *Wiederentdeckung des heiligen Geistes. Der Heilige Geist in der charismatische Erfahrung und theologischen Reflexion,* Oekumenische Perspektiven 6, ed. M. Lienhard and H. Meyer (Frankfurt: Otto Lembeck, 1974) 29–30.

36. Flynn, *Irish Experience,* 184. Father Carrillo's paper is included as Appendix III, 167–88.

37. Ibid., 176.

38. Ibid.

39. Ibid., 178.

40. Ibid., 181–82.

41. O'Connor, *Pentecostal Movement*.

42. L. Schmieder, *Geisttaufe. Ein Beitrag zur neueren Glaubensgeschichte* (Paderborn: Schöningh, 1982) 412.

43. O'Connor, *Pentecostal Movement*, 216.

44. Ibid.

45. Ibid., 134–35.

46. J. Massingberd (*sic*) Ford, "Pentecostal Catholicism," in *Concilium: Spirituality*, ed. C. Duquoc and C. Geffré (London: Burns and Oates, 9 [8, 1972]) 89.

47. J. Massyngberde Ford, "The New Pentecostalism: Personal Reflections of a Participating Roman Catholic Scholar," in *Perspectives on the New Pentecostalism*, ed. R. P. Spittler (Grand Rapids: Baker, 1976) 211. (Dr. Ford changed the spelling of her middle name to its original form. That is why both spellings are found.)

48. Ibid., 211 n. 4 and 211–15.

49. Ranaghan, *Catholic Pentecostals Today*, 97.

50. Ibid., 98.

51. Ibid., 104.

52. Ibid., 102.

53. Laurentin, *Catholic Pentecostalism*, 36.

54. Ibid., 45.

55. Ibid., 47.

56. Spittler, "Suggested Areas," 40.

57. D. L. Gelpi, *Experiencing God: A Theology of Human Emergence* (New York: Paulist, 1978); and *The Divine Mother: A Trinitarian Theology of the Holy Spirit* (Lanham, MD: University Press of America, 1984).

58. D. L. Gelpi, *Pentecostalism: A Theological Viewpoint* (New York: Paulist, 1971); and *Charism and Sacrament: A Theology of Christian Conversion* (New York: Paulist, 1976).

59. Gelpi, *Pentecostalism*, 223–26.

60. Ibid., 182–83.

61. Ibid., 180–82.

62. Gelpi, *Charism and Sacrament*, 97.

63. Ibid., 150.

64. Ibid., 151.

65. D. L. Gelpi, "American Pentecostalism," in *Concilium: Spiritual Revivals*, ed. C. Duquoc and C. Floristan (New York: Herder, 1973) 101–2.

66. Ibid., 108.

67. D. L. Gelpi, "Pentecostal Theology: A Roman Catholic Viewpoint," in *Perspectives on the New Pentecostalism*, ed. R. P. Spittler (Grand Rapids: Baker, 1976) 103.

68. Ibid.

69. S. Tugwell, *Did You Receive the Spirit?* (New York: Paulist, 1972). Tugwell also regularly writes in *New Blackfriars* and *The Heythrop Journal*.

70. Ibid., 85–86.

71. Ibid., 87.

72. P. Hocken, "Catholic Pentecostalism: Some Key Questions I," in *HeyJ* 15 (2, 1974) 137.

73. Tugwell, *Did You Receive the Spirit?* 93.

74. Ibid., 92.

75. Ibid., 89.

76. Ibid., 90. Tugwell is, of course, not using the term "Neo-Pentecostals" in the specific sense it is used in this study. It could here probably be equated with "charismatics."

77. S. Tugwell, "Catholics and Pentecostals," in *New Blackfriars* 52 (612, 1971): 214.

78. Ibid.

79. S. Tugwell, "The Speech-Giving Spirit," in S. Tugwell, P. Hocken, G. Every, and J. O. Mills, *New Heaven? New Earth?* (Springfield, IL: Templegate, 1976) 133.

80. Ibid., 128.

81. O'Connor, *Pentecostal Movement,* 23.

82. Hollenweger, *New Wine in Old Wineskins,* 48.

83. Tugwell, "The Speech-Giving Spirit," 151.

84. S. Tugwell, "Reflections on the Pentecostal Doctrine of 'Baptism in the Holy Spirit' II," *HeyJ* 13 (4, 1972): 407.

85. Ibid., 407–8.

86. Hollenweger, *The Pentecostals,* 508.

87. W. J. Hollenweger, preface to *New Heaven? New Earth?* 9.

88. Ibid., 10.

89. Hocken, "Pentecostals on Paper II," 165.

90. Hocken, "Significance and Potential," 48.

91. Tugwell, "Reflections II," 406.

92. Lindberg, *Third Reformation?* The major study referred to is L. Christenson (ed) *Welcome, Holy Spirit. A Study of Charismatic Renewal in the Church* (Minneapolis: Augsburg, 1987). Unfortunately I only procured a copy of this book as the present study was in its final proof stage.

93. B. R. Hoffman, *Luther and the Mystics: A Re-examination of Luther's Spiritual Experience and His Relationship to the Mystics* (Minneapolis: Augsburg, 1976) 230–31.

94. Ibid., 231–32.

95. L. Christenson, *The Charismatic Renewal Among Lutherans: A Pastoral and Theological Perspective* (Minneapolis: Lutheran Charismatic Renewal Services, 1976) 9.

96. McDonnell, "Established Denominations," 229.

97. Ibid., 228.

98. Lindberg, *Third Reformation?* 220.

99. L. Christenson, "Baptism with the Holy Spirit," in *International Lutheran Renewal* 62 (January, 1985): 1–3 (unnumbered). I was unable to procure a copy of the third revised edition of *The Charismatic Renewal among Lutherans* published in 1985.

100. Lindberg, *Third Reformation?* 226.

101. Christenson, *The Charismatic Renewal among Lutherans,* 37–38.

102. Ibid., 50.

103. Ibid., 38.

104. Ibid.

105. Ibid., 49–50.

106. Ibid., 49, and "Baptism with the Holy Spirit," 1.

107. Christenson, *The Charismatic Renewal among Lutherans,* 51.

108. Schmieder, *Geisttaufe,* 385–88.

109. Ibid., 387.

110. Lindberg, *Third Reformation?* 227.

111. T. R. Jungkuntz, "A Response to Scott H. Hendrix's 'Charismatic Renewal: Old Wine in New Skins,'" *Currents in Theology and Missions* 5 (1, 1978): 57.

112. The Missouri-Synod Document can be found in Opsahl, *The Holy Spirit in the Life of the Church,* 271–87. Jungkuntz's reply is entitled "A Response," in *The Cresset: Occasional Paper II* (Valparaiso, IN: Valparaiso University Press, 1977) 3–11.

113. Lindberg, *Third Reformation?* 227.

114. T. R. Jungkuntz, "Secularization, Theology, Charismatic Renewal, and Luther's Theology of the Cross," *Concordia Theological Monthly* 42 (1, 1971): 20a. Also quoted in Jungkuntz, "A Response," 55.

115. T. R. Jungkuntz, "Charismatic Worship: Challenge or Challenged,"*Response* 16 (1–2, 1976): 5b. Also quoted in Jungkuntz, "A Response," 55, and Lindberg, *Third Reformation?* 228.

116. T. R. Jungkuntz, "Testing the Spirit of the Charismatic Renewal," *Lutheran Charismatic Renewal Newsletter* 1 (7, 1975): 3a–b. Also quoted in Jungkuntz, "A Response," 55.

117. Lindberg, *Third Reformation?* 228.

118. T. R. Jungkuntz, *Confirmation and the Charismata* (Lanham, MD: University Press of America, 1983).

119. Ibid., 91.

120. Ibid., 92.

121. Ibid., 96.

122. Ibid., 97.

123. Bradford, *Releasing the Power.*

124. Ibid., 23.

125. Ibid., 15.

126. Ibid., 13.

127. Ibid., 12.

128. E. A. Stephanou, "The Charismata in the Early Church Fathers," *GOTR* 21 (1976): 126.

129. Ibid., 143.

130. Ibid. The only reference given to the source is *Catechesis* 9.

131. K. T. Ware, "Orthodoxy and the Charismatic Movement," *Eastern Churches Review* 5 (2, 1973): 183.

132. M. T. Kelsey, *Tongue Speaking: An Experiment in Spiritual Experience* (New York: Doubleday, 1964) 6–7, 42–43.

133. E. E. Plowman, "Mission to Orthodoxy: The 'Full' Gospel," *Christianity Today* 18 (April 26, 1974): 45.

134. E. Kovalevski, "Gnadengaben in der Kirchengeschichte. Die Charismen in der Geschichte der orthodoxen Kirche," *Kirche und Charisma* (1966): 78–88; and "Gnadengaben in der Kirche heute. Die Charismen in der orthodoxen Kirche heute," *Kirche und Charisma* (1966): 129–37.

135. Ibid., 80–81.

136. J. W. Morris, "The Charismatic Movement: An Orthodox Evaluation," *GOTR* 28 (1983): 118.

137. Ibid., 134.

138. Ibid., 125.

139. Ibid., 129.

140. Williams, *Gift of the Holy Spirit Today,* 5 n. 7.

141. Morris, "Charismatic Movement," 130–31.

142. Ibid., 131.

143. A. F. S. Emmert, "Charismatic Developments in the Eastern Orthodox Church," in *Perspectives on the New Pentecostalism,* ed. R. P. Spittler (Grand Rapids: Baker, 1976) 42.

144. Ibid., 36.

145. Ibid., 38.

146. Ibid., 39.

147. Ibid., 38.

148. F. P. Möller, *Die Diskussie oor die charismata soos wat dit in die Pinksterbeweging geleer en beoefen word* (Braamfontein, South Africa: Evangelie Uitgewers, 1975) 15, 338 n. 32.

149. Emmert, "Charismatic Developments," 41–42.

150. Ibid., 40.

151. J. Gunstone, *Greater Things than These: A Personal Account of the Charismatic Movement* (Leighton Buzzard, England: Faith Press, 1974) 7.

152. Ibid., 30.

153. Ibid., 31.

154. Ibid., 35.

155. Ibid., 32–33.

156. J. W. Jones, *Filled with New Wine: The Charismatic Renewal of the Church* (New York: Harper and Row, 1974). See also his next book, *The Spirit and the World* (New York: Hawthorn, 1975).

157. Ibid., 44.

158. Ibid., 80–81.

159. Ibid., 70.

160. Ibid., 70–71.

161. Ibid., 117.

162. See n. 156.

INTEGRATIVE INTERPRETATIONS
OF SPIRIT-BAPTISM

═ **4** ════════════════════════════

Apart from the two large charismatic reinterpretations of Spirit-baptism, namely the neo-Pentecostal view, which is really just a slight adaptation of the Pentecostal teaching, and the sacramental interpretation, there are a variety of other perspectives that do not have such broad support. In this chapter views of Spirit-baptism as the final stage of Christian initiation, the fullness of the Spirit, or a spiritual renewal (e.g., parish renewal) will be discussed. There will be much less uniformity among these groups than among those subscribing to a sacramental interpretation, although there is some variance there too. Generally speaking the scene also moves geographically. The majority of charismatic authors discussed in chapters 2 and 3 were American; chapter 4 focuses on Europe—especially Britain and Germany. Denominational affiliations are by no means decisive in determining interpretations of Spirit-baptism. Catholic, Lutheran, Anglican, and Reformed theologians are found in chapters 2, 3, and 4. Apart from their being largely European, the only other common denominator among the groups discussed in this chapter is a strong critique of the rigid two-stage pattern for Christian experience (especially as presented by American neo-Pentecostals) and a simultaneous awareness, in a much more vague way, that not every momentous or significant work of God's Spirit need be tied to the sacraments. Chapter 4 will also lay the foundation for my own interpretation of Spirit-baptism. The basic element common to these "integrative" interpretations of Spirit-baptism is that they wish to integrate this teaching organically into the historic Christian faith without necessarily doing this in a specifically sacramental way.

4.1 The Joint Statement: Gospel and Spirit (Anglican)

A joint statement was issued in 1977 by the body responsible for the furthering of the charismatic renewal in Britain, the Fountain Trust (which closed down voluntarily in 1980 so as not to become a divisive factor within the Church of England) and the Church of England Evangelical Council, which represents the traditional stream of Anglican Evangelicalism.[1] The statement was developed by leaders from these two institutions at a series of day conferences. Among them were prominent evangelicals such as J. I. Packer and John Stott and charismatics such as John Baker, Michael Harper, David Watson, and Tom Smail. A remarkable degree of unanimity was achieved resulting in restored fellowship across the so-called charismatic divide.

Theologically the statement can probably best be described as Reformed in doctrine. The participants agreed that "all gospel blessings (are) given in Christ"; the idea that in the Spirit one receives something more wonderful than Christ or something apart from him and the fullness of his saving grace was roundly rejected.[2] An important insight is presented with respect to initiation into Christ:

> We are all convinced that according to the New Testament Christian initiation, symbolized and sealed by water-baptism, is a unitary work of God with many facets. This work is expressed by a cluster of partly overlapping concepts, including forgiveness, justification, adoption, regeneration, conversion (embracing repentance and faith in Jesus Christ as Lord and Savior), new creation, death, burial and resurrection in and with Christ, and the giving and reception of the Holy Spirit. . . .God's initiatory work is itself apprehended and experienced by different individuals in differing ways and time-scales. . . .But essentially the concepts all belong together, since together they express the single full reality of the believer's incorporation into Christ, which leads to assurance of sonship, and power to live and serve in Christ. We are agreed on the need (i) to avoid trying to stereotype or straitjacket either the work of the Holy Spirit or the experience of individual Christians into a one, two or three-stage experience; (ii) to avoid presenting the work of the Spirit in separation from the work of the Son, since the Son gives the Spirit and the Spirit both witnesses to the Son and forms him in us; and (iii) to present the full range of Christ's salvation and gift for us in all our evangelism and teaching—i.e. to preach a complete, rather than a truncated, gospel.[3]

This could be seen as a new perspective, for "the giving and reception of the Holy Spirit" are seen as an integral part of a cluster of partly overlapping concepts describing Christian initiation. But to what does this refer? We have here stumbled on an inner ambiguity which one should probably expect in a document that attempts to reach a compromise.

If "reception of the Spirit" refers merely to the work of the Spirit in regeneration and conversion we are back to the traditional evangelical position. If, however, "reception of the Spirit" refers to the charismatic experience or dimension then Spirit-baptism is being regarded as part of a *process* of Christian initiation, most likely its completion.

Another significant aspect of this part of the *Joint Statement* is that the stereotype of forcing the experience of individual Christians into a one-stage pattern is rejected. It is common to find charismatics rejecting the two- and three-stage patterns which correlate with the Baptistic and Wesleyan-Holiness traditions of classical Pentecostalism. One stage as a stereotype would probably

not refer to the Augustinian heritage of much of Christianity in which sanctification is seen as an ongoing process. It would more likely refer to the
complacent attitude which some evangelicals may express over against charismatics in words such as: "I have it all" implying that in conversion they have
"arrived" and have no need of further growth.

The next section of the *Joint Statement* expresses the remaining differences.
It is stated as a fact that many Christians have experienced "a fresh enrich-
ment" of their Spirit-given experience of Christ, and in many cases they have
called it "baptism in the Holy Spirit."[4] Problematically, such terminology
would, according to the Statement, suggest that a long interval between new
birth and any conscious realization or reception of the Spirit's power is normal,
whereas the New Testament regards this as sub-normal. Another problem is
that the words "baptize into" have an initiatory content and context. (Of
course this objection would not apply if Christian initiation were seen as a long
process completed by an experiential Spirit-baptism.)

Next the Statement acknowledges the difficulty of changing a widely
accepted terminology. Perhaps it would be sufficient if the term "baptism in
the Spirit" could be employed in such a way that the reality of the Spirit's
work in regeneration in others was not implicitly questioned.

The *Joint Statement* delineates three positions on Spirit-baptism:

> Some who speak of a post-conversion "baptism in the Spirit" think of it mainly
> in terms of an empowering for service similar to the disciples' experience at Pente-
> cost, though all are agreed that we should not isolate this side of the Spirit's work
> from his other ministries to and in the believer.

> Some, stressing the experiential content of the term "baptism in the Spirit," value
> it as having played a unique part in awakening Christians out of spiritual lethargy
> and bondage, and regard it as still having such a role in the future.

> Others, concentrating rather upon its initiatory implications, prefer to use it only
> to describe one aspect of new birth.

> None of us wishes to deny the possibility or reality of subsequent experiences of
> the grace of God.[5]

Once again one needs to look at the wording with care. The first position
resembles the common neo-Pentecostal position that sees Spirit-baptism as
post-conversion and as an enduement with power. It differs from neo-
Pentecostalism in that it is not locked into a two-stage framework, since the
reality of subsequent experiences of God's grace is recognized by all. From a
later section of the document[6] it is clear that the position of glossolalia as the
initial evidence of Spirit-baptism is rejected.

The second position is difficult to pinpoint. It appears to view Spirit-
baptism as spiritual renewal—here termed awakening. If this is accurate Spirit-
baptism is being interpreted in terms similar to the views of Heribert Mühlen
and Arnold Bittlinger, who will be discussed later in this chapter.

The third position holds that Spirit-baptism is one aspect of Christian
initiation. This in all likelihood represents the traditional evangelical position;

146

but Spirit-baptism could also be interpreted here as the experiential side or dimension of Christian initiation. The only justification for this reading in the Statement itself (apart from the fact that this view is found among charismatic evangelicals and can be clearly illustrated in their writings) is the section already quoted earlier:

> God's initiatory work is itself apprehended and experienced by different individuals in differing ways and time-scales. . . . But essentially the concepts all belong together, since together they express the single full reality of the believer's incorporation into Christ, which leads to assurance of sonship, and power to live and serve in Christ.[7]

That "God's initiatory work" can be experienced in differing time-scales by different individuals, and the statement that the full reality of Christian initiation leads to power to live and serve in Christ strongly suggest something conscious and "charismatic"–something other than the work of the Spirit in regeneration, which is usually conceived of as not being humanly perceptible.

The importance of the *Joint Statement* for this study is that we have here an example of some interpretations of Spirit-baptism that are neither neo-Pentecostal nor sacramental. They are still very much in kernel form. It will be necessary to look at individual charismatic writers to get more insight into these perspectives on Spirit-baptism.

4.2 Thomas Smail (Presbyterian/Anglican)

Thomas Smail was one of the more prominent theologians who worked on the *Joint Statement: Gospel and Spirit.* He was also editor of *Theological Renewal* and played a role as catalyst in resolving some of the tensions surrounding the charismatic renewal in Britain. He declared that being neither Anglican nor Evangelical (with a capital E, at any rate), he was privileged to take part in the consultations.[8] At the time Smail was Presbyterian–a member of the Church of Scotland. Subsequently after moving to St. John's, Nottingham, he joined the Church of England and may now even be capitalizing the "e" of his evangelical position!

In *Reflected Glory. The Spirit in Christ and Christians,* Tom Smail presents his unique perspective on Spirit-baptism. In 1977 Culpepper described this book as "the most important theological work to come out of the charismatic movement."[9] Although I would not concur with this judgment (and I suspect Culpepper would no longer make this claim today), the contribution of Smail is remarkable since he pioneered the break with the theology of subsequence in Protestantism. He, in fact, provided a new basis for charismatic theology by seeking to replace the "second blessing" approach with the controversial Christology of Edward Irving. Smail warns of the danger of charismatics "in the first flush of their new thing" becoming a great trial to other Christians and generating the misunderstanding that they are a type of "first-class" Christian.[10]

Smail's Reformed heritage (although he has joined the Church of England after leaving Scotland, his theology remains Reformed which, of course, has always been an option within Anglicanism since Cranmer) leads him to object to any glorifying of the Spirit that obscures the centrality of Christ. The task of the Spirit is to glorify Christ. He criticizes Pentecostalism as being

> in danger of dividing the Christian life into a salvation which is gift to the sinner, and the fullness of the Spirit which is reward of the saint, and thus maligning the central gospel principle that from beginning to end is all of grace.[11]

Personally I doubt whether this is a real danger but rather one which emanates from reading Bruner's overstated critique of Pentecostalism!

Smail may be clear of his rejection of Pentecostal teaching but he does not allow the issue of terminology to dominate. He quotes John Taylor:

> It is better to call it incorrectly a second blessing and lay hold of the reality of new life in Christ than to let the soundness of our doctrine rob us of its substance.[12]

Smail goes on to give his last chapter the title: "By Whatever Name—Receive!"[13]

The terminology of the release of the Spirit is also found in Smail's analysis.

> The New Testament assumption is that all Christians are in the full experiential flow of the Spirit's life and power, because in being initiated into Christ they have come to know *the full release of the Spirit* as well (my emphasis).[14]

But this does not make his approach typically sacramental. He does, in fact, accept the validity of the term "baptism in the Spirit," which is questioned by both the Catholic sacramental charismatics and Protestant evangelicals.[15]

Basically Smail contends that the Spirit's work in us is the reflection of the Spirit's work in the manhood of Christ. Sharing in the human nature we can model ourselves on Christ and his relationship to the Spirit. Smail argues convincingly:

> In both Christ and us the Spirit is working with the stuff of our common humanity; because he is man and we are man, it becomes possible and credible that what the Spirit did first in him, he should be able to do again in us.[16]

This perspective is akin to both Karl Barth and Edward Irving.[17] The human nature which Christ assumed was the one characterized by the Fall. Irving's Christology was officially rejected by the Church of Scotland of his time (early nineteenth century), and there is some debate about his exact meaning. Did he teach that Jesus' human nature was actually sinful in the sense of culpable or that it was similar to ours in that it had the same disadvantages caused by sin and was weakened by the Fall? Smail acknowledges that this Christology may need correction, but as a basic model he finds it to be the solution that charismatic theology is seeking.

This focus on Christ's human nature makes it understandable that Smail can "revive" the old Pentecostal concepts of a parallel between Christ's virgin birth and our regeneration and between his "Spirit-baptism" at the Jordan and the Christian's Spirit-baptism. Barth also taught this.[18] Nevertheless this does not lead to a reintroduction of the two-stage pattern in Smail's charismatic theology.

What implications does this have for Smail's view of Spirit-baptism? In his chapter on "Birth and Baptism in the Spirit" Smail argues for the unity of Christian initiation. This includes regeneration, the sacramental act which expresses our union with Christ and the entry by confession, faith, and repentance into full, experiential participation in Christ and the Holy Spirit.[19] Smail expresses the hope that the renewal of the church will result in God's joining these aspects together again which man has put asunder.[20]

In his concluding chapter Smail draws everything together. He makes a very valid point:

> Throughout this book, we have tried to show that the charismatic dimension of the Spirit's work does not depend upon a few special phrases or incidents in Acts, but is integral to the whole New Testament grasp of the work of Christ. When Paul speaks in Ephesians 1:19 of "The immeasurable greatness of Christ, of his power in us who believe" and prays in Ephesians 3:20 to "him who by the power at work within us is able to do far more abundantly than all that we can ask or think," he uses none of the Pentecostal clichés, and does not even speak of the Spirit, but clearly says in principle everything that charismatics want to see recognized in the life of the Church.[21]

Nevertheless Smail still considers "baptism in the Spirit" as a legitimate description of the charismatic experience and dimension. His definition of Spirit-baptism reiterates his Irvingite and Barthian Christology:

> Baptism in the Holy Spirit is that aspect of Christian initiation in which, through expectant and appropriating faith in Christ's promises, the indwelling Holy Spirit manifests himself in our experience, so that he works in and through us with freedom and effectiveness, as he first worked with complete freedom and full effectiveness in the manhood of Christ.[22]

To Smail Spirit-baptism is thus an experiential aspect of Christian initiation that could be seen as the "crowning glory" of becoming a Christian, the ongoing completion of Christian initiation. Clearly it is no mere second stage but is the full life in Christ and his salvation. Smail, nevertheless, feels the need to give further content to this concept and thereby runs the risk of being interpreted as remaining basically Pentecostal. Smail explains that Spirit-baptism does not just point to the regenerating, justifying, and sanctifying activity of the Spirit. There is an experiential dimension which denotes an overwhelming by the Spirit in terms of personal experience. This is the essential New Testament content of Spirit-baptism according to Smail—the released power and energy of the Spirit and charismatic manifestations. Smail states his case in the context of the disciples in Acts 2:

> . . .what is actually described is their entering into an overwhelming experience of the manifested presence and power of the Lord through the Holy Spirit, to give

them boldness and ability to witness in word and deed in ways that could be seen and heard. This, not regeneration or sanctification, is the focus of their being baptized or filled with the Spirit. It has to do with manifestation rather than relation, witnessing act rather than ethical disposition.[23]

Interestingly, Smail here uses "baptized" and "filled with the Spirit" interchangeably and does not relate either of these concepts to "ethical disposition."

Jonker points out that by emphasizing this experiential element Smail is moving beyond Barth. Instead of two stages Smail has two aspects of the one salvation in Christ–the incorporation into Christ and experiencing the effect thereof.[24] One should, however, always keep Smail's whole argument in mind. He is pleading for the recognition of the "charismatic dimension of the Spirit's work"–not for isolated experiences. Smail invites Christians to open themselves up to all that the Spirit wants to do in them. This, he says, remains as actual and urgent as ever, even if the phrase "baptism in the Spirit" were abolished and banished.[25] It is not so much an emphasizing of a particular experience of the Spirit but the pointing out of a dimension of New Testament Christianity that is sadly lacking. For this reason I find Jonker's comments that "special experience of the Spirit and the manifestation of the gifts of the Spirit are seen [by charismatics] as essential" unsatisfactory.[26]

In her study, *Geisttaufe* [Spirit-baptism], Schmieder also discusses eight Protestant charismatic writers. Surprisingly, she gives the briefest attention–hardly half a page–to Smail (who in my opinion warrants the most attention). Just as questionable is her assessment that his view is similar to that of Michael Harper.[27]

Larry Hart, on the other hand, gives serious attention to Smail in his dissertation, "A Critique of American Pentecostal Theology." Hart writes:

> Thus, Thomas Smail has moved further away from the "second blessing" fallacy than any other Protestant neo-Pentecostal. He has evinced the most adequate response to the criticism of the salient inadequacies of Pentecostal religion. The most disappointing aspect of his presentation is his refusal to give up the phrase, baptism in the Holy Spirit, to refer to one's personal appropriation of spiritual renewal.[28]

Hart also points out the contradictory position into which Smail wedged himself: Spirit-baptism is seen as an aspect of Christian initiation but not all Christians have entered into it.[29] Unfortunately, in elaborating his definition of Spirit-baptism Smail gives the impression that the manifested power of the Spirit operates very much like the second-stage experience of neo-Pentecostalism. A last quotation from Smail may help to dispel the misgiving about him slipping back into an event-centered two-stage pattern, while at the same time it may bring into sharper relief the fact that Smail is not only referring to "the charismatic and experiential dimension of Christian reality" but to a distinctive experience:

> The particular experience is significant because it marks a breakthrough into a fresh dimension of their experiential relationship with Christ.

It may be sudden, critical and sensationally transforming; it may be slow and quiet and spread over a period. . . . Even when the Spirit comes quietly, we shall be aware that he has come, and his manifestation will be known also in the Body of Christ around us.[30]

In the last chapter a view will be developed that is not far removed from this perspective of Smail and yet in the final analysis the differences will be seen to be crucial. It is the choice between charismatic experience and a charismatic experience.

4.3 David Watson (Anglican)

David Watson discusses the issue of Spirit-baptism in his book, *One in the Spirit* (1973). His views significantly influenced the charismatic debates of the decade following its release.[31] He declares that more has probably been written and spoken about the phrase "baptism of the Spirit" recently than about any other phrase in the Bible.[32] Like the *Joint Statement* he later endorsed, Watson seeks to delineate the areas of agreement and disagreement. He states that all Christians agree that every Christian *has* the Spirit but not every Christian is *filled* with the Spirit. In the last analysis Watson underscores that it is the love, power, and reality of the Spirit that counts, not the terminology. He then proceeds to guide the reader seeking the fullness of the Spirit through the steps: Repent, Obey, Thirst, and Ask, using Luke 11:13b for the last step.[33]

The crux of Watson's view suggests that the term "baptize" has a rich meaning in the New Testament and that these elements of meaning encompass both "initiated into" and "overwhelmed by." The former referring to becoming a Christian, a status in Christ, and the latter to an experience.[34]

Watson declares that we must not be frightened of experience:

How can you have a vital relationship with the living Lord Jesus without some experience? How can you be filled with the mighty Spirit of God without some experience? How can you worship God in spirit and truth without some experience? Certainly we must beware of seeking experiences just for their own sake, but the New Testament portrait of the Christian is full of superlatives: the peace which passes understanding, the love which surpasses knowledge, unutterable and exalted joy.[35]

This experience of being overwhelmed by the Spirit correlates with Smail's view of the experiential dimension of life in Christ. Smail, in fact, refers to Watson in this regard.[36] Watson wishes to keep the elements of *initiation* and *overwhelming* in balance.

They are ideally and potentially one – though not necessarily experientially so. One is reminded of Kilian McDonnell's distinction between the theological and experiential aspects of Spirit-baptism, although Watson never develops this in any strictly sacramental way of understanding God's work in us. To counter the argument that being initiated into Christ without any overwhelming is enough, Watson quotes Martyn Lloyd-Jones with approval:

151

Got it all? Well, if you have "got it all" I simply ask, in the name of God, why are you as you are? If you have got it all, why are you so unlike the New Testament Christians? Got it all! Got it at your conversion! Well, where is it, I ask?[37]

Once again, one could possibly describe Watson's view of Spirit-baptism as that of full initiation into Christ. Whether one should build so much on the two elements of meaning in the word baptize is to be questioned. An etymological study of New Testament words could readily supply a number of other facets of meaning which play no part in this theologizing. It is not even clear that these are the fundamental elements in the meaning of this concept. At the same time it is apparent that Watson's view is neither neo-Pentecostal nor sacramental. He advocates Spirit-baptism as an experience which has a legitimate role to play in Christianity and doesn't seem to make any distinction between the baptism and the fullness of the Spirit. If Watson had rather spoken of the experiential dimension of the Christian life instead of calling the aspect of overwhelming an experience over against initiation as a status he could have avoided the criticism of espousing an "event-centeredness."

Hart expresses the same problem that I have with Watson in a different way:

Watson, at least, recognizes that in the sense of Christian initiation every Christian is baptized in the Spirit; although he still holds to an additional experiential sense.

The fallacious implication of this approach is the initiatory connotation – as though one needed only one such empowering experience rather than a continuing experience of such "empowerings" over a lifetime.[38]

4.4 Michael Harper (Anglican)

Next we turn to, perhaps, the most renowned leader of the charismatic renewal in Britain, Michael Harper. As founder of Fountain Trust he played a major role in promoting the renewal. He has also published widely.[39]

When Grossmann describes the greater part of the charismatic movement in the United Kingdom as being neo-Pentecostal he mentions Harper as an exception who "disagrees with the Pentecostals on some points."[40] At the same time, Harper makes a clear distinction between regeneration and Spirit-baptism. Harper sees the failure to distinguish between these two concepts as the main hindrance to people claiming and receiving Spirit-baptism.[41]

In one of his earliest writings, *Power for the Body of Christ,* Harper comes very close to classical Pentecostalism.[42] He discusses the five cases from Acts and then rejects three views which he sees as not in accordance with the evidence from Acts: (1) that every Christian receives Spirit-baptism at conversion; (2) that it is given at water baptism or later at confirmation; and (3) that Spirit-baptism refers to sanctification. Over against this Harper sees Spirit-baptism as a normative, discernible empowerment promised to every believer.[43]

With respect to initial evidence Harper considers the evidence that in the early church glossolalia normally accompanied the receiving of the Spirit if not conclusive, then very compelling.[44] He even uses the shibboleth "conditions" when discussing the receiving of Spirit-baptism, but he actually only mentions repentance, belief, faith, and prayer.[45]

Walter Hollenweger would probably group Harper in terms of this present study with the neo-Pentecostals. He writes:

> The literature by the Fountain Trust (London) shows that these churches have taken over not only the experience, but also the theological interpretation placed upon it by Pentecostals, that is, the two-stage way of salvation and speaking in tongues as a necessary sign of the baptism of the Spirit.[46]

Hollenweger supports this statement with references to Harper and I. Cockburn.

In his book *As at the Beginning* (1965) Harper points out that the receiving or baptism of the Spirit (note again the *of*—a sign of the early stages of the charismatic movement and/or Pentecostal Holiness influences) was part of normal Christian initiation from the earliest days.[47] He supports this from the church fathers. When discussing the debt the church owes to Pentecostals he mentions "all their theological ignorance," but his warning is double-edged:

> It is true that it is dangerous to accept a doctrine solely on the grounds of experience. But doctrine without experience is dangerous also.[48]

An important feature of Harper's doctrine is his use of Luke 11:9–13.[49] Watson also uses this text in the same fashion. It refers to a father giving his children good gifts. Verse 13 reads:

> If you then, who are evil, know how to give good gifts to your children, how much more will the heavenly Father give the Holy Spirit to those who ask him!

Alfred Kuen takes Harper to task about his use of this text.[50] Kuen denies that this can refer to the experience of receiving the Spirit or Spirit-baptism. Why does Jesus exhort his disciples to pray or ask for the Spirit? Kuen points out that this took place before Pentecost. Today it would be applicable to nominal Christians who still need to receive the Holy Spirit in order to become regenerate. However, Kuen goes on to point to some additional exegetical insights from F. F. Bruce:

> F. F. Bruce draws our attention to the fact that the article is missing in front of the word "Holy Spirit." That brings us to the conclusion that the reference is not to the person of the Holy Spirit but to his gifts. This interpretation is all the more likely when we find Jesus saying, in the parallel passage in Matthew 7:11: "How much more will your Father who is in heaven give good things to those who ask him!" The good things are the gifts of the Holy Spirit, and the command to pray for them is just as valid today as it was on the day Jesus pronounced it (see 1 Cor 12:31; 14:1; Jas 1:5ff). Furthermore in one of our oldest manuscripts—in Papyrus 45—we find "a good gift" instead of "Holy Spirit" in Luke 11:13.[51]

Plainly Harper cannot legitimately build a call to pray for Spirit-baptism on this pericope. Moreover, it is often pointed out that the New Testament *never* exhorts us to be baptized with the Holy Spirit—only to be filled with the Spirit.

Later Harper develops his categorizing of views on Spirit-baptism. In Britain the book is called *This Is the Day. A Fresh Look at Christian Unity;* whereas the American edition has the more expressive title, *Three Sisters. A Provocative Look at Evangelicals, Charismatics, and Catholic Charismatics and Their Relationship to One Another.*[52] Under the rubric "Christian Initiation" Harper discusses four approaches to Spirit-baptism. These views will help us to clarify his own position.[53] The first approach contends that Spirit-baptism is the same as the sacrament of water baptism or the experience of regeneration. Under this heading Harper groups people as widely divergent as John Stott, Simon Tugwell, and James Dunn.

Secondly, some accept the experience of Spirit-baptism but reject the terminology. Harper mentions Watson as a representative here, but in his book Watson does not state this explicitly. Watson does, nevertheless, seem to prefer the terminology of infilling. Cardinal Suenens and Michael Green are cited as other examples.

Harper views the third position as representing the majority of charismatics. I would seriously question this—given the rapid and widespread growth of the sacramental interpretation. This view accepts both the experience and the terminology of "baptism in the Holy Spirit."

The fourth position, Pentecostalism, sees Spirit-baptism as quite distinct from baptism in water and regeneration. This position insists that glossolalia is initial evidence of Spirit-baptism. Harper points out that Dennis Bennett also adopts this position—an inaccurate assessment, since Bennett does have some reservations about Pentecostalism and is more accurately termed neo-Pentecostal in his theology.

More attention needs to be given to Harper's own position. He states that accepting both the experience and the terminology of Spirit-baptism sympathizes with the classical Pentecostal view of initial evidence and a theology of subsequence, but it also differs somewhat:

> Its teaching is much more of a twin-aspect initiation, rather than a two-stage blessing. It is incorporated into the older structure of sacramental teaching. It sees baptism in the Spirit as part of Christian initiation rather than something completely separate from it. Some would reject altogether the idea that speaking in tongues is the only or necessary evidence of Spirit-baptism, though it (*sic*) would accept that it often is. Most of the Roman Catholic charismatics would adopt this position. This is roughly the view of Thomas A. Smail in Chapter 10 of his book *Reflected Glory.*[54]

Obviously Harper is working along lines that do not fit the categorizing of this study. The basic dichotomy between a neo-Pentecostal and a sacramental approach escapes him. This makes his views difficult to classify. He wishes, like Hocken, to keep the best of both worlds—Pentecostalism and historic Christianity, for which he need not be faulted.

Nevertheless, it is not possible to combine eclectically diametrically opposed elements. We have already noted that Harper sees initial evidence as "very compelling" and that he speaks of "conditions"—one of them being praying or asking on the basis of Luke 11:13. If these points are consistently and logically applied they lead to a two-stage pattern. It is impossible, logically, to have Christians whose Christianity is acknowledged but who have not undergone Christian initiation. If Harper claims that Spirit-baptism is the second part of a twin-aspect initiation he must conclude that those who have not experienced it (and this is certainly evidential for him even if tongues is not insisted on) are, at least in some sense, not fully initiated Christians. In evaluating this rather confused position one needs to keep in mind how pervasive the temptation is to generalize from personal experience. Very often the nature of a particular experience tends to cloud one's attempts to analyze the broader range of the experiential dimension of Christianity.

Harper also does not acknowledge a shift in his thinking. He states in a footnote in 1978 concerning his book *Power for the Body of Christ:*"Although this book was written in 1964 in the formative stage of the development of my thinking, it still substantially reflects my present view of this matter."[55] Some parallels exist between Harper and Christenson, but whereas Christenson would almost certainly acknowledge a development in his thought, Harper does not. Consequently Christenson could be discussed under the neo-Pentecostal and sacramental positions, while it seemed best to deal with Harper's views as a whole under the rubric of integrative views.

Furthermore, it needs to be stated that Harper is unquestionably wrong when he claims that most of the Roman Catholic charismatics would adopt the same position he does. He fails to notice how different their sacramental view is. Harper does not mention the concepts "the release of the Spirit" or "the manifestation of baptismal grace" in his summary of his position. There are Catholics who would support his view but they certainly do not represent the majority position.

There is some agreement between Smail and Harper. Especially in chapter 10 of Smail's *Reflected Glory,* where we find the same ambiguity regarding Spirit-baptism as part of Christian initiation (thus rejecting two classes of Christians), and yet also being seen as a particular experience which some Christians still need to seek. Nonetheless, Smail's rather unique view is set in a very distinct christological framework (which Harper nowhere reflects), and it is questionable whether there is much inner agreement. That both could support the *Joint Statement: Gospel and Spirit* rather tends to underscore the unresolved nature of some of the underlying theological tensions in that document of compromise.

The basic ambiguity in Harper's position can also be illustrated by the widely differing assessments that have been made of his position. Walter Hollenweger claims that the Fountain Trust position defended by Harper has taken over Pentecostal theology and has accepted the two-stage pattern of salvation and initial evidence. Lucida Schmieder comes to the very opposite conclusion:

> He (Harper) advocates the retaining of the Pentecostal designation "Spirit-baptism," but rejects the two-stage theory as well as the conception that speaking

in tongues is the only and essential sign for validly determining the reception of "Spirit-baptism."[56]

Harper defends his retention of the term "baptism in the Spirit" and attaches great importance to this. Thus he can annex the majority of Catholic charismatics so easily for his own position without realizing that many of them may be using Spirit-baptism terminology merely out of convenience or custom. The crucial point is surely the theological content given to the term, and that is where Harper and the sacramental interpretation part ways.

In his discussion of the expression Harper initially concedes that "The phrase 'to be baptized in the Spirit' is probably used exclusively in the New Testament to describe the event of Pentecost."[57] This view accords with much of contemporary New Testament scholarship—certainly within the Reformed tradition. He develops this line further historically by stating that the early Christians set a pattern for the usage of this phrase that was followed rather consistently till the advent of the Holiness movement in the nineteenth century.

Harper's subsequent remarks point in the direction of a different approach, although he does not follow it up in this context. He writes:

> The reality of Pentecostal experience has been part of the life of the Church. But for various reasons, which we can only guess, it was seldom, if ever, called by this name.[58]

This implicitly acknowledges "Pentecostal experience" as a dimension of Christian reality. Harper's point is that this reality can now be described with the term "baptism in the Spirit." He does not see much danger today of a gnostic approach with several stages of initiation into higher forms of spiritual life as would have been the case in the early church. The divisive influence of the charismatic movement in many congregations fails to validate this assessment. Remarkably, Harper himself wrote an article in *Logos* in 1972, "Are you a Gnostic?" in which he warns charismatics against elitism.[59]

In 1979 we find that rather than still fearing gnostic elitism Harper wishes to employ the term Spirit-baptism with a specific purpose and agenda in mind:

> In all this the popular use of the phrase "baptism in the Spirit" today has been instrumental in bringing many evangelicals out of their cozy and lackadaisical view of initiation, and sacramentalists from their quasi-magical approach to water baptism. We should be thankful for this and not be too hasty in throwing out the expression before it has completed its work.[60]

Harper also discusses the alternative "filled with the Holy Spirit." Since it is used in Acts 2:4 to describe what happened to the church on the day of Pentecost, it is a perfectly legitimate alternative to Spirit-baptism. However, Harper points out some snags! The expression is often used in a non-initiatory sense (e.g. Ephesians 5:18). He also considers it more subjective than being baptized in the Spirit. The most serious objection I find in the following observation:

Besides, being "filled with the Spirit" has strong ethical overtones to it, which creates problems in its use. It is much harder to say "I am a Spirit-filled believer" than to say "I am Spirit-baptized." Spirit-baptism does not partake of degrees, whereas the notion of being Spirit-filled does.[61]

I presume that it is in the interests of Christian humility that Harper says it is more difficult to claim to be Spirit-filled than Spirit-baptized because the latter does not have ethical overtones. This is a significant insight.

Why Harper introduces the issue of degree which seems to nullify the point of the argument is not clear to me. If one does not want to boast of Spirit experience it would be logical rather to opt for the term that does partake of degrees and not the one that can give the impression of having arrived spiritually.

In his book *Let My People Grow! Ministry and Leadership in the Church* (1977) Harper writes a chapter on the charismatic dimension of the church. Harper first points out that it was the sociologist, Max Weber, who "discovered" the word charisma in 1947, and that it was first internationally applied to President John Kennedy. In the fifties the word began to be used in the church outside of the technical theological sense to describe the "Pentecostal" renewal within the historic churches.[62] Harper goes on to describe the charismatic dimension in the ministry of Christ, the early church, and today. He presents the following definition in conclusion:

Perhaps the word charisma could be defined as, the sovereign gift of God the Spirit to a man or woman to be and to do what he has called them to be and to do in service to the Body of Christ and the world. It is the divine equipping of someone for a task of ministry in the Body of Christ.[63]

Harper sees this charismatic dimension as a crucial factor in the renewal of the ministry of the church today. Unfortunately, Harper does not indicate any relationship between this charismatic dimension and what he prefers to call "the baptism in the Spirit," although we saw how he aligned Spirit-baptism with "the reality of Pentecostal experience" in *Three Sisters*.[64] That very relationship could introduce clearer thinking in the confusion around Spirit-baptism. Harper refers in this same book to a statement of George Orwell from *1984*: "Double think means the power of holding two contradictory beliefs in one's mind simultaneously and accepting both of them."[65] This could be a timely (though unintentional) warning to most reinterpretative charismatic theology.

4.5 Michael Cassidy (Anglican)

South African Michael Cassidy stands in the same tradition of Evangelical Anglicanism. Cassidy's *Bursting the Wineskins* tries to unravel the problem of Spirit-baptism.[66] He clearly accepts the experience of Spirit-baptism but rejects the terminology, replacing it with being "filled with the Spirit." He sees the Cornelius story of Acts 10 as particularly relevant to present renewal. He classifies three views concerning the timing of Spirit-baptism—akin to Harper's analysis but with significant differences.[67] View one is that regeneration and Spirit-baptism synchronize and take place at conversion. Stott is quoted as an example. View two is the two-stage pattern of Pentecostalism and neo-Pentecostalism (as understood in this study) with an adaptable view on initial evidence, some insisting on glossolalia, others not.

View three accepts the renewal experience but refuses to call it Spirit-baptism. Like David Watson, Cassidy prefers the phrase being "filled with the Spirit." Both Cardinal Suenens and Michael Green are representatives of this view. Like Harper, Cassidy neglects to differentiate further. Under such a rubric as accepting the experience but rejecting the terminology, the sacramental view and a variety of "integrative" views could potentially be discussed.

Cassidy writes:

> Apart from anything else the idea and desirability of being filled with the Holy Spirit is shared by both so-called "camps" (cf. Views One and Two) and it is one both can embrace, even if the understanding relating to timing and mechanics may vary somewhat. The term therefore has the advantage of being widely serviceable and of not being divisive.[68]

Cassidy, who leans heavily on David Watson's insights, also considers it acceptable as an alternative to utilize

> the dual meaning of the Greek word *baptizō* as both being "initiated into something" (which would seemingly speak of a *status*) and of being "overwhelmed by something" (which speaks of an *experience*).[69]

Another insight of Watson that Cassidy finds helpful is the idea of New Testament initiation being a single work of God with many facets which together constitute a cluster of overlapping spiritual realities including inter alia repentance, justification, baptism in the Spirit, baptism in water, new life in the Spirit.[70] This idea also influenced the *Joint Statement*.

A few more aspects of Cassidy's concept are needed to complete the picture. Without discussing the issue in detail, Cassidy acknowledges the ethical overtones of being filled with the Spirit. Of the process of sanctification and the kingship of Christ in our lives he writes:

> In many ways this must of necessity be a lifetime matter, but sometimes God may make extremely dramatic breakthroughs when all at once we allow Him by our surrender to capture and occupy massive and hitherto unsurrendered tracts of our lives.[71]

Cassidy is very aware of the role of surrendering in the Christian life. He sees that varying degrees of understanding and of surrender lead to various degrees of spiritual control and spiritual power. In this context he refers to 1 Corinthians 2:14 and 3:1, but it would be wrong to associate this recognition of "carnal" and "spiritual" Christians with the old Pentecostal stage theory whereby the differences in level are externalized and focused on particular individual event-centered experiences.

Cassidy writes:

> What this says to me at any rate is that our fullness in the Holy Spirit is in proportion to the degree of our surrender. We are as full of the Holy Spirit as our surrender. We are as full of the Holy Spirit as our commitment permits. Disobedience therefore can both "quench the Spirit" (1 Thess 5:19) and "grieve" Him (Eph 4:30). This we do when we fail to allow Him to do in us that for which He has been given.[72]

Clearly Cassidy is bringing out the aspect of sanctification as an ongoing process which is part of the concept of "fullness" (which for Cassidy is interchangeable with being "baptized in the Spirit!").

Cassidy also introduces a new element possibly hinted at above by Harper. He states:

> In fact to the best of my knowledge no one in Scripture ever claims to be filled with the Spirit and on the whole I suspect that most truly Spirit-filled men are largely unaware of what to others is quite evident. This has made me wonder whether the question–"Are you filled with the Spirit?"–does not border on the illegitimate. The questioner ought to know. . . .Could it also be a corollary of this that if or when we claim to be filled with the Spirit we become just a little less filled at that moment?[73]

This reticence stemming from Christian humility places Spirit-baptism, now called the infilling of the Spirit, in a new framework. Of a particular experience one can say quite matter of factly whether one has had it or not, while the fullness of the Spirit with its ethical overtones introduces an entirely different angle. Apparently switching terminology in this case has also changed the content and mood of the discussion.

F. D. Bruner is known in charismatic circles for his strong critique of Pentecostalism, *A Theology of the Holy Spirit*. More recently he has co-authored *The Holy Spirit–Shy Member of the Trinity*.[74] In it he also addresses the issue of humility (or rather by implication the lack of it) which he finds among some charismatics.[75]

Cassidy purposely chooses for fullness because he believes it

> can fit either the once-for-all non-repeatable experience or the on-going experience of appropriation, rededication and, as it were, refilling–an understanding preferred by many, who have difficulties getting the New Testament data to support any rigid two-stage doctrine of Christian growth and experience.[76]

In the end, however, Cassidy reserves his use of Spirit-baptism for the non-repeatable initiatory Christian experience (e.g. Pentecost and Cornelius' household) and fullness of the other kind. The compromise of trying to accommodate the neo-Pentecostal view of Spirit-baptism (which is also non-repeatable in the sense of being foundational for the second stage), however, clouds the issue terminologically. Fullness is incapable of incorporating both views at the same time and has the added disadvantage of further complicating the issue with its ethical overtones. Cassidy's own preference is nonetheless lucid. He reserves Spirit-baptism for Christian initiation.[77]

4.6 Tormod Engelsviken (Lutheran)

One of the leading Lutheran charismatic theologians of Norway, Tormod Engelsviken, does not opt for the sacramental approach like his American colleague, Ted Jungkuntz, but instead espouses a very particular form of Spirit-baptism as "fullness" of the Spirit. He has written an extensive thesis on charismatic theology: "The Gift of the Spirit. An Analysis and Evaluation of the Charismatic Movement from a Lutheran Theological Perspective."[78] He analyzes five interpretations of the charismatic experience in his homeland: (1) the views of Pentecostal charismatics—especially Edvardsen; (2) Prof. Hallesby's preparation of a Lutheran charismatic theology; (3) the non-confessional Lutheran charismatics of the Agape Foundation (cf. H. J. Frøen who was discussed in chapter 2); (4) and (5)—two groups of Confessional Lutheran charismatics, i.e., students at the Free Faculty of Theology in Oslo and those responsible for the Holy Spirit Seminars—especially Søvik. Next he explores the doctrine of the Holy Spirit in the writings of the Old and New Testaments to come eventually to a biblical evaluation. He basically distinguishes between the Pentecostal type, (1) and (3) above, and Lutheran type (2, 4, and 5) of interpretations of the charismatic experience. He finds the Pentecostal type to contain elements distinctly contrary to the biblical evidence while the Lutheran interpretations are in accordance with the New Testament.[79]

In this context our interest is in the Lutheran interpretations because they represent Engelsviken's position in a general sense. A clear distinction is made between baptism in the Spirit and being filled with the Spirit. Some influence of the basic sacramental stance is illustrated in these words:

> The baptism of the Spirit is always thought to be integrally related to Christian initiation. It may be closely associated with baptismal regeneration (2 and 5), or with the initial, salvation-historical bestowal of the Spirit on the church once for all (Luke) and the individual's incorporation in the body of Christ, the reality of the Spirit, through baptism (Paul) (4). In this view all initiated, believing Christians are Spirit-baptized. Christians are not encouraged to seek the baptism of the Spirit.

> While the baptism of the Spirit represents the Spirit's indwelling in the Christian as a person, applying equally to all Christians, the fullness of the Spirit is seen under a double aspect: the fullness of the Spirit in terms of sanctification (2, 4, 5) and the fullness of the Spirit in terms of power (2, 5) or the Spirit's manifestation (4). The latter aspect of the fullness of the Spirit, which has as its aim missions and ministry, is identified with the Charismatic experience.[80]

This is a very significant statement of a theological position. It is puzzling that the inaccurate term "baptism of the Spirit" is still being used, since most charismatics see Spirit-baptism as a baptism by Jesus in or with the Spirit, whether they take it as referring to Christian initiation or to a second-stage experience. Nevertheless, there are more important perspectives than this minor aspect of terminology. The Norwegian Lutheran charismatics undoubtedly associate Spirit-baptism with Christian initiation. However, instead of speaking of the charismatic dimension or experience as a Spirit-baptism "experientially speaking" or as "the actualization or manifestation of baptismal grace" as in the sacramental position, they use quite a different term for it–the biblical concept of being filled with the Spirit (Ephesians 5:18). This is then understood in a twofold sense of *sanctification* and *endowment*. According to the theology of Søvik, who played a prominent role in the Holy Spirit Seminars in Norway, sanctification relates to the Holy Spirit as Person and aims at producing the fruit of the Spirit in the life of the believer, also called "Christ-qualities." Endowment, though, relates to the Spirit as power and is aimed at giving the charisms or charismatic gifts to the believer, also called "Christ-abilities."[81]

Not the sanctification but the endowment with power and charisms is seen as the charismatic experience, which can come as an instantaneous act or as a continuous process. This "reality" which neo-Pentecostals have consistently called "baptism in the Spirit"–a second-stage crisis experience, distinct from and subsequent to conversion–and which sacramental charismatics have called "the release of the Spirit"–an actualization of grace received in Christian initiation–is here called the second aspect (apart from sanctification) of the infilling with the Spirit. The most serious problem of this position lies in the relationship between sanctification and this charismatic element or dimension. Experience indicates that one can move powerfully in the charisms and yet have very limited growth in sanctification. Perhaps more important is the exegetical question, does the biblical metaphor of fullness/infilling really correlate with this twofold concept of holiness and giftedness for ministry?

Engelsviken points out that all three Lutheran interpretations that he is analyzing on the Norwegian charismatic scene hold that it is possible to be baptized with the Spirit (be a Christian) without being filled with the Spirit. Consequently Christians are never exhorted to be *baptized* with the Spirit, but they are encouraged to be *filled*, which implies a decision both to grow in fruitfulness and to seek the charismatic experience.[82] An almost unexpected but quite logical division of Christians into the "haves" and the "have-nots" inescapably results.[83]

This is a very sensitive point in charismatic dialogue, and not surprisingly Carter Lindberg, who states that Engelsviken's work only became available to him at a very late stage, nevertheless picked up this point.[84] Unquestionably Scripture itself makes distinctions among Christians–the issue has always been the nature and status of these distinctions.

Engelsviken has actually overstated his case since the twofold concept of infilling or fullness really does preclude two distinct classes of Christians based on the fact of their being filled or not. If sanctification is part of this fullness and not only endowment, and sanctification is a process in which every Christian is involved (premises which I expect Engelsviken would accept), there are actually no Christians who are not in the process of experiencing the fullness of the Spirit in some or other measure. One could form two classes if one were to group those who are only filled in the sense of sanctification over against those who are filled in the sense of being sanctified and endowed (which can occur as an event); but this really seems a very paltry criterion for forming two classes of Christians – especially given the gradual nature of most sanctification. (If one worked with the Holiness movement's concept of sanctification this may be more distinct, but then one could envisage Christians who are endowed but not yet sanctified. This is in fact the position of the Norwegian Frøen who was discussed under the neo-Pentecostals.)

Engelsviken himself states that the two aspects of the Spirit's work relating to the fullness of the Spirit may not be separated and are mutually dependent on one another.[85] This makes it virtually impossible to have two classes of Christians according to Engelsviken's own approach. All of this further underlines the precarious nature of Engelsviken's twofold concept of fullness. It may, in fact, have the unexpected and unacknowledged advantage of actually preventing a division into two classes of Christians; but is there any convincing exegetical argument for such a view of fullness?

Engelsviken's assessment of the charismatic renewal is positive but guarded:

> Provided a "two-stage-model" of the Christian life is avoided and it is recognized that all believing Christians have received the gift of the Spirit at their initiation into the Christian life, the emphasis of the Charismatic Movement on the openness, expectancy and prayer for the Spirit's continuous coming and manifestation throughout the Christian life should be a part of all genuine Christian spirituality.[86]

Engelsviken considers the Lutheran type interpretations of the charismatic experience as identified with the fullness of the Spirit as biblically valid. He points out that the initial gift of the Spirit (in Christian initiation or Spirit-baptism), which he sees as the "indicative," forms the basis for the exhortation to the continuous reception of the Spirit and the walk according to the Spirit (the "imperative" or the fullness of the Spirit).[87] There must be a balance between the initial and the subsequent comings of the Spirit. Engelsviken remarks:

> The history of dogma shows a difficulty with regard to this balance: either all the emphasis is placed on the initial coming of the Spirit, usually in connection with baptism [in water], or all the emphasis is placed on the subsequent coming(s) usually in connection with a spiritual experience.[88]

Engelsviken presents his own view of the work of the Spirit in the form of an *ordo salutis* chart. Under the rubric of "New Experiences of the Spirit" he gives his definitive view of the charismatic experience (which has been termed Spirit-baptism in this study for the sake of convenience, but is called the fullness of the Spirit by Engelsviken). He sums it up in these words:

The indwelling Spirit grants new experiences of the power of the Spirit in terms of sanctification aimed at producing the fruit of the Spirit and in terms of charismatic equipment aimed at ministry and mission. The Spirit's will is to produce the same fruit in all believers: love, peace, joy, etc., and to grant various gifts to the different members of the one body. Since the same Spirit produces fruit and grants gifts they cannot be separated, though distinguished. The ever new coming of the Spirit may be experienced as quiet, continuous growth in the Spirit or as instantaneous crisis-experiences. In either case it is an experience of being filled with the Spirit on the basis of the initial baptism of the Spirit. The Spirit is possessed by being repeatedly received.[89]

Engelsviken's idea of the "ever new coming of the Spirit" either as "quiet, continuous growth" or "instantaneous crisis-experiences" is rather similar to the position which will be defended in the last chapter, a difference is the coupling of this (and the twofold concept of sanctification and endowment) with the biblical metaphor of Spirit-fullness.

4.7 Charles Hummel (Episcopal)

Charles Hummel of Inter-Varsity Christian Fellowship has written a helpful overview on the charismatic movement: *Fire in the Fireplace: Contemporary Charismatic Renewal.*[90] Although he is not attempting to present his own inter-pretation of Spirit-baptism but rather to clarify the basic issues, it will be worthwhile to take note of some of his insights. He rejects the two-stage pat-tern of Pentecostalism and neo-Pentecostalism. His main contribution is to point out that Luke and Paul use the phrase "baptize in the Spirit" differently:

> According to Luke's teaching, the baptism in the Spirit for the disciples was an empowering for prophetic witness. According to Paul, the baptism in the Spirit for the Corinthians was their incorporation into the body of Christ. Luke's context is the unfolding of redemptive history and the mission of the church, while Paul's is the experience of individual believers when they become members of Christ's body. The distinction—the two meanings of baptize in the Spirit—helps clarify the significance of Pentecost for the church today.[91]

This dual meaning of Spirit-baptism is reminiscent of Watson's dual mean-ing of baptize, namely *initiation* and *overwhelming*. In terms of Engelsviken's view, the incorporation concept of Paul would correlate with his view of Spirit-baptism as initiation, while Luke's empowering concept would correspond with the endowment aspect of Spirit-fullness. Hummel acknowledges the legitimacy of the experiences of Christians in the charismatic renewal. The experience may be better than the doctrinal explanation given to it, the medi-cine may be powerful even though the label on the bottle is incorrect.[92] He continues with respect to the charismatic renewal:

> What, then, is the biblical description for this evident, powerful working of the Holy Spirit? For many this life-changing experience is their conversion, the begin-ning of personal faith in Jesus Christ. For others it is a rededication or a full commitment to his lordship. For still others it is a new openness to the Spirit's manifestations of power in worship, witness and service. This wide range of experi-

ences also occurs in evangelistic revivals under the label of "decision for Christ." A theology of Christian growth must have room for crises and dramatic workings of the Spirit as well as for the slower maturing of his fruit called sanctification.[93]

Hummel argues that the New Testament does not teach *the* baptism in the Spirit. Paul teaches *a* Spirit-baptism involving Christian initiation. Hummel continues:

Luke teaches a baptism in the Spirit which is a pouring out and a filling of the Spirit to endue with power for witness and service. From his perspective it is neither the first nor the second stage of salvation in the life of the individual. Rather it is a repeated filling with the Spirit which manifests his presence as a sign of the New Age. Paul also teaches a repeated filling with the Spirit, although his characteristic language is "charism or manifestation of the Spirit."[94]

For Hummel then there are at least two different Spirit-baptisms—one for Christian initiation or incorporation into the body of Christ, another for empowering for service, the latter also a "filling." Apart from that there is also a Pauline filling which seems to correlate with charisms. It is not clear to what extent these two concepts of filling can be seen as basically the same.

In conclusion, another quotation from Hummel in which he makes the significant observation that Spirit-baptism is not of cardinal importance to the charismatic renewal:

The heart of the charismatic renewal is not the question of speaking in tongues or even baptism in the Spirit (about which there is marked difference of opinion even within the renewal). Rather it is the commitment to the full range of charisms as manifestations of the Holy Spirit to meet the needs of the Christian community. The charismatic renewal affirms the New Testament teaching that all of these spiritual gifts are essential to the life and mission of the church. It expects these charisms and witnesses to their presence today.[95]

In a study which is focused on Spirit-baptism it is refreshing to hear that this is not (as is usually claimed) the heart of the charismatic renewal. To seek this "heart" rather in a commitment to the full range of charisms is an insight which has important ecumenical ramifications. The relationship (if any) between Spirit-baptism and the charisms is not addressed by Hummel and must also be referred to the last chapter. Although Hummel is Episcopal, he represents a broad evangelical perspective.

4.8 Culpepper, Hart, Bridge and Phypers (Baptist)

Next, we turn to some Baptists. Most of the theologians being discussed in this study themselves espouse a charismatic perspective and identify with the movement to some degree, Kilian McDonnell as sympathetic observer being a notable exception. His inclusion was made necessary by the important role that he played in Catholic renewal thought. Culpepper also does not wish to be seen as a charismatic, but he has written a very fair assessment of the renewal to which brief attention will now be given.[96]

As can be expected of a Southern Baptist, Culpepper finds fault with the theology of subsequence. He sees Spirit-baptism as an initiatory experience for *all* Christians, not a second-stage experience for *some* Christians.[97] To become a Christian is to receive Spirit-baptism:

> It is significant that the New Testament never enjoins Christians to be baptized in the Spirit. The reason seems to be that the fundamental presupposition is that they have already been so baptized.[98]

Culpepper makes a sharp distinction between Spirit-baptism and being filled by the Spirit. He illustrates his view by quoting from John Stott:

> As an initiatory event the baptism [in the Spirit] is not repeatable and cannot be lost, but the filling can be repeated and in any case needs to be maintained. If it is not maintained, it is lost. If it is lost, it can be recovered. The Holy Spirit is grieved by sin (Eph 4:30) and ceases to fill the sinner. Repentance is then the only road to recovery.[99]

Culpepper also points out that the distinction between carnal and spiritual Christians is not between those who have received Spirit-baptism and those who have not, but between Christians filled by the Spirit and those dominated by the flesh.[100]

Culpepper's view of the Pentecostal experience comes out in his critique of charismatics:

> The Pentecostal experience is expressed in terms of a defective theology. At this point, generally speaking, Catholic charismatics, apart from their strong insistence that the Holy Spirit is mediated through what they call the sacraments of initiation (baptism and confirmation), are theologically more correct than their Protestant counterparts. They usually see more clearly than Protestant charismatics that what is involved in the Pentecostal experience is a deeper appropriation of that which is given through the "in Christ" relationship which begins when one becomes a Christian.[101]

Culpepper seemingly accepts the legitimacy of an experience (not called Spirit-baptism) whereby the relationship with Christ that begins in Christian initiation is more deeply appropriated. This is not the sacramental position of the manifestation of sacramental grace but an evangelical counterpart.

Culpepper graciously acknowledges that many charismatics have had valid experiences that have

> revitalized their relationship to God in Christ, deepened their devotional lives, opened their hearts to the teachings of Scripture. . .given them. . .a new boldness in witness.[102]

His objection is that charismatics have no theological basis to assume that everyone must have the same kind of experience which they have had. He regards this as putting the Holy Spirit in a box and programming his operation.[103] To those whose spiritual lives have grown dry and stale one need not advocate a standard type of experience but exhort them in words like these:

> There are riches in Christ that you haven't begun to appropriate. It is time for you to start possessing your possessions. Reach down, brother or sister, and draw fresh water from the well of salvation. Open your heart to the movement of Christ's Spirit that rivers of living water may ever flow through you.[104]

Culpepper's perspective is ecumenically important. He apparently understands the charismatic teaching better than most and feels that what is legitimate and valuable in it can be accommodated within evangelical Christianity.

Oral Roberts University faculty member Larry Hart's dissertation, "A Critique of American Pentecostal Theology," deals with the charismatic movement.[105] He gives a helpful assessment of the dialogue with Pentecostalism.

> There is no Biblical basis at all for a Spirit-baptism subsequent to conversion that places one on a higher plane than can be reached by those only having been converted, so that one may regard himself as "Spirit-baptized" or "Spirit-filled" and possessing an increment of spiritual power not yet bestowed upon the merely once-initiated non-Pentecostal.
>
> Additionally, there is no Scriptural evidence for an experience subsequent to Christian initiation by which—and only by which—one may enter into spiritual gifts. These are the fallacies of Classical Pentecostal theology primarily, but Pentecostal and Catholic neo-Pentecostal theology has not escaped being tainted by these theological aberrations.[106]

After these and other equally devastating conclusions Hart affirms that the vital spirituality of the Pentecostal movement is authentic. The concept and experience of being "filled with the Spirit" is one of the most useful. For Hart

> fruitful and effective life in the Spirit becomes available to every believer willing to appropriate what he already possesses, and false ideas about "arrival points" and a specially blessed pneumatic group are avoided—there is the further need, of course, to grasp the charismatic nature of the Church and to raise expectations as to how the Spirit can manifest Himself, and the Church clearly owes a debt to Pentecostalism in this respect.[107]

Of particular importance is Hart's observation that Pentecostals (and probably also neo-Pentecostals) contend that spiritual gifts or charisms appear *only* after a Spirit-baptism subsequent to conversion. This issue needs to be dealt with further—especially if Hummel's assertion that the heart of the charismatic renewal is a commitment to the full range of charisms is correct. Hart, in fact, adds to the list of charisms:

> Even doing theology can be a charism, if the lists of spiritual gifts found in the New Testament are only representative (and there is no indication that they are intended to be exhaustive).[108]

It is also salient that Hart, too, refers to the charismatic nature of the church and the task of raising expectations of the manifestations of the Spirit.

Before leaving the Baptists, one more book needs to be examined: *Spiritual Gifts and the Church* by Donald Bridge and David Phypers.[109] Their position resembles Culpepper's and Hart's. They analyze "the two most commonly-held views"[110] on Spirit-baptism: the two-stage pattern and the standard evangelical approach:

> If this second line of approach is followed [the evangelical one], then "baptism with the Holy Spirit" will be regarded as one New Testament description among many of the change which God works in the life of an individual when he or she becomes a true Christian and is thus incorporated into the body of Christ. This change produces holiness of character and power for service. It comes, in normal circumstances, not through prayer and the laying on of hands, but through repentance toward God and faith in our Lord Jesus Christ.[111]

Bridge and Phypers (who wrote their whole book together) also highlight the Pentecostal/neo-Pentecostal concept that the gifts or charisms are received through Spirit-baptism:

> Those so baptized demonstrate their baptism by speaking with tongues. Speaking with tongues is the gateway into the exercise of all the other gifts. If Christians would exercise gifts they must first seek and receive the baptism.[112]

This facet of the neo-Pentecostal approach is very important. Oddly, it is very seldom mentioned – functioning more as an axiom that is implied rather than expressed. Bridge and Phypers point out that when gifts in general and tongues in particular are linked inseparably to Spirit-baptism this leads to a false yardstick of spirituality, namely:

> The presence or absence of gifts (generally the more dramatic ones are in mind)....Those who exercise such gifts are those who are spiritual, while those without such gifts are unspiritual....Yet this is most dangerous teaching. Gifts are not self-authenticating. The mere presence of something seemingly supernatural or dramatic proves nothing, otherwise there would be no need to test apparent gifts by the Word of God and the exercise of love (1 Cor 13).[113]

Over against this attitude the authors of *Spiritual Gifts and the Church* bring in contemporary and historical witnesses that have exercised a variety of the charismata without having a theology of a post-conversion Spirit-baptism. They refer to the Montanists, Saxon missionaries, Martin Luther, and the Anabaptists. A modern example is the Evangelical Lutheran Sisters of Mary in Darmstadt, Germany.[114] This same point has been made by Peter Wagner of the Church Growth school at Fuller Seminary. He speaks of a Third Wave of the Spirit (Pentecostalism and the charismatic movement being the first two waves of this century) in which traditionally evangelical churches are experiencing especially the charisms of healing.

Wagner, a Congregational theologian and former missionary from a Scofield Bible dispensational background, first became interested in Pentecostalism from the perspective of church growth. He found that worldwide there is a close relationship between the growth of churches and the healing ministry of the church – especially in new areas where the gospel has just begun to penetrate. Without the supernatural power of the Spirit churches just don't make much headway in regions where the devil has had full sway for centuries.

Wagner does not limit this to the missionary context either. He explains this with his concept third wave:

> I see the third wave of the eighties as an opening of the straight-line evangelicals and other Christians to the supernatural work of the Holy Spirit that the Pentecostals and charismatics have experienced, but without becoming either charismatic or Pentecostal. I think we are in a new wave of something that now has lasted almost through our whole century.[115]

This opening up the non-Pentecostal and non-charismatic Christians leads to the same results but not the same theology. Wagner writes:

> But what I see is a lowering of traditional barriers between those of us who are evangelicals, and charismatics and Pentecostals, so that we can have the same results, the same work of the Holy Spirit in both groups, even though we tend to explain what is happening in a slightly different way.

He goes on to explain that he prefers to think of Spirit-baptism as occurring at conversion and that this is followed by subsequent intermittent fillings. At such occasions

> the power is activated in the life of a Christian who in the past hasn't been an open channel for that power and God begins doing a new thing in his or her life. My charismatic friends say that is the baptism of the Holy Spirit. I say, great; whatever you call it, I believe in it.[116]

The importance of Wagner's observations is that charismata, healing, and glossolalia appear in groups that do not accept Pentecostal theology. Instead, they see Spirit-baptism as connected with conversion; however, they do recognize multiple "fillings" or experiences of the Spirit as intermittent spiritual breakthroughs. The presence of charisms is not directly connected to a second-stage Spirit-baptism or to these intermittent breakthroughs.

Bridge and Phypers, like Hummel, also accept the legitimacy of the experiences that have been interpreted by those affected as the second stage of a theology of subsequence. They reinterpret these experiences as falling into four categories: (1) They were actually conversion experiences or (2) experiences that ended a period of coldness and backsliding. (3) They could also refer to a time when rapid progress was made in the Christian life because few Christians just progress steadily in Christian growth throughout their lives. (4) They could refer to a point in one's spiritual life when one was empowered in a specific way for some particular kind of service. [117]

With respect to the last category Bridge and Phypers also caution that one should not raise expectations of Christians to such a degree that everyone thinks he can become a Whitefield, Moody, or Graham just by renewing vows of dedication:

> . . . such startling results follow only in a tiny number of cases. If all are encouraged to expect such fruitfulness as a result of their experience many are likely to be discouraged and disillusioned when the promised fruit does not materialize, and some may give up the Christian life altogether.[118]

Here a careful balance must be kept–people should be freely inspired by what God has done in other peoples' lives without evoking a rigid pattern of cause and effect that God will do exactly the same if one prays, repents, etc., in the same manner as the "heroic" example quoted. An overly "realistic" approach unfortunately often results in inhibiting a much needed rise in expectation.

The bottom line seems to be that Christians of all traditions must resist the temptation to force the experiences of others into a pattern based on their own experience, especially when it seems to be contrary to biblical guidelines. The conclusion of Bridge and Phypers again has relevancy for our concluding chapter.

> It is our contention that what many Christians may call a "baptism of the Spirit" is in fact an experience which comes into one of these categories which we have listed. There can be no scriptural objection to any of these, for none of them implies that regeneration is an incomplete work of the Holy Spirit, and none of them divides Christians into two distinct categories in an unscriptural manner. Some writers do indeed recognize that in what many Christians call a baptism of the Spirit experience they are simply appropriating more of what potentially become theirs at their conversion and the difference between their position and that taken by this book is very small indeed.[119]

In 1982 Bridge and Phypers again jointly published a book on the charismatic renewal. *More Than Tongues Can Tell. Reflections on Charismatic Renewal*[120] is the personal story of how they, as a result of experiencing renewal, moved from being deeply hesitant about Pentecostalism to reassessing their position, which was reflected in a more objective way in *Spiritual Gifts and the Church*.

4.9 Robert Tuttle, Jr. (Methodist)

For some reason Methodists have not featured prominently in formulating interpretations of Spirit-baptism from a charismatic perspective. (Only Merlin Carothers was briefly referred to under neo-Pentecostalism.) This does not mean that the renewal movement has not made a sizable impact on Methodism. Possibly this is explained by the Methodist tradition's rather unique relationship to Pentecostalism. Out of it developed the Wesleyan-Holiness movement which was, as it were, a midwife at the birth of Pentecostalism. This connection has, however, been overstated by Vinson Synan. Non-Wesleyan revivalist and Keswick-Holiness influences were certainly also significant from the very beginning of Pentecostalism. Nevertheless it is very widely acknowledged that the basic two-stage pattern of Pentecostalism has historical roots traceable to Methodism. Even if this were proved to be somewhat inaccurate on an academic level, the fact remains that this theory has had a not insignificant impact on Methodist attitudes towards the renewal. Whereas Methodist charismatics cultivate the connection, for example, by calling their charismatic conferences "Aldersgate" gatherings–a reference to the place where John Wesley's heart was "strangely warmed"–other Methodists felt somewhat embarrassed and inhibited by the "reproach" that Pentecostalism developed out of a background related to their tradition.

Robert G. Tuttle, Jr., has written on the charismatic renewal and Spirit-baptism from a United Methodist perspective. Unfortunately he has not formulated an extensive exposition on Spirit-baptism, and what follows has been gleaned from short references in three sources.[121] Tuttle contends that although Pentecostalism has its own well-defined theological system, the charismatic renewal does not have a theology of its own.

Charismatics interpret their gifts and experiences in the light of their respective denominational theologies. An unfortunate exception to this are some charismatics who apparently have no theology at all, but seem to have substituted experience for doctrine. Tuttle acknowledges that charismatics do stress the work of the Spirit beyond conversion but they do not insist that Spirit-baptism must be distinct from and follow conversion.[122] Tuttle's expressed desire is found in these words:

> The task of the Charismatic Renewal, if it is to remain a movement of the Spirit, is to retain its traditional church base. It cannot become just another denomination.[123]

When commenting on the view of John Fletcher (a contemporary of John Wesley) Tuttle states that he partly disagrees with Fletcher's view that the Holy Spirit baptizes the faithful follower with power subsequent to conversion: "It is my conviction that the Holy Spirit baptizes us with power usually at the moment of conversion."[124] Tuttle also breaks with the neo-Pentecostal view on tongues. He not only does not see glossolalia as the sign of Spirit-baptism, he even asserts that it is not universally available to Christians.[125] Those more flexible neo-Pentecostals who make no necessary connection between tongues and Spirit-baptism almost always believe that as a devotional prayer language tongues is available to all believers.

Tuttle's own perception of Spirit-baptism is decidedly Methodist. In the document *Guidelines,* approved by the 1976 General Conference of the United Methodist Church, this large body (which acknowledges that it is theologically pluralistic) encourages its members to seek the gifts of the Spirit which enrich life and ministry; it accepts that the charismatic renewal, like other new movements in church history, has a valid contribution to make to the ecumenical church.[126] In an analysis "commended to the church for study" Tuttle attempts to work out a Wesleyan framework for charismatic gifts and experiences. He maintains that although charismatics are open to all spiritual gifts and experiences subsequent to conversion, they should not try to isolate those gifts and experiences as marks of superior spirituality. Tuttle quotes the renowned Methodist scholar, Albert Outler, as having stated that the charismatic movement might be the catalyst for a third great awakening (after the first and second great awakenings of the eighteenth and nineteenth centuries).[127]

Tuttle interprets Spirit-baptism in the light of Wesley's theology of grace. After the gentle wooing of the Spirit from the moment of conception in *pre-*

venient grace, the Spirit prompts one's freedom to say yes to God. Then the Spirit imputes to the believer the righteousness that was in Christ—*justifying grace.* Tuttle continues:

> For Wesley this begins a *lifelong movement* from imputed to imparted righteousness in which the Holy Spirit moves the believer from the righteousness of Christ attributed through faith to the righteousness of Christ realized within the individual—*sanctifying grace.* [128]

Within this realm of sanctifying grace what this study has called Spirit-baptism finds its place. Tuttle underscores the gradual nature of this work of grace, admitting that Wesley was "a bit unguarded at times when referring to sanctification as an instantaneous experience subsequent to justification."[129] Tuttle surmises:

> If he [Wesley] were writing today he would probably place even more emphasis on sanctification as a gradual work of grace characterized by many experiences that keep conversion contemporary.[130]

Tuttle states that grace is continual, even though it may be perceived episodically.

> The Spirit-filled life is, rather, a sustained line of gifts, experiences, and divine support, beginning with conversion, constantly moving us toward that goal. Many charismatics have come to believe that being filled with the Holy Spirit is an experience which begins with justification and continues as a lifelong motivating experience for the believer. For the charismatic, Spirit-baptism is not one but many gifts, not two but many experiences, intended to sustain one day after day.[131]

Apparently Tuttle sometimes uses *filled with the Spirit* and *baptized with the Spirit* interchangeably. In a technical sense he would probably prefer Spirit-baptism for Christian initiation or conversion and then see the rest of Christian life as a gradual, continual work of God's sanctifying grace and infilling which is characterized by a charismatic element—expressed in a sustained line of many gifts (charisms) and experiences. All in all this Methodist perspective blends easily into the integrative views of this chapter being clearly non-Pentecostal and non-sacramental in nature.

4.10 Arnold Bittlinger (United: Lutheran and Reformed)

Arnold Bittlinger is one of the most important thinkers in the charismatic renewal. He served in Geneva as the representative of the charismatic renewal at the World Council of Churches and has been very influential in Europe. That European (especially German-speaking European) charismatics did not merely take over the neo-Pentecostal framework for the charismatic renewal which they "received" from America is largely due to Bittlinger. In 1978 he completed a dissertation on the Roman Catholic-Pentecostal dialogue, *Papst und Pfingstler* [The Pope and the Pentecostals];[132] he has also done much exegetical study on charisms and ministries in the New Testament. He has published on the liturgy of the early church and edited *The Church Is Charismatic* for the WCC and its consultations on the Pentecostal renewal.[133]

To describe the history of Bittlinger's trip to America where he "discovered" the manifestation of New Testament charisms in mainline churches and how this influenced his ministry in Germany does not belong to the aim of this study. This interesting development has been related well elsewhere.[134] What is of relevance is that Bittlinger realized that the meaning of these charisms had to be appropriated differently in the German situation. From the very beginning the renewal in Germany was propagated within the heart of the churches—not in small groups on the fringes of the mainstream of Christianity. Bittlinger also managed to involve a series of prominent theologians, inter alia, Professors Bohren, Ewald, Hollenweger, Locher, Meyendorff, and Rohrbach, as well as church leaders such as D. M. Niemöller.[135] He kept a strong ecumenical representation at his consultations involving Lutherans, Catholics, Reformed, Baptists, Anglicans, and Eastern Orthodox. The work of New Testament scholars such as E. Käsemann and E. Schweizer was also studied. Back in 1949 Käsemann had already written:

> But the problem which should concern us most closely is this: why even Protestantism itself, as far as I can see, has never made a serious attempt to create a church order which reflected the Pauline doctrine of charisma, but has left this to the sects.[136]

A theological-pastoral workshop put together a list of *Guidelines* for the charismatic renewal. Aspects that were emphasized are the following: All regenerate Christians are charismatic because the Spirit dwells in them and wishes to become manifest in them; the charisms are focused on the edification and building up of the congregation; whoever operates in a gift does so as a member of the body of Christ; there is no gradation in the manifestation of charisms. The main theological issue was seen as the following:

> How can the institutional churches, the established groups and traditional movements obtain a charismatic structure? How can they become dynamic and mobile, charismatically "transparent" (or permeable), i.e. become permeated by the will and activity *of God* so that the Lordship of Christ can make visible progress in space and time? How can the Church become a credible and authentic testimony to her Lord?[137]

Next, attention must be given to the concept of Spirit-baptism. The most remarkable fact is that the word, and to some extent the concept, *Spirit-baptism* was purposefully avoided. The German-speaking renewal chose consciously not to be a continuation of the mood and style of charismatic renewal in the English-speaking world. Not only was the Pentecostal heritage rejected, but also the whole framework and theology of Anglo-American neo-Pentecostalism.

In Bittlinger's own theologizing on Spirit-baptism there seems to have been a slight development. In his early article, published together with Kilian

McDonnell's article on the same topic, namely, "The Baptism in the Holy Spirit as an Ecumenical Problem," Bittlinger gives classic expression to the sacramental position. He states that Christian baptism is always a baptism with water and with Spirit.[138] There are three main aspects to Christian initiation connected with and symbolized by baptism, namely *conversion,* the *charismatic aspect* (which involves the operating of the Spirit in the Christian's life through the exercise of charismata), and thirdly, the *union aspect:* identification with the dying and rising Christ in love.[139] Bittlinger points out that the efficacy of baptism is not tied to the moment of time at which it was administered. What God has given in baptism must be *actualized* in the life of the individual.[140] This is an ongoing process including the element of backsliding.

> The normal Christian life is a life between conversion actualized and conversion unactualized, between charismata actualized and charismata unactualized, between union with Christ actualized and union with Christ unactualized.[141]

Bittlinger rejects Spirit-baptism as a second, additional stage for Christians:

> Actualizing the charismatic aspect of baptism is not an act of receiving, but of releasing the Spirit who is already dwelling in the Christian.[142]

If the term Spirit-baptism is to be reserved for Christian initiation then that element of Christian initiation which involves the exercise of charisms must be expressed in a different way. Bittlinger speaks of "a charismatic experience":

> the essence of a charismatic experience is the experience of encountering Jesus Christ as the Head of His Body, which is the Church, who gave gifts and ministries to men.[143]

To some extent we have the sacramental view united with the concept of charismatic experience as part of complete initiation. Like Smail, Bittlinger not only sees this charismatic aspect as part of Christian initiation, but he also gives it a distinctly experiential setting. Lindberg, discussing Bittlinger (just after Jungkuntz), simply states, "Bittlinger. . .also relates baptism in the Spirit to sacramental baptism."[144]

The point of the charismatic dimension of Christian initiation or even baptism should not be pressed since Bittlinger moves with apparent ease between describing *conversion, charisms,* and *union* as elements of Christian initiation[145] and then as elements of Christian life.[146] This ambiguity does open one up to the reproach that people who have not fully actualized these three elements are incomplete Christians.

One thing is clear—Bittlinger does not tie the charismatic experience to glossolalia. Bittlinger has a rather "down-to-earth" interpretation of speaking in tongues. He emphasizes that it is completely "normal," not compulsively ecstatic or mystical.

He sees its significance as lying especially in private devotions and as a phenomenon through which people often gain access to the charismatic dimension. This leads him to keep the following two statements in balance, accepting the truth of both: "The charismatic movement is not a Tongues movement"; and: "Without tongues (glossolalia) there would be no charismatic renewal."[147]

Bittlinger gives a working definition of a charism:

> A charism is a gratuitous manifestation of the Holy Spirit, working in and through, but going beyond, the believer's natural ability for the common good of the people of God.[148]

Later he develops this within the framework of the specific ideal of charismatic congregational renewal. In a paper[149] for the WCC sub-unit on renewal and congregational life, which met at Stony Point, New York, in 1978, Bittlinger distinguishes charismatic congregational renewal from neo-Pentecostalism by underscoring that it interprets its spiritual awakening within denominational theological traditions and does not seek to establish prayer groups independent of local congregations. He points out the variety of charisms. Pietistically inclined charismatics look for charisms chiefly in prayer circles, the liturgically interested find them in liturgical worship, the psychologically concerned charismatics seek charisms in therapeutic teams, while the socially committed and politically engaged focus on charisms of action groups. Like Hart, Bittlinger also incorporates the charismatic theologian who hopes for deeper insights into theology. The same is applicable to parents, teachers, doctors, etc.[150]

This broad approach leads one to ask, What then is a charism? Bittlinger proceeds to give a more comprehensive description:

> Purely as a phenomenon, nothing whatever is in itself "charismatic" or "spiritual." All phenomena are the realization of possibilities within this world. But everything, however ordinary or extraordinary, can be made use of by God for the neighbor's or the world's salvation, and thereby becomes a charism (there is no Christian who always acts charismatically, but there is also no Christian who never acts charismatically).[151]

Within this broadening of perspectives we find Bittlinger's concept of "Spirit-baptism" (rather: the charismatic dimension) moving beyond the Spirit-baptism interpretation of actualization of baptismal grace. The concept of charismatic renewal is replaced by congregational or parish renewal. The renewal is seen as a spiritual awakening or renewal without any definitive type of experience as prerequisite. This is the result of taking even more seriously the initial guideline that every Christian has the Holy Spirit indwelling him or her and manifests the charisms of the Spirit to some or other degree. What is needed then is a spiritual awakening and congregational renewal so that we may possess the possessions we have in Christ. It is difficult to pinpoint this development in Bittlinger, but it is significant and was the deciding factor for discussing him in this chapter rather than the previous one.

In March 1976, the coordinating committee for Charismatic Congregational Renewal in the Evangelical (Protestant) Church of Germany meeting at Würzburg drew up a list of *Theological Guidelines*.[152] This list is a development of the first set of Guidelines mentioned above. Although it is a team document, it is reasonable to assume that Bittlinger, who undoubtedly at the time was the most prominent Protestant leader in the renewal in Germany, played an important role in formulating these points. At any rate it is safe to assume that they reflect his position. A few quotations will suffice to illustrate the theology behind this document:

> Charismatic parish renewal is a movement of spiritual revival within the church. (4) Every Christian who has been reborn through faith and baptism exists within this charismatic reality. The Holy Spirit dwells in him and wishes to become visible through him for the edification of the parish and for service in the world.
> (8) All charisms are signs of the renewal of creation–not a supernatural occurrence. (12) Charismatic experiences are given where people admit their helplessness and emptiness before God and consequently expect everything from God and from his concrete direction and gifts. This admission above can operate in theology and deaconate, in parish life and ecumenism as the precondition for a spiritual awakening and for the active involvement of the Holy Spirit (2 Cor 12:9f.)

> A people's or established national church (Volkskirche), which is characterized by the passivity and indifference of the majority of its members, is challenged by the charismatic renewal. Nevertheless charismatic parish renewal is part of the mainstream of the church and stands in continuity with its confessional tradition. It seeks to be involved in dialogue with all streams in theology which contribute to the renewal of the church. Its aim is a charismatically renewed church which will make a separate charismatic movement superfluous.[153]

Even though not specifically stated, the acceptance of these *Theological Guidelines* implicitly replaces the concept of Spirit-baptism with the concept "Geisterneuerung" or "renewal in the Spirit." (The English translation "spiritual renewal" tends to have other connotations. "Renewal of the Spirit" is sometimes used for Geisterneuerung but is also, in my opinion, ambiguous.)

Bittlinger's view is actually quite different from anything we have come across yet, although it does have some similarities with the approach of charismatics like Bridge and Phypers. Bittlinger adopts a cautious approach to exercising the charismatic dimension in church life. One should be considerate towards those church members who still find the charisms of 1 Corinthians 14:26ff. strange. Consequently Bittlinger advocates their being exercised not in the main services but in separate smaller services which could be held from time to time in local parishes. In order to prevent these meetings from becoming exclusive they should remain fundamentally open to all church members.[154] In all likelihood this should be seen as a temporary measure.

Why is the German approach so different? This question becomes more pressing when one notes that the German Catholic charismatic renewal has taken the same line. This question has been partially answered above with references to an awareness of the different European context. To this one could add a concerted effort to resist American influence, which is generally thought of in pejorative terms in many European circles–especially on the continent. Schmieder seems to discern theological and philosophical factors:

Above all the influence of the historical-critical method of exegesis is clearly discernible in German speaking countries. In like manner we also have, since Kant, the prevailing critical philosophy with the result that the renewal in German speaking countries takes place within a different intellectual and religious framework.[155]

A random example of such acceptance of more recent biblical scholarship that would certainly surprise many American charismatics (especially neo-Pentecostals) is Bittlinger's remark in his article on Christian initiation:

It is not necessary to argue with people who say that certain words in the Bible were not spoken by the historic Christ, but by the early Church.[156]

From the context it is clear that "not necessary to argue with" means, in fact, "One can agree with."

Yet another factor has determined the German context historically since early in this century and has led to an inordinate fear of and reaction against anything that smacks of Pentecostalism. In his book . . . *bis alle eins werden* [Until all become one],[157] Ludwig Eisenlöffel tells the story of the Berliner Erklärung [Berlin Declaration] of 1909. This was a particularly extreme rejection and defamation of early Pentecostalism in Germany. The fledgling movement was denounced as proceeding from an evil spirit. In order to demonstrate the fanatical level of criticism and "overkill" a brief section of this Berlin Declaration needs to be cited:

The so-called Pentecostal movement is not from above, but from below. It has many manifestations in common with spiritism. Within it there are demons operative that are being cunningly directed by Satan to mingle lies and truth in order to lead the children of God astray. In many cases it has afterwards become apparent that those who were seen as possessing spiritual gifts were in fact possessed.[158]

The Declaration poisoned the atmosphere against anything remotely like Pentecostalism in Germany, and it would be fair to say that it has caused a legacy of harshness still discernible in the criticism from certain sections of German Christianity today. It is not unlikely that this tradition of anti-Pentecostalism also played a role in the almost immediate rejection of the neo-Pentecostal interpretation of Spirit-baptism found among German charismatic leaders. I am not suggesting that they shared the sentiment of the Berlin Declaration, but having been made aware of the problematic nature of much of distinctive classical Pentecostalism, they were more likely to evaluate critically the theological framework within which the charismatic experience was interpreted by the first Protestant charismatics.

Bittlinger's role as leader of the charismatic congregational renewal in Germany has been taken over by the Lutheran, Wolfram Kopfermann. In a booklet, *Charismatische Gemeinde-Erneuerung. Eine Zwischenbilanz* [Charismatic renewal. An interim statement],[159] he gives a clear analysis of the distinctive approach which he abbreviates as CHARGE (*Char*ismatische Gemeinde-*Er*neuerung in der *e*vangelischen Kirche [Charismatic parish renewal in the evangelical church]). He points out that new spiritual experiences are to be interpreted within a traditional doctrinal framework and that the "Stufen-theorien" (two-stage approaches) are unacceptable.[160] Of particular importance in our study is Kopfermann's section on Spirit-baptism. It is likely that his view also represents Bittlinger's convictions. Although they recognize that the concept Spirit-baptism is biblical in its verbal form, the congregational renewal exponents in the Lutheran Church in East Germany and the Catholic and Evangelical (Protestant) churches in West Germany purposefully choose not to use it. Kopfermann gives four reasons: (1) The use of the term Spirit-baptism generally implies a necessary connection between the experience of the fullness and power of the Spirit and speaking in tongues. (2) This concept of Spirit-baptism is legalistic since it seeks to reduce the freedom of the divine distribution of grace to one basic pattern – an approach which causes pastoral problems. (3) Another result is a division of Christians into those "merely" regenerate and, on the other hand, those who are Spirit-baptized. (4) The use of the term Spirit-baptism usually implies a depreciation of baptism in water.[161]

Kopfermann goes on to remark that the apostolic call to be filled with the Spirit is still applicable, but as an alternative expression the choice falls on "Renewal in the Spirit":

> To refer terminologically to "Renewal in the Spirit" instead of to Spirit-baptism has stood the test. By this one means an all-encompassing occurrence which has at least three aspects to it:
> 1. Conversion and personal commitment of faith;
> 2. (Renewed) acceptance of baptismal grace, in other words the experience of justification;
> 3. Opening one's self up to the power of the Holy Spirit and to his gifts.[162]

This reminds one somewhat of Bittlinger's three aspects of Christian initiation/Christian life.

Kopfermann mentions that one of these three aspects can receive the main emphasis. Renewal in the Spirit is an encounter with the living God, rather than special experiences. Although God may grant one vivid emotional experiences, the focus is on faith, not on experiences.[163]

In conclusion it needs to be said that Bittlinger (and Kopfermann) represent an approach rather different from the other theologians whose views have been discussed in this chapter. Whereas the others would all probably fit under the rubric "evangelical" (with Smail the only one who might be slightly uncomfortable with such a label), the German charismatics represent a broader perspective. They emanate from mainstream Christianity. They are not only in good standing in their denominations but are often recognized leaders. Heribert Mühlen, who leads the Catholic wing of the charismatic renewal in Germany, has long been recognized as a prominent theologian. His views will still be dealt with in this chapter. Another quite remarkable feature of this "German" approach is that the ideals of congregational renewal have penetrated not only the large Lutheran and Catholic bodies but also the so-called

Free Churches. Furthermore, although this approach typified by Bittlinger and Mühlen started in Germany, the same style and basic presuppositions have also been accepted among charismatics in Eastern Europe, specifically in the German Democratic Republic, Poland, Hungary, and Yugoslavia.

The name of Wolf-Eckart Failing should also be noted. He is mentioned by Hollenweger as one of the few "Protestant neo-Pentecostals" who like Bittlinger rejects a fundamentalist position. Hollenweger is, of course, not using the term "neo-Pentecostal" in the sense in which it is being employed in this study. Failing has written an article, "Neue charismatische Bewegung in den Landeskirchen" [New charismatic movement in the national church] about the German charismatic context.[164] He gives a good overview citing Becker and Bittlinger, but he does not develop any independent position of his own. Obviously he sympathizes with Bittlinger's approach.

4.11 Wilhard Becker and Siegfried Grossmann (Free Church/Baptist)

In 1965 an important ecumenical conference on Church and Charisma took place in Königstein/Taunus.[165] The charismata in the New Testament, in church history, and in the present were dealt with from Orthodox, Catholic, and Protestant perspectives. At this early stage the Orthodox and Catholic churches had not really been touched by the charismatic renewal. Pastor Wilhard Becker gave the Protestant perspective. His background is that of the so-called Free churches which are Baptist in their persuasion.

Although he does not address Spirit-baptism specifically, his contribution is worthy of note. He mentions the effective suppression of Pentecostalism at the beginning of the century, pointing out that that was followed by a relative dearth of charismatic phenomena, a situation changed only by the Second World War. The war and post-war period brought the elements of lay involvement, ecumenism and eschatology to the fore. In small groups people started experiencing the charisms—without having sought them or having reflected on them. Tongues, prophecies, and healings surfaced in communities such as the Sisters of Mary (a Lutheran Sisterhood). Becker fails to mention the significant fact that here we have charisms without the previous occurrence of Spirit-baptism—at least not in any obvious or clear-cut manner. Next, another impulse is received from America—through Bittlinger and Christenson at the Enkenbach conference. Of the experience of charisms there Becker remarks:

> In truth much was not entirely new. Here and there there had already been experiences of prophecy and also of the healing of the sick without one perhaps having particularly labelled it as charismatic. We had often prayed with the sick in our pastoral ministry, often with the laying on of hands when it had been requested. In some cases we had experienced that they were healed, by several this even happened quite spontaneously and suddenly. We kept these experiences secret. Only later on did we realize that we had here been dealing with the exercising of the gifts of the Spirit.[166]

Becker points out that in the manifestation of charisms there are no "experts." He also experienced no ecstatic or fanatical manifestations. He also underscores that there is no fixed pattern to follow. It goes without saying that he should reject the idea of a theology of subsequence, requiring a second experience with tongues as "sign" by which one gains access to the charisms.

Siegfried Grossmann is a German charismatic with a background similar to Becker, namely belonging to the Evangelical Free churches. He devotes a chapter to Spirit-baptism in his book *Stewards of God's Grace*.[167] He advocates a unified concept of Christian initiation incorporating conversion, regeneration, water baptism and the reception of the Spirit.[168] All the passages in the New Testament which record a considerable time interval Grossmann sees as describing exceptional situations.[169] He clearly rejects the neo-Pentecostal view and equates baptism in the Holy Spirit with the reception of the Holy Spirit.[170]

Grossmann furthermore denies any connection between glossolalia as a kind of sign of initiation and the reception of the Spirit. With respect to tongues the same basic rule applies, namely that the charisms are distributed so that no one has all the charisms. It is only the full congregation that has received the promise of the fullness of all the gifts.[171] Although Grossmann does not specifically point this out, the distribution principle also implies that no one gift would be given to every member of the congregation for this would reduce their interdependence.

Grossmann highlights the fact that Pentecostals and neo-Pentecostals alike have the same "horizon of expectation" with respect to tongues. He explains why so many of them do speak in tongues:

> Since speaking in tongues can also occur as a purely human phenomenon, it is reasonable to suppose that where people expect it as an essential sign of Spirit baptism, what they often experience is in fact a merely emotional glossolalia, a function of the human unconscious. That this is the case becomes even clearer when it is deliberately practiced as is normal in some parts of the Pentecostal movement.[172]

Grossmann blames the almost universal neglect of the charismatic dimension by churches for the development of Spirit-baptism into a separate stage of salvation. This led people who rediscovered it to conclude that the conscious and perceptible reception of the Spirit was an independent experience. In this sense the churches need to rediscover and proclaim the fundamental Christian experience in its totality—one could rephrase this as Christian initiation in all its aspects including the dimension of the Holy Spirit. Grossmann sees this call as applicable not only to the traditional churches that practice infant baptism but also to his own heritage although to a lesser extent:

> Both national [established regional] churches which practice infant baptism and Free churches which practice believers' baptism ought therefore to reflect together on the nature of the fundamental Christian experience in the early church. Churches which practice believers' baptism ought really to find it easier within their own structures to re-establish the fundamental Christian experience in its original sense. In our age of the orientation crisis it is especially important that the

Christian life should begin with a conscious experience involving every level of the personality—not with a purely intellectual decision nor with a purely emotional event. The fundamental Christian experience, with its full content of conversion, regeneration, water baptism and reception of the Spirit, with its balance between the action of God and the action of man, between work and sign, between intellect and emotion, is worthy of being reached and practiced afresh in all its original power.[173]

The term "fundamental Christian experience" is also used in this sense of full Christian initiation by Heribert Mühlen, and the cultural component of involving every level of the personality—not merely the intellect—is a line that will also be developed further under the views of Morton Kelsey.

Grossmann has not specified in any detail his view of "Spirit-baptism" or rather of the charismatic dimension. This is, perhaps, because he does not wish to see it as a separate, distinct experience but rather as a rediscovery of the charismatic, experiential dimension of normal Christian life. In this context he sees the charismatic renewal movement (as congregational renewal) as pointing the way to a better future.[174] In Grossmann the perspective initiated by Bittlinger received further development. Next we turn to the Catholic version of this "German" approach.

4.12 Heribert Mühlen (Catholic)

Through the work of Professor Mühlen of Paderborn the most advanced form yet of the integration of charismatic theology into the structures of established Christianity has been achieved. That this should happen in the Roman Catholic Church is particularly impressive. The charismatic movement was in its first few years a decidedly Protestant phenomenon and in its theology not even Protestant in the sense of the so-called magisterial Reformation of Luther, Calvin, or Cranmer but in the Free Church sense with revivalistic and fundamentalistic heritage.

Before entering into the charismatic renewal Mühlen had already published widely on the Holy Spirit and had achieved recognition as a scholar of international standing.[175] Mühlen reflects both a sacramental interpretation of Spirit-baptism and a full integration of the charismatic dimension into the life of the Catholic Church in Germany.

The interesting history of this development has been documented by the Benedictine sister, Lucida Schmieder, who worked under Mühlen and completed her dissertation, *Geisttaufe. Ein Beitrag zur neueren Glaubensgeschichte,* in systematic theology and the history of doctrine at Paderborn in 1981–82. For that reason the development of Mühlen's insights will not be extrapolated in any detail here. It has consistently been the aim of this study to concentrate more on the systematic theological concepts than on the relating of historical developments whether contemporary or from previous centuries.

The renewal movement started in 1972 in German-speaking Catholicism with prayer groups developing in West Germany, Austria, Switzerland, and

German-speaking Alsace (France). In 1975 Mühlen prepared a report for the German Bishop's Conference on the Catholic-charismatic parish renewal.[176] Even at this early stage German Catholics are clearly taking a different route, not only from neo-Pentecostalism but also from many Catholics in the English-speaking world. There is a conscious attempt to avoid the "Free Church mentality" of America and its vocabulary.[177] The expression "Catholic Pente-costalism" is frowned on. The terminology chosen is that of Catholic charis-matic parish renewal.[178]

Mühlen sets about developing a theology for this renewal movement. He works out two seven-week seminar courses called "Einübung in die christliche Grunderfahrung" [Training in the fundamental Christian experience], the first one dealing with doctrine and exhortation and the second one with prayer and expectancy.[179] Simon Tugwell in a review article expresses surprise at the Eng-lish title of this course book, namely, A Charismatic Theology, since he says Mühlen specifically denies that any such thing as a new "charismatic the-ology" exists.[180]

Mühlen uses the concept "Geist-Erneuerung" [renewal in the Spirit] for the first time in these seminar courses—according to Schmieder.[181] He sees the Spirit-baptism of Jesus as a pattern for our renewal in the Spirit (but does not work this out in an Irvingite sense as Smail does). The basic Christian experience (Christian initiation) has several overlapping aspects. One of these, the charismatic-missionary aspect of the "basic Christian experience" he calls Spirit-baptism and relates this to the sacrament of confirmation. But this Spirit-baptism and confirmation can and should be renewed. Mühlen argues:

> Since sacraments are God's offers and are effective in us only to the extent that we accept the offer, the graces promised in the sacrament of confirmation must be con-tinually freshly welcomed and accepted in the course of our life-history. This accep-tance we call renewal of the baptism of the Spirit/renewal of confirmation or renewal of the Spirit. The same holds for confirmation and other forms of baptis-mal renewal in the reformed churches.[182]

This approach is unquestionably sacramental. Renewal in the Spirit is used as the encompassing concept, which is a life-long process and really approxi-mates the basic Christian experience. It includes components such as (1) con-version, (2) baptism in water for the forgiveness of sins, (3) Spirit-baptism—in the sense of missionary witnessing, (4) guidance by the Spirit, and (5) the Eucharist.[183]

Mühlen's theology is permeated by an ecumenical pathos. His Einübung in die christliche Grunderfahrung was revised with the co-operation of Protestants. Bittlinger, Erhard Griese, and Manfred Kiessig worked on the course book, adding, where applicable, the necessary Protestant comments. The ideals of parish renewal and renewal in the Spirit are also employed by the German Protestants. One technical ambiguity does remain. Mühlen seems to use "renewal in the Spirit" for all of Christian life, in some context incorporating something like the Eucharist under it and seeing it as a life-long process, while in other contexts he seems to associate it with the renewal of Spirit-baptism or confirmation which he has described as being only a part of renewal in the Spirit. This kind of ambiguity should perhaps be expected in the pioneering phase of new theological development. The basic intention is clear enough.

Tugwell writes a sharply critical review of Mühlen's book. He concludes that the concept of the basic Christian experience should be abandoned.[184] Mühlen is not, Tugwell suspects, distinguishing clearly between experience and the object of experience.[185] Tugwell also objects to Mühlen's terminology:

> But since he recognizes the need not to make the specific forms of Pentecostalism binding on all Catholics, he is trapped into saying that "the initiation into the basic Christian experience does not claim to be the sole way to the living parish" (p. 17), which is, on the face of it, absurd. How can there be a living parish which was not initiated into the basic Christian experience (assuming, for the moment, that such talk is appropriate at all)?[186]

It must be conceded that Tugwell has a valid point. The trouble seems to be that Mühlen sometimes uses basic Christian experience in an encompassing sense and sometimes seems to be focusing on the one element, namely the charismatic dimension. He would wish to disclaim the latter as the only way to a living parish, acknowledging that God is not tied to human limitations and that the Christian faith takes on a different appearance in different historical epochs—as Mühlen mentions in the context of the quote given by Tugwell. The major problem with Tugwell's statement above is that he can call what Mühlen is envisaging "the specific forms of Pentecostalism." This indicates a basic misunderstanding. In the light of the discussion of Tugwell's position above and Mühlen's whole contribution to the debate I would venture to say that Tugwell's position is much closer to "the specific forms of Pentecostalism" than Mühlen's—a clear case in point being glossolalia. To deal adequately with Tugwell's assessment of Mühlen having "subjectivized" and "psychologized" Christianity[187] a much more thorough analysis of Mühlen's book and Tugwell's review would be called for. This is not to be undertaken since the focus is here only on the concept of Spirit-baptism and its significance.

The problem of Mühlen's ambiguity is somewhat relativized by his slight shifts in emphasis as he continues to formulate a theology for the Catholic charismatic renewal. In his "Leitlinien der Gemeindeerneuerung" [Guidelines for parish renewal][188] in the periodical of the parish renewal approach, *Erneuerung in Kirche und Gesellschaft* [Renewal in church and society], he no longer uses the word Spirit-baptism and sees "renewal in the Spirit" as incorporating (1) conversion, (2) renewal of baptismal promises and grace, and (3) the acceptance of charisms.[189] This third aspect was not previously mentioned in any explicit form in the aspects of the basic Christian experience.

Mühlen underscores the significance of local parish renewal. Parish renewal is not to be seen as a new movement in the church but as the church in movement.[190] Peter Hocken objects to this perspective stating that total integration of the charismatic renewal into the church is not possible.[191] Mühlen warns against elitist separation into groups. His view is unequivocal:

> Parish renewal in the vivification and intensification of the spirituality of baptism which all Christian have in common and does not lead to division within the Church, the local parish or religious community.

> Even through the exercising of the gifts of the Spirit (which are hardly in existence in the traditional established regional churches) one does not become a member of a new spiritual community or "movement." This is so because all the gifts of the Spirit are given for the edification of the specific parish in which the individual is living at that time. Even when we find that small groups are initially being formed in a parish as an introduction to renewal in the Spirit, the goal is nevertheless an ongoing evangelization of the parish through which all members of the parish will be addressed in due time.[192]

Elitist separation is not seen as coming from the Holy Spirit but from human feelings of superiority. The aim of the charismatic renewal is not a new charismatic church but a charismatically renewed church.[193]

The basic difference to the practice of neo-Pentecostals in America is the approach of presenting a spirituality for every Christian rather than grouping together those who have had similar spiritual experiences.

With Mühlen's approach as background, the German Catholic Bishop's Conference remarkably accepted and officially approved a document "Erneuerung der Kirche aus dem Geist Gottes" [The Renewal of the Church through the Spirit of God] in May 1981. This differs from all other official statements by churches about the renewal. Here was not a statement pointing out positive and negative elements in the charismatic renewal but a document of a national conference of Catholic Bishops espousing that charismatic renewal be officially accepted.

Schmieder comments, "The basic trend is towards a full integration of the charismatic awakening with the local parishes and the religious orders."[194] The approach of Bittlinger and Mühlen is patently discernible in the document, for example, in the use of the word charismatic:

> The adjective "charismatic" means "gracious": over against human exertion it focuses on the gift-character of the abilities, over against mere human spontaneity on the capacity to allow oneself to be directed by the Spirit of God; over against enthusiastic excesses on the sobriety of service. In this sense every Christian is a "charismatic." Consequently one should not use the words "charismatic," "a charismatic" in an elitist sense to divide a particular group of people from other Christians.[195]

A new distinction is introduced in "Erneuerung der Kirche aus dem Geist Gottes." "Geist-Erfahrung" [experience of the Spirit] is seen as a sovereign work of God's grace – a gift which is given. "Geist-Erneuerung" [renewal in the Spirit] is the human reaction to this. Humanity has no control over the experience of the Spirit – it remains a mystery. The aim of renewal in the Spirit is the encounter with the living God, not a special experience.[196]

In this definitive document renewal in the Spirit is seen as incorporating three aspects. They are very similar to those distinguished above by Mühlen. First there is the basic decision–conversion. Baptism is the sacrament of conversion and a new start. Next there is the renewed acceptance of the sacramental offer of God's grace. Third, renewal in the Spirit involves becoming open to the Spirit and his gifts.[197] This third aspect which can be seen as charismatic is a further development in the process of becoming a Christian. The Christian becomes open to the full working of the Holy Spirit which touches all the facets of one's life to an ever increasing extent. In this regard the document makes reference to Thomas Aquinas's distinction between the abiding indwelling of the Spirit imparted in baptism, and a renewal through grace which involves a new coming of the Spirit. This insight, so crucial for understanding Francis Sullivan's concept of Spirit-baptism, will be discussed later on in this chapter.

Finally, this official Catholic document's position on Spirit-baptism must be examined. The document was authored by a co-ordinating team of the charismatic parish renewal in co-operation with the theological committee for charismatic parish renewal (with no names mentioned). It is safe to conclude that Heribert Mühlen played an important part in the writing. The authors remark that when one experiences an initial breakthrough of God's presence it feels like a baptism into the stream of divine joy and love. This makes it understandable why many call the experience Spirit-baptism. However, the witness of the New Testament and the Fathers of the church is that the Spirit is already received in baptism in water. They continue:

> The phenomenon designated as "Spirit-baptism" to the extent that it refers to a breakthrough experience is seen in these guidelines as a form of the experience of the Spirit. This conscious experience of being deeply moved by the Holy Spirit can also be combined with the complex occurrence of renewal in the Spirit. Due to the misunderstandings that it causes one should totally avoid the term "Spirit-baptism."[198]

In his article, "Geist-Erfahrung und Oekumene [Experience of the Spirit and ecumenism]," Mühlen indicates that the perspectives of parish renewal have to some extent also penetrated the Catholic churches in Eastern Europe.[199] Because no new theological insights are mentioned it is not necessary to refer to this development in any detail.

Mühlen is also acutely aware of the socio-political dimensions of the gospel. Even the title of the German renewal magazine, *Erneuerung in Kirche und Gesellschaft* [Renewal in church and society], has a different ring to it than most of the American renewal magazines. Mühlen speaks of "socio-critical charisms" which are dangerous in nature. He says of them:

> They lead one through prophetic programs and strategies (the spiritual nature of which needs to be tested according to the rules of discernment) towards prophetic signs of an alternative society.[200]

Mühlen mentions that examples of this perspective, involving structural issues such as land reform, agricultural policy, etc., are to be found in Pentecostal congregations in Latin America.

Mühlen decries the reluctance for renewal in the large established churches of Germany and the lack of involvement by theologians:

> With respect to numbers Germany represents rock bottom when compared with global developments. Many theologians and office bearers persist in the attitude of Gamaliel: if the matter is of God it will accomplish its aims even without my help! As theologians we may heap up new guilt upon ourselves if we do not recognize the kairos (moment of decision) and remain at a distance in a critical and external evaluatory stance over against the charismatic awakening.[201]

One finds the anomalous situation that where the groundwork has been most thoroughly and reflectively done by theologians (such as Bittlinger and Mühlen) the harvest of renewal as far as the number of renewed lives is concerned seems disproportionately smaller than in places where the theological basis for renewal is an inadequate tottering edifice. The causes for this state of affairs would be diverse and are not the focus of this study.

In her concluding statement Schmieder underscores that the official Catholic bishops' document on the renewal represents a departure from Pentecostal and neo-Pentecostal positions as well as from many Catholic circles in the English-speaking world. She continues:

> In the context of renewal in the Spirit one can "from time to time" receive an experience of infilling or a spiritual breakthrough (compare 2.1.2) but such an experience of infilling by no means necessarily forms part of the basic ingredients of the fundamental Christian experience. It need also not be connected to a specific moment in time but can become apparent through a process of gradual growth. This breakthrough experience is "a form" of experience in the Spirit and there is no way that the prayer language can be seen as visible proof for the validity of experience in the Spirit.[202]

This new approach to Spirit-baptism, or rather renewal in the Spirit, is of the utmost significance to Schmieder, particularly with respect to its potential impact upon pastoral care in the mainline churches.[203]

Most charismatics discussed in this chapter (and probably also in Chapter 3) would go along with the German pathos for congregational renewal although they may not be as insistent on rejecting all separate organizing of renewed individuals. Even the *Joint Statement: Gospel and Spirit* declared that "the goal of renewal is not merely renewed individuals but a renewed and revived Church."[204]

4.13 Francis Sullivan (Catholic)

Francis A. Sullivan, SJ, is professor of dogmatic theology at the Gregorian University in Rome. He has published a monograph, *Charisms and Charismatic*

Renewal. A Biblical and Theological Study, and several articles on the charismatic renewal.[205] He was also involved in a debate with Simon Tugwell, OP, on the nature of a Pentecostal experience.[206]

Sullivan represents a unique position in Catholic thought on Spirit-baptism. We have seen that some Catholics espouse a neo-Pentecostal view, others – the majority – interpret Spirit-baptism as an experiential manifestation of sacramental grace received in baptism and/or confirmation. This is often expressed as representing "a release" or breaking forth into conscious experience of the Spirit. Then there is the Middle and Eastern European approach advocated by Heribert Mühlen. This is also sacramental in nature but functions within the framework of parish renewal, and the expression Spirit-baptism is replaced by renewal in the Spirit in an encompassing sense. René Laurentin mentioned three other theological interpretations which were referred to in chapter 3 – two were sacramental in nature in a rather technical sense – the other is Sullivan's view.

Tugwell has described the basic problem that Sullivan has with the sacramental position aptly. The Spirit should not be treated as a kind of commodity that can be stored away.[207] Sullivan argues as follows:

> What people experienced in the charismatic renewal is a change that took place in their lives. This experience is later interpreted theologically. When a person has been baptized but never personally ratified that commitment and received confirmation without any personal commitment either, one could say that person's Christian initiation still needs to be completed.[208]

This is similar to the view expressed by some Anglican evangelicals.

Catholics, however, were reticent to call this completion of Christian initiation "the baptism in the Holy Spirit" as neo-Pentecostal Protestants had done. The first Malines Document's solution was to distinguish between a theological and experiential sense of Spirit-baptism. Sullivan writes:

> The solution which has been most commonly adopted in the literature of the Catholic charismatic renewal is to see the "giving" or "imparting" of the Holy Spirit as taking place exclusively in the sacraments. There is an evident reluctance to speak of a new imparting of the Spirit except through the reception of a sacrament, as though this would be incompatible with Catholic theology.[209]

This is the point where Sullivan wishes to differ, calling on no one less than Thomas Aquinas to support his position. Sullivan explains:

> Perhaps the best way to express my own opinion on this question is to say that I believe that what happens to people in the charismatic renewal is that they are baptized in the Spirit in the biblical sense of this term, and that the biblical sense includes both the theological and the experiential senses. In other words, in my view, what people are receiving in the charismatic renewal is a real imparting of the Spirit, a new "outpouring of the Spirit" (the theological sense), which typically has effects that make them aware that the Spirit is working in a new way in their lives (the experiential sense).[210]

What is this "biblical sense" of Spirit-baptism? After discussing the references in the Gospels and Acts, Sullivan concludes that to say Jesus baptizes in the Spirit simply means he sends, pours out, or gives us the Spirit.[211]

Sullivan disagrees with two ideas implicit in the Malines Document, namely that it would be unorthodox (for a Catholic) to receive "a new sending of the Spirit in answer to.a prayer that was not a sacrament."[212] The second idea is that one receives a "total gift" of the Spirit in sacramental initiation so that there can be no question of another coming of the Spirit, merely of a release or coming into conscious experience of the Spirit. This traditional approach of the Catholic renewal implies that the charismatic experience is not really a new powerful sending of the Spirit but merely a change in one's subjective consciousness. Sullivan points out that nothing in Catholic theology necessitates one believing that the coming of the Spirit can take place only through the reception of a sacrament.

Sullivan appeals, as stated above, to the leading Catholic theologian of the thirteenth century, Thomas of Aquino. Thomas discusses the mission of the divine Persons in Question 43 of the first book of his *Summa Theologiae*.[213]

Thomas explains that the mission of a divine Person (such as the Holy Spirit) is becoming present where he already is by a new kind of presence rather than a movement to a place where he has not been before. This new kind of presence involves a new relationship between human and divine (here the Holy Spirit). Sullivan emphasizes Thomas's words *inhabitatio* and *innovatio* in the *Summa Theologiae*:

> Accordingly in the destinary of a mission we should take into account both the indwelling (inhabitationem) by grace and a quality of newness (innovationem) brought about by grace.[214]

Such an invisible sending results in an increase of grace and a growth in virtue. Thomas continues:

> Still there is a special instance of an invisible mission based on an increase in grace when someone advances to a new act or new stage of grace, e.g. to the grace of miracles or prophecy or to delivering himself in the favor of his charity to martyr-dom.or to renunciation of all he possesses or to taking up any sort of heroic task.[215]

When quoting from this source Sullivan, who has probably made his own translation from the Latin, renders "statum gratiae" as *state* of grace. Personally I prefer the rendering given above: *stage* of grace. To modern ears a new state of grace could imply something as fundamental as the primary concept of regeneration where our state in the eyes of God is fundamentally changed. Such an association should be avoided with respect to the charismatic experience to distinguish this approach from the Pentecostal pattern of two distinct experiences.

The examples that Thomas gives, namely miracles, prophecy, and martyr-dom, show plainly that Thomas is not thinking within Spirit-baptism categories. These new acts or stages of grace are related to charisms. Sullivan adds a word of caution here:

> However, it must be noted that if we follow the lead of St. Thomas, we cannot interpret the new sending of the Spirit as simply the conferring of a charism. As he explains it, a new sending of the Spirit must involve a new way of the Spirit's indwelling in the soul, and this has to mean a real innovation of the person's relationship with the indwelling Spirit. Therefore, in Thomas' view, it has to mean a more intimate and "experiential" knowledge of God as present in the soul, a knowledge that "breaks out into more ardent love."[216]

Sullivan makes several important conclusions from this teaching of Thomas on the divine missions. Of particular significance for the position to be developed in chapter 5 of this study is the first:

> First, there is good reason to believe that such new "sendings of the Spirit" or "baptisms in the Spirit" have been happening to people all through Christian history. The life-story of practically any holy person, canonized or not, will usually include some turning-point, some conversion, that marked a decisive change in that person's life.[217]

The second conclusion is that a new sending or coming of the Spirit can be repeated in a person's lifetime. Sullivan also feels that an experiential confirmation is necessary so that we may know that such a mission has taken place. The mere fact that one has prayed for it or been prayed over is not sufficient if one cannot detect any change or new experience of God's power in one's life. A sacramental baptism does not require such confirmation, but the charismatic dimension has an experiential side to it. As can be expected, Sullivan does not believe that glossolalia must be part of this experiential element. With respect to terminology Sullivan prefers to call the charismatic experience (which we have been calling Spirit-baptism for convenience) a new outpouring of the Spirit. If the word baptism cannot be avoided it would be best to speak of "a new baptism in the Spirit."[218]

Donald Gelpi, whose views were dealt with in chapter 2, also makes reference to this doctrine of Thomas, but develops it from a slightly different angle:

> Aquinas correctly distinguished two aspects of the Spirit's mission: His permanent indwelling and His "surprises" (innovationes). The indwelling of the Spirit is His constant, pre-conscious presence to the believer as a sustaining and healing life-source. His "surprises" are the pneumatic breakthroughs He effects, especially by means of the gifts of service. Every time a believer is visibly transformed by some new gift of service, one may, then, speak appropriately and meaningfully of a "new sending" of the Spirit. The sacrament of confirmation pledges the believer to stand in lifelong openness to the Spirit's surprises. And it affirms such openness to be binding on all who are covenanted to God in the image of Jesus.[219]

This distinction between the indwelling of the Spirit following after regeneration or Christian initiation as the initial sending of the Spirit and the "surprises" of new pneumatic breakthroughs closely resembles the position which considers Spirit-baptism to be the start of Christian life. This initiation is followed by a process of sanctification whose experiential element comes in the form of charismatic breakthroughs and gradual ongoing growth; both of these can involve the exercise of charisms.

Harold Hunter, who also gives the above quotation from Gelpi when discussing Thomas, states:

> Aquinas does not relegate "charismatic" "surprises" of the Spirit to "actualizations" of sacramentally conferred graces, but he most usually would have preferred that they operate in that fashion.[220]

In the light of Sullivan's exposition Hunter seems merely to be reflecting the traditional Catholic reticence to which Sullivan refers above. Hunter does not substantiate the remark that Thomas "most usually" would have preferred the innovations to operate as actualizations of sacramental grace. Sullivan's contention that nothing in Catholic theology obliges one to believe that new "sendings" of the Spirit can only take place via the sacraments is convincing.[221]

Gelpi has translated "innovationes" as "surprises." Sullivan grapples with this:

> Unfortunately there is no English word which fully expresses the meaning of St. Thomas' innovatio; "renewal" is about as close as we can come, but it does not have the same sense of "going forward into something new."[222]

Schmieder points out that Sullivan's approach is rather unique among Catholics:

> According to Sullivan a Catholic need not necessarily relate Pentecostal experience to baptism or confirmation. With this view Sullivan is nevertheless in a rather isolated position within Catholic ranks.[223]

If this was accurate it is no longer the case. Schmieder writing in 1981–82 does not refer to Sullivan's book *Charisms and Charismatic Renewal* (1982), merely to his articles. With the appearance of this book this approach has become more widely disseminated. In at least one recent publication it is the preferred interpretation. I am referring to Alan Schreck's *Catholic and Christian. An Explanation of Commonly Misunderstood Catholic Beliefs.*[224] Schreck states:

> God can pour out the Holy Spirit in a new and significant way many times in a person's life if he wishes. The first time that this happens to a person is often the most dramatic, because it may be experienced by the person as a totally "new thing."[225]

He then goes on to cite Sullivan and Thomas, also underscoring that unlike the sacraments, in which Catholics believe that God unfailingly confers his grace, the prayer for "Spirit-baptism" may or may not lead to one receiving this gift.[226]

Schreck fully supports Sullivan's interpretation and encourages Catholics seeking a deeper knowledge of God and a fuller release of the Spirit's power to pray for Spirit-baptism:

> . . .they are right to pray to God and seek the prayers of others to be "baptized in the Holy Spirit." They open themselves to receive the full range of gifts (charisms) and other manifestations of the Holy Spirit.[227]

Sullivan gives the new Catholic teaching on charisms in "The Ecclesiological Context of the Charismatic Renewal." He explains the development at the Second Vatican Council:

> As on many other issues, the teaching of Vatican II on the charisms marks a break with a commonly held view, but in doing so returns to an authentic tradition solidly based on scripture.[228]

In a widely publicized speech, Cardinal Suenens repudiated the traditional view of charisms (championed by Cardinal Ruffini) that charisms became extremely rare and altogether exceptional after the apostolic era and have no role to play in the life of the modern church.

Suenens's view that charisms are, on the contrary, of vital importance reflected a notion of charism that had been advanced by Catholic scholars such as Yves Congar and Karl Rahner. The fruit of Suenens's contribution can be seen in the following section of the Council's *Dogmatic Constitution on the Church (Lumen Gentium)*:

> It is not only through the sacraments and church ministries that the same Holy Spirit sanctifies and leads the People of God and enriches it with virtues. Allotting His gifts "to everyone according as he will (*sic*)" (1 Cor 12:11), He distributes special graces among the faithful of every rank. By these gifts He makes them fit and ready to undertake the various tasks or offices advantageous for the renewal and upbuilding of the Church, according to the words of the Apostle: "The manifestation of the Spirit is given to everyone for profit" (1 Cor 12:7). These charismatic gifts, whether they be the most outstanding or the more simple and widely diffused, are to be received with thanksgiving and consolation, for they are exceedingly suitable and useful for the needs of the Church.[229]

Next Sullivan discusses the implications of a charismatic renewal of the church asking, too, whether the "Catholic Pentecostal Movement" is such a charismatic renewal of the church. He concludes that there are several ways of speaking in this movement that may alienate the rest of Catholicism. As one would expect, Sullivan mentions the term "baptism in the Holy Spirit." The problem lies in the implicit corollary that other Christians have not been Spirit-baptized. Sullivan adds:

> It is equally misleading to use the terms "Spirit-filled" or "living in the Spirit" in such a way as to imply that it is only through the Pentecostal experience that one becomes "Spirit-filled" or enters into "life in the Spirit."[230]

Sullivan also points out that the way the word charismatic is used has inevitably led to distinguishing the two categories of "charismatics" and "non-charismatics" in the church. Sullivan rejects this distinction and indicates that such a distinction resurrects the restrictive notion of charism advanced by Cardinal Ruffini. Sullivan's conclusion is worthy of full citation:

Who, then, is a "charismatic"? Is it not clear that anyone who has received any one of these manifold gifts of grace and is using it in the service of God and his neighbor can rightly be called "charismatic"? I am afraid that the current use of the term "charism" and "charismatic" in the "charismatic renewal" reflects the restricted idea of charism defended by Cardinal Ruffini, rather than the broad concept which the Second Vatican Council recognized to be the authentic Pauline idea, and adopted as its own.

Inevitably a narrow concept of charism is going to result in a narrow concept of who and what is charismatic. And this, in turn, results in too narrow a concept of what a charismatic renewal of the Church would involve, and how it can come about. While I believe that God is using the Catholic Pentecostal movement as an instrument for the charismatic renewal of his Church, I am also convinced that it is crucial for the future of this movement that people involved in it realize that as there are other ways of being charismatic than "speaking in tongues" and "prophesying," so there are other ways to a charismatic renewal of the church than through the narrow gate of Pentecostalism.[231]

These perspectives are crucial to the position which will be developed in the last chapter. To some extent they are identical to the approach I wish to develop there.

It will be abundantly clear that Sullivan sees the need that Catholics reinterpret their "Pentecostal experiences" within a broader context. He goes so far as to indicate that these experiences are really basically Christian in a general sense:

The fact that the Pentecostal experience can be fruitfully interpreted in the light of other Christian traditions—a fact which I believe is becoming more and more clear—suggests that it is a basically *Christian* experience, and not something distinctively Evangelical Protestant.[232]

This quotation needs some clarifying. By "other Christian traditions" Sullivan is most probably referring to denominational traditions such as Catholic, Lutheran, Anglican, etc. When he sees "Pentecostal" as being directly related to "Evangelical" Protestant I would beg to differ. As mentioned previously, both Hollenweger and Edward O'Connor have pointed out a distinctly "un-Protestant" aspect of Pentecostalism, although this receives little acknowledgement. But that is not really the issue here. Sullivan seemingly identifies "Evangelical Protestantism" with concepts such as fundamentalism, rejection of infant baptism, revivalism, insistence on a crisis born-again experience, providing a date for conversion, etc. Sullivan does associate "evangelical" with "the necessity of an adult conversion experience for salvation and rejection of the practice of infant baptism."[233] This may be somewhat closer to the truth with respect to American evangelicals, but there certainly is an evangelical tradition outside of the U.S. which would not recognize itself as being fundamentalist or revivalist and clearly practices infant baptism, e.g., evangelical Anglicans, Presbyterians, etc. Even in America many confessional Lutheran and Reformed Christians would call themselves "evangelical" and yet would be very far removed from Pentecostalism. Furthermore, some Free Church evangelicals with Baptist doctrine are the most vehement in their criticism of Pentecostals and charismatics. The neo-evangelical movement compounds the objections to this association of Sullivan. Nevertheless that was not Sullivan's point–it is merely a critique of his terminology. Another difference with Sullivan's terminology is his argument for the term "neo-Pentecostal" rather than "charismatic" for Catholics and Protestants in what he still calls "the Pentecostal movement."[234] Sullivan is reflecting Yves Congar's objections, namely that all Christians are charismatic. There is validity to this argument, but in a sense all Christians are also Pentecostal, which then seems to relativize the usefulness of neo-Pentecostal. Naturally Sullivan is not using neo-Pentecostal in the sense it is being employed in this study. To a large extent such terminology is a dated matter of convenience. The important thing is not to use the words in an unreflected way and always to explain the content given to them. By using "charismatic renewal" in the title of his book Sullivan seems to accept the reality that it is usually not theologians but the majority of people that determine common usage of terms.

Although his insistence on moving away from the Pentecostal theological interpretation of what he calls the Pentecostal experience (and I have been calling the charismatic experience or dimension) it should not be concluded that Sullivan sees no merit in Pentecostalism. In fact, he sounds a warning in this regard:

> At the same time, in the process of interpreting the Pentecostal experience in the light of our own traditions, we also have to avoid the danger of so "domesticating" it as to recognize in it only what we ourselves have had all along, with the danger of eliminating what is most vital in this movement and what could be its most important contribution to the renewal of ourselves and our Church.

> There is now a Pentecostal tradition in Christianity by which our own tradition can be enriched; but we have to discern where the wealth of the Pentecostal tradition really lies. Surely it is not in its theology or exegesis; rather, its richness is to be found in its openness to the powerful working of the Spirit through the whole community, its participative and creative worship, its extraordinary effectiveness in communicating the good news of Jesus Christ. It is in these areas that the Pentecostals are leading the way, and that we of the more venerable and "respectable" Christian traditions must have the humility to learn and to follow their lead.[235]

With this background the scene has been sufficiently prepared to look at the debate between Sullivan and Tugwell–perhaps the most subtle and interesting exchange of ideas that has taken place between theologians on the charismatic renewal and its integration into mainstream Christianity.

The debate consists of a series of articles in 1976 and 1977. In reaction to Sullivan's article in *Gregorianum* (1974), Tugwell responds in *New Blackfriars* with "So Who's a Pentecostal Now?" This title conveys his dissatisfaction with the charismatic revisionism of Pentecostalism that leaves it devoid of distinctive elements. Sullivan replies in *Theological Renewal* with an article on "What is a Pentecostal Experience? A Reply to a Question Raised by Simon Tugwell."

This is followed, finally, by a further response by Tugwell: "Is there a 'Pentecostal Experience'? A Reply to Fr. Francis A. Sullivan, SJ," in the next edition of *Theological Renewal*.

It is quite difficult to pinpoint the essential difference between the views of Tugwell and Sullivan. Tugwell is upset by the "massive institutionalizing that has been going on within Catholic Pentecostalism,"[236] and he fears that the "charismatic leaders" are usurping the authority of official church leaders. He sees the act whereby the Fountain Trust disbanded itself as achieving far more in the long run to serve the renewal of the church. Tugwell seems to prefer grappling with the challenge presented by classical Pentecostalism rather than introducing a Catholic renewal movement into the Roman Catholic Church. This leads him to challenge the process of reinterpretation undertaken by so many Catholic theologians. Oddly, he does not direct his objections against the main thrust of Catholic charismatic thought, namely the sacramental interpretation given by the first Malines Document. Sullivan's interpretation is not the most influential interpretation of Spirit-baptism in Catholic circles (although it may yet become that), and he is also acutely aware of the danger of so "domesticating" Pentecostalism that it no longer presents a challenge, as pointed out above.

When Tugwell argues for the rediscovery "in ourselves and in our churches what it means to be so totally 'led by the Spirit' that every thought, even, is brought into subjection to Christ,"[237] he comes rather close to Sullivan's plea that we have the humility to learn and follow the Pentecostal tradition:

> ...in its openness to the powerful working of the Spirit through the whole community, its participative and creative worship, its extraordinary effectiveness in communicating the good news of Jesus Christ.[238]

To summarize the line of argument in this debate: Tugwell questions the existence of something called "the Pentecostal experience." To him this only makes sense as a reference to glossolalia as practiced in the classical Pentecostal churches. He also doubts whether one can peel off interpretations to leave an experience "bare" and then just clothe it differently. Tugwell points out that Thomas found it preferable to reserve speaking of a new sending of the Spirit for occasions where there is clear evidence of change in the person's life.

The central argument of Tugwell is reflected in the following paragraph:

> The neo-Pentecostals, by and large, have given up the insistence on tongues as the evidence of "baptism in the Holy Spirit." But it is far from clear that any coherent doctrine remains. The tendency in Catholic Pentecostalism, at least, seems to have been a move away from any such specificity, so that more and more phenomena, and more and more elusive "experiences" are allowed to count as "baptism in the Spirit." Eventually it seems likely that absolutely any kind of Christian experience will count. And that is, in itself, not unfitting: after all, if it is the basic theological characteristic of Christian behavior that it proceeds from the indwelling of the Holy Spirit, then "Pentecostal" does simply equal "Christian."[239]

Once again I wish to point out how close Tugwell and Sullivan are to one another by quoting again from Sullivan's remarks on tradition:

> The fact that the pentecostal experience can be fruitfully interpreted in the light of other Christian traditions—a fact which I believe is becoming more and more clear—suggests that it is a basically Christian experience, and not something distinctively Evangelical Protestant [read: Pentecostal].[240]

The full integration of the charismatic renewal into authentic Christianity in the next chapter will demonstrate that "Pentecostal" (or charismatic if one prefers) and "Christian" should increasingly overlap.

When Tugwell then tries to define the specificity of "Pentecostal" within the Catholic charismatic movement his reproaches become more serious.

> The only specificity of the "Pentecostal" is social, an experience is "pentecostal" because it happens in a "pentecostal" (or "charismatic") group. The more any group identifies itself simply with the characteristics of "mere Christianity," the more inevitably will it have to tend towards becoming a sect. This is the common element in the genesis of almost all sects. As an institution comes to have fewer and fewer real distinguishing features, it has to rely more and more on mere institutional separation to preserve its raison d'être.[241]

Here we seem to have stumbled into a "hidden agenda." Perhaps Tugwell has the same fears about what Josephine Ford called "Type 1 Pentecostals" and their ecumenical covenant communities. This would certainly tie in with his reproach that official Catholic leaders are having their authority "usurped" by charismatic leaders. Ford finds these communities such as the Word of God in Ann Arbor and Ypsilanti, Michigan, to be elaborately structured depending upon unquestioning submission to the majority of male co-ordinators[242] and the Catholics in them not sufficiently orthodox in their doctrine and practice. She also suggests that they operate in an Anabaptist type setting, influenced by Benjamin Zablocki's book, *The Joyful Community*.[243] I have no way of knowing whether this dispute between Ford and the covenant community leaders really does form the background to this debate between Tugwell and Sullivan. Ford's contentious book was published in 1976 making the assumption that it could have played a role in this discussion more likely.

Sullivan's response to this element of Tugwell's attack is guarded. He acknowledges that the charismatic renewal is not altogether immune from any danger of tending toward becoming a sect. In his article, "The Ecclesiological Context of the Charismatic Renewal," Sullivan pointed out the real danger of alienation from the rest of the Catholic Church. This has been referred to above and stems from 1975, i.e., before the debate we are now discussing. Nevertheless, Sullivan does not see the strongly social character of the charismatic renewal, i.e., the important role of its prayer groups and covenant communities, as a potentially dangerous development.

Sullivan sees the danger of sectarianism elsewhere:

> In my opinion, the danger of tending toward becoming a sect does not lie in seeking or promoting a Pentecostal experience [within a social context], but rather in

laying down rules as to how, when, and with what manifestations such an experience must necessarily be had. The more such rules are laid down, the more inevitable it is going to be that only the privileged few are going to qualify, as having had that particular kind of experience of the power of the Spirit.[244]

Here Sullivan is referring to rules such as insisting on glossolalia, which he calls in Smail's terminology the "law of tongues."[245] Precisely this fear of sectarian tendencies inspired the whole process of reinterpretation of Spirit-baptism within Catholic charismatic circles. Sullivan concludes: "What some are inclined to fear as the beginning of a sect may well turn out to be a pillar of strength for the Church of the future."[246] Sullivan further points out that he too favors some experiential evidence in a Christian's life. He also explains that not any kind of Christian experience can be described as a "Pentecostal experience" in the way he was using the term. He does acknowledge a great variety of manifestations finding the common factor in the power of the Spirit transforming people into effective witnesses. What this means in individual lives will depend on variables such as state of life, natural talents, opportunities for witnessing and particular charisms which the sovereign Spirit distributes as he chooses.[247] Sullivan does see this experience as available to every Christian and something every Christian should want to have, again indicating that the experience is basically Christian rather than being exclusively Pentecostal.

In the last round of the debate Tugwell points out that there is a distinction between interpreting experience and interpreting an experience. This somewhat technical distinction leads him to focus on learning from the whole experience of Pentecostals rather than from Spirit-baptism or what Sullivan calls "the Pentecostal experience."

Tugwell also wishes to maintain that "baptism in the Spirit" is not an experience, but a doctrinal interpretation of the experience of glossolalia. Therefore he wishes to devote his energy to reinterpreting speaking in tongues, which is pivotal to the whole experience of Pentecostals. Like the Catholic sacraments, Pentecostal glossolalia is bodily and can free us from "the tyranny of our half-baked emotions and confused intuitions."[248] These ideas are further developed in Tugwell's article in *New Heaven? New Earth?* [249] The last round in the debate does not contribute much to the furthering of insights, except the revealing statements by Tugwell that he finds the massive institutionalizing of Catholic Pentecostalism with its para-ecclesial institutions, "which effectively claim to contain within themselves all that is essential to the Christian life," truly terrifying.

This leads me to reiterate my question: Why does Tugwell take up his pen against Sullivan's Thomistic reinterpretation of Spirit-baptism and not against the sacramental interpretation of the first Malines Document and the pervasive "release of the Spirit" theory? Surely the proponents of that view are also overlooking the "important distinction between interpreting experience and interpreting an experience" and neglecting the useful task of reinterpreting glossolalia and the richness of its symbolic and sacramental potential? It may even be that they are also supportive of the "massive institutionalizing" of

Catholic charismatics. In short, I find Tugwell's attack misplaced and wonder if he would not have been more effective if he had launched his critique not against Sullivan's interpretation theory of Spirit-baptism but against the practical over-institutionalizing of charismatic para-ecclesial structures and their tendency to alienate the rest of Catholicism by an in-group mentality. In such a critique, I suspect, Tugwell would have found in Sullivan a willing ally.

4.14 Morton Kelsey (Episcopal)

Morton T. Kelsey is an Episcopal scholar who has played a significant role in the charismatic renewal. He has never published on Spirit-baptism and, I suspect, never even used the word in his many publications except possibly, to refer to the Pentecostal approach which he rejects. Nonetheless Kelsey has provided an academic framework for "the spiritual dimension" of reality which has supported the "theology" of the charismatic movement in a very general sense. When the Lutheran Richard Jensen sought to find an interpretative framework for understanding the meaning of spiritual experience and the gifts of the Spirit he found two schemes of interpretation dominating the horizon, namely Pentecostal theology and what he calls *The Kingdom Within*.[250] This framework was devised by Kelsey based on insights from Plato and, especially, C. G. Jung.

In his major work, *Encounter with God*,[251] Kelsey provides a scholarly analysis of Western theology and philosophy. He argues for the existence and reality of the spiritual world. The Western mind-set has created a theoretical framework which operates with a monistic concept of the world as a space-time box and a closed system of materialistic causality. With the heritage of Aristotle, who limited knowledge to the empirical and the rational, humankind lost the Platonic epistemological insights that recognized other avenues of knowledge including non-rational elements such as intuition, prophecy, artistic inspiration, and love. There is the possibility of an individual making direct contact with God and participating in the realm of the Spirit.

Kelsey points out that through a capitulation to the rationalism of the Enlightenment and dispensationalism, Christianity has become blind to the "supernatural" elements in the New Testament, such as the Holy Spirit, angels, demons, the devil, heaven and hell, miracles, healings, dreams, prophecy and tongues. He calculates that 49% of the verses in the New Testament are concerned with this dimension of reality.[252] Either by spiritualizing, demythologizing, or limiting these aspects to the apostolic age the church has managed to avoid facing them as an integral part of the gospel. The charismatic dimension of Christian life always encounters skepticism and open opposition because the existence of such manifestations of the Spirit questions our modern concept of reality, which is founded on scientivism and positivism.

The irony of the church's capitulation before these forces of rationalistic humanism is underscored by recent developments in the scientific world that are moving away from empiricism and the positivistic approach. In medicine the psychosomatic factor is attracting attention. Emotions like grief, bitterness, or anger do cause physical pain. Non-Euclidean geometry sees space as curved, and quantum physics (Bohr and Heisenberg) rejects the rationalistic polarity between subject and object. Most significant have been the discoveries of depth psychology and the analysis of dreams. The school of C. G. Jung recognizes the importance of God and the individual's relationship to God in therapeutic treatment. This rather generalized summary of Kelsey's perspective cannot hope to do justice to his profound insights and perspectives. Suffice it to say that Kelsey opens up a new dimension of reality in which phenomena such as charismatic gifts are able to be integrated. Kelsey wrote *Tongue Speaking* [253] in 1964, in which he drew together insights from the Bible, church history, and psychology. In his chapter on "Understanding Tongues" he writes:

> There are two fundamentally different ideas about the way man comes to know God. Both have had wide currency in the Christian tradition. One of them has been accepted by Western Christianity, both Catholic and Protestant, for the past five centuries and it has supplied the groundwork for our unique Western civilization. But it has little place for direct experience of God and, so, little place for tongues. If we are to find value in this recurring experience of tongues, we must turn to the other world view about how man knows God. . . . [this] other view. . . maintains that man has knowledge of the world in which he lives not only through sense experience and reason, but also through direct experience of the non-physical world. This view adds another dimension to experience and introduces a greater complexity to human experience.

> This point of view sees man as standing between two worlds, an outer one of material reality with endless potentiality, and an inner one of spiritual reality, equally potent and inexhaustible. [254]

Kelsey maintains that the second approach was the world view of Jesus and for that reason the early church could so easily conceptualize their first attempts at theology within the framework of Platonic philosophy. Kelsey does not seem to be aware of the disadvantages which Platonic concepts brought with them as a tool to understand Scripture. Modern theological enterprise has expended much energy explaining for example that Plato's immortality of the soul is not the same as the Christian doctrine of the resurrection of the body, and that Christian anthropology sees the individual as an integrated being rather than dualistic. Platonic thinking has also influenced our doctrine of God, leading to a predicative approach where attributes that are "worthy" of God are predicated to him rather than deduced from Scripture. The whole debate about anthropomorphisms boils down to the Platonic heritage of ancient and scholastic theology.

For Kelsey, Jung plays a major role in the rediscovery of the spiritual world:

> Jung found that no permanent health, maturity, or freedom were achieved in any of his patients until something new emerged from the collective unconscious. . . .

The person who loses touch with the unconscious and the powers which it mediates sooner or later falls into mental, physical, or moral illness. . . .

When religion is alive, it brings the individual to vital contact with the Holy Spirit, the creative center of spirituality, and the same results occur [healing]. Those who have participated in the Pentecostal movement remark on the healings in mind and body which occur along with tongues. From the earliest days of Pentecostal groups there has been as much interest in the physical, mental, and moral healings which have taken place as in the phenomenon of tongues itself.[255]

To make a critical analysis of Kelsey's view would take us beyond the aims of this study. This "introduction" to his approach was deemed necessary merely because he has played a significant part in providing an intellectual defense for the reality of religious experience. About "Spirit-baptism" he has said practically nothing. From his perspective one could perhaps interpret Spirit-baptism as a breakthrough into experiencing the realm of the spiritual or, equally, the process of living in both worlds, being continually open to the spiritual dimension of reality which means being open to and experiencing direct encounters with God. It is to be expected that some or other charismatic theologian will in the future rise to the challenge and develop a charismatic theology using Kelsey's perspectives. Unmistakably there seems to be a rise in interest in Kelsey's work in American charismatic circles which—I might add—is not only appreciative and sympathetic. There is also a growing dissatisfaction with this perspective correlating with the rise in Kelsey's influence. Jensen's critique of "the kingdom within" is not worked out in any detail, but he does make two major points. As a good Lutheran he protests against any concept of salvation other than salvation by grace alone. He finds in Kelsey's concept of "openness" a plus to grace! One needs to work at keeping one's psyche open by a training system with rules such as working with a spiritual director, fasting, keeping a journal, recording dreams, giving generously of one's material goods, seeking solitude, developing imagination, loving deeply, etc.[256] Kelsey and his supporters would protest that these are guidelines not legalism, but one does get the impression that the better one keeps these rules the more spiritual experiences one will have. Jensen writes:

The New Testament talks of speaking in tongues and other spiritual experiences as *gifts* of the Spirit. The temptation in interpretations like that of Kelsey and Nee is to understand spiritual experiences as a *reward* for spiritual openness and obedience.[257]

Jensen furthermore points out that God's Spirit is present in outer, visible signs—an incarnational principle expressed in the preaching of the Word and the celebration of the sacraments. Jensen remarks:

We don't become spiritual people by entering into the depths of our own invisible being. We become spiritual people by being encountered by God and his Spirit as he encounters us again and again through the outer outerness of words and bread and wine and people.[258]

Jensen's criticism does not invalidate Kelsey's approach. Everything Kelsey teaches can be couched in a thorough evangelical setting if evangelical is taken to mean relying on grace not works. If the danger of works righteousness does lurk in the background it needs to be recognized; but this does not mean that Kelsey's basic approach should be rejected. We may also benefit by being fore-warned that the Spirit is not to be identified with "innerness"–possibly this warning is more apposite to Watchman Nee whom Jensen discusses in the same context. It does not, however, apply to Kelsey who, as an Episcopalian priest, is strongly sacramental in his theology. Even a glance at the "rules" mentioned above by Jensen shows the respect for outer, visible elements such as help-ing the poor, fasting, talking to a companion, writing, loving. In other contexts Kelsey underscores the value of studying and reflecting on Scripture and partaking of the sacraments. Although his contribution is more indirect than immediate, Morton Kelsey has also contributed to an interpretation of Spirit-baptism as a *breakthrough* or openness to the spiritual dimension of reality.

4.15 Donald Griffioen and Barbara Pursey (Reformed/Presbyterian)

In conclusion a brief look will be taken at two Reformed scholars. Donald J. Griffioen of the Christian Reformed Church has written a D.Min. thesis for Fuller Theological Seminary. It is published under the title *Open Windows and Open Doors. Open to Renewal and Growth*.[259] Griffioen sees it as: A strategy for renewal and growth of Grand Rapids area Christian Reformed churches. Within the context of the charisms (chapter 5) Griffioen introduces his thoughts on renewal. Significantly he does not even discuss Spirit-baptism as a particular "second stage" experience giving access to the charisms. He pro-ceeds from the understanding that Christians have the Spirit dwelling in them under the new covenant. They do, nonetheless, need spiritual renewal. Part of this renewal is an openness to God's gifts. Griffioen explains:

> Spiritual renewal results in spiritual gifts for all believers equipping them for min-istry. . . .The Holy Spirit equips believers for ministry by giving them spiritual gifts.
>
> Spiritual renewal occurs wherever an outpouring of the Holy Spirit occurs. The outpouring of the Spirit is not merely a one-time event in history at the time of Pentecost, nor is it a one-time experience in an individual. . . .
>
> . . .When the Holy Spirit of God comes, he comes with spiritual gifts which equip the recipient for worship, communion with God, fellowship with God's people, and ministry and witness in the name of Jesus. The spiritual gifts equip the Spirit-filled person for effective service. One cannot be Spirit-filled without receiving spiritual gifts. One cannot receive spiritual gifts without being Spirit-filled. Spiritual gifts need daily spiritual empowerment or else they will become mere human abilities devoted to human endeavors. Renewal requires that we be "open to gifts."[260]

Griffioen uses the concept of renewed outpourings of the Spirit as the way in which God brings spiritual renewal to individuals. This is seen as a daily filling relating, I suspect, in all probability to the practice of daily devotions, although not necessarily tied to it. Griffioen sees a necessary relationship between being Spirit-filled and receiving charisms. This works both ways: Spirit-filled people will receive gifts and gifted people will be Spirit-filled. Not only the Christians but also the gifts need daily spiritual empowerment.

I do have a reservation about the very first sentence from the above quotation. It can be acceptable as it stands, but it is possible to read it as though a Christian could be devoid of any gift before a process of renewal commences. However if renewal is related to daily infillings this objection falls away. This just leads one to realize that "being a Christian" and "being a renewed Christian" not only overlap but are ideally identical.

Central to Griffioen's approach to renewal is his rejection of clericalism and clergy professionalism, and his propagation of the Reformation ideal of the office or priesthood of all believers. This distinction between clergy and laity which he sees as developing at the start of the Constantinian era led to a "deemphasis on the Spirit-filled character and giftedness of all believers."[261]

Viewing the "two-class system of priest and people, clergy and laity, professional and amateur" as "disastrous in stifling the growth of the church and in quenching the life of the Spirit,"[262] Griffioen is obviously striving after the full integration of charismatic impulses into the Reformed tradition. He does not find it necessary to refer to Pentecostal practices. He finds the necessary resources in his own tradition but seeks to revitalize them. The same can be said of Henry Wildeboer, who completed his D.Min. at Fuller in the same year as Griffioen. His study is entitled: "First Christian Reformed Church Renewal: Its Reformed Theological Basis, Its Development, and Its Implications for Other Congregations." Griffioen gives the following quotation from Wildeboer:

> Scriptural confession leads to the recognition that all Christians are gifted by God for praise and ministry. To be truly Reformed is to be biblically charismatic and, though the categories of charismatic and non-charismatic are frequently used, in reality any distinction is invalid since all Christians are charismatic.[263]

The rest of Griffioen's analysis in his chapter on "Renewal for Ministry" is devoted to the charisms, the great variety, fraudulent manifestations, the issue of natural talents and supernatural gifts, etc. He does, however, also use the phrase "a new outpouring of the Holy Spirit" in the more usual sense, namely of special periods of renewal in the church.[264] This contrasts with his more individualistic concept of *daily* outpourings and infillings.

In conclusion I wish to underline Griffioen's concept of expectancy—an element which was also focused on by Hummel. Griffioen expresses this well in his first proposition on renewal and spiritual gifts:

> Church renewal is born in the midst of an expectant people—pregnant with a hope and anticipation that are conceived by the Spirit of God. Amidst such an expectant people potential for the manifestation of any of the gifts of the Holy Spirit is present. We must not set any limitations on the Spirit's power and potential in our

lives, nor in the congregation of God's people. We should pray for and be open to receive and appreciate all spiritual gifts in the congregation.[265]

Griffioen exemplifies the final stage of reinterpretation of Spirit-baptism. This Pentecostal concept has fallen away completely and the focus is instead on charisms, on expectancy for the full range of charismatic gifts.

The last person in this long line of writers is the Presbyterian elder and ministerial candidate, Barbara A. Pursey. Unfortunately she has not been in a position to publish as widely as she would have liked. Her only published monograph is *Gifts of the Holy Spirit*.[266] Perhaps it is significant that the charisms, again, have been focused on as a matter of priority. Pursey has, nonetheless, lectured widely on the whole scope of charismatic theology and has an extensive survey on cassette tapes and in manuscript form. Apart from her booklet on the charisms I shall be referring to two unpublished articles: "Toward an Understanding of Baptism in the Spirit," and "Charismatic Power and Social Relevance."[267] Because they are not (yet) available in print, extensive quotations will be given.

Pursey rejects the neo-Pentecostal interpretation of Spirit-baptism and goes further, lamenting that the word charismatic has been so misused by some Pentecostal groups that it can no longer be utilized for what she used to mean by it. That is why the Presbyterian Charismatic Communion was renamed Presbyterian and Reformed Renewal Ministries International. Pursey underscores the diversity in a person's experience with God and the Spirit. She also accepts Hummel's analysis (which has been referred to previously) that Luke emphasizes the Spirit's work to empower service whereas Paul focuses on his sanctifying and unifying work.

With regard to Christian history Pursey states:

> There has never been a time in the history of the Church when the Spirit was not moving among the people of God and giving gifts of power and love.[268]

She points out that John Calvin was ambivalent on Spirit-baptism, in one place holding Spirit-baptism as more or less identical with the saving work of the Spirit, but elsewhere seeing Spirit-baptism as giving visible graces, which include miraculous powers that could be present in the church at any time if God willed it.[269] The core of the problem with respect to spiritual experience is that what started out as elements of personal experience hardened into doctrinal stands. Pursey concludes:

> One important thing to recognize is that the Pentecostal teaching on the baptism in the Spirit with the evidence of speaking in other tongues came out of a human desire to know in an absolute way what is neither given in an absolute way in the Bible nor experienced in absolute ways in Christian history.[270]

Pursey develops a new approach to Spirit-baptism which relativizes the fixed patterns of the past. It is the *reality* that needs to be communicated, not the *terminology*. Pursey summarizes her approach in the following way:

As a modern term, "baptism in/with the Spirit" describes in the language of experience one form of visitation or breakthrough by the Holy Spirit into the totality of our being. Spiritual breakthrough experiences are found in all ages of the church, but these deepening and transformational works of the Spirit have been given different names at different times. The essential feature of such breakthrough experiences is that the individual is initiated into a new level of awareness of God and effectiveness in Christian discipleship. These "baptisms" are in contrast to a gradual almost imperceptible work of the Spirit in the soul which precedes and follows the breakthrough experiences. As a matter of observation the gracious gifts of the Spirit can occur with or without such breakthrough experiences as a prelude. In earlier centuries of the church, "Baptism" experiences were connected with a call to religious life, contemplative life, the priesthood or missionary activity. Last century they were connected with holiness and spiritual perfection. Today they are primarily connected with power for ministry and particular charismatic gifts. Clearly it is a matter of the religious context of the Christian experiencing the "baptism of the Spirit" how he/she interprets it. The same Spirit is involved in all of the manifestations mentioned.[271]

Reminiscent of Tom Smail, Pursey also accords the humanity of Jesus the role of example for us:

Even Jesus, the man perfectly open to the Spirit at all times, had breakthrough experiences—in the temple at his bar mitzvah, and at the river Jordan with John. The first of these locked his sights on his life work—the Father's business. The second experience gave him the spiritual power to carry out his mission in adult life. At each point he was full of the Holy Spirit. There was no deficiency to be made up by "more Spirit," but there was a fresh "coming" of the Spirit.[272]

Pursey also refers to Thomas Aquinas—like Sullivan—in developing the idea of many "comings" of the Spirit that are both in continuity and discontinuity with one's previous experience of the Spirit.

She points out that the nature of our religious experiences is also influenced by personality factors. "Thus baptism/release/infilling of the Spirit can never be just one thing, one type of experience, one set event."[273] Note the relativizing of the positions labeled neo-Pentecostal, sacramental, and integrative in this study. Pursey also points out that, like conversion, Spirit-baptism comes in many different shapes and time slots.

Although recognizing the value of glossolalia as a liberating experience in our modern rationalistic society, Pursey is emphatic about cutting tongues down to size:

There is a pressing need today among mainline church charismatics to separate "baptism in the Spirit" experiences from the tongues experience, both in theological understanding and in practical ministry to those seeking empowerment by the Spirit. There is no reason on earth for us as Reformed Christians to interpret our experiences of the release of power and presence of the Holy Spirit in 19th century holiness/pentecostal terms. Especially if there no sound biblical footing for tongues as a necessary sign of the infilling of the Spirit. Possible—yes; helpful—often; necessary—no! There is in fact no biblical warrant for making the Acts 2 event a normative experience for 20th century Christians. Even if we restrict ourselves to the accounts in Acts, prophecy, healing, powerful evangelism and earth-shaking prayer are more prominent than tongues. Today some Pentecostal theologians are also having second thoughts about tongues as the essential sign of the baptism in the Spirit.[274]

Here Pursey refers to the minority position in the Pentecostal tradition dating back to Leonhard Steiner and represented today by leading Assemblies of God theologians such as Gordon Fee and Russ Spittler. By strange irony, while some classical Pentecostals are departing from this approach, a Catholic theologian such as Simon Tugwell (as we have seen previously) seems to be arguing that Spirit-baptism should indeed be considered as characterized by glossolalia–although I am not hereby implying that he has accepted the Pentecostal interpretation given to tongues. Pursey is also committed to the full integration of the charismatic renewal into Christianity at large:

> If we divest ourselves of Pentecostal theological doctrines, then we can stand in continuity with the church universal through the ages in affirming many infillings of the Spirit, many "comings," many evidences of the Spirit's release in our lives. Spiritual breakthrough experiences are like human growth experiences.[275]

Pursey presents the following challenge to charismatic Christians in the Reformed tradition. She says we should not rest content with what was received at infant baptism. Nor should we claim that we have "more" of the Spirit than others due to our experiences. She continues:

> It is incumbent on us all to continue our growth in grace, seeking ever-deepening openness to the Spirit, and ever-increasing willingness to be used by the Spirit in ministry. It is essential that we not reify our own experiences of the Spirit, and make them canonical for everyone else. In particular we need to be careful about defining our baptisms in the Spirit solely in terms of emotional states or physical manifestations–which diverge from the biblical teaching about the Spirit. It is also important that we not unthinkingly adopt another tradition's definition for infilling or release of the Spirit as our own–it may not fit![276]

Pursey is also true to her Calvinist heritage in calling for a prophetic witness in all areas of life under the sovereign Lordship of Christ:

> As charismatic Christians in a transformationist Reformed tradition, it is vital that we recover the union of love and justice, prayer and action, in the outworking of our baptism in the Holy Spirit, that we do justice as well as love mercy and walk humbly with our God.[277]

She develops this aspect further in her article "Charismatic Power and Social Relevance." Evaluating the charismatic renewal after 25 years, Pursey acknowledges that its early agenda was that of personal renewal. She sounds a call for compassionate charismatic servanthood including social and structural dimensions. The renewal must avoid grace without discipleship. The secret of empowerment lies in the desert experience: "In the desert we learn to be faithful lovers of God, even when there is no pleasure in being a Christian, and no miracles to excite us."[278]

Pursey notes that powerful charisms without a loving servant heart do more harm than good. We should also understand the realities of the political process so that we do not fail to be effective merely due to political naiveté. Intercession is not a cop-out but a form of action to precede other forms. Pursey states that the structural ministry in which a Christian is to get involved is the one God calls him or her to in a kingdom ministry—not necessarily the most fashionable cause of the moment.

Pursey appeals to the Reformed heritage in developing her case:

> Reformed Christians have always recognized that life is all of a piece under the universal Lordship of Christ and that there are no areas of life exempt from his kingly reign. To us, Christ is the "transformer of culture." It is time for the artificial barriers between personal and structural ministry to be dismantled. It is time for Presbyterian and Reformed Christians who have been renewed in the Spirit to bring their charismatic power to the social, economic and political issues of our times. The gifts of the Spirit are meant to be used wherever the Spirit is active—and that means both the church and the world.[279]

With this last remark Pursey focuses on the important perspective that the Spirit's work is not limited to the church. Her concept of the dimension of the Spirit and obedient walking in the Spirit is all-encompassing. If charismatic Christians do not involve themselves increasingly in costly servanthood the movement will be little more than an enthusiastic footnote in religious history.[280]

Pursey mentioned above that the gifts of the Spirit are not related to a breakthrough experience such as Spirit-baptism in any direct manner. She thus rejects the notion that Spirit-baptism opens one up to experiencing the charismata. Consequently it is not necessary to discuss Pursey's booklet on charisms in a study on Spirit-baptism. A few remarks will be sufficient. Pursey steers a middle course with respect to the natural/supernatural debate on the gifts of the Spirit:

> The biblical evidence is that charismata are not simply to be absorbed into the offices of the church or the natural abilities of believers. The same biblical teaching also discourages an excessively "miraculous" interpretation of the gifts—which somehow makes the Holy Spirit "unnatural."[281]

Pursey sees the fruit and the gifts of the Spirit as interrelated:

> The indwelling Holy Spirit has the twofold purpose of making us like Jesus Christ and enabling us to do his works. Gifts and fruits are meant to work together in a balanced way in our lives. We cannot choose between them. We can see the relationship of gift and fruit in 1 Cor. 12–14, where the famous "love chapter" is sandwiched in between two chapters on gifts (12 and 14).[282]

With respect to the question, Who is eligible to receive the charismatic gifts? balance is again the watchword:

> On the one side the church can lock the gifts up into ordained offices—as happened in the medieval church. On the other side, an individual may view the gifts as his/her private possession to be used as that individual desires.
>
> A balanced biblical view is that the gifts come personally through individual Chris-

tians, but they are not individualistic gifts. The gifts as a whole are endowments to the church as a whole, but they are distributed as the Spirit wills to individuals in the church, whether ordained or not.[283]

Pursey goes on to underscore that the charisms are for service in the Christian community and the kingdom of God in the world. Significantly, the work of the Spirit in the world has been emphasized in this study with respect to Pursey's views. She surely represents one of the clearest examples of charismatic theology fully integrated into a mainline church background (Presbyterian).

This concludes the survey of charismatic interpretations of Spirit-baptism or the dimension of the Spirit. Clearly in this chapter, charismatic theologians were introduced with whom the perspective adopted in this study was increasingly in agreement. The final assessment now remains to be given.

Endnotes 4

1. *Gospel and Spirit* (London: The Fountain Trust and the Church of England Evangelical Council, 1977). I shall be quoting from this statement as reproduced in an appendix to *Those Controversial Gifts: Prophecy, Dreams, Visions, Tongues, Interpretation, Healing*, ed. G. Mallone (Downers Grove, IL: Inter-Varsity, 1983) 155–72.
2. Ibid., 158.
3. Ibid., 158–59.
4. Ibid., 159.
5. Ibid., 160.
6. Ibid., 161.
7. Ibid., 159.
8. Ibid., 156.
9. Culpepper, *Evaluating the Charismatic Movement*, 188.
10. Smail, *Reflected Glory*, 19.
11. Ibid., 47.
12. Ibid., 35. The quote is from J. V. Taylor, *The Go-between God: The Holy Spirit and the Christian Mission* (London: SCM, 1972) 202.
13. Smail, *Reflected Glory*, 134. See the whole of ch. 10, 134–53.
14. Ibid., 41.
15. Ibid., 49.
16. Ibid., 62.
17. W. J. Jonker, *Die Gees van Christus* (Pretoria: NGKB, 1981) 226–27, also points out the role of Barth and Irving in Smail's thinking.
18. Ibid., 227.
19. Smail, *Reflected Glory*, 86–88.
20. Ibid., 87.
21. Ibid., 135–36.
22. Ibid., 138.
23. Ibid., 140.
24. Jonker, *Die Gees van Christus*, 227.
25. Smail, *Reflected Glory*, 136.
26. Jonker, *Die Gees van Christus*, 227.
27. Schmieder, *Geisttaufe*, 389.
28. Hart, "American Pentecostal Theology," 181–82.
29. Ibid., 182.

30. Smail, *Reflected Glory,* 150.

31. D. C. K. Watson, *One in the Spirit* (London: Hodder and Stoughton, 1973) 65–74.

32. Ibid., 65.

33. Ibid., 71–74.

34. Ibid., 65, 69.

35. Ibid., 69.

36. Ibid., 68. The reference is to Smail, *Reflected Glory,* 139.

37. Ibid., 70.

38. Hart, "American Pentecostal Theology," 183.

39. Some of Harper's books are: *Power for the Body of Christ* (1964); *As at the Beginning; The Baptism of Fire; Life in the Holy Spirit; Walk in the Spirit* (1968); *Spiritual Warfare; None Can Guess; Glory in the Church; A New Way of Living; Let My People Grow: Ministry and Leadership in the Church* (London: Hodder and Stoughton); *Bishops' Move* (ed.); *This is the Day: A Fresh Look at Christian Unity* (London: Hodder and Stoughton, 1979); *You Are My Sons; The Love Affair; That We May Be One* (London: Hodder and Stoughton, 1983). They are mostly published by Hodder and Stoughton or Logos.

40. Grossmann, *Stewards of God's Grace,* 53.

41. M. Harper, *Walking in the Spirit* (Minneapolis: Bethany, 1981) 35. This book contains Harper's earlier works *Power for the Body of Christ* and *Walk in the Spirit.*

42. Compare the chapter "Receiving the Promise" from *Walking in the Spirit,* 39–67, originally in *Power for the Body of Christ.*

43. Ibid., 53.

44. Ibid., 55.

45. Ibid., 60–65.

46. Hollenweger, *The Pentecostals,* 186.

47. Harper, *As at the Beginning,* 92.

48. Ibid., 95.

49. Harper, *Walking in the Spirit,* 36.

50. Kuen, *Die charismatische Bewegung,* 20–21.

51. Ibid., 21 n. 6.

52. Harper, *This is the Day,* and *Three Sisters: A Provocative Look at Evangelicals, Charismatics and Catholic Charismatics and Their Relationship to One Another* (Wheaton, IL: Tyndale, 1979). I shall be quoting from *Three Sisters.*

53. Harper, *Three Sisters,* 55–57.

54. Ibid., 57.

55. Ibid., 145 n. 19.

56. Schmieder, *Geisttaufe,* 389.

57. Harper, *Three Sisters,* 57.

58. Ibid., 58.

59. M. Harper, "Are You A Gnostic?" *Logos* (1972): 42f.

60. Harper, *Three Sisters,* 60.

61. Ibid.

62. Harper, *Let My People Grow,* 88.

63. Ibid., 100.

64. Harper, *Three Sisters,* 58.

65. Harper, *Let My People Grow,* 34.

66. M. Cassidy, *Bursting the Wineskins* (London: Hodder and Stoughton, 1983). Cassidy addresses this issue in ch. 14, "A Filling or the Baptism," 143–57, and especially in Appendix A, "What is the Baptism in the Holy Spirit?" 249–71.

67. Ibid., 257–70.

68. Ibid., 267.

69. Ibid.
70. Ibid., 268.
71. Ibid., 147.
72. Ibid., 149.
73. Ibid., 149–50.
74. F. D. Bruner and W. Hordern, *The Holy Spirit—Shy Member of the Trinity* (Minneapolis: Augsburg, 1984).
75. Ibid., 13; see his appeal to Charles Erdman.
76. M. Cassidy, *Bursting the Wineskins,* 151.
77. Ibid., 154.
78. Engelsviken, "Gift of the Spirit."
79. Ibid., 566–71.
80. Ibid., 310.
81. Ibid., 296.
82. Ibid., 311.
83. Ibid.
84. Lindberg, *The Third Reformation?* 226. Lindberg, however, incorrectly gives the reference as 260. The quotation from Engelsviken is, in fact, to be found on 311.
85. Engelsviken, "Gift of the Spirit," 569.
86. Ibid., 584.
87. Ibid., 569.
88. Ibid.
89. Ibid., 571.
90. Hummel, *Fire in the Fireplace.*
91. Ibid., 182.
92. Ibid., 185–86.
93. Ibid., 186.
94. Ibid., 188.
95. Ibid., 229.
96. Culpepper, *Evaluating the Charismatic Movement.*
97. Ibid., 62.
98. Ibid. See also 72.
99. Ibid., 63. The reference is to Stott, *Baptism and Fullness,* 25.
100. Ibid., 62.
101. Ibid., 68.
102. Ibid.
103. Ibid.
104. Ibid.
105. Hart, "American Pentecostal Theology."
106. Ibid., 222.
107. Ibid., 223.
108. Ibid., 225.
109. D. Bridge and D. Phypers, *Spiritual Gifts and the Church* (London: Inter-Varsity, 1973).
110. Ibid., 103.
111. Ibid., 115.
112. Ibid., 107.
113. Ibid., 134.
114. Ibid., 137–38.
115. C. P. Wagner, "A Third Wave? Signs Point to a Rediscovery of the Spirit's Power by Christians Outside the Pentecostal and Charismatic Movements: An Interview with C. Peter Wagner," *Pastoral Renewal* 8 (1, 1981): 5.

116. Ibid., 4.

117. Bridge and Phypers, *Spiritual Gifts and the Church,* 140–42.

118. Ibid., 134.

119. Ibid., 144.

120. D. Bridge and D. Phypers, *More Than Tongues Can Tell: Reflections on Charismatic Renewal* (London: Hodder and Stoughton, 1982).

121. R. G. Tuttle, *Wind and Flame: A Study of the Holy Spirit* (Nashville: United Methodist Publishing House [Graded Press], 1978); *Help is on the Way: Overcoming Barriers to Spirit-Assisted Prayer* (Nashville: The Upper Room, 1983); and *Guidelines: The United Methodist Church and the Charismatic Movement* (Nashville: Discipleship Resources, 1976).

122. Tuttle, *Wind and Flame,* 74.

123. Ibid., 79.

124. Tuttle, *Help is on the Way,* 76.

125. Ibid., 105.

126. From the section "Guidelines for All" *Guidelines,* 2 (see n. 121).

127. *Guidelines,* 8. The reference is A. Outler, *Evangelism in the Wesleyan Spirit* (Nashville: Tidings, 1971) 82.

128. *Guidelines,* 7. This section of *Guidelines,* namely "The Charismatic Movement: Its Historical Base and Wesleyan Framework," is not directly by Tuttle. The Introductory Statement, 1, says it "derived by the Executive Committee. . .and the editors from a paper by Dr. Robert G. Tuttle."

129. Ibid.

130. Ibid.

131. Ibid.

132. A. G. Bittlinger, *Papst und Pfingstler: Der römich-katholisch-pfingstliche Dialog und seine ökumenische Relevanz* (Bern: Peter Lang, 1978).

133. Among the most important works of Bittlinger are *Im Kraftfeld des Heiligen Geistes. Gnadengaben und Dienstordnungen im Neuen Testament* (Marburg an der Lahn: Edel, 1968); *Gifts and Graces: A Commentary on 1 Corinthians 12–14* (Grand Rapids: Eerdmans, 1968); *Gifts and Ministries* (Grand Rapids: Eerdmans, 1973); "Baptized in Water and in Spirit: Aspects of Christian Initiation," in *The Baptism in the Holy Spirit as an Ecumenical Problem,* ed. K. McDonnell and A. Bittlinger (Notre Dame: Charismatic Renewal Services, 1972); "Der frühchristliche Gottesdienst und seine Wiederbelebung innerhalb der reformatorischen Kirchen der Gegenwart," *Oekumenische Texte und Studien* 30 (1964); and *The Church is Charismatic: The World Council of Churches and the Charismatic Renewal,* ed. A. Bittlinger (Geneva: World Council of Churches, 1981).

134. Schmieder, *Geisttaufe,* 390–91, 435–38; and W. E. Failing, "Neue charismatische Bewegung in den Landeskirchen," in *Die Pfingstkirchen. Selbstdarstellungen, Dokumente, Kommentare,* ed. W. J. Hollenweger (Stuttgart: Evangelisches Verlagswerk, 1971) 131–45.

135. Failing, "Neue charismatische Bewegung," 143 n. 15.

136. Ibid., 139. From E. Käsemann, *Exegetische Versuche und Besinnungen* I, 133 [Exegetical Experiments and Reflection] Vol. 1, 4th ed. Göttingen: Vandenhoeck & Ruprecht, 1965, p. 133. The quotation from the first German edition that Failing used is exactly the same as the one given here. The English translation given is by W. J. Montague (based on the second German edition) and is from *Essays on New Testament Themes* (London: SCM, 1964) 93.

137. Ibid., 142.

138. Bittlinger, "Baptized in Water and in Spirit," 6.

139. Ibid., 10.

140. Ibid., 11.

141. Ibid., 18.

142. Ibid., 20.
143. Ibid., 14.
144. Lindberg, *The Third Reformation?* 229.
145. Bittlinger, "Baptized in Water and in Spirit," 25–26.
146. Ibid., 18.
147. A. Bittlinger, ——*Und sie beten in anderen Sprachen. Charismatische Bewegung und Glossolalie* (Metzingen: Heinzelmann, 1979) 4–5.
148. Bittlinger, *Gifts and Ministries,* 20.
149. Bittlinger, "Charismatic Renewal?" 7–13.
150. Ibid., 10–11.
151. Ibid., 11.
152. Reproduced in "Anhang: Dokumente 1," in W. Kopfermann, *Charismatische Gemeinde-Erneuerung. Eine Zwischenbilanz* (Metzingen: Heinzelmann, 1981) 53–55.
153. Ibid., 54.
154. Bittlinger, *Oekumenische Texte und Studien,* 26–27.
155. Schmieder, *Geisttaufe,* 437.
156. Bittlinger, "Baptized in Water and in Spirit," 3.
157. L. Eisenlöffel, ——*bis alle eins werden. Siebzig Jahre Berliner Erlkärung und ihre Folgen* (Erzhausen: Leuchter, 1979).
158. Ibid., 23.
159. Kopfermann, *Charismatische Gemeinde-Erneuerung.* See n. 152.
160. Ibid., 24–25.
161. Ibid., 16–17.
162. Ibid., 17.
163. Ibid., 18.
164. See n. 134.
165. The Conference proceedings were published as *Kirche und Charisma. Die Gaben des Heiligen Geistes in Neuen Testament, in der Kirchengeschichte und in der Gegenwart,* ed. R. F. Edel (Marburg an der Lahn: Edel, 1966).
166. W. Becker, "Die Charismen in der evangelischen Kirche heute," in *Kirche und Charisma. Die Gaben des Heiligen Geistes in Neuen Testament, in der Kirchengeschichte und in der Gegenwart,* ed. R. F. Edel (Marburg an der Lahn: Edel, 1966) 164–65.
167. The original German title is *Haushalter der Gnade Gottes. Von der charismatischen Bewegung zur charismatischen Erneuerung der Gemeinde,* or Stewards of God's grace. From the charismatic movement to the charismatic renewal of the congregation.
168. Ibid., 75 (Original German edition, pp. 81, 82).
169. Ibid., 76 (Original German edition, p. 83).
170. Ibid., 77 (Original German edition, p. 84).
171. Ibid., 78 (Original German edition, p. 85).
172. Ibid., 78 (Original German edition, p. 86).
173. Ibid., 80, 81 (Original German edition, p. 88).
174. Ibid., 79 (Original German edition, p. 87).
175. Among his important publications are *Die Heilige Geist als Person; in der Trinität, bei der Inkarnation und im Gnadenbund: ich, du, wir* (Münster: Aschendorff, 1967); *Die abendländische Seinsfrage als der Tod Gottes und der Aufgang einer neuen Gotteserfahrung* (Paderborn: Schöningh, 1968); *Una mystica persona. Die Kirche als das Mysterium der Heilsgeschichtlichen Identität des Heiligen Geistes in Christus und den Christen; eine Person in vielen Personen* (Paderborn: Schöningh, 1968); *Die Veränderlichkeit Gottes als Horizont einer zukunftigen Christologie. Auf dem Wege zu einer Kreuzestheologie in Auseinandersetzung mit der altchristliche Christologie* (Münster: Aschendorff, 1969).
176. H. Mühlen, "Die katholisch-charismatische Gemeinde-Erneuerung," *Stimmen der Zeit* 193 (12, 1975): 801–12.

177. Ibid., 803.

178. I am rendering the word "Gemeinde" as "Parish" in Catholic contexts and as "Congregation" in most Protestant contexts.

179. H. Mühlen, *Einübung in die christliche Grunderfahrung* I and II (Mainz: Matthias Grünewald, 1976); with the cooperation of A. Bittlinger, E. Griese, and M. Kiessig. The English translation is *A Charismatic Theology: Initiation in the Spirit* (New York: Paulist, 1978).

180. Tugwell, "Faith and Experience I," 360.

181. Schmieder, *Geisttaufe*, 440.

182. Mühlen, *A Charismatic Theology*, 93–94 (Original German edition, Vol. 1, also 93–94).

183. Ibid., 133–34 (Original German edition, Vol. 1, 133–34).

184. Tugwell, "Faith and Experience II," 427.

185. Ibid., 422.

186. Tugwell, "Faith and Experience I," 360.

187. Tugwell, "Faith and Experience II," 427.

188. H. Mühlen, "Leitlinien der Gemeindeerneuerung," *Erneuerung in Kirche und Gesellschaft* 1 (1977): 2–7.

189. Ibid., 3–4.

190. Ibid., 5. See also H. Mühlen, "A Church in Movement–Not a Movement in the Church," *Theological Renewal* 9 (June/July, 1978): 15–21.

191. Hocken, "Charismatic Renewal," 310–21, esp., 314.

192. Mühlen, "Leitlinien der Gemeindeerneuerung," 5.

193. Ibid., 6.

194. Schmieder, *Geisttaufe*, 447.

195. "Erneuerung der Kirche aus dem Geist Gottes" is reproduced in *Erneuerung in Kirche und Gesellschaft* 10 (1981): 2–31. See 9, sec. 1.2.4.3.

196. Ibid., 13, sec. 2.1.2.

197. Ibid., 13–17, sec. 2.2, 2.3, and 2.4.

198. Ibid., 19, sec. 2.6.2.3.

199. H. Mühlen, "Geist-Erfahrung und Oekumene. Zum Verhältnis zwischen 'Charismatischer Erneuerung' und Gemeinde-Erneuerung," *Erneuerung in Kirche und Gesellschaft* 7 (1980): 27–32, here specifically, 32.

200. H. Mühlen, "Die Geisterfahrung als Erneuerung der Kirche," in *Theologie des Geistes,* ed. O. A. Dilschneider (Gütersloh: Gerd Mohn, 1980) 69–94, here esp., 94.

201. Ibid.

202. Schmieder, *Geisttaufe*, 461. The Reference in this quotation is to the official document *Erneuerung der Kirche aus dem Geist Gottes*. In the *Erneuerung in Kirche und Gesellschaft* reproduction it is on 12–13.

203. Schmieder, *Geisttaufe*, 461.

204. Mallone, *Those Controversial Gifts*, 171.

205. F. A. Sullivan, *Charisms and Charismatic Renewal: A Biblical and Theological Study* (Dublin: Gill and Macmillan, 1982); "The Ecclesiological Context of the Charismatic Renewal," in *The Holy Spirit and Power: The Catholic Charismatic Renewal,* ed. K. McDonnell (New York: Doubleday, 1975) 119–38; and "The Role of Tradition," in *Theological Reflections on the Charismatic Renewal: Proceedings of the Chicago Conference October 1–2, 1976,* ed. J.C. Haughey (Ann Arbor: Servant, 1978) 79–93.

206. S. Tugwell, "So Who's a Pentecostal Now?" *New Blackfriars* 57 (1976): 415–20; F. A. Sullivan, "What is a Pentecostal Experience? A Reply to a Question Raised by Simon Tugwell," *Theological Renewal* 6 (1977): 21–25; and S. Tugwell, "Is there a 'Pentecostal Experience'? A Reply to Fr. Francis A. Sullivan, SJ," *Theological Renewal* 7 (1977): 8–11.

207. Tugwell, "Faith and Experience I," 363.
208. Sullivan, *Charisms and Charismatic Renewal*, 61.
209. Ibid., 62.
210. Ibid., 63.
211. Ibid., 66.
212. Ibid., 69.
213. Thomas Aquinas, *Summa Theologiae*, Vol. 7: Father, Son, and Holy Ghost, ed. T. C. O'Brien (London: Blackfriars, 1976).
214. Ibid., 227 S.T. 1a. 43, 6, responsio.
215. Ibid., S.T. 1a. 43, 6, ad 2.
216. Sullivan, *Charisms and Charismatic Renewal*, 72.
217. Ibid.
218. Ibid., 72–75.
219. Gelpi, *Charism and Sacrament*, 148–49.
220. Hunter, *Spirit-Baptism*, 159.
221. Sullivan, *Charisms and Charismatic Renewal*, 70.
222. F. A. Sullivan, "'Baptism in the Holy Spirit': A Catholic Interpretation of the Pentecostal Experience," *Gregorianum* 55 (1, 1974): 66.
223. Schmieder, *Geisttaufe*, 414.
224. A. Schreck, *Catholic and Christian. An Explanation of Commonly Misunderstood Catholic Beliefs* (Ann Arbor: Servant, 1984).
225. Ibid., 106.
226. Ibid., 108.
227. Ibid., 109.
228. Sullivan, "Ecclesiological Context," 122–23.
229. "Dogmatic Constitution on the Church (Lumen Gentium)" ch. 2, 12., in *The Documents of Vatican II. All Sixteen Official Texts Promulgated by the Ecumenical Council 1963–1965*, ed. W. M. Abbot (London: Geoffrey Chapman, 1966) 30.
230. Sullivan, "Ecclesiological Context," 134.
231. Ibid., 136.
232. Sullivan, "The Role of Tradition," 91.
233. Sullivan, *Charisms and Charismatic Renewal*, 51.
234. Ibid.
235. Sullivan, "The Role of Tradition," 91–92.
236. Tugwell, "Pentecostal Experience," 11.
237. Ibid., 10.
238. Sullivan, "The Role of Tradition," 92.
239. Tugwell, "Who's a Pentecostal?" 418.
240. Sullivan, "The Role of Tradition," 91.
241. Tugwell, "Who's a Pentecostal?" 418–19. The emphasis in the quotation is mine, not Tugwell's.
242. Ford, *Which Way for Catholic Pentecostals?* 18.
243. B. D. Zablocki, *The Joyful Community. An Account of the Bruderhof, A Communal Movement now in its Third Generation* (Chicago: University of Chicago Press, 1971).
244. Sullivan, "What is a Pentecostal Experience?" 25.
245. Ibid., 21.
246. Ibid., 25.
247. Ibid., 24.
248. Tugwell, "Pentecostal Experience," 10.
249. Tugwell, "The Speech-Giving Spirit," 119–59.
250. Jensen, *Touched by the Spirit*, 87–128.
251. M. Kelsey, *Encounter with God: A Theology of Christian Experience* (Minneapolis: Bethany, 1972).

252. Ibid., 242–45.
253. Kelsey, *Tongue Speaking.*
254. Ibid., 169–70.
255. Ibid., 194–95.
256. Jensen, *Touched by the Spirit,* 92. The reference is to Kelsey, *Encounter with God,* 171–212.
257. Ibid., 99.
258. Ibid., 101.
259. D. J. Griffioen, *Open Windows and Open Doors: Open to Renewal and Growth* (Grand Rapids: Christian Reformed Board of Evangelism of Greater Grand Rapids, 1984).
260. Ibid., 100.
261. Ibid., 103.
262. Ibid. The reference is to D. Watson, *I Believe in the Church* (London: Hodder and Stoughton, 1978) 259.
263. Ibid., 101. The reference is to H. Wildeboer, "First Christian Reformed Church Renewal: Its Reformed Theological Basis, its Development, and its Implications for Other Congregations" (D.Min. diss., Fuller Theological Seminary, 1983) 61. Unfortunately I was not able to get access to this dissertation from the library at Fuller in time for publication.
264. Ibid., 104.
265. Ibid., 101.
266. B. A. Pursey, *The Gifts of the Holy Spirit* (Oklahoma City: Presbyterian and Reformed Renewal Ministries International, 1984).
267. B. A. Pursey, "Toward an Understanding of Baptism in the Spirit" and "Charismatic Power and Social Relevance: The Way of Renewal Discipleship," unpublished articles.
268. Pursey, "Toward an Understanding," 2.
269. Ibid., 4.
270. Ibid., 5.
271. Ibid., 6.
272. Ibid., 7.
273. Ibid., 8.
274. Ibid., 9.
275. Ibid.
276. Ibid., 10.
277. Ibid.
278. Pursey, "Charismatic Power," 8.
279. Ibid., 20.
280. Ibid., 12.
281. Pursey, "Gifts of the Holy Spirit," 31.
282. Ibid., 6.
283. Ibid., 33.

═ 5 ═══════════════════════

5.1 General Overview

This study has critically examined the views on Spirit-baptism of more than forty writers. Chapter 2 introduced an excursus on the issue of neo-Pentecostalism and denominational structures as well as an excursus on my interpretation of what the New Testament texts mean by "baptized in the Holy Spirit." That these two digressions were necessary in chapter 2 is indicative of the fact that the neo-Pentecostal interpretation of Spirit-baptism is the least acceptable among the charismatic interpretations. The distance between my perspective and those views discussed in chapter 3 and, especially, chapter 4 is much less than it is between the pre-charismatic and neo-Pentecostal approaches of chapters 1 and 2. Nevertheless, it was essential to evaluate the rather heterogeneous complex of views dealt with in chapter 4.

One major task remains: to develop more fully the implications of my own interpretation of "Spirit-baptism." Due to the nature of my view on Spirit-baptism some attention must also be given to the issue of charisms. At the same time, the ecumenical focus of this study must be kept in mind. This study aims to be ecumenical not only in the sense that a wide variety of theologians and church leaders have been discussed in it; this, in itself, is not insignificant though, and it is important to notice that denominational ties have been relativized by the scheme of categorizing. Notice, for example, that Roman Catholics are well represented in all three chapters on charismatic interpretations. To a somewhat lesser degree this also applies to Anglicans, Reformed, and Lutherans. Baptists are found only in chapters 2 and 4. One would not expect them to use a sacramental framework since they do not use the concept "sacrament," preferring to speak of ordinances which they give the character of human response rather than divine impartation. The Eastern

Orthodox and Methodist communions are here only represented by one or two persons each. They just have not given much attention to developing theories of Spirit-baptism thus far. Equally important to remember, even though this study is focused on charismatics, is that Pentecostals, too, are far from being monolithic. The theological interpretations which have been termed Pentecostal and neo-Pentecostal are both clearly present in classical Pentecostal denominations. More noteworthy is a minority tradition in Pentecostalism stretching from Steiner in the 1930s to Fee (contemporary) which, had it been included, would probably have found its theological locus in chapter 4 (being akin to some Baptist/Free Church approaches). Although these views have not been thoroughly analyzed here, it is safe to conclude that it would be highly unlikely for any Pentecostal thinker to endorse a sacramental interpretation of Spirit-baptism (except, possibly, if glossolalia were taken to be a sacrament in the sense given to it by Simon Tugwell but that, of course, is quite a different matter).

Obviously there was an ecumenical aspect to the categorizing and discussing of the various writers on Spirit-baptism. Although not exhaustive, every attempt was made to try to represent all major published approaches. The one "glaring omission" was the absence of the views of the black independents. Especially among researchers in England (or from England) such as Hollenweger and Hocken there is an acute awareness of the importance of this perspective. The black independent Christians comprise a very large group in modern Christianity. My only defense for not having dealt with them is that their views are not easily accessible (since so much of it is oral tradition rather than written), but, more especially, their perspective is not really associated with the charismatic movement. The charismatic movement, although penetrating all groups and societal classes was, and is, largely a middle-class white phenomenon except possibly among the Catholics in South America and India. In the USA, black involvement was prominent from the very beginning in Pentecostalism, but black charismatics have never formed a substantial percentage of either the denominational or non-denominational charismatic groupings. (Some exceptions that come to mind are individual leaders such as Joseph Garlington of Mobile, Alabama, and Prentice Tipton of Ann Arbor, Michigan, but they certainly do not represent a different theological perspective from the other charismatics in the groupings to which they belong.)

As hinted above, this study wishes to make another contribution towards ecumenical theology besides having an ecumenical scope. This is on the level of doctrinal reflection. This study seeks to some degree to help bridge the rift that has developed between the Pentecostal and charismatic movements on the one hand and the rest of Christianity, mainline Protestant, Catholic, Orthodox, and evangelical on the other hand.

From even a superficial knowledge of the different divisions of Christianity it is apparent that there are three main elements of contention between Pentecostals and mainline churches: the doctrines of believer's baptism by immersion, Spirit-baptism, and the so-called extraordinary charisms of the Spirit. These doctrines will now be examined in turn.

The differences concerning baptism in water, of course, divide Christianity along lines other than Pentecostal-charismatic versus the rest. Baptists, most (but not all) Pentecostals, and some smaller Evangelical Free Church groups are united in rejecting infant baptism. The vast majority of Christians do not. With the unique position of the Presbyterian Church in New Zealand, defended by Samuel McCay,[1] of a Celebration of baptism (so as to allow an adult appropriation of "baptismal grace"), some ecumenical progress has been made – at least the hardening of the two classical positions has been questioned. This approach is also espoused elsewhere in the world and in many other denominational contexts, but the Presbyterians of New Zealand led the way and have produced the most sophisticated theological backing. By this new venture, which received its strongest impulses from the Reformed denominational charismatic movement, a significant measure of ecumenical progress has been made. The "big divide" between most Pentecostals and the mainline churches has been narrowed by the realization that both camps advocate a church-related ceremony for infants (infant baptism or the blessing and dedication of babies) and for people who have reached the age of discernment (believer's baptism, confirmation or the public profession of faith). The difference becomes apparent when we notice in which of the two ceremonies – the earlier or the later one – water is used. McCay upsets the apple cart by advocating water in both when he develops a rite for celebrating infant baptism at a later date by immersion to mark a spiritual breakthrough where faith has been newly appropriated (often through the charismatic movement). Although one should not overestimate the significance of this development, it is an example in practice of ecumenical theology at a deeper level.

This study aims to provide a similar contribution with respect to Spirit-baptism. With the concept of Spirit-baptism towards which this study has been progressing, an interpretation is given which could facilitate the total integration of the legitimate elements (in my opinion) of the charismatic movement into all sections of Christianity. The details of this position will be developed presently, but through the discussion of various theologians in chapter 4 whose views tend in this direction some inkling of what this would entail has already been supplied to the reader. Where Spirit-baptism is divested of its Pentecostal mystique and definitiveness, where it is stripped of its elitist tendency and interpreted as a spiritual growth experience or the charismatic dimension of Christian life, it can be directly incorporated and recognized as an element in the general Christian doctrine of sanctification (as an ongoing process which allows for both crisis-experiences and gradual step-by-step advancement).

The essential reality which Spirit-baptism represents is then not the second stage of a "Stufentheorie," but the essential insight that the Christian life should have an experiential dimension to it. In openness to the Spirit and in the acceptance of the full range of spiritual gifts or charisms lies the genius of

215

the Pentecostal and charismatic movements. It is encouraging that "avant garde" Pentecostal theologians are coming to this same realization today, and lonely prophetic voices from within classical Pentecostalism like Leonhard Steiner have been defending a position which amounts to much the same as this since the 1930s.

Consequently, this study contends the heartbeat of the charismatic contribution to Christianity at large is not Spirit-baptism but the acknowledging of the dimension of the Spirit which is experientially manifested in spiritual gifts or charisms. The expectancy of a broader range of charisms granted for the upbuilding and encouragement of the gathered congregation forms a key element in the contemporary renewal of Christian churches.

Now content can be given to the heading used in this chapter and in the book's title itself, *Treasures Old and New*. The impetus for this came ultimately from Matthew 13:52:

> And he said to them, "therefore every scribe who has been trained for the kingdom of heaven is like a householder who brings out of his treasure what is new and what is old."

This enigmatic little parable may be a reference to the use of the Hebrew Bible and the New Testament writings or the old and the new covenants, but be that as it may, the idea here is to apply these words to the charismatic movement. This international renewal movement, now a quarter of a century old, is in general assessed positively in this study. The charismatic Christian (i.e. the Christian involved in the charismatic movement) is like the householder referred to in Matthew 13. He has a rich treasure-house – the heritage of Christianity. Out of this treasure-house he brings forth treasures old and new. The *old treasures* mentioned second in the verse from Scripture[2] are the classic doctrines of the Christian faith like the Trinity, justification by faith, salvation, creation, the kingdom of God on earth, grace, the church as Christ's interdependent body, sanctification, the cross and the resurrection of Christ, the Lord's Supper, the indwelling of the Holy Spirit, etc. These are all part of the heritage of the Christian involved in the charismatic renewal. He or she learns to appreciate the value of them afresh. Part of these old treasures are also concepts such as "baptized in the Spirit," which refers to regeneration and the outpouring of Christ's Spirit on the church in Acts 2, and charisms such as service, teaching, giving aid, acts of mercy, and administration.

There are also the *new treasures* that the householder discovered for the first time in the charismatic renewal: charisms such as prophecy, healings, miracles, discernment, and speaking in tongues. Perhaps these were accompanied by a new depth in one's relationship to Christ, or doxological praise, fresh power to serve, new enthusiasm to pray, a deeper sense of God's presence and involvement in our lives, a new openness to being led and being guided by the Spirit, etc. Many of these elements were not totally new but became renewed. The new and the old interplay, new facets of old doctrines are discovered and old

216

familiar elements in new doctrines are recognized. Eventually the new and the old are acknowledged in everything. One is reminded of "the old, old story" that is ever new at the same time. So much for the reinterpretation of "treasures old and new."

The same metaphor can also, yet again, be extended in an ecumenical sense – the storehouse contains treasures from the wide variety of Christian churches, the old from one is rediscovered and the new from the other can be acknowledged – in both cases as the "gospel intention" behind them is recognized more clearly. The charismatic movement with its grassroots outburst of ecumenical enthusiasm certainly contained this element in its ecumenical prayer groups, covenant communities, and conferences. In the work of its theologians the same ecumenical ardor can often be found, attested to above by the fact that different interpretations of Spirit-baptism drew support across the board of denominational distinctives.

5.2 Summary of the Critical Findings of this Study

5.2.1 Chapter 1

The pre-charismatic interpretations of the Christian life where a two-stage pattern was employed were discussed to indicate the roots of the basic misunderstanding expressed in the neo-Pentecostal interpretation of Spirit-baptism. The unified pattern of Christian experience is considered as normative. The interpretation placed upon Christian experience by the two-stage patterns is questioned – not the reality of the actual religious experiences. The experiential encounter with God which the Reformed Sealers experienced as a sealing of the assurance of their salvation, and which was advocated by Martyn Lloyd-Jones as well, can be interpreted within the perspective defended later in this chapter as a powerful religious growth experience affirming the specific need for assurance of so many people both in the seventeenth century and today. Where the experience rather than the assurance is being sought (for assurance of our being children of God can surely come in other ways than through an experience), this Puritan approach becomes the forerunner of the Wesleyan, Keswick, and Pentecostal two-stage patterns. When the changes which this experience brings are viewed as necessarily permanent, the danger of an event-centered approach to the Christian life looms large. This entails a shift from the mainstream of Reformed teaching and is ultimately based on the individual experiences of certain prominent Puritans who then fell prey to the temptation of generalizing and, in time, hardened the particular experiential pattern of God's work in their lives into a fixed doctrine.

In the Wesleyan doctrine of pure love the duality of Christian experience is expressly taught. Human intentionality is perfected in the crisis experience of entire sanctification. Here one needs to take issue not only with the event-centeredness and incipient elitism, but also with a superficial doctrine of sin. The fact that this "blessing" could be lost and regained needs to be interpreted against the background of the general Arminian approach to salvation taken by Wesley. In the Wesleyan-Holiness tradition the expression "baptism with the Holy Spirit" came to designate the "second blessing." This movement eventually became separatist and was characterized by moralistic legalism and the avoidance of culture.

The ideal of the Higher Life was pursued by the Keswick movement. The second step inaugurating "the victorious life" brought, not an eradication of sinfulness from the heart (like the Wesleyan teaching), but perfection of performance. This freedom from actual sinning is achieved through willfully "resting" in Christ. In time the element of being endued with power dominated in the Keswick-Holiness tradition as an indication of the Spirit-filled life. As a movement it did not become separatist. The inherent triumphalism of this viewpoint is, however, unacceptable.

In Pentecostalism we find the full-fledged form of the event-centered, two-stage pattern for Christian experience. Doctrinally the distinction is made between the three-stage Pentecostals from the Wesleyan-Holiness tradition, who added Spirit-baptism after sanctification, and the two-stage Pentecostals, who saw Spirit-baptism as the culminating event after conversion. A rigid pattern for the experience of Spirit-baptism evolves: it must be distinct from and subsequent to conversion, attested to by water baptism, and manifested by the initial physical evidence of glossolalia, reached after meeting a series of "conditions." Once again we find legitimate experiences generalized into rules. Here the elitism is crudely evident. Whether one has had the "experience" or not is apparent from external evidence manifested by speaking in tongues as a sign. Pentecostalism was forced by the rejection it experienced from mainline Christianity into separatist structures. The event of Spirit-baptism is generally conceived of as leading to a higher level of Christian life evidenced by the "extraordinary" charisms of the Spirit. Within Pentecostalism the permanency of the experience is in all probability dependent on the Arminian/Calvinist division with respect to soteriology. All three basic elements of common Pentecostal doctrine: the so-called theology of subsequence, "conditions," and initial evidence need to be repudiated theologically. The evidence from New Testament texts do not support a second-stage reception of the Spirit after meeting "conditions" and with one particular charism as essential manifestation. Although not usually explicit, the Pentecostal teaching generally conceives of Spirit-baptism as being the pre-condition for the operation of the charisms. This underscores a theoretically superior attitude over against the rest of Christianity, which is then conceived of as practically devoid of charisms since only the more exceptional charisms are being focused on. Again there is no biblical support for any particular crisis experience or event being the gateway to the functioning of the gifts of the Spirit.

5.2.2 Chapter 2

The difference between Pentecostalism and neo-Pentecostalism is more one of degree than one of principle. The issue of separatism is keenly debated.

Consequently an excursus is devoted to it. The major dividing line among neo-Pentecostals is the "stay in" or "come out" debate which groups the denominational neo-Pentecostals together over against the various non-denominational or independent groups. Although the legitimacy of "coming out" in circumstances that would force one to be untrue to one's faith are recognized, the major issue seems to be the interpreting of the circumstances in order to determine the nature of the particular case in hand. My conviction is that the incipient elitism of neo-Pentecostalism has caused a significant number of neo-Pentecostals to become separatist where circumstances did *not* necessitate their leaving their denominations. When advancement in sanctification is externalized and objectified to such a degree that it can be measured by the experiencing of a particular event, the logical conclusion in practice (even though strictly avoided in theory) is that the "traditional" churches are "dead" and one should separate from them, coming together in a new structure formed by people who have all reached the second stage of Spirit-baptism. This argument is supported in practice by the actual experience of vibrant Christianity in such new formations. It usually takes some time before the recognition surfaces that regardless of the number of crisis experiences a Christian remains *simul iustus et peccator* and that true advancement in sanctification depends on the fruit of the Spirit, not charisms, and that one cannot gather together the more spiritually "advanced" and separate them off from the "less advanced." The reason for this latter state of affairs is that such a distinction cannot really be accurately made by men or women. Only God knows our hearts, and since humility is central to the gospel, the most advanced in sanctification seldom realize that they are more advanced and seldom evaluate themselves accurately in this regard. One fact can be categorically stated: there is no biblical or experiential reason to suppose that one can identify the more advanced or holy Christians by establishing whether or not they have had a particular second-stage experience, usually evidenced by glossolalia. Experience itself soon shows that on either side of this dividing line one finds carnal and spiritual Christians.

The neo-Pentecostal argument from Scripture was found wanting; an alternative interpretation was given in an excursus. It should be recognized that neo-Pentecostals have given up any suggestion of "conditions" (other than faith in Christ) for receiving Spirit-baptism. In fact, it is to be questioned whether the Pentecostal concept of "conditions" ever really functioned as an unevangelical works righteousness. At any rate, this point has been vastly overstated by most Reformed critics of Pentecostalism. It should furthermore be acknowledged that neo-Pentecostals have generally conceded that there should not be, what Smail has called, the "law" of tongues. Believing, however, that tongues will generally be given if there is an openness for glossolalia, neo-Pentecostals in practice place almost as much emphasis on tongues as Pentecostals. This is related to the mistaken exegesis that the wish expressed by Paul in 1 Corinthians 14:5, "Now I want you all to speak in tongues, but even more to prophesy," implies that every Christian could be granted this particular gift (at least as a devotional prayer language). Firstly this approach disregards the principle of distribution by the Spirit and the concept of interdependence among the members of the body (1 Corinthians 12). Secondly it fails to acknowledge fully that Paul is actually desiring that prophecy be sought rather than tongues while we generally find less emphasis on prophecy among neo-Pentecostals than on glossolalia. Thirdly Paul, in a similar vein, expresses the wish in 1 Corinthians 7:7 that all would remain unmarried. This is not made applicable in the same way as his desire that all speak in tongues. In the fourth and last place Paul clearly points out in 1 Corinthians 12:29, 30 that not all work miracles, possess gifts of healing, speak in tongues or interpret, etc.

The basic objections against neo-Pentecostal teaching can be summarized under the following points:

(1) All Christians have received the Holy Spirit at regeneration and are indwelt by him. This is the primary meaning of baptized in the Spirit, and it is confusing to use the term for any later experiences of the Spirit's power.

(2) There is no fixed pattern for Christians to experience in their process of sanctification. To prescribe fixed events or experiences has no warrant in Scripture and also leads to much unnecessary agonizing and searching, creating serious pastoral problems for many. Under group pressure people will sometimes fabricate the desired manifestations often leading to self-deception and an acute sense of unreality.

(3) The much disputed but valuable gift of glossolalia has no particular role to play in Christian experience. It may be used of God more frequently than other gifts in particular contexts such as the breaking through of elements such as prejudice and reserve against the spiritual which are so deeply embedded in the rationalistic culture of the West today. Nevertheless, speaking in tongues is not the "sign" or "initial evidence" of any second-stage development in the Christian life. It is a charism among other charisms—not to be despised or overrated.

(4) The event-centeredness of much of neo-Pentecostalism focusing on conversion and Spirit-baptism as experiences with a particular structure limits the inexhaustible variety of the ways in which God works in human lives. This is the unfortunate heritage of American revivalism, which often leads to these experiences being couched in overly emotional contexts as well. The event is too easily seen as a panacea. This generates much frustration when spiritual problems reappear after the glow of the experience has worn off.

(5) Another serious objection against neo-Pentecostalism could be called the "Trojan horse" syndrome. It represents the secret importation of a foreign theological framework and foreign doctrinal concepts into particular traditional backgrounds without the possibility of integration. This causes an ongoing tension often resulting in separatism. A good percentage of charismatics who have interpreted their renewal experience in neo-Pentecostal categories have, after a time, felt compelled to leave their denominations without sufficient reason. This is due to the incompatibility of this interpretation with anything but classical Pentecostal theology.

(6) Neo-Pentecostal doctrine leads to two clearly discernible classes of Christians – those who have received Spirit-baptism and those who have not (yet). Enough has already been said about this gnostic elitism, which not only causes those on the outside to feel antagonistic or inferior because they have not experienced a particular event, but also leads many on the inside later to wonder about the validity of their experience since they don't always conceive of themselves on a higher moral level or plateau. In neo-Pentecostal circles the effects of this second-stage event are generally considered to be permanent.

(7) A very important problem with neo-Pentecostal teaching is the implicit concept that Spirit-baptism is the gateway to life in the Spirit and the exercising of the charisms. Although it may be true in many individual cases that such a particular experience did open the person up to the experiencing of a whole new range of charisms, the problem again lies with the generalization. There is no biblical warrant for any experience providing the only access to the charismatic dimension of the Spirit.

(8) Finally, in close connection with the previous point, I object to the division of biblical charisms into extraordinary, supernatural gifts and ordinary, natural gifts. This may not be taught in that precise form by neo-Pentecostals, but it functions as a corollary to their position of two classes of Christendom. This is not a distinctive view of neo-Pentecostals but rather the uncritical taking over of the traditional dispensationalist framework. Neo-Pentecostals do not relegate the supernatural charisms such as miracles, tongues, and healings to a bygone age, but they do seem to use the words: charisms, gifts, charismata, etc., as always referring to the "supernatural" gifts, seldom giving sufficient attention to other gifts such as most of those mentioned in Romans 12. The "ordinary" class of gifts are either stringently "supernaturalized" or not considered as gifts, but merely as human talents and part of traditional Christianity.

In the evaluative statements made thus far the impression can be given of a one-sidedly negative approach to Pentecostal and neo-Pentecostal perspectives. This can be remedied by referring to the more lengthy treatment of the same issues in chapters 1 and 2. In order to place matters in perspective it must be noted that what I consider to be the legitimate contribution of Pentecostalism and neo-Pentecostalism is dealt with below in my own interpretation of Spirit-baptism as the charismatic dimension of the Christian life.

It is also necessary to keep the following points in mind when evaluating: much of Pentecostalism was purposefully anti-intellectual and anti-theological. There were significant reasons for this development. The fact remains that what they wrote was most often not conceived of as theology and should thus not be pressed or stringently analyzed as to logical conclusions and formulation. To a degree this also applies to early neo-Pentecostals. They wished to explain an experience rather than evolve a theology. This should, however, not detract from the fact that they were constructing a theology and presenting a theological interpretation of an experience. The mere naming the experience "baptism in the Holy Spirit" was a theological decision – unfortunately an incorrect one. Early Pentecostals saw Pentecostal and Spirit-baptism as an experience not as a denomination. Their perspective was ecumenical – this "experience" should be shared by all. Soon, however, it was theologically interpreted, albeit in a rudimentary form, and the event or experience of Spirit-baptism became the supreme distinctive of a set of denominations classified as Pentecostalism. Furthermore in Pentecostal and neo-Pentecostal writings there is an element of propaganda – the experience needs to be "sold" and this attitude does not tend to further careful explication. The totally novel nature of the first years of "Pentecost" probably contributed to the need for "tarrying meetings" and "conditions." Their importance fell away as people became more accustomed to the Pentecostal experience in the second generation of classical Pentecostals. Another factor that needs to be taken into consideration is that the keynote of their experience was that of jubilant freedom – the break with the confinements of previous traditional styles of Christianity and a refusal to be limited again in any way in their faith experience.

Quite possibly much of neo-Pentecostalism lies on the level of a lack of conscious awareness. In many the Pentecostal framework has been absorbed on a largely unconscious level; this makes its operation actually more dangerous! Many people who think, operate, and write from the perspective of a theology of subsequence would be surprised to hear that they are doing so. They often have no idea of the theological consequences of their positions. This does not justify their taking such an approach, but it does make it more understandable.

Certain neo-Pentecostal theologians have achieved a high degree of sophistication. With the new generation of upcoming Pentecostal scholars a better defense of the basic Pentecostal premises will be forthcoming. To my mind it would be more valuable if such scholars worked along the lines indicated by Pentecostals such as Gordon Fee and Russ Spittler.

5.2.3 Chapter 3

The dozen or so theologians discussed in chapter 3 have consciously rejected the neo-Pentecostal position. They are involved in the ongoing task of the reinterpretation of Spirit-baptism. Some of them have made peace with the inherited terminology of a "baptism in the Holy Spirit," others seek to supplant this confusing phrase with a more suitable one. This does not really indicate a theological difference. (It is more likely the parting of ways between realists and idealists.) We are still in a pioneering phase. It has become patently clear that the High Church tradition is incompatible with the neo-Pentecostal framework offered as an interpretive tool for the renewal experience. The easily predictable solution which was developed is that the sacramental framework of the High Church tradition should supplant the doctrine of subsequence. This approach would be expected from Eastern Orthodox, Roman Catholic, Anglican, and Lutheran communions, and it would also be possible for Presbyterian, Reformed, and Methodist charismatics, although sacramental structures are somewhat less pronounced in these latter groupings. In practice, however, no Methodist representative was forthcoming.

My basic objection to this perspective, which has excellent defenders— especially in the Catholic Church, is that although the sacramental interpretation allows for the integration of Catholic charismatics into the Catholic Church, the categories just do not fit well. Sacramental theology was seemingly not designed to accommodate Spirit-baptism. There is a sense of unreality in telling someone who has just had a powerful renewal experience that theologically nothing has happened at that particular time or that the Holy Spirit did not come in any new way at all, and all that transpired was that the Spirit, received at infant baptism, was experientially "released." (I have succumbed to the temptation to describe this as the "time bomb" theory thereby expressing, perhaps, more a Reformed impatience (!) with the constant preoccupation of many High Church theologians with the sacraments than anything else.) Catholics such as Tugwell and Sullivan acknowledge the problem of conceiving of the Holy Spirit as a kind of commodity that can be stored away for decades and then "taken off the shelf" in an experiential release. Fortunately no one less than Thomas Aquinas has acknowledged fresh "comings" or "surprises" by the Spirit, even to those whom, by another metaphor, he is already indwelling. I concur with Sullivan that there is no reason to limit the manifested workings of the Spirit to the sacraments, taking solace in the fact that he is more competent to judge whether this statement applies also to those espousing a sacramental theology than I am. Thus, there is no need to spell out a lengthy list of objections to the sacramental interpretation of Spirit-baptism. The case has been stated by Catholics already. My objection is merely that it does not fit the sacramental categories themselves. The first Malines Document's distinction between Spirit-baptism in the theological and experiential senses is rather precarious, as is the implicit assumption that God works predominantly through the sacraments with the result that a later renewal experience must be "a flowering of baptismal grace" or a renewal of confirmation, etc. The strength of this sacramental position lies in its affirmation of Christian initiation and its relating the rest of Christian experience to these beginnings. Also significant is that the primary meaning of the New Testament texts on "baptized in the Spirit" is acknowledged as referring to Christian initiation. The richness of the New Testament usage of the concept baptism is also underscored by those adopting a sacramental interpretation. Another merit of this view is that it clarifies that all who wish to accept the legitimacy of renewal experiences need not fall prey to fundamentalism, revivalism, or a moralistic attitude towards culture and society. In this sense this initial reinterpretation of Spirit-baptism paved the way for later attempts to integrate this experience into non-Pentecostal backgrounds. Furthermore, this first attempt at reinterpretation received support from Orthodox, Catholic, and Protestant theologies. It was in that sense an ecumenical endeavor, even though it did not necessarily evolve with that specific aim. Because it was so broadly applied, it could also be the fruit of the large degree of ecumenical interchange that had already taken place in the charismatic movement at large on all levels.

5.2.4 Chapter 4

This chapter presented miscellaneous "integrative" views. The inability to fit writers and concepts into neatly prescribed categories is frustrating, but I do regard accuracy more valuable than neat categories. Looking back on this chapter it is, perhaps, possible now to introduce some sub-classifications; as a result we will not be left with almost twenty supposedly widely differing perspectives. It has already been suggested that several of the theologies discussed can be termed "evangelical." However, this is not really all that helpful. The focus should rather be on the theological interpretations given to "Spirit-baptism." Or rather, as has become increasingly clear, it would be better to designate the reality referred to under the term "Spirit-baptism" as a charismatic or renewal experience; or even better, the charismatic dimension of Christian life; or alternatively, the charismatic dimension of the Holy Spirit in Christian experience. If evangelical describes a more encompassing but less useful theological viewpoint, what rubrics can be selected to classify the approaches to "Spirit-baptism" of the theologians discussed in this chapter?

Four positions seem to emerge:

(1) One approach views "Spirit-baptism" as the final stage of Christian initiation (and I shall henceforth be consistently placing the term in quotation marks to indicate that it is being employed as a convenient description for the charismatic element of life, even though I consider the term to be used properly only of regeneration, Christian initiation, or the unique events of Acts 2). According to this view, a series of overlapping concepts all form part of becoming a Christian, e.g., conversion, regeneration, repentance, justification, new birth, and being baptized in the Spirit. This view of "Spirit-baptism" as the completion of Christian initiation needs to be assessed. Such an approach has the advantage of considering the experiential charismatic dimension as an essential ingredient of the Christian life. Taken to its logical conclusion, however, it would imply that those who miss this element are either incomplete Christians or not Christians at all. In itself such a position is tenable. The problem appears when we claim to be able to establish by means of a particular type of externally verifiable experience whether such an element is present or not. Here the questionable event-centered heritage of neo-Pentecostalism and its pervasive influence must be discerned. Both Smail and Watson slip back into formulations centering on a particular charismatic experience as necessary to complete Christian initiation. I contend that charismatic experience as a dimension of the Spirit is an essential part of the Christian life; however, this does not necessarily imply a charismatic experience, even though many may be receiving it in a particular form due to cultural factors. Although Smail employs a very interesting christological model based on Irving and Barth, this does not, in

essence, affect his view on this particular point. (Something of Smail's focus on the humanity of Jesus and his relationship with the Spirit as an example to us is also found in Mühlen and Pursey.) In the final analysis Smail remains ambiguous—some formulations defining "Spirit-baptism" as what I have come to call the charismatic element and others seeing it as a particular experience which would then be needed by all to complete Christian initiation.

(2) The next position identifies "Spirit-baptism" with "filled with the Spirit." Although the expressions actually seem to be used interchangeably in Acts—with the Acts 2 experience being referred to as both "being baptized" and "being filled," this position has the advantage of leaving "Spirit-baptism" as a concept free for its proper initiatory meaning, while the charismatic experience or element is then described as an infilling or fullness. Another advantage of this perspective is that one can point to an imperative in Scripture—Ephesians 5:18. This is not the case with being baptized in the Spirit. Describing the charismatic experience/element as the fullness of the Spirit removes the major stumbling block of event-centeredness. Fullness or infilling can happen by degrees—it is not final, definitive, initiatory, or complete. Fullness must be conceived of as a dimension rather than an event or a delineated experience. Yet this view is not free from serious objections. The basic problem is that being filled with the Spirit has clear ethical overtones. To claim that one is Spirit-filled can be seen as a lack of humility, but even more important is the relationship between being Spirit-filled and sanctification. The Norwegian Lutheran approach of Engelsviken underlines the problem. He is forced to evolve a twofold fullness encompassing both sanctification and the charismatic element or dimension representing the Spirit's power and gifts. The solution may be ingenious but it is exegetically suspect. Besides, how would the two elements correlate? The charismata are said to be irrevocable (Romans 11:29) and there does not seem to be a direct relationship between advancement in gifts and in holiness. Although avoiding an event-centeredness and locating "being baptized in the Spirit" in its proper initiatory context as a metaphor for regeneration, Engelsviken's use of the term "fullness" causes more problems than it solves. This has brought me to the conclusion that specific biblical terminology is not essential or even desirable in order to describe the legitimate elements of "Spirit-baptism." The desire to find biblical backing and support should be stripped of the fundamentalist notion that to be "biblical" one needs to use biblical terminology.

(3) The next concept of "Spirit-baptism" defended in this chapter is the so-called German approach. Here "baptism in the Spirit" is expressly acknowledged as part of Christian initiation, and the charismatic dimension is given a new name, viz., "Geisterneuerung" or renewal in the Spirit. This effectively counters the problem of event-centeredness. Furthermore we have here a conscious rejection of the approach that one needs a particular experience in order to start exercising spiritual gifts. The most remarkable feature of this Middle-European model is that it became influential in mainline Protestant, Roman

Catholic, and Free Church circles. The latter is particularly important since the sacramental interpretation received no support from the Baptist or independent churches and this "German" approach can, in a certain sense, be seen as a further step towards fuller integration of the renewal into the church at large subsequent to the development of the sacramental approach. There is some development in Mühlen's position with respect to "Spirit-baptism." It is consequently difficult to conceive of the German approach as being totally homogeneous. In his early work Mühlen adopts the sacramental approach, focusing on the renewal of the sacrament of confirmation. He also follows the avenue of seeing "Spirit-baptism" as one component of Christian initiation. The criticisms leveled at these views above apply here equally. In the more recent phase of Mühlen's approach we find him presenting instead "a spirituality for every Christian." In the official German Catholic document, *Erneuerung der Kirche aus dem Geist Gottes* (May 1981), Geist-Erneuerung [renewal in the Spirit], seen as the human reaction to God's sovereign work of Geist-Erfahrung [experience in the Spirit], incorporates as a third element the charismatic dimension described as openness to the Spirit and his charisms. The possibility of a "spiritual breakthrough" or crisis experience is acknowledged as part of this dimension, but it is not made normative. In the "mature" phase of its Catholic version this German approach of parish renewal is rather similar to the Protestant versions thereby legitimizing this approach as representing a theological (rather than merely geographical!) model of "Spirit-baptism." This approach presents "Spirit-baptism" as the dimension of the Spirit but still has the sacramental concept of the renewal of the sacraments of Christian initiation as a preparatory stage or an aspect in the definitive Catholic representation of this view.

(4) The last theological interpretation discussed is basically similar to the previous one. It does have one important difference in that it sees no necessity for any sacramental renewal as background to the experiential dimension of the Christian life. Focusing on the nature of particular spiritual experiences we find that this approach sees them as "comings" of the Spirit in the Thomistic tradition. Experiences of this nature have taken place throughout the history of the church, and what is called a "Pentecostal" experience can just as aptly be described as a Christian experience. Event-centeredness is avoided and the right of particular breakthrough experiences is recognized without making them prescriptive.

In some versions of this view the particular cultural and societal factors which influence the nature of such experiences is taken squarely into account and the charismatic dimension is described in Jungian terms as encountering the psychoid or spiritual reality of the unconscious. Although not explicit, it would seem apparent that in the Kelseyan version a particular experience does in effect form the gateway to experiencing spiritual reality (in the form of charisms). This probably is an unacceptable generalization, but it should be remembered that it is not a universal generalization. It is applicable only to rationalistic Western culture since the Enlightenment.

In yet another version of this position the charismatic dimension is described by the term "Spirit-filled." The objection to this terminology has been spelled out above. Here the openness to the charismatic dimension is related to receiving charisms. This is acceptable; the problem only comes in when the receiving of charisms is tied to a particular type of experience or event. In the last theologian discussed in the chapter we find a conscious rejection of a necessary correlation between breakthrough experiences and charisms. The terminology of infilling, "comings," and release of the Spirit sometimes describes the charismatic dimension of the Spirit. The important thing is that they be given content in such a way as to avoid a rigid event-centered pattern and the notion that a particular type of experience is essential (both in itself and as a prelude to receiving charisms). The most acceptable terminological variation is reached, in my opinion, when Pursey states quite simply that spiritual breakthrough experiences are like *human growth experiences*.[3] After such an experience the charisms may flow more fully, but this is not to deny the possibility of their presence beforehand. Gifts and the fruit of the Spirit do not necessarily correlate but are meant to work together.

5.3 "Spirit-Baptism" as the Charismatic Dimension of Normal Integrated Christian Life

As an alternative to the many interpretations of "Spirit-baptism" already discussed and in the line with perspectives developed in approaches (3) and (4) I wish to present the charismatic dimension of normal Christian life as a reinterpretation of what a large section of the charismatic movement has called "baptism in the Spirit." Under this concept I wish to include everything that I consider legitimate in charismatic experiences, as well as providing a new theological framework for understanding such renewal experiences and the functioning of charisms. What is meant by "the charismatic dimension" of Christianity? Simply this: the Christian life has an experiential faith dimension to it. By this I do not mean that people who have not had heavy, emotional encounters with God, seen visions, spoken in tongues, etc., are not Christians —far from it. Nevertheless, I insist that where faith in accountable Christians is not experiential or "real" it does not exist in a healthy form. (The qualifications "accountable" accommodates situations of very young or very old people or those physically, psychologically, or mentally so handicapped or diseased that they may not be able to give account of their faith.)

This experiential or charismatic dimension of the life and faith of Christians is characteristic of all forms of vibrant Christianity. It expresses itself in trusting prayer, experiencing the grace of Christian fellowship, worshiping, meditating on Scripture, celebrating the sacraments, prophetically witnessing, rendering deeds of compassion, etc. The human spirit is sometimes more receptive to the workings of God than at other times. This can be influenced by personal or corporate sinfulness or by individual or systemic factors of a psychological or societal nature.

The normal integrated Christian life is living the life of Christ or walking in the Spirit. This is graciously granted us by God who calls us to "stay in tune" and "keep in step" with the Spirit. On this pathway of grace God showers the church with his spiritual gifts and ministries. The power of God becomes experientially manifested in various ways, not the least of them being that the Spirit distributes his gifts or charisms to the body of Christ. The concept of charisms employed here includes the whole spectrum of gifts designated as charismata in the New Testament, and then goes on to encompass other facets of Christian existence in which the energizing power of God operates. I believe there is a large diversity of charisms such as intercession, helping the aged, promoting justice and equity, breaking the power of evil spirits, practicing a profession, rearing children, doing theology or physics, witnessing to the great deeds of God, and propagating ecological balance and global peace. In this sense every Christian is, and should be increasingly, charismatic. This charismatic dimension includes elements that are at times more common and usual than others. The church should strive towards expressing the fullness of life in the Spirit and exercising all its charisms. The concept charism here functions in the broadest possible sense. The great service of the charismatic renewal has been to rediscover several New Testament charisms that had fallen into disuse. This draws attention to the great variety of charisms the Spirit distributes and the need for the church to rediscover the full range of charisms.

God usually distributes his gifts within the human parameters of openness and expectancy, but being sovereign he is not obligated to restrict himself to our receptivity. The charisms are elements of the new creation—Bittlinger's attempt to avoid the dilemma of natural or supernatural. It may be good to recall both his definition and description of charisms given above in 4.10:

> A charism is a gratuitous manifestation of the Holy Spirit, working in and through, but going beyond, the believer's natural ability for the common good of the people of God.

> Purely as a phenomenon, nothing whatever is in itself "charismatic" or "spiritual." All the phenomena are the realization of possibilities within this world. But everything, however ordinary or extraordinary, can be made use of by God for the neighbor's or the world's salvation, and thereby becomes a charism (there is no Christian who always acts charismatically, but there is also no Christian who never acts charismatically).[4]

This last statement should not be interpreted as if authentic Christian life is divided dualistically into charismatic and non-charismatic sections. Life in the Spirit is charismatic, life in the flesh is not. This ideal radicalization of the concepts charismatic dimension and charism does present us with some problems. First, it tends to blur the distinction between the fruit and the gifts of the Spirit. Second, there is the temptation (which is always present) either to reduce the charismatic dimension just to the "natural" or else to limit it to the "supernatural" and extraordinary. Let us first deal with the second point. This dilemma must be avoided. *Christian life* and *life* could be synonymous if sin were not a factor. The charismatic dimension of living in the Spirit is that quality of life which sees life as a gift, which leads one to do all things as good works out of gratitude towards God, which acknowledges the kingly rule of Christ over the whole cosmos, which seeks to serve the neighbor and the world rather than self, etc. This is the broadest, or "kingdom-perspective," usage of the concepts charismatic dimension and charism. Here Christian, spiritual, and charismatic are almost synonyms, spiritual naturally focusing on the Holy Spirit just as Christian points to Christ.

However, it is still possible to use the terms charismatic and charism in a more restricted sense without limiting it to the traditional stereotypes of supernaturalism and emotionalism. Theoretically, it is possible to reserve charism only for the charisms listed in Scripture and to reserve charismatic dimension for particular experiences of spiritual breakthrough or "infilling." The temptation to restrict the terms in this manner is very real. I believe, nonetheless, that it should be consistently resisted. The normal Christian life should always be full of the charismatic dimension, i.e. be thoroughly Spirit-energized even though one acknowledges that this is not possible due to sin and because we still live in the eschatological tension between the already and the not yet.

Even in this broad concept of the charismatic dimension it is necessary to preserve the interdependence of the body of Christ, i.e. what has been called the distribution principle of 1 Corinthians 12. No matter how many or how few charisms there are, we still need one another (and the gifts that God has given to others) in order to experience the fullness of God's grace in his body. He does not give all gifts to any one person or any one gift to everyone. The broadening of the concept of charism really underscores the element of mutual interdependence rather than lessening it.

With regard to the distinction between the gifts and the fruit of the Spirit we need to keep in mind that the ideal pattern is that they should develop and work together. God in his sovereignty can grant many gifts to individuals, withdrawing them or still maintaining them when these individuals resist that work of the Spirit which is aimed at producing fruit in their lives. Similarly God can let some people grow in the fruit of the Spirit even while they may be resisting the charisms through a lack of receptivity. There are no fixed rules or patterns here except that one can generally expect that growth in either charisms or fruit should have an advantageous influence on the whole life of the person and lead to further dedication and docility to the Spirit in other areas as well.

The basic intention of the charismatic renewal is compatible with all sections of Christianity. It lies in vibrant, expectant faith; openness to the Holy Spirit and the wide range of his gifts; and a refusal to deny the experiential aspect of Christianity in order to appease rationalistic Western culture. If, however, the impression has been given that the charismatic renewal can fit into much of mainline Christianity with ease that impression is misleading and incorrect. The charismatic movement is a revival, a spiritual awakening, which needs to revitalize, energize, disturb, and renew the contemporary expressions of the faith of the church. There are attempts in some circles to domesticate the charismatic renewal—to "tame" it so that it amounts to roughly the same as traditional Christianity. Walter Hollenweger has made reference to this in his preface to *New Heaven? New Earth?*[5] This has been referred to previously and will not be discussed again here. What is necessary is to look at two discussions of the charismatic renewal from an evangelical perspective by Andrews and Packer, who came to a conclusion very different from those arrived at in this study.

After a perceptive analysis of the classical Pentecostal, neo-Pentecostal, Reformed Sealers' and traditional Reformed viewpoints, E. H. Andrews opts for a return to dispensationalism. In the final chapter of his book, *The Promise of the Spirit,* he concludes that the "foundational" charismata have ceased; yet he wishes to maintain "the charismatic principle."[6] This should, however, by no means be confused with what is called in this study the charismatic element or dimension. Andrews sees this "principle" as involving the continued distribution of the Spirit's gifts (1 Corinthians 12:11)—which is surely acceptable, but then he limits this to the non-miraculous! He sees the cessation of miraculous charisms as progress—leaving behind the "childhood" phase of the church.[7] This is an overt return to antiquated dispensational doctrine. Accordingly, the manifestations displayed among Pentecostals and charismatics can be explained as satanic imitation or as psychological productions.[8] By implication he sees authentic glossolalia as limited to the apostolic era, but he makes a small concession:

> Having said this, we do not condemn others. In one matter, that of private tongues-speaking, we have not in fact been able to come to any clear view as to their cessation.[9]

Since this study is focused on Spirit-baptism it is, unfortunately, not possible to deal further with the arguments of dispensationalism here.

J. I. Packer shows an even deeper understanding of the charismatic movement than Andrews, but he also ends up discounting the likelihood that New Testament gifts of tongues, interpretation, healing, and miracles have been restored.[10]

Packer notes the basic flaw of neo-Pentecostal teaching. On the one hand he sees most Protestant and lay Roman Catholic charismatics as espousing a form of restorationism and introducing Wesleyan-Pentecostal thought patterns.

On the other hand he groups together those who see Spirit-baptism in terms of "realization":

> ...those with their roots in Catholic theology (Roman, Orthodox, Anglican) follow a different path at crucial points, as do also some Reformed thinkers who are involved.[11]

By "realization" Packer means the release of something previously latent—the sacramental pattern of interpretation—although Packer does not use that term for it. His opinion is that charismatic experience is less distinctive than is sometimes made out. Packer, as a clear "outsider," makes some interesting and noteworthy observations about the direction in which the charismatic renewal is going:

> Charismatics, while maintaining spiritual solidarity with other charismatics, are more and more seeking theological solidarity with their own parent segment of Christendom.[12]

> These emphases also have the effect of moving charismatic thought into line with the mainstream Christian tradition which sees grace not as overriding or destroying nature, but rather as restoring and perfecting it, eliminating our radical sinfulness but not our rational humanity.[13]

Packer concludes that any divisiveness or hypercritical attitudes among charismatics are temporary and that what God is doing through the experience of charismatics is essentially what he is doing in the lives of all believing, regenerate people everywhere, namely, working to renew the image of Christ in them[14].

In all these points Packer's view is essentially accurate. In his interpretation of Spirit-baptism he reveals his Puritan roots. He sees the experience in essence as a deepened awareness of the Spirit of adoption bearing witness to the Father's love in Christ (Romans 8:15–17). Such an experience of assurance is in continuity with the rest of one's Christian existence.[15] I would question whether this is the only correct interpretation or type of "Spirit-baptism," but I agree with the basic thrust of Packer's argument. That is why it comes as such a surprise when he rejects the openness to the full range of biblical charisms as an objectionable super-supernaturalism.

When Packer questions the ultimacy sometimes assumed by exponents of the charismatic renewal, and notes a lack of humility, and cautions against an insufficient realization of God's holiness and the sinfulness of sin, I can only agree that this applies in many cases. Unfortunately Packer does not seem to notice that he, too, falls prey to the temptation of generalizing and fails to recognize that there are leading exponents of charismatic theology who are not guilty of the flaws of neo-Pentecostalism that he is continually addressing. His oversight is compounded when he acknowledges the exceptional nature of "particular segments of it [the charismatic movement] in Britain and Germany."[16] If he sees the differences, why is his rejection couched in such blanket statements? One can only hope that after studying Bittlinger, Grossmann,

Mühlen, Sullivan, or Pursey, Packer will at least partially retract statements such as,

> The charismatic movement is theologically immature, and its public speech and style seem on occasion half-baked as a result.[17]

> The movement's intellectual and devotional preoccupation with the Holy Spirit tends to separate him from the Son.[18]

> ...the charismatic life stream still needs an adequately biblical theology and remains vulnerable while it lacks one.[19]

While these remarks do apply to some segments of the worldwide renewal movement, there are vast areas where they do not. Some of these statements can also be made of many non-charismatic groups as well.

The major problem with Packer, however, is not that he does not sufficiently take notice of the nuance and diversity of the charismatic renewal. Such faults can be expected in research on a movement so young and dynamic. The most serious objection is that in his enthusiasm to reject the Pentecostal ideal of restorationism (with its arrogant view of church history that the Spirit "abandoned" the church between the apostolic era and the renewal of this century) Packer throws out the proverbial baby with the bath water. Theoretically he states that the question as to whether God's withdrawing of the so-called sign gifts after the apostles' ministry was over (in my opinion already an incorrect assumption) meant that God would never under any circumstances restore them as they were, is unanswerable;[20] but the answer that he would prefer to give to the question is transparent from his rejection of what he calls super-supernaturalism and his statement,

> ...nobody can be sure, nor does it seem likely, that the New Testament gift of tongues, interpretation, healing, and miracles have been restored.[21]

Neither do I consider his point significant that most Catholic and some Protestant charismatics who do not have a restorationist perspective "go no further than to claim that current charismatic phenomena are analogous to [rather than the same as] those mentioned in the New Testament."[22] If one operates with the view that the New Testament lists of charisms are not closed or definitive but merely examples (as has been the case in this study), it really makes little difference whether glossolalia today is exactly the same as in Acts 2, or in Corinth for that matter. The issue is: Is one open to acknowledging that God can and does grant charisms of a supernatural, non-rational nature today?

It should remain clear that in arguing for "Spirit-baptism" as the charismatic dimension of the normal integrated Christian life this openness to the full range of charisms is not negotiable. It is the very heart of the matter. The broadening of the concept charismatic has important implications for the way in which we view pneumatology and Christology. I will return to this presently, but first further attention needs to be given to the aspect of particular spiritual experiences.

Within this charismatic dimension of the Christian life there is room, not only for charisms, however broadly conceptualized, but also for a wide range of spiritual experiences. The most common form of particular spiritual experience in the charismatic renewal involves a crisis experience or spiritual breakthrough where the non-rational elements of faith experience a sudden "release" from the inhibiting forces of the rationalistic cultural patterns of contemporary Western civilization. In many cases this is expressed in a newfound avenue of doxological praise, usually manifested in glossolalia. The nature of the most common type of spiritual experiences will, in all probability, be culturally and societally determined; but a variety of experiences do nevertheless still occur in Christianity today. Factors of individual personality structure sometimes play an important role as regards the nature of religious experiences. Hocken writes:

> There are two dominant models for spiritual growth: the "break-through" and the "gradual." The former represents the crisis-experience, the sudden irruption and invasion of the Spirit of God, the moment of crucial decision; the latter the step-by-step advance, the slowly eroding or gently filling work of the same Spirit.[23]

To explore the nature of religious experience—even charismatic experience—is not the task of this study. I merely wish to give some pointers regarding another interpretive framework for "Spirit-baptism."

The charismatic dimension with its openness to charisms as well as particular experiences can be followed throughout the history of the church. Unfortunately most new historical surveys of the eras of the Christian church written from a charismatic perspective seem to focus on specific charisms of a more spectacular nature such as miracle healings and glossolalia. It would be valuable to ferret out less spectacular charisms like the "gift of tears" throughout church history, or infused contemplation, or prophecy, or being single for the Lord (celibacy).

When commenting on the book of Acts, Reformed scholar J. H. Bavinck speaks of intense spiritual experiences under the heading: "Filled with the Spirit." He writes:

> In the normal everyday life they [the disciples] were not always "filled," but nevertheless the Spirit always dwelt in them. They were always "guided" by Him. The same also applies to us: we are being led by the Spirit day by day (Rom 8:14), but we are only "filled" at a few special moments when God deems it necessary. This "being filled" is actually a foretaste of heaven, when God will be "all in all" (1 Cor 15:28).[24]

It may be debatable whether the concepts "infilling" or "fullness" of the Spirit are the best to apply here, but Bavinck underscores the value of such intermittent moments as milestones in one's spiritual life. They are different to the daily Christian walk. One could say that the daily Christian walk has a charismatic dimension to it through the experiencing of God's charisms or his guidance (as Bavinck acknowledges). On occasion there may be the more

233

intense spiritual experience when one's being is flooded by the presence of God. Such experiences are generally emotional and the temptation is always to seek them for themselves. Such misguided endeavor results in an event-centered concept of the Christian life.

Experiences such as Bavinck describes are given by grace. They are not "necessary" in any strict sense. They do not indicate spiritual superiority. They may even tend to happen more to those who suppress the gradual ongoing working of God and then need to experience sudden releases or spurts of growth when their temporary resistance has been overcome by a fresh act of commitment and dedication. These experiences are not the key to the charisms, but it is quite understandable that the exercising of the charisms may be benefited or increased by such growth experiences.

After a quarter of a century it seems as if the charismatic movement is entering the phase in which it can now be fully integrated into the mainstream of Christianity. Through theological reflection and wise pastoral guidance this integration is being facilitated. The ultimate aim is the charismatic renewal of the whole of Christianity. This is a long way off, but the rediscovery by many Christians of what I am calling the charismatic nature or dimension of the Christian life is a powerful tool in working towards this goal.

In *Unordained Elders and Renewal Communities* Steve Clark explores the early ascetic movement of the fourth and fifth centuries, which, as a renewal movement, was successfully and constructively integrated into the church as a whole.[25] He highlights the role of lay (unordained) elders in this monastic movement and the great contribution it made to missionary zeal and social service. It also produced prominent leaders who became saints and doctors of the church: Basil, Augustine, Jerome, John Chrysostom, Gregory of Nazianzus, and Gregory the Great.[26] The future will have to show whether the charismatic movement could also overcome the obstacles to full integration, stem the tide of separating off into new charismatic denominations, and thus become an effective instrument in God's hand for renewing the whole church and for establishing the kingly rule of Christ in the world.

We now need to return to the issue of the full integration of the charismatic renewal into historic Christianity, or the problem of distinguishing between Christian and charismatic. From another perspective this can be called the issue of relating Christology and Pneumatology.

A long tradition of lamenting the lack of emphasis on the Spirit exists in theology. The Germans have called it "Geistvergessenheit." Renewal movements often see themselves as reestablishing the balance by underscoring the work of the Spirit. Unfortunately this generally develops into an unhealthy tension between our conceptions of the second and third Persons of the Trinity. The position found among some early Pentecostals that one receives Christ at conversion and the Spirit at a subsequent experience is completely misguided. This would make the Spirit "superior" since Christ then just does the preparatory work while the Spirit only comes to hearts already converted and sanctified (cf. the original three-stage Wesleyan-Holiness Pentecostals). Over against this attitude the pendulum has sometimes swung to seeing the Spirit as subordinate to Christ (in practice, if not acknowledged in theory). Of course, those who emphasize the work of the Spirit usually see themselves as reacting against such subordination of the Spirit in traditional Christianity. In some Reformed circles the Spirit is seen as being "modest" or even "shy" as Bruner describes him in his latest book, *The Holy Spirit—Shy Member of the Trinity.*[27] This modesty of the Spirit is enlisted as a safeguard over against what is considered to be an overinflated pneumatology or to preserve what "rightfully" belongs to Christ. The exegetical defense for the "modesty" of the Spirit seems to be John 16:13: "When the Spirit of truth comes, he will guide you into all the truth; for he will not speak on his own authority." The words "he will not speak on his own authority" are rendered by the Authorized Version "for he shall not speak of himself." The point is not that the Spirit does not speak about himself but that he does not speak on his own, or on his own authority. It is surely correct to state that the Spirit is modest or humble (I would hesitate about shy!), but then not modest or humble in contrast to Christ who is just as modest and humble (cf. Philippians 2), and one might add, just as bold and forthright too!

In chapters 14–16 of John's Gospel we not only find the reference to the Spirit not speaking on his own authority (just quoted above) but also exactly the same idea expressed about the Son in relationship to the Father:

> Do you not believe that I am in the Father and the Father in me? The words that I say to you I do not speak on my own authority; but the Father who dwells in me does his works. (John 14:10)

The basic misunderstanding behind it all involves a wrong doctrine of the Trinity. Not only are the Persons of the Trinity conceived of as separate individuals (persons in the modern sense of the word), but one also gets the impression that they could vie against one another so that people arise to champion the cause of the Son, the Father, or the Spirit. It is possible that in our theology we can place incorrect emphases. Many have seen the charismatic movement as being too Spirit-centered, while more perceptive observers have pointed out that it is the Son who is at the center.[28] Others have spoken of *The Forgotten Father,*[29] pointing to a neglect of the role of God the Father in the charismatic movement.

In the light of the structure of the history of salvation it is necessary to deny that the Spirit has come to do something "extra" or additional to what the Son has accomplished. The dangers of such spiritualism have been historically illustrated in the excesses of the radical Anabaptists and Spiritualists of the Reformation era. This eventually leads to a separation of Word and Spirit as well. The essential unity of divine operation must be clearly recognized.

The Spirit does not work on his own but neither does the Son do anything that He did not receive from the Father, i.e., Father, Son and Spirit do one divine work. It can be viewed from the perspective of each Person, but all are involved in every aspect of God's work, even if it is also true that each one is not involved in the same way. It is not really helpful to designate for example, creation, as the Father's work. John tells us all things were made by the Word—the Son (John 1). Augustine proclaimed *"opera trinitatis ad extra indivisa sunt."* In every aspect of Christ's work we can also recognize the sending of the Father and the supportive and anointing presence of the Spirit. Consequently it makes no sense to try to diminish the role of the Son to enrich the Spirit or the Father.

From this two conclusions can be made: First, it is not necessary to downgrade the Spirit so that the Son may receive his due honor as the center of our faith (which, in any case, we happen to call the Christian faith!). Second, in order to do justice to the Spirit we do not need to create a separate, extra work for him to do. His work is already as encompassing as that of the Father and the Son. One could theoretically accept that possibly one Person of the Trinity is more on the foreground than another in some particular facet of salvation for instance, but this is not really helpful in my opinion. One needs rather to guard against the natural tendency to forget that the other two members of the Trinity are fully involved in that aspect as well. This danger is illustrated in the approach of Hendrikus Berkhof (who furthermore also rejects the traditional concept of the Trinity).[30] Berkhof finds it necessary to speak, reacting against a "neglect" in traditional theology, of "an additional working" of the Spirit beyond justification and sanctification.[31] This can easily create the impression that this "third element" which has to do with the Spirit's infilling and gifts is something the Spirit adds to the works of justification and sanctification which rest in Christ's atonement. The real problem is not that we have neglected the Spirit but that our view of the work of God in Christ has been too limited! It is not right to restrict the benefits of Christ's saving deeds to the traditional concepts of justification and sanctification. There is "more," but that "more" is not so much an additional working of the Spirit (over against the work of Christ) as a deeper and broader realization of the implications of Christ's work of reconciliation. The saving grace of Jesus Christ also brings us the benefits of spiritual renewal, guidance and the fruit and charisms of the Spirit. It is Jesus who sends the Spirit. It is the risen and glorified Lord who pours out the Spirit on the Church on the day of Pentecost:

> This Jesus God raised up, and of that we all are witnesses. Being therefore exalted at the right hand of God, and having received from the Father the promise of the Holy Spirit, he has poured out this which you see and hear. (Acts 2:32, 33)

This is why Pentecostals like the late David du Plessis underscore that Jesus is the Baptizer, the agent in Spirit-baptism. A consequence of this focus has been the preference for the preposition *in* as a translation of the Greek *en* in the phrase "baptized *in* the Holy Spirit," rather than the instrumental alternative *by.*

One finds in the New Testament a remarkable parallel between christo-logical and pneumatological categories. The whole Christian life can be expressed in terms of Christ and his salvation (e.g. in Romans 6). The same applies to the Holy Spirit. This is illustrated by the parallelism in Romans 8 where the phrases "in Christ" and "in the Spirit" are used as alternatives denoting the same things, compare, for example, verses 1 and 9–11. The believers are seen as in Christ and in the Spirit as well as having Christ and the Spirit living in them. The ethical categories of the Pauline indicative and imperative are also expressed christologically and pneumatologically.

For this reason it is possible to give a theological outline of the Christian life using the incorporation into Christ, the participation by faith in his death and resurrection as the start or initiation into the life of Christ, which then continues in sanctification as abiding in Christ (John 15). Similarly using pneumatological concepts the life in the Spirit can be seen as starting with Spirit-baptism or regeneration through the Spirit—a participation by faith in the initial outpouring of the Spirit on the church and continuing in being filled with the Spirit, bearing the fruit of the Spirit, and receiving his charisms or gifts. (The same can even be done with reference to "theological" categories and God the Father by using concepts such as incorporation into the covenant and the people of God.)

The charismatic dimension of the Christian life is a crucial part of life in the Spirit. Consequently it is a crucial part of life in and through Christ—the normal integrated Christian life. One should also recognize that life in the Spirit is, of course, broader than the charismatic element or dimension. However widely one conceives of the charisms there is more to the Christian life (and life in the Spirit) than charismatic gifts and experiences. Pneumatologically one can point to the realm of the fruit of the Spirit which provides the style in which the gifts are to be exercised. Although one cannot choose between the fruit and gifts of the Spirit as alternatives (as many evangelicals are tempted to do, saying they will focus on the fruit and thus the gifts) one could say that in sanctification the fruit is primary. Due to the nature of this study much emphasis has been given to the charisms. Other non-charismatic aspects of life in the Spirit include the inner testimony of the Spirit, guidance, inspiration, assurance, but the ninefold fruit of the Spirit probably makes up the major part of life in the Spirit that can be distinguished from charisms and spiritual experiences.

We have seen above that *Christo*logy and *Pneuma*tology (and for that matter "*Theo*logy" as the doctrine of the Father) in a very real sense deal with the same work of the one triune God. If Christology happens to be worked out in greater detail in theological textbooks that is of historical, rather than prin-cipial, significance. It is due to the pivotal position of Jesus Christ in the history of salvation, not because he is either more or less important than the Spirit. The Spirit, as the Heidelberg Catechism states: "is also given me, to make me, by a true faith, partaker of Christ and all His benefits."[32] The Spirit does this here and now and he was also fully involved in every facet of Christ's life on earth from his birth to his ascension, as well as being involved in Pentecost and the second coming of Christ. Likewise he is involved in every aspect of the believer's life. The relationship between the Spirit's work in Jesus and its reflection in the life of the believer has been developed by Tom Smail and to some degree also dealt with by Mühlen.

Thus, there is no theological impediment to describing the dimension of the Spirit in a believer's life simply as Christian and the charismatic element in it as a crucial part of the normal Christian life. For too long the Spirit and his work have been conceived of in a limited sense. There was a capitulation at the beginning of the modern era in which faith became restricted to the private devotional life and the latter was then described as "spiritual." McDonnell writes that we now await a mature theology of the Spirit.[33] The Spirit should not be limited to "spiritual experiences" and charisms—even though it needs to be recognized that the element of "experiences" and charisms still awaits acknowledgement in much of Christianity. We need, however, to set our sights much higher. Not only the realm rediscovered by Pentecostalism needs to be reclaimed but also the cosmic dimensions of the Spirit's work. Large areas of societal life and contemporary culture need to be reappropriated. The Spirit is at work in the world and should not be degraded into an ornament of piety.[34]

Within this more encompassing framework it is necessary to return to what has been called the "proper" understanding of Spirit-baptism and the relationship of this to the charismatic dimension of Christian life. The view taken in this study is that "baptized in the Spirit" properly refers primarily to the communal "initiation" of the early church at Pentecost when the Spirit was poured out and secondarily to Christian initiation. Spirit-baptism is thus one of the metaphors used to describe the way a person becomes a Christian. The dominant concept in Christian initiation, however, is that of baptism in water.

The New Testament often includes all the other overlapping concepts under the rubric baptism. Christian baptism speaks of the forgiveness of sins, purification, regeneration, becoming the possession of Christ, receiving the Spirit, being incorporated into Christ's body—the church, and into the covenant of grace.[35] It also includes in a very real sense a union with and participation in the life of Jesus Christ. König develops this in his book on baptism, *Die doop as Kinderdoop én Grootdoop* [Baptism as Infant Baptism and Adult Baptism]. He sees the baptized believer as taking part in Christ's history, being united to him in his crucifixion, death, burial, resurrection, present position in heaven, and his return.[36] Unfortunately König fails to refer to Pentecost in this regard, but he could easily have developed this as well. In our union with Christ, the anointed and Spirit-filled Lord, we partake of the charisms serving and building up his body through them. By being united with the life of Christ it is no longer we who live but Christ who lives in us (cf. Galatians 2:20).

This calls us to the task of then living this life. This christological balance between the indicative and the imperative is equally applicable to pneumatological categories. The charisms of the Spirit are gifts that are distributed, yet we are called to earnestly desire these gifts and to exercise them. One is reminded of Augustine's maxim: Lord, first grant me what you desire from me and then require whatever you wish.

What is then, firstly, the relationship between baptism and Spirit-baptism? When baptism in water is seen in this very encompassing sense it can be considered to include Spirit-baptism as one element among others. It is also possible to see Spirit-baptism specifically as the receiving of the Spirit in regeneration. This would imply that Spirit-baptism is the meaning or significance of baptism in water. The ritual act of baptism itself should not be seen as an automatic guarantee of salvation (the doctrine of baptismal regeneration). The New Testament, however, does not separate the true meaning or significance (Spirit-baptism or regeneration) from the actual act of baptism itself. This is probably because the New Testament was written within a first generation mission context that cannot be applied on a one-to-one basis to the situation of a covenantally structured Christian life.

Secondly, how does this now relate to what has been called the charismatic dimension of life? Christian initiation is the prerequisite for life in the charismatic dimension of the Spirit. One could almost say that this is a doctrine of subsequence! This is naturally not meant in the sense of a second step or "event" but in the sense that the Christian life, also called the process of sanctification, is the ongoing development after one becomes a Christian. Nevertheless, there is always some ambiguity about this distinction. This has been illustrated in the previous chapter by theologians who want to see Spirit-baptism as the completion of Christian initiation landing up with the logical deduction that some Christians are then "incomplete" Christians. Even Karl Barth, who was referred to in the first chapter as representing the unitary position in which Spirit-baptism is considered synchronous with regeneration, does not escape this ambiguity. He sometimes expresses the idea that Spirit-baptism is the start of Christian life while at other times it seems to include the whole Christian life.[37] Calvin and Kuyper also used the concept regeneration (which is usually seen as the start of the Christian life) in an all-inclusive sense encompassing the whole of Christian life. The work of the Spirit in people seems to defy rigid classifications—a point amply illustrated by the cases of so-called Spirit-baptism in the book of Acts. Consequently, there is a sense in which that which has been termed the charismatic dimension of life cannot be completely sealed off from baptism and Christian initiation. There is something about the *simul iustus et peccator* nature of Christian life which continually brings us back to "square one" again! For example, those who consider themselves advanced in spirituality probably need to relearn the initial exercise of humility. Perhaps this is another way of saying that we live, as Christians, not by merit but by grace. Thus, there is no great principal need to hermetically seal off the start from the rest of Christian life. In this sense one can relate Spirit-baptism as part of Christian initiation more directly to "Spirit-baptism" as signifying the charismatic dimension.

Barth always returned to the forgiveness of sins as the primary element of Christian life and Luther saw the Christian's existence as a "stete Busse"[38] or continual repentance. Nevertheless, I still believe that it was important to reject the neo-Pentecostal exegesis of Spirit-baptism as a subsequent stage or event. The locus of Spirit-baptism is Christian initiation but, in retrospect, it is perhaps good to relativize the rigidity of our categories by acknowledging that the charismatic dimension (which I see as the authentic heritage of the neo-Pentecostal position) is really quite closely related to Spirit-baptism in Christian initiation. The dimension of life in the Spirit is the ongoing fruit of Spirit-baptism much like the correlation of faith and works in James 2. To paraphrase accordingly:

> What does it profit, my brethren, if a man says he has received Christian initiation but has not the charismatic dimension? Can his Spirit-baptism (alone) save him? So baptism by itself, if it renders no charisms or life in the Spirit, is dead.

This needs to be balanced by Galatians 2 in similar paraphrase:

> Yet we know that a man is not justified by charisms of the Spirit but through initiation into Jesus Christ, even we have been baptized into Christ Jesus, in order to be justified by becoming a Christian, and not by spiritual experiences, because by experiences and charisms shall no one be justified.

I do not mean to suggest at all that faith and works really correlate with the two senses of Spirit-baptism as used here. The only conclusion that needs to be drawn is their interrelatedness and interdependence for the normal integrated Christian life. This brings us to the close of the discussion of my interpretation of "Spirit-baptism." This model of interpretation which sees "Spirit-baptism" neither as a second event in a theology of subsequence nor as a release of the Spirit, neither as an infilling or fullness nor the completion of Christian initiation, has its benefits. It provides the possibility of full integration into the various non-Pentecostal sections of Christianity and also presents the revitalization of an old, but very minor position, in Pentecostalism itself—in other words, I believe it could be ecumenically useful to Christian theology at large. The view of "Spirit-baptism" as the dimension of the Spirit, the charismatic element of normal Christian life should, however, not be seen as a panacea. All the theological problems of the charismatic movement will not be solved if this becomes the pervasive interpretation of Spirit-baptism. Mercifully the blessing of God has never been dependent on "good theology." Possibly other interpretations of Spirit-baptism will continue to dominate the scene and the few places where this approach is, to some degree, already being implemented, will continue to involve small numbers of Christians. This study is just one attempt among several to contribute to the ongoing development of charismatic theology (and Christian theology) from an ecumenical perspective. The triune God renews his church and transforms the face of the earth: *soli Deo gloria*, or, in the charismatic idiom, "Praise the Lord!"

Endnotes 5

1. S. J. D. McCay, "Charismatic Renewal and Requests for a Second Baptism," *Theological Renewal* 8 (Feb./Mar., 1978): 13–21; "Celebrating Renewal and Appropriation of Baptism by Immersion (Paper 6)," in *Infant Baptism? The Arguments for and against. Proceedings of a Theological Congress held at UNISA 3–5 October 1983,* ed. A. König, H. I. Lederle, and F. P. Möller (Roodepoort, South Africa: CUM, 1984) 125–38; see also from the same collection of essays H. I. Lederle, "First Response to Paper 6," 139–43. The best defense of this position is McCay's "Celebrating Renewal by Appropriating Baptism" (M.Th. thesis, University of South Africa, Pretoria, 1986).

2. I have chosen to reverse the word order in Matthew in this reinterpretative usage not only because it sounds better on the tongue but since my basic point with respect to the charismatic movement is that charismatics need to discover that what they consider to be all new is actually a revitalization of the "old treasures" of Christianity. Traditional Christianity needs to discover the same fact–that much which they find novel or strange in the renewal movement is part of the heritage of historic Christianity. These old facets do need to be renewed and are thus in a sense old and new at the same time. The context and impetus of the charismatic movement is, however, new and, in its particular form, unique in the history of the church.

3. Pursey, "Toward an Understanding," 9.

4. The references are from Bittlinger, *Gifts and Ministries,* 20, and *The Church is Charismatic,* 11.

5. Tugwell, et al., *New Heaven? New Earth?* 9.

6. Andrews, *Promise of the Spirit,* 249–51.

7. Ibid., 248.

8. Ibid., 252.

9. Ibid., 253.

10. Packer, *Keep in Step,* 229.

11. Ibid., 181.

12. Ibid., 220.

13. Ibid., 221.

14. Ibid., 221–22.

15. Ibid., 225–26.

16. Ibid., 228.

17. Ibid., 232.

18. Ibid., 233.

19. Ibid., 231.

20. Ibid., 218.

21. Ibid., 229.

22. Ibid., 183.

23. P. Hocken, *You He Made Alive: A Total Christian View of Prayer, Communal, Individual and with Special Reference to the Work of the Spirit in Prayer Groups* (London: Darton, Longman and Todd, 1974) 69.

24. J. H. Bavinck, *Geschiedenis der Godsopenbaring. Het Nieuwe Testament,* 3rd ed. (Kampen: Kok, 1955) 513.

25. S. B. Clark, *Unordained Elders and Renewal Communities* (New York: Paulist, 1976) 6.

26. Ibid.

27. Bruner and Hordern, *The Holy Spirit.*

28. Compare, e.g., K. McDonnell, "The Determinative Doctrine of the Holy Spirit," in *Theology Today* 39 (2, 1982): 160.

29. Compare the book of T. A. Smail, *The Forgotten Father* (London: Hodder and Stoughton, 1980).

30. H. Berkhof, *The Doctrine of the Holy Spirit* (Atlanta: John Knox, 1976) 111–21.

31. Ibid., 87.

32. *Heidelberg Catechism*, Lord's Day XX Question 53.

33. McDonnell, "Determinative Doctrine," 142–43.

34. Ibid., 143.

35. A. König, *Die Doop as Kinderdoop én Grootdoop* (Pretoria: NGKB, 1985) ch. 2.

36. Ibid., 21–31.

37. K. Barth, *Die Kirchliche Dogmatik IV, 4. Das christliche Leben (Fragment). Die Taufe als Begründung des christlichen Lebens* (Zürich: EVZ-Verlag, 1967) 34,40 en 42.

38. The first of Luther's 95 theses reads as follows:

Wenn unser Herr und Meister Jesus Christus sagt: "Tut Busse" usw., so will er, dass das ganze Leben seiner Gläubigen auf Erden eine stete Busse sein soll. [When our Lord and Master Jesus Christ said: "Repent," etc., it is his desire that those who believe in him will live their entire earthly lives in an ongoing state of repentance.]

LIST OF SOURCES

This list of sources includes all works cited and referred to in the endnotes of the chapters of this study as well as a selected list of other sources consulted, arranged in one consecutive alphabetical list according to the last name of author or editor. Primary sources of a corporate and institutional origin are listed separately at the end according to title.

Abbott, W. M., ed. *The Documents of Vatican II. All Sixteen Official Texts Promulgated by the Ecumenical Council 1963–1965*. London: Geoffrey Chapman, 1966.

Agrimson, J. E., ed. *Gifts of the Spirit and the Body of Christ. Perspectives on the Charismatic Movement*. Minneapolis: Augsburg, 1974.

Anderson, R. M. *Vision of the Disinherited: The Making of American Pentecostalism*. New York: Oxford University Press, 1979.

Andrews, E. H. *The Promise of the Spirit*. Welwyn, England: Evangelical Press, 1982.

Archer, Antony, OP. "Teach Yourself Tonguespeaking." *New Blackfriars* 55 (1979): 357–64.

Askew, T. A., and Spellman, P. W. *The Churches and the American Experience: Ideals and Institutions*. Grand Rapids: Baker, 1984.

Backman, M. V. *Christian Churches of America. Origins and Beliefs*. Rev. edition. New York: Charles Scribner's Sons, 1983.

Baker, J. P. *Baptized In One Spirit. The Meaning of 1 Cor. 12:13*. London: Fountain Trust, 1967.

Barabas, S. *So Great Salvation: The History and Message of the Keswick Convention*. London: Marshall, Morgan & Scott, 1952.

Barnard, R. T. "Die Fenomeen 'Doop met die Heilige Gees': 'n Eksegeties-dogmatiese evaluering." M.A. thesis. University of Port Elizabeth, South Africa, 1984.

Barrett, D. B. *World Christian Encyclopedia: A Comparative Study of Churches and Religions in the Modern World A.D. 1900–2000*. Nairobi: Oxford University Press, 1982.

Barth, K. *Die Kirchliche Dogmatik. Das christliche Leben (Fragment). Die Taufe als Begründung des christlichen Lebens*. IV,4. Zürich: EVZ-Verlag, 1967.

Basham, D. *A Handbook on Holy Spirit Baptism. 37 Questions and Answers on the Baptism in the Holy Spirit and Speaking in Tongues*. Springdale, PA: Whitaker, 1969.

Baumert, N. "Aus dem Leben der Kirche. Zum charismatischen Aufbruch." *Geist und Leben* 55 (1, 1982): 55–60.

Bavinck, J. H. *Geschiedenis der Godsopenbaring. Het Nieuwe Testament*. 3rd Rev. Edition. Kampen: Kok, 1955.

Becker, W. "Die Charismen in der evangelischen Kirche heute." In *Kirche und Charisma. Die Gaben des Heiligen Geistes in Neuen Testament, in der Kirchengeschichte und in der Gegenwart*. Edited by R. F. Edel. Marburg an der Lahn: Edel, 1966.

Bennett, D. J. *Moving on in the Spirit*. Eastbourne: Kingsway, 1982.

———. *Nine O'Clock in the Morning*. Plainfield, NJ: Logos, 1970.

Bennett, D., and Bennett, R. *The Holy Spirit and You: A Study Guide to the Spirit-Filled Life*. Plainfield, NJ: Logos, 1971.

———. *Trinity of Man. The Three Dimensions of Healing and Wholeness*. Plainfield, NJ: Logos, 1979.

Berkhof, H. *The Doctrine of the Holy Spirit.* Atlanta: John Knox, 1976.

————. "Der Vorschuss des Geistes. Aktuelle Tendenzen in der Pneumatologie." *Evangelische Kommentare* 8 (1975): 658–62.

Bittlinger, A. "Baptized in Water and in Spirit: Aspects of Christian Initiation." In *The Baptism in the Holy Spirit as an Ecumenical Problem.* Edited by K. McDonnell and A. Bittlinger. Notre Dame: Charismatic Renewal Services, 1972.

————. "Charismatic Renewal: An Opportunity for the Church." *The Ecumenical Review* 31 (1979): 247–51.

————. "Charismatic Renewal–An Opportunity for the Church?" In *The Church is Charismatic.* Edited by A. Bittlinger. Geneva: World Council of Churches, 1981.

————, ed. *The Church is Charismatic.* Geneva: World Council of Churches, 1981.

————. "Der frühchristliche Gottesdienst und seine Wiederbelebung innerhalb der reformatorischen Kirchen der Gegenwart." *Oekumenische Texte und Studien* 30 (1964): 1–32.

————. *Gifts and Graces: A Commentary on 1 Corinthians 12–14.* Grand Rapids: Eerdmans, 1968.

————. *Gifts and Ministries.* Grand Rapids: Eerdmans, 1973.

————. *Im Kraftfeld des Heiligen Geistes. Gnadengaben und Dienstordnungen im Neuen Testament.* Second rev. edition. Marburg an der Lahn: Oekumenischer Verlag Edel, 1968.

————. *Papst und Pfingstler. Der römisch-katholisch-pfingstliche Dialog und seine ökumenische Relevanz.* Bern: Peter Lang, 1978. Studien zur interkulturellen Geschichte des Christentums 16.

————. . . . *Und sie beten in anderen Sprachen. Charismatische Erneuerung und Glossolalie.* Fourth rev. edition. Koordinierungsausschuss für Charismatische Gemeindeerneuerung in der Evangelischen Kirche. Metzingen: Heinzelmann, 1979. Charisma und Kirche series 2.

Bloch-Hoell, N. *The Pentecostal Movement: Its Origin, Development and Distinctive Character.* New York: Humanities Press, 1964. Also Oslo: Universitetsforlaget, 1964.

Bloesch, D. G. "The Charismatic Revival: A Theological Critique." *Religion in Life* 35 (1966): 377–80.

Boer, J. de. *De verzegeling met de Heilige Geest volgens de opvatting van de Nadere Reformatie.* Rotterdam: Bronder, 1968.

Boer, C. den. "De doop met de Heilige Geest." In *Profetie of fantasie?* Edited by J. van der Graaf and C. Snoei. Amersfoort: Echo, 1978.

Bouyer, L. "Some Charismatic Movements in the History of the Church." In *Perspectives on Charismatic Renewal.* Edited by E. D. O'Connor. Notre Dame: University of Notre Dame Press, 1975.

Bradford, B. *Releasing the Power of the Holy Spirit.* Oklahoma City: Presbyterian Charismatic Communion, 1983.

————. Review of J. R. Williams, *The Gift of the Holy Spirit Today.* In *Renewal News for Presbyterian and Reformed Churches* 64 (Jan./Feb., 1981): 14.

Bridge, D., and Phypers, D. *More Than Tongues Can Tell: Reflections on Charismatic Renewal.* London: Hodder and Stoughton, 1982.

————. *Spiritual Gifts and the Church.* London: Inter-Varsity, 1973.

Brumback, C. *"What Meaneth This?" A Pentecostal Answer to a Pentecostal Question.* Springfield, MO: Gospel Publishing House, 1947.

Bruner, F. D. "The Holy Spirit: Conceiver of Jesus." *Theology, News and Notes* (March, 1974): 9–13.

————. *A Theology of the Holy Spirit: The Pentecostal Experience and the New Testament Witness.* Grand Rapids: Eerdmans, 1970.

Bruner, F. D., and Hordern, W. *The Holy Spirit–Shy Member of the Trinity.* Minneapolis: Augsburg, 1984.

Byrne, J. E. *Living in the Spirit. A Handbook on Catholic Charismatic Christianity.* New York: Paulist, 1975.

Calvin, J. *Institutes of the Christian Religion* (LCC: XX, XXI). Translated by F. L. Battles. Philadelphia: Westminster, 1960.

Carothers, M. *Prison to Praise: Spiritual Power through Praise.* Plainfield, NJ: Logos, 1970.

Cassidy, M. *Bursting the Wineskins.* London: Hodder and Stoughton, 1983.

Chantry, W. J. *Signs of the Apostles. Observations on Pentecostalism Old and New.* Second rev. edition. Edinburgh: Banner of Truth, 1976.

Christenson, L. "Baptism with the Holy Spirit." *International Lutheran Renewal* 62 (January, 1985): 1–3 (unnumbered).

_____. "Bericht aus der Lutherischen Kirche in Amerika." In *Kirche und Charisma. Die Gaben des Heiligen Geistes in Neuen Testament, in der Kirchengeschichte und in der Gegenwart.* Edited by R. F. Edel. Marburg an der Lahn: Edel, 1966.

_____. *The Charismatic Renewal among Lutherans: A Pastoral and Theological Perspective.* Minneapolis: Lutheran Charismatic Renewal Services, 1976.

_____. *A Message to the Charismatic Movement.* Minneapolis: Bethany, 1972.

_____. "Pastoral Guidelines." *Theology, News and Notes* (March, 1974): 22–23.

_____. "Pentecostalism's Forgotten Forerunner." In *Aspects of Pentecostal-Charismatic Origins.* Edited by V. Synan. Plainfield, NJ: Logos, 1975.

_____. *Speaking in Tongues and Its Significance for the Church.* Minneapolis: Bethany, 1968.

_____. *Social Action Jesus Style.* Minneapolis: Bethany, 1976. Original title: *A Charismatic Approach to Social Action,* 1974.

Christenson, L. ed. *Welcome, Holy Spirit. A Study of Charismatic Renewal in the Church.* Minneapolis: Augsburg, 1987.

Clark, M. S. "A Critical Evaluation of the Doctrine of the Rhema Bible Church." B.D. thesis. Pretoria, University of South Africa, 1983.

Clark, S. B. *Baptized in the Spirit and Spiritual Gifts. A Basic Explanation of the Key Concepts and Experiences of the Charismatic Renewal.* Ann Arbor: Servant, 1976. First published 1969.

_____. *Confirmation and the Baptism of the Holy Spirit.* Pecos, NM: Dove, 1969.

_____. *Unordained Elders and Renewal Communities.* New York: Paulist, 1976.

_____. *Where Are We Headed? Guidelines for the Catholic Charismatic Renewal.* Ann Arbor: Servant, 1973. Book two of the Servant series.

Clement, A. J. *Pentecost or Pretense? An Examination of the Pentecostal and Charismatic Movements.* Milwaukee: Northwestern, 1981.

Congar, Y. *I Believe in the Holy Spirit. II "He Is Lord and Giver of Life."* New York: Seabury, 1983. Original title: *Je crois en l'Esprit Saint II Il est Seigneur et Il donne la vie.* Les Editions du Cerf, 1979.

Conn, C. W. *Like A Mighty Army Moves the Church of God.* Cleveland, TN: Church of God Publishing House, 1955.

Cottle, R. E. "All Were Baptized." *JETS* 17 (1974): 75–80.

Cox, L. G. "John Wesley's Concept of Perfection." Ph.D. diss., Iowa State University, 1959.

Culpepper, R. H. *Evaluating the Charismatic Movement. A Theological and Biblical Appraisal.* Valley Forge, PA: Judson, 1977.

_____. "A Survey in Some Tensions Emerging in the Charismatic Movement." *SJT* 30 (5, 1977): 439–52.

Damboriena, P., SJ. *Tongues as of Fire: Pentecostalism in Contemporary Christianity.* Washington, DC: Corpus, 1969.

Davis, R. *Locusts and Wild Honey: The Charismatic Renewal and the Ecumenical Movement.* Geneva: World Council of Churches, 1978.

Dayton, D. W. "From Christian Perfection to the 'Baptism of the Holy Ghost.'" In *Aspects of Pentecostal-Charismatic Origins*. Edited by V. Synan. Plainfield, NJ: Logos, 1975.

Dilschneider, O. A. "Gnoseologie oder vom Verstehen im Geiste." In *Theologie des Geistes*. Edited by O. A. Dilschneider. Gütersloh, Gerd Mohn, 1980.

———, ed. *Theologie des Geistes*. Gütersloh, Gerd Mohn, 1980.

du Plessis, D. J. *A Man Called Mr. Pentecost*. As told to Bob Slosser. Plainfield, NJ: Logos, 1977.

———. *The Spirit Bade Me Go. The Astounding Move of God in the Denominational Churches*. Revised edition. Plainfield, NJ: Logos, 1970.

Dunn, J. D. G. *Baptism in The Holy Spirit: A Reexamination of the New Testament Teaching on the Gift of the Spirit in Relation to Pentecostalism Today*. London: SCM, 1970.

———. *Jesus and the Spirit: A Study of the Religious and Charismatic Experience of Jesus and the First Christians as Reflected in the New Testament*. London: SCM, 1975.

Duquoc, C., and Floristán, C., eds. *Charisms in the Church*. New York: Seabury, 1978. Concilium. Religion in the Seventies.

———, ed. *Spiritual Revivals*. New York: Herder, 1973. Concilium. Religion in the Seventies.

Durasoff, S. *Bright Wind of the Spirit: Pentecostalism Today*. Plainfield, NJ: Logos, 1972.

Dusen, H. P. van. "The Third Force." *Life* 44 (June 9, 1958): 122–24.

Eaton, M. A. "The Direct Witness of the Spirit in the Theology of David Martyn Lloyd-Jones (1899–1981)." M.Th. thesis. University of South Africa, Pretoria, 1984.

Edel, R. F. "Die Charismen in der Geschichte der evangelischen Kirche." In *Kirche und Charisma. Die Gaben des Heiligen Geistes in Neuen Testament, in der Kirchengeschichte und in der Gegenwart*. Edited by R. F. Edel. Marburg an der Lahn: Edel, 1966.

Edel, R. F., ed. *Kirche und Charisma. Die Gaben des Heiligen Geistes in Neuen Testament, in der Kirchengeschichte und in der Gegenwart*. Marburg an der Lahn: Edel, 1966.

Edwards, J. *A Treatise on Religious Affections*. repr., Grand Rapids: Baker, 1982.

Eisenlöffel, L. . . . *bis alle eins werden. Siebzig Jahre Berliner Erklärung und ihre Folgen*. Erzhausen: Leuchter, 1979.

Emmert, A. F. S. "Charismatic Developments in the Eastern Orthodox Church." In *Perspectives on the New Pentecostalism*. Edited by R. P. Spittler. Grand Rapids: Baker, 1976.

Engelsviken, T. "The Gift of the Spirit: An Analysis and Evaluation of the Charismatic Movement from a Lutheran Theological Perspective." (Part 1 and 2). Ph.D. diss., Aquinas Institute of Theology, Dubuque, IA, 1981. University Microfilms International, Ann Arbor, 1982.

Ervin, H. M. *Conversion-Initiation and the Baptism in the Holy Spirit: A Critique of James D. G. Dunn, Baptism in the Holy Spirit*. Peabody, MA: Hendrickson, 1984.

———. *These Are Not Drunken, as Ye Suppose*. Plainfield, NJ: Logos, 1968.

Failing, W. E. "Neue charismatische Bewegung in den Landeskirchen." In *Die Pfingstkirchen. Selbstdarstellungen, Dokumente, Kommentare*. Edited by W. J. Hollenweger. Stuttgart: Evangelisches Verlagswerk, 1971.

Farah, C. *A Critical Analysis: The "Roots and Fruits" of Faith-Formula Theology*. Tulsa: Insight Ministries, 1980.

———. *From the Pinnacle of the Temple: Faith or Presumption*. Plainfield, NJ: Logos, n.d. (ca. 1980).

Faupel, D. W. "The Function of 'Models' in the Interpretation of Pentecostal Thought." *Pneuma* 2 (1, 1980): 51–71.

———. *The American Pentecostal Movement: A Bibliographic Essay*. Society for Pentecostal Studies Monograph Series 1, 1972.

Fee, G. D. "Baptism in the Holy Spirit: The Issue of Separability and Sequence." In Toward a Pentecostal/Charismatic Theology: "Baptism in the Holy Spirit." Society for Pentecostal Studies's Fourteenth Annual Meeting, November 15–17, 1984, at Gordon-Conwell Theological Seminary.

_____. *The Disease of the Health and Wealth Gospels.* repr., Costa Mesa, CA: The Word for Today, 1979.

_____. "Hermeneutics and Historical Precedent. A Major Problem in Pentecostal Hermeneutics." In *Perspectives on the New Pentecostalism.* Edited by R. P. Spittler. Grand Rapids: Baker, 1976.

Ferreira, I. L. *Die charismata en die Nederduitse Gereformeerde Kerk.* Pretoria: NG Kerkboekhandel, 1975.

Fichter, J. H. *The Catholic Cult of the Paraclete.* New York: Sheed and Ward, 1975.

Fickett, J. D. *Confess It, Possess It: Faith's Formula? Reflection on Faith-Formula Theology.* Oklahoma City: Presbyterian and Reformed Renewal Ministries International, 1984.

Firet, J. "Psychologische notities met betrekking tot de 'Geestesdoop.'" *Gereformeerd Theologisch Tijdschrift* 78 (1, 1978): 77–91.

Fischer, B. "'Baptism of the Spirit.' The Meaning of the Expression 'Baptism of the Spirit' in the Light of Catholic Baptismal Liturgy and Spirituality." *One in Christ* 10 (1974): 172–73.

Flew, R. N. *The Idea of Perfection in Christian Theology: An Historical Study of the Christian Ideal for the Present Life.* Oxford: Clarendon, 1934.

Flynn, T. *The Charismatic Renewal and the Irish Experience.* London: Hodder and Stoughton, 1974.

Ford, J. M. *Baptism of the Spirit: Three Essays on the Pentecostal Experience.* Techny, IL: Divine Word, 1971.

_____. "Catholic Pentecostals." *Catholic Digest* (June, 1974): 44–48.

_____. "The Charismatic Gifts in Worship." In *The Charismatic Movement.* Edited by M. P. Hamilton. Grand Rapids: Eerdmans, 1975.

_____. "Neo-Pentecostalism within the Churches." *The Ecumenist* 13 (3, 1975): 33–36.

_____. "The New Pentecostalism: Personal Reflections of a Participating Roman Catholic Scholar." In *Perspectives on the New Pentecostalism.* Edited by R. P. Spittler. Grand Rapids: Baker, 1976.

_____. "Paul's Reluctance to Baptize." *New Blackfriars* 55 (654, 1974): 517–20.

_____. "Pentecostal Catholicism." In *Spirituality.* Edited by C. Duquoc and C. Geffré. London: Burns and Oates, 9 (8, 1972). Concilium. Religion in the Seventies.

_____. *Which Way for Catholic Pentecostals?* New York: Harper and Row, 1976.

Frøen, H. J. "What is the Baptism in the Holy Spirit?" In *Jesus, Where Are You Taking Us? Messages from the First International Lutheran Conference on the Holy Spirit.* Edited by N. L. Wogen. Carol Stream, IL: Creation House, 1973.

Gaffin, R. B. "The Holy Spirit and Charismatic Gifts." In *The Holy Spirit Down to Earth.* Grand Rapids: Reformed Ecumenical Synod, 1977.

_____. *Perspectives on Pentecost: Studies in New Testament Teaching on the Gifts of the Holy Spirit.* Phillipsburg, NJ: Presbyterian and Reformed, 1979.

Gee, D. "To Our New Pentecostal Friends." *New Covenant* (Sept., 1974): 21–22. Originally in *Pentecost* (Dec., 1961/Feb., 1962).

Gelpi, D. L. "American Pentecostalism." In *Spiritual Revivals.* Edited by C. Duquoc and C. Floristán. New York: Herder, 1973. Concilium. Religion in the Seventies.

_____. "Can You Institutionalize the Spirit?" *New Catholic World* 217 (1301, 1974): 254–58.

_____. *Charism and Sacrament: A Theology of Christian Conversion.* New York: Paulist, 1976.

_____. "Conversion: The Challenge of Contemporary Charismatic Piety." *TS* 42 (1982): 606–28.

_____. *The Divine Mother: A Trinitarian Theology of the Holy Spirit*. Lanham, MD: University Press of America, 1984.

_____. "Ecumenical Problems and Possibilities." In *The Holy Spirit and Power: The Catholic Charismatic Renewal*. Edited by K. McDonnell. New York: Doubleday, 1975.

_____. *Experiencing God: A Theology of Human Emergence*. New York: Paulist, 1978.

_____. "Pentecostal Theology: A Roman Catholic Viewpoint." In *Perspectives on the New Pentecostalism*. Edited by R. P. Spittler. Grand Rapids: Baker, 1976.

_____. *Pentecostalism: A Theological Viewpoint*. New York: Paulist, 1971.

Gérest, C. "The Hour of Charisms: The Development of the Charismatic Movements in America." In *Charisms in the Church*. Edited by C. Duquoc and C. Floristán. New York: Seabury, 1978. Concilium. Religion in the Seventies.

Gerlach, L. P., and Hine, V. H. "Five Factors Crucial to the Growth and Spread of a Modern Religious Movement." *JSSR* 7 (1968): 23–40.

Ghezzi, B. "The Charismatic Renewal and Church Renewal." *New Covenant* (Sept., 1974): 29–31.

Graaf, J. van der, and Snoei, C., eds. *Profetie of fantasie?* Amersfoort: Echo, 1978.

Green, M. *I Believe in the Holy Spirit*. London: Hodder and Stoughton, 1975. I Believe series.

Greet, K. G. *When the Spirit Moves*. London: Epworth, 1975.

Griffioen, D. J. *Open Windows and Open Doors: Open to Renewal and Growth*. Grand Rapids: Christian Reformed Board of Evangelism of Greater Grand Rapids, 1984.

Gritsch, E. W. *Born Againism: Perspectives on a Movement*. Philadelphia: Fortress, 1982.

Grossmann, S., ed. *Der Aufbruch. Charismatische Erneuerung in der katholischen Kirche*. Kassel: Rolf Kühne, n.d.

_____. *Stewards of God's Grace*. Exeter, Devon: Paternoster, 1981. German original: *Haushalter der Gnade Gottes. Von der charismatischen Bewegung zur charismatischen Erneuerung der Gemeinde*. Wuppertal: Oncken, 1977.

Gunstone, J. *Greater Things than These: A Personal Account of the Charismatic Movement*. Leighton Buzzard, England: Faith Press, 1974.

Haenchen, E. *Die Apostelgeschichte*. 7. Auslegung, 16. Auflage. Göttingen: Vandenhoeck & Ruprecht, 1977. English translation: *Acts of the Apostles. A Commentary*. Oxford: Basil Blackwell, 1971.

Hamilton, M. P., ed. *The Charismatic Movement*. Grand Rapids: Eerdmans, 1975.

Harper, M. "Are You A Gnostic?" *Logos Journal* 40 (3, May/June, 1972): 42–43.

_____. *As At the Beginning: The Twentieth Century Pentecostal Revival*. Plainfield, NJ: Logos, 1971.

_____. "Bericht aus der anglikanischen Kirche Englands." In *Kirche und Charisma. Die Gaben des Heiligen Geistes in Neuen Testament, in der Kirchengeschichte und in der Gegenwart*. Edited by R. F. Edel. Marburg an der Lahn: Edel, 1966.

_____. "Charismatic Renewal–A New Ecumenism?" *One in Christ* 9 (1, 1973): 59–65.

_____. *Let My People Grow: Ministry and Leadership in the Church*. London: Hodder and Stoughton, 1977.

_____. *That We May Be One*. London: Hodder and Stoughton, 1983.

_____. *Three Sisters: A Provocative Look at Evangelicals, Charismatics and Catholic Charismatics and Their Relationship to One Another*. Wheaton, IL: Tyndale, 1979. British edition: *This Is the Day: A Fresh Look at Christian Unity*. London: Hodder and Stoughton, 1979.

_____. *Walking in the Spirit*. Minneapolis: Bethany, 1981.

Harrell, D. E. *All Things Are Possible: The Healing and Charismatic Revivals in Modern America*. Bloomington, IN: Indiana University Press, 1975.

Hart, L. D. "A Critique of American Pentecostal Theology." Ph.D. diss., Southern Baptist Theological Seminary, Louisville, 1978.

_____. "I am a Charismatic and . . . Tough questions for Charismatics and Other Evangelicals." *Christianity Today* 28 (April 20, 1984): 51.

_____. "Problems of Authority in Pentecostalism." *RevExp* 75 (1978): 249–66.

Haughey, J. C., ed. *Theological Reflections on the Charismatic Renewal: Proceedings of the Chicago Conference October 1–2, 1976.* Ann Arbor: Servant, 1978.

Heath, R. W. "Persuasive Patterns and Strategies in the Neo-Pentecostal Movement." Ph.D. diss., University of Oklahoma, 1973.

Heitmann, C., and Mühlen, H., eds. *Erfahrung und Theologie des Heiligen Geistes.* München: Kösel, 1974.

Hendrix, S. H. "Charismatic Renewal: Old Wine in New Skins." *Currents in Theology and Mission* 4 (1977): 158–66.

_____. "Reply to Jungkuntz." *Currents in Theology and Mission* 5 (1, 1978): 58–60.

Heron, A. *The Holy Spirit. The Holy Spirit in the Bible in the History of Christian Thought and in Recent Theology.* London: Marshall, Morgan and Scott, 1983. Foundations for Faith series: An Introduction to Christian Doctrine.

Hesselink, J. "The Charismatic Movement in the Reformed Tradition." *Reformed Review* 28 (3, 1975): 147–56.

Hocken, P. "Catholic Pentecostalism: Some Key Questions I." *HeyJ* 15 (2, 1974): 131–43.

_____. "Catholic Pentecostalism: Some Key Questions II." *HeyJ* 15 (3, 1974): 271–84.

_____. "The Charismatic Experience." *The Way* 18 (1978): 44–55.

_____. "The Charismatic Movement and the Church. A Response to Heribert Muhlen *(sic)*." *Theological Renewal* 13 (Oct., 1979): 22–29.

_____. "Charismatic Renewal, the Churches and Unity." *One in Christ* 15 (1979): 310–21.

_____. "Charismatics and Mystics." *Theological Renewal* 1 (Oct./Nov., 1975): 12–17.

_____. "Jesus Christ and the Gifts of the Spirit." *Pneuma. Journal of the Society for Pentecostal Studies* 5 (1, 1983): 1–16.

_____. "The Pentecostal-Charismatic Movement as Revival and Renewal (Catholic Church)." *Pneuma. Journal of the Society for Pentecostal Studies* 3 (1, 1981): 31–47.

_____. "Pentecostals on Paper I: Character and History." *The Clergy Review* 59 (11, 1974): 750–67.

_____. "Pentecostals on Paper II: Baptism in the Spirit and Speaking in Tongues." *The Clergy Review* 60 (3, 1975): 161–83.

_____. "Pentecostals on Paper III: The Gifts of the Spirit and Distinctive Catholic Features." *The Clergy Review* 60 (6, 1975): 344–68.

_____. "The Significance and Potential of Pentecostalism." In *New Heaven? New Earth? An Encounter with Pentecostalism,* by S. Tugwell, P. Hocken, G. Every, and J. O. Mills. Springfield, IL: Templegate, 1977.

_____. "The Spirit and Charismatic Prayer." *Life and Worship* 43 (1974): 1–10.

_____. "Wiser than Human Wisdom." *Theology, News and Notes* (March, 1984): 8–12,34.

_____. *You He Made Alive: A Total Christian View of Prayer, Communal, Individual and with Special Reference to the Work of the Spirit in Prayer Groups.* London: Darton, Longman and Todd, 1974.

Hoek, A. L. "Bericht über die reformierte Vuur-bewegung in Holland." In *Kirche und Charisma. Die Gaben des Heiligen Geistes in Neuen Testament, in der Kirchengeschichte und in der Gegenwart.* Edited by R. F. Edel. Marburg an der Lahn: Edel, 1966.

Hoekema, A. A. *Holy Spirit Baptism.* Grand Rapids: Eerdmans, 1972.

Hoffman, B. R. *Luther and the Mystics: A Re-examination of Luther's Spiritual Experience and his Relationship to the Mystics.* Minneapolis: Augsburg, 1976.

Hollenweger, W. J. "Charismatische und pfingstlerische Bewegungen als Frage an die Kirchen heute." In *Wiederentdeckung des Heiligen Geistes. Der Heilige Geist in der charismatischen Erfahrung und theologischen Reflexion.* Edited by M. Lienhard and H. Meyer. Frankfurt: Otto Lembeck, 1974. Oekumenische Perspektiven 6.

————. "Creator Spiritus. The Challenge of Pentecostal Experience to Pentecostal Theology." *Theology* 81 (679, 1978): 32–40.

————. "Kirche und Charisma." In *Kirche und Charisma. Die Gaben des Heiligen Geistes in Neuen Testament, in der Kirchengeschichte und in der Gegenwart.* Edited by R. F. Edel. Marburg an der Lahn: Edel, 1966.

————. *New Wine in Old Wineskins: Protestant and Catholic Neo-Pentecostalism.* Gloucester, England: Fellowship, 1973.

————. *Pentecost between Black and White. Five Case Studies on Pentecost and Politics.* Belfast: Christian Journals, 1974.

————. *The Pentecostals.* London: SCM, 1972.

————. *Die Pfingstkirchen. Selbstdarstellungen, Dokumente, Kommentare.* Stuttgart: Evangelisches Verlagswerk, 1971. Die Kirchen der Welt. Reihe A Band VII.

————. Preface: "Towards a Charismatic Theology." In *New Heaven? New Earth? An Encounter with Pentecostalism,* by S. Tugwell, P. Hocken, G. Every, and J. O. Mills. Springfield, IL: Templegate, 1977.

————. "'Touching' and 'Thinking' the Spirit: Some Aspects of European Charismatics." In *Perspectives on the New Pentecostalism.* Edited by R. P. Spittler. Grand Rapids: Baker, 1976.

Hummel, C. E. *Fire in the Fireplace.* Downers Grove, IL: Inter-Varsity, 1978.

Hunter, H. D. *Spirit-Baptism: A Pentecostal Alternative.* Lanham, MD: University Press of America, 1983.

Hutchenson, R. G. *Mainline Churches and the Evangelicals. A Challenging Crisis?* Atlanta: John Knox, 1981.

Jensen, P. F. "Calvin, Charismatics and Miracles." *EvQ* 51 (3, 1979): 131–44.

Jensen, R. A. *Touched by the Spirit: One Man's Struggle to Understand his Experience of the Holy Spirit.* Minneapolis: Augsburg, 1975.

Johnston, R. K. "Pentecostalism and Theological Hermeneutics: Evangelical Options." *Pneuma. Journal of the Society for Pentecostal Studies* 6 (1, 1984): 51–66.

Jones, C. E. *A Guide to the Study of the Holiness Movement.* Metuchen, NJ: Scarecrow Press, 1974. ATLA bibliography series no. 1.

Jones, J. W. "The Charismatic Renewal after Kansas City." *Sojourners* 6 (1977): 11–13.

————. *Filled with New Wine: The Charismatic Renewal of the Church.* New York: Harper and Row, 1974.

————. *The Spirit and the World.* New York: Hawthorn, 1975.

Jonker, W. J. *Die Gees van Christus.* Pretoria: NG Kerkboekhandel, 1981. Wegwysers in die dogmatiek series.

————. "Kritiese verwantskap? Opmerkings oor die verhouding van die pneumatologie van Calvyn tot dié van die Anabaptisme." In *Calvyn aktueel? 'n Bundel opstelle onder.* Edited by E. Brown. Cape Town: NG Kerk-Uitgewers, 1982.

Jorstad, E., ed. *The Holy Spirit in Today's Church: A Handbook on the New Pentecostalism.* Nashville: Abingdon, 1973.

————. "Pro and Con on the Charismatic Movement." Review article. *Christianity Today* 23 (Dec. 15, 1978): 34–35.

Judisch, D. *An Evaluation of Claims to the Charismatic Gifts.* Grand Rapids: Baker, 1978.

Jungkuntz, T. R. *Confirmation and the Charismata.* Lanham, MD: University Press of America, 1983.

_____. "A Response." (to *The Lutheran Church and the Charismatic Movement: Guide-lines for Congregations and Pastors: A Report of the Commission on Theology and Church Relations of the Lutheran Church – Missouri Synod April 1977*). In *The Cresset: Occasional Paper II*. Valparaiso, IN: Valparaiso University Press, 1977.

_____. "A Response to Scott Hendrix's 'Charismatic Renewal: Old Wine in New Skins.'" *Currents in Theology and Mission* 5 (1, 1978): 54–57.

Kantzer, K. S. "The Charismatics Among Us. The Christianity Today Gallup Poll Identifies Who they are and What they Believe." *Christianity Today* (Feb. 22, 1980): 25–29.

Kelsey, M. "Courage, Unity and Theology." In *Perspectives on the New Pentecostalism*. Edited by R. P. Spittler. Grand Rapids: Baker, 1976.

_____. *Discernment: A Study in Ecstasy and Evil*. New York: Paulist, 1978.

_____. *Encounter with God: A Theology of Christian Experience*. Minneapolis: Bethany, 1972.

_____. *Healing and Christianity: In Ancient Thought and Modern Times*. New York: Harper and Row, 1973.

_____. *The Other Side of Silence: A Guide to Christian Meditation*. New York: Paulist, 1976.

_____. *Tongue Speaking: An Experiment in Spiritual Experience*. New York: Doubleday, 1964.

Knox, R. A. *Enthusiasm: A Chapter in the History of Religion with Special Reference to the XVII and XVIII Centuries*. London: Oxford University Press, 1950.

König, A. *Die Doop as kinderdoop én grootdoop*. Pretoria: NGKB, 1985.

Koenig, J. "Documenting the Charismatics." *Word and World: Theology for Christian Ministry* 1 (1981): 287–89.

Kopfermann, W. *Charismatische Gemeinde-Erneuerung. Eine Zwischenbilanz*. Metzingen: Heinzelmann, 1981. Charisma und Kirche series 7/8.

Kovalevski, E. "Gnadengaben in der Kirche heute. Die Charismen in der orthodoxen Kirche heute." In *Kirche und Charisma. Die Gaben des Heiligen Geistes in Neuen Testament, in der Kirchengeschichte und in der Gegenwart*. Edited by R. F. Edel. Marburg an der Lahn: Edel, 1966.

_____. "Gnadengaben in der Kirchengeschichte. Die Charismen in der Geschichte der orthodoxen Kirche." In *Kirche und Charisma. Die Gaben des Heiligen Geistes in Neuen Testament, in der Kirchengeschichte und in der Gegenwart*. Edited by R. F. Edel. Marburg an der Lahn: Edel, 1966.

Kruger, M. A. "'n Blywende teologiese onderstroming onder gereformeerdes." *In die Skriflig* 15 (60, 1981): 43–50.

Krust, C. "Geistestaufe." In *Die Pfingstkirchen. Selbstdarstellungen, Dokumente, Kommentare*. Edited by W. Hollenweger. Stuttgart: Evangelisches Verlagswerk, 1971.

Kuen, A. *Die charismatische Bewegung. Versuch einer Beurteilung*. Wuppertal: Brockhaus, 1976.

Küng, H., and Moltmann, J., eds. *Conflicts about the Holy Spirit*. New York: Seabury, 1979. Concilium. Religion in the Seventies.

Kydd, R. *Charismatic Gifts in the Early Church*. Peabody, MA: Hendrickson, 1984.

_____. "Pentecostals, Charismatics and the Canadian Denominations." *Église et Theologie* 13 (1982): 211–31.

Lauréntin, R. *Catholic Pentecostalism*. New York: Doubleday, 1977. Original edition: *Pentecôtisme chez les Catholiques: Risques et Avenir*. Editions Beauchesne, 1974.

_____. "The Charismatic Movement. Prophetic Renewal or Neo-Conservatism?" In *Neo-Conservatism: Social and Religious Phenomenon*. Edited by G. Baum. New York: Seabury, 1981. Concilium. Religion in the Eighties.

Lederle, H. I. "Be Filled with the Spirit of Love: An Update on the State of the Charismatic Renewal and Some Reflections on its Central Experiential Teaching." *Theologia Evangelica* 15 (3, 1982): 33–48.

———. "The Charismatic Movement." Study guide for the B.Th. Honors paper STH 408–Y. Pretoria, UNISA, 1983.

———. "First Response to Paper 6." ("Samuel McCay: Celebrating Renewal and Appropriation of Baptism by Immersion.") In *Infant Baptism? The Arguments For and Against. Proceedings of a Theological Congress Held at UNISA 3–5 October 1983.* Edited by A. König, H. I. Lederle, and F. P. Möller. Roodepoort: CUM, 1984.

———. "Fruitio Dei or Getting Blessed right out of your Socks!" (A somewhat personal review article on the second renewal conference at Milner Park, Johannesburg, January 1–6, 1980.) *Theologia Evangelica* 14 (1, 1981): 23–31.

———. "Wat is wonderwerke? 'n Sistematies-teologiese besinning oor wonder en werklikheid." In *Dit is Ek, die Here, wat julle gesond maak.* Edited by H. Lederle and J. Theron. Pretoria: Christelike Lektuursentrum, 1985.

Lindberg, C. *The Third Reformation? Charismatic Movements and the Lutheran Tradition.* Macon, GA: Mercer University Press, 1983.

Lloyd-Jones, D. M. *God's Ultimate Purpose: An Exposition of Ephesians 1:1–23.* Edinburgh: Banner of Truth, 1978.

Logan, J. C. "Controversial Aspects of the Movement." In *The Charismatic Movement.* Edited by M. P. Hamilton. Grand Rapids: Eerdmans, 1975.

Lovelace, R. F. *Dynamics of Spiritual Life: An Evangelical Theology of Renewal.* Downers Grove, IL: Inter-Varsity, 1979.

MacArthur, J. F. *The Charismatics: A Doctrinal Perspective.* Grand Rapids: Zondervan, 1978.

Mallone, G., ed. *Those Controversial Gifts: Prophecy, Dreams, Visions, Tongues, Interpretation, Healing.* Downers Grove, IL: Inter-Varsity, 1983.

———. "Tidy Doctrine and Truncated Experience." In *Those Controversial Gifts: Prophecy, Dreams, Visions, Tongues, Interpretation, Healing.* Edited by G. Mallone. Downers Grove, IL: Inter-Varsity, 1983.

———. "Tongues: The Biggest Christian Friendship and Oneness Buster of the Century." In *Those Controversial Gifts: Prophecy, Dreams, Visions, Tongues, Interpretation, Healing.* Edited by G. Mallone. Downers Grove, IL: Inter-Varsity, 1983.

Martin, D., and Mullen, P. *Strange Gifts? A Guide to Charismatic Renewal.* Oxford: Blackwell, 1984.

Martin. G. *An Introduction to the Catholic Charismatic Renewal.* Ann Arbor: Servant, 1975.

———. *Scripture and the Charismatic Renewal. Proceedings of the Milwaukee Symposium December 1–3, 1978.* Ann Arbor: Servant, 1979.

Martin, R. "Baptism in the Holy Spirit: Pastoral Implications." In *The Holy Spirit and Power: The Catholic Charismatic Renewal.* Edited by K. McDonnell. New York: Doubleday, 1975.

———. "God is Restoring his People." *New Covenant* 4 (3, 1974): 3–6.

———. *The Spirit and the Congregation: Studies in 1 Corinthians 12–15.* Grand Rapids: Eerdmans, 1984.

Mascarenhas, F. "At the Heart of the Church." In *At the Heart of the Church. International Leaders Conference Proceedings.* Rome: ICCRO, 1984.

Mason, A. J. *The Relation of Confirmation to Baptism as Taught in Holy Scripture and the Fathers.* London: Longmans, Green & Co., 1891.

McCay, S. J. D. "Celebrating Renewal and Appropriation of Baptism by Immersion (Paper 6)." In *Infant Baptism? The Arguments for and against. Proceedings of a Theological Congress held at UNISA 3–5 October 1983.* Edited by A. König, H. I. Lederle, and F. P. Möller. Roodepoort, South Africa: CUM, 1984.

_____. "Charismatic Renewal and Requests for a Second Baptism." *Theological Renewal* 8 (Feb./Mar., 1978): 13–21.

_____. "Celebrating Renewal by Appropriating Baptism." M.Th. thesis, University of South Africa, Pretoria, 1986.

McDonnell, K. "Baptism in the Holy Spirit as an Ecumenical Problem." In *The Baptism in the Holy Spirit as an Ecumenical Problem*. Edited by K. McDonnell and A. Bittlinger. Notre Dame: Charismatic Renewal Services, 1972.

_____. "Catholic Charismatic Renewal: Reassessment and Critique." *Religion in Life* 44 (1975): 138–54.

_____. "Catholic Charismatics. The Rediscovery of a Hunger for God and the Sense of his Presence." *Commonweal* 96 (1972): 207–11.

_____. "Catholic Pentecostalism: Problems in Evaluation." *Dialog* 9 (1970): 35–54.

_____. *Charismatic Renewal and the Churches*. New York: Seabury, 1976.

_____. *The Charismatic Renewal and Ecumenism*. New York: Paulist, 1978.

_____. "Die charismatische Bewegung in der katholischen Kirche." In *Wiederentdeckung des Heiligen Geistes. Der Heilige Geist in der charismatische Erfahrung und theologischen Reflexion*. Edited by M. Lienhard and H. Meyer. Frankfurt: Otto Lembeck, 1974. Oekumenische Perspektiven 6.

_____. "Classical Pentecostal/Roman Catholic Dialogue: Hopes and Possibilities." In *Perspectives on the New Pentecostalism*. Edited by R. P. Spittler. Grand Rapids: Baker, 1976.

_____. "The Determinative Doctrine of the Holy Spirit." *Theology Today* 30 (2, 1982): 142–61.

_____. "The Experience of the Holy Spirit in the Catholic Charismatic Renewal." In *Conflicts about the Holy Spirit*. Edited by H. Küng and J. Moltmann. New York: Seabury, 1979. Concilium. Religion in the Seventies.

_____. "The Experiential and the Social: New Models from the Pentecostal/Roman Catholic Dialogue." *One in Christ* 9 (1, 1973): 43–58.

_____. "The Function of Tongues in Pentecostalism." *One in Christ* 19 (4, 1983): 332–54.

_____. "The Holy Spirit and Christian Initiation." In *The Holy Spirit and Power: The Catholic Charismatic Renewal*. Edited by K. McDonnell. New York: Doubleday, 1975.

_____, ed. *The Holy Spirit and Power: The Catholic Charismatic Renewal*. New York: Doubleday, 1975.

_____. "If One has Jesus and the Gospel does one need the Church? Ecclesiological Reflections on the Catholic Charismatic Renewal." *One in Christ* 11 (2, 1975): 106–20.

_____. "Introduction. Parameters, Patterns, and the Atypical." In *Presence, Power, Praise: Documents on the Charismatic Renewal*. Vol 1. Collegeville, MN: Liturgical Press, 1980.

_____. "Katholische Charismatiker." In *Der Aufbruch. Charismatische Erneuerung in der katholischen Kirche*. Edited by S. Grossmann. Kassel: Rolf Kühne, n.d. Translation of "Catholic Charismatics" in *Commonweal* 96 (1972): 207–11.

_____. "Pentecostal Culture: Protestant and Catholic." *One in Christ* 7 (4, 1971): 310–18.

_____, ed. *Presence, Power, Praise: Documents on the Charismatic Renewal*. 3 vols. Collegeville, MN: Liturgical Press, 1980.

_____. "The Relationship of the Charismatic Renewal to the Established Denominations." *Dialog: A Journal of Theology* 13 (3, 1974): 223–29.

_____. "Towards a Critique of the Churches and the Charismatic Renewal." *One in Christ* 16 (4, 1980): 329–37.

McGuire, K. H. "People Prayer and Promise. An Anthropological Analysis of a Catholic Charismatic Covenant Community." Ph.D. diss., Ohio State University, 1976.

McNamee, J. J. "The Role of the Spirit in Pentecostalism. A Comparative Study." Ph.D. diss., Eberhard Karls University, Tübingen, 1974.

Mederlet, P. E. "Die Charismen in der römisch-katholischen Kirche heute." In *Kirche und Charisma. Die Gaben des Heiligen Geistes in Neuen Testament, in der Kirchengeschichte und in der Gegenwart.* Edited by R. F. Edel. Marburg an der Lahn: Edel, 1966.

Menzies, W. M. "The Non-Wesleyan Origins of the Pentecostal Movement." In *Aspects of Pentecostal-Charismatic Origins.* Edited by V. Synan. Plainfield, NJ: Logos, 1975.

Michell, J. *Church Ablaze: The Hatfield Baptist Church Story.* Basingstoke, England: Marshalls, 1985.

Mills, W. E., ed. *Speaking in Tongues: A Classified Bibliography.* Franklin Springs, GA: SPS, 1974.

_____ , ed. *Speaking in Tongues: Let's Talk about It.* Waco, TX: Word Books, 1973.

Möller, F. P. *Die diskussie oor die charismata soos wat dit in die Pinksterbeweging geleer en beoefen word.* Braamfontein, South Africa: Evangelie Uitgewers, 1975.

_____. "Faith and Experience. Roman Catholic-Pentecostal Dialogue: Papers from the Rome Meeting, October 1977." *One in Christ* 19 (4, 1983): 306–15.

Molenaar, D. G. *De Doop met de Heilige Geest.* Kampen: Kok, 1963.

Montague, G. T., SM. "Baptism in the Spirit and Speaking in Tongues: A Biblical Appraisal." *Theology Digest* 21 (4, 1973): 342–60, 92.

_____. "Hermeneutics and the Teaching of Scripture." In *Scripture and the Charismatic Renewal. Proceedings of the Milwaukee Symposium December 1–3, 1978.* Edited by G. Martin. Ann Arbor: Servant, 1979.

_____. *The Holy Spirit: Growth of a Biblical Tradition.* New York: Paulist, 1976.

_____. *Riding the Wind. Learning the Ways of the Spirit.* Ann Arbor: Servant, 1977. First published 1974.

_____. *The Spirit and his Gifts: The Biblical Background of Spirit-Baptism, Tongue-Speaking, and Prophecy.* New York: Paulist, 1974.

Moonie, P. M. "The Significance of Neo-Pentecostalism for the Renewal and Unity of the Church in the United States." Ph.D. diss., Boston University, 1974.

Moore, J. "The Catholic Pentecostal Movement." *A Sociological Yearbook of Religion in Britain* 6 (1973): 73–90.

Morris, J. H. "The Charismatic Movement: An Orthodox Evaluation." *GOTR* 28 (1983): 103–34.

Moule, C. F. D. *The Holy Spirit.* Grand Rapids: Eerdmans, 1979. Original British edition Oxford: Mowbray, 1978.

Mühlen, H. "The Charismatic Renewal as Experience." In *The Holy Spirit and Power: The Catholic Charismatic Renewal.* Edited by K. McDonnell. New York: Doubleday, 1975.

_____. *A Charismatic Theology: Initiation in the Spirit.* London: Burns and Oats, 1978. *Einübung in die christliche Grunderfahrung. Erster Teil: Lehre und Zuspruch, Zweiter Teil: Gebet und Erwartung.* Unter mitarbeit von Arnold Bittlinger, Erhard Griese und Manfred Kiessig. Mainz: Matthias Grünewald, 1976. Topos-Taschenbücher Bd 40, 49.

_____. "Charismatisches und sakramentales Verständnis der Kirche. Dogmatische Aspekte der charismatischen Erneuerung." *Catholica* 28 (3, 1974): 169–87.

_____. "A Church in Movement–Not a Movement in the Church." *Theological Renewal* 9 (June/July, 1978): 15–21.

_____. *Dokumente zur Erneuerung der Kirchen.* Mainz: Matthias Grünewald, 1982.

_____ , ed. *Erfahrungen mit dem Heiligen Geist. Zeugnisse und Berichte.* Mainz: Matthias Grünewald, 1979. Topos-Taschenbücher Bd 90.

_____. "Die Geisterfahrung als Erneuerung der Kirche." In *Theologie des Geistes.* Edited by O. A. Dilschneider. Gütersloh: Gerd Mohn, 1980.

_____. "Geisterfahrung und Oekumene. Theologische Aspekte." *Erneuerung in Kirche und Gesellschaft* 7 (1980): 27–32.

_____. "Gemeinde-erneuerung und überkonfessioneller 'charismatischer Aufbruch.'" *Erneuerung in Kirche und Gesellschaft* 15 (1983): 41–46.

_____. "Die katholisch-charismatische Gemeinde-Erneuerung." *Stimmen der Zeit* 193 (12, 1975): 801–12.

_____. "Leitlinien der Gemeinde-erneuerung." *Erneuerung in Kirche und Gesellschaft* 1 (1977): 2–7.

_____. "Mysterium-Mystik-Charismatik." *Geist und Leben* 47 (1974): 247–56.

_____. "Neue Gestalt des Christseins." *Erneuerung in Kirche und Gesellschaft* 10 (1981): 46–53.

Nee, W. *The Release of the Spirit*. Bromley, Kent: Send the Light, 1965.

Nichol, J. T. *Pentecostalism*. New York: Harper and Row, 1966.

Niebuhr, H. R. *Christ and Culture*. New York: Harper and Row, 1951.

O'Connor, E. D., CSC. "The Hidden Roots of the Charismatic Renewal in the Catholic Church." In *Aspects of Pentecostal-Charismatic Origins*. Edited by V. Synan. Plainfield, NJ: Logos, 1975.

_____. "The Holy Spirit, Christian Love, and Mysticism." In *Perspectives on Charismatic Renewal*. Edited by E. D. O'Connor. Notre Dame: University of Notre Dame Press, 1975.

_____. "The Literature of the Catholic Charismatic Renewal 1967–1975." In *Perspectives on Charismatic Renewal*. Edited by E. D. O'Connor. Notre Dame: University of Notre Dame Press, 1975.

_____. *Pentecost in the Modern World*. Notre Dame: Ave Maria, 1972.

_____. *The Pentecostal Movement in the Catholic Church*. Notre Dame: Ave Maria, 1971.

_____, ed. *Perspectives on Charismatic Renewal*. Notre Dame: University of Notre Dame Press, 1975.

_____. "When the Cloud of Glory Dissipates." *New Catholic World* 217 (1301, 1974): 271–75.

Olivier, D. F. "The Baptism with the Holy Spirit: An Exposition, Comparison and Evaluation of the Subsequent and Synchronous Concepts of the Baptism with the Holy Spirit with Reference to the Relation Christ-Spirit as Foundation of Man's Experience of God." pre-doctoral thesis, Free University of Amsterdam, 1980.

Opsahl, P. D., ed. *The Holy Spirit in the Life of the Church, from Biblical Times to the Present*. Minneapolis: Augsburg, 1978.

Packer, J. I. "Charismatic Renewal: Pointing to a Person and a Power." *Christianity Today* 24 (March 7, 1980): 16–20.

_____. *Keep in Step with the Spirit*. Old Tappan, NJ: Revell, 1984.

_____. "Theological Reflections on the Charismatic Movement, Part 1." *The Churchman* 94 (1, 1980): 7–25.

_____. "Theological Reflections on the Charismatic Movement, Part 2." *The Churchman* 94 (2, 1980): 108–25.

Parratt, J. K. "An Early Baptist on the Laying on of Hands." *Baptist Quarterly* 21 (7, 1966): 325–27.

_____. "The Holy Spirit and Baptism. Part I: The Gospel and the Acts of the Apostles." *ExpTim* (May, 1971): 231–35.

_____. "The Holy Spirit and Baptism. Part II: The Pauline Evidence." *ExpTim* (June, 1971): 266–71.

_____. "The Laying on of Hands in the New Testament: Contributions and Comments." *ExpTim* (April, 1969): 151–52, 210–14.

_____. "The Seal of the Holy Spirit in the New Testament Teaching." Ph.D. diss., University of London, 1965.

_____. "The Witness of the Holy Spirit: Calvin, the Puritans and St. Paul." *EvQ* (July, 1969): 161–68.

Parry, D. OSB. *This Promise is for You: Spiritual Renewal and the Charismatic Movement.* London: Darton, Longman and Todd, 1977.

Peckam, C. N. "An Investigation into Some of the Terms and Texts Used by Exponents of the 'Deeper Life' Teaching." M.Th. thesis, University of South Africa: Pretoria, 1984.

Piepkorn, A. C. *Profiles in Belief. The Religious Bodies of the United States and Canada. Vol. 3. Holiness and Pentecostal.* New York: Harper and Row, 1979.

Pinnock, C. H. "Charismatic Renewal for the Radical Church." *Post American* 4 (1975): 16–21.

_____. "An Evangelical Theology of the Charismatic Renewal." *Theological Renewal* 7 (Oct./Nov., 1977): 28–35.

_____. "The New Pentecostalism: Reflections of an Evangelical Observer." In *Perspectives on the New Pentecostalism.* Edited by R. P. Spittler. Grand Rapids: Baker, 1976.

_____. "The New Pentecostalism: Reflections by a Well-Wisher." *Christianity Today* 17 (Sept. 14, 1973): 6–10.

_____. "Opening the Church to the Charismatic Dimension." *Christianity Today* 25 (June 12, 1981): 16.

Plowman, E. E. "Mission to Orthodoxy: The 'Full' Gospel." *Christianity Today* 18 (April 26, 1974): 44–45.

Poloma, M. M. *The Charismatic Movement: Is there a New Pentecost?* Boston: Twayne, 1982.

Purkiser, W. T. *The Gifts of the Spirit.* Kansas City, MO: Beacon Hill, 1975.

Pursey, B. A. "Charismatic Power and Social Relevance: The Way of Renewed Discipleship." Unpublished article.

_____. *The Gifts of the Holy Spirit.* Oklahoma City: Presbyterian and Reformed Renewal Ministries International, 1984.

_____. "Toward an Understanding of Baptism in the Spirit." Unpublished article.

Quebedeaux, R. *The New Charismatics. The Origins, Development and Significance of Neo-Pentecostalism.* New York: Doubleday, 1976.

_____. *The New Charismatics II. How a Christian Renewal Movement Became Part of the American Religious Mainstream.* Rev. edition. New York: Harper and Row, 1983.

_____. "The Old Pentecostalism and the New Pentecostalism." *Theology, News and Notes* (March, 1974): 6–8,23.

Ranaghan, K., and Ranaghan, D. *Catholic Pentecostals Today.* South Bend: Charismatic Renewal Services, 1983.

Rea, J., ed. *The Layman's Commentary on the Holy Spirit.* Rev. edition. Plainfield, NJ: Logos, 1974.

Reed, D. "Aspects of the Origins of Oneness Pentecostalism." In *Aspects of Pentecostal-Charismatic Origins.* Edited by V. Synan. Plainfield, NJ: Logos, 1975.

Ridderbos, H. *Paulus. Ontwerp van zijn theologie.* Kok: Kampen, 1966. English translation: *Paul: An Outline of His Theology.* Grand Rapids: Eerdmans, 1975.

Robeck, C. M. "The Charismatic Renewal of the Church." *Theology, News and Notes* 2 (March, 1983): 33–34.

_____. *Pentecostal/Charismatic Literature: A Survey of the Last Ten Years.* Dickson, Australia: Zadok Centre, 1984. Previously "The Decade (1973–1982) in Pentecostal-Charismatic Literature: A Bibliographic Essay." *Theology, News and Notes* 30 (1, 1983): 24–29.

Roberts, O. *The Baptism with the Holy Spirit and the Value of Speaking in Tongues Today.* Tulsa: Oral Roberts Evangelistic Association, 1964.

Robinson, W. A. *I Once Spoke in Tongues*. Wheaton, IL: Tyndale, 1973.

Rondelle, H. K. La. *Perfection and Perfectionism: A Dogmatic-Ethical Study of Biblical Perfection and Phenomenal Perfection*. Kampen: Kok, 1971.

Runia, K. "De doop met de Heilige Geest." *Rondom het Woord* 16 (1, 1974): 37–55.

_____. "The 'Gifts of the Spirit.'" *Reformed Theological Review* 29 (1976): 82–94.

Russell, T. *Why Some Catholics Join Evangelical Protestant Churches*. Pretoria: South African Catholic Bishops Conference, n.d. Series: Pastoral Action No. 34.

Samarin, W. J. *Tongues of Men and Angels: The Religious Language of Pentecostalism*. New York: Macmillan, 1972.

Sandidge, J. L. "Roman Catholic/Pentecostal Dialogue. A Contribution to Christian Unity." In *Toward a Pentecostal/Charismatic Theology: "Baptism in the Holy Spirit."* Society for Pentecostal Studies's Fourteenth Annual Meeting, November 15–17, 1984, at Gordon-Conwell Theological Seminary.

Schep, J. A. *Baptism in the Spirit according to Scripture*. Plainfield, NJ: Logos, 1972. First edition 1969. Dutch original: *Geestesdoop en tongentaal. Het standpunt van de Calvinistische traditie getoetst aan de Heilige Schrift*. Franeker: T. Wever, n.d.

Schmieder, L. *Geisttaufe. Ein Beitrag zur neueren Glaubensgeschichte*. Paderborn: Schöningh, 1982.

Schoonenberg, P. "Het doopsel met Heilige Geest." In *Leven uit de geest. Theologische peilingen aangeboden aan Edward Schillebeeckx*. Hilversum: Gooi en Sticht, 1975. English translation "Baptism with the Holy Spirit." In *Experience of the Spirit*. Edited by P. Huizing and W. Bassett. New York: Seabury, 1974. Concilium. Religion in the Seventies.

Schreck, A. *Catholic and Christian. An Explanation of Commonly Misunderstood Catholic Beliefs*. Ann Arbor: Servant, 1984.

_____. "Ronald Knox's Theory of Enthusiasm and its Application to the Catholic Charismatic Renewal." Ph.D. diss., University of St. Michael's College, Toronto, 1979.

Schrotenboer, P. G., ed. *The Holy Spirit Down to Earth*. Grand Rapids: Reformed Ecumenical Synod, 1977.

Schutz, C. *Einführung in die Pneumatologie*. Darmstadt: Wissenschaftliche Buchgesellschaft, 1984.

Schwarz, H. "Reflections on the Work of the Spirit outside the Church." *Neue Zeitschrift für Systematische Theologie* 23 (1981): 197–211.

Sherrill, J. L. *They Speak with Other Tongues*. New York: McGraw-Hill, 1964.

Smail, T. A. "1 Corinthians 12, 13 Revisited." *Theological Renewal* 9 (June/July, 1978): 2–6.

_____. *The Forgotten Father*. London: Hodder and Stoughton, 1980.

_____. *Reflected Glory. The Spirit in Christ and Christians*. London: Hodder and Stoughton, 1975.

Smith, T. L. "The Disinheritance of the Saints." Review article on *Vision of the Disinherited*, by R. M. Anderson. *RelSRev* 8 (1, 1982): 22–28.

Sneck, W. J. *Charismatic Spiritual Gifts: A Phenomenological Analysis*. Washington, D.C.: University Press of America, 1981.

Spittler, R. P. "Bat Mizvah for Azusa Street: Features, Fractures and Futures of a Renewal Movement Come of Age." *Theology, News and Notes* (March, 1983): 13–17, 35.

_____. "Competent Charismatic Theology." *Agora* 3 (3, 1980): 21–22. A review of D. L. Gelpi, *Experiencing God: A Theology of Human Emergence*.

_____ , ed. *Perspectives on the New Pentecostalism*. Grand Rapids: Baker, 1976.

257

_____. "Suggested Areas for Further Research in Pentecostal Studies." *Pneuma. Journal of the Society for Pentecostal Studies.* 5 (2, 1983): 39–56.

_____. "The Theological Opportunity lying before the Pentecostal Movement." In *Aspects of Pentecostal-Charismatic Origins.* Edited by V. Synan. Plainfield, NJ: Logos, 1975.

Stagg, F., Hinson, E. G., and Oates, W. E. *Glossolalia: Tongue Speaking in Biblical, Historical and Psychological Perspective.* Nashville: Abingdon, 1967.

Steiner, L. "Glaube und Heilung." In *Die Pfingstkirchen. Selbstdarstellungen, Dokumente, Kommentare.* Edited by W. Hollenweger. Stuttgart: Evangelisches Verlagswerk, 1971.

_____. "Die Pfingstbewegung und die anderen Kirchen." In *Die Pfingstkirchen. Selbstdarstellungen, Dokumente, Kommentare.* Edited by W. Hollenweger. Stuttgart: Evangelisches Verlagswerk, 1971.

Stendahl, K. "The New Pentecostalism: Reflections of an Ecumenical Observer." In *Perspectives on the New Pentecostalism.* Edited by R. P. Spittler. Grand Rapids: Baker, 1976.

Stephanou, E. A. "Charismata in the Early Church Fathers." *GOTR* 21 (1976): 125–46.

Stott, J. R. W. *The Baptism and Fullness of the Holy Spirit: An Explanation and Exhortation to Christians.* London: Inter-Varsity, 1964. Also Downers Grove: Inter-Varsity, 1964, and Leicester: Inter-Varsity, 1975.

Strachan, C. G. *The Pentecostal Theology of Edward Irving.* London: Darton, Longman and Todd, 1973.

_____. "Theological and Cultural Origins of the Nineteenth Century Pentecostal Movement." *Theological Renewal* 1 (Oct./Nov., 1975): 17–25.

Stronstad, R. *The Charismatic Theology of St. Luke.* Peabody, MA: Hendrickson, 1984.

Suenens, L. J. Cardinal. *Ecumenism and Charismatic Renewal: Theological and Pastoral Orientations.* Malines Document 2. Ann Arbor: Servant, 1978.

_____. *Essays on Renewal.* Ann Arbor: Servant, 1977.

_____. *A New Pentecost?* Glasgow: Collins, 1977. Original edition, *Une Nouvelle Pentecôte?* Desclée de Brouwer, 1974.

Sullivan, F. A. "'Baptism in the Holy Spirit': A Catholic Interpretation of the Pentecostal Experience." *Gregorianum* 55 (1, 1974): 49–68.

_____. *Charisms and Charismatic Renewal: A Biblical and Theological Study.* Dublin: Gill and Macmillan, 1982.

_____. "The Ecclesiological Context of the Charismatic Renewal." In *The Holy Spirit and Power: The Catholic Charismatic Renewal.* Edited by K. McDonnell. New York: Doubleday, 1975.

_____. "The Pentecostal Movement." *Gregorianum* 53 (2, 1972): 237–66.

_____. "Pentecostalism." English original of article in *Dictionnaire de Spiritualité.* Paris: Beauchesne, 1984. Tome XII, Première Partie: 1036–52.

_____. "The Role of Tradition." In *Theological Reflections on the Charismatic Renewal: Proceedings of the Chicago Conference October 1–2, 1976.* Edited by J. C. Haughey. Ann Arbor: Servant, 1978.

_____. "What is a Pentecostal Experience? A Reply to a Question Raised by Simon Tugwell." *Theological Renewal* 6 (1977): 21–25.

Sweetman, L. "The Gifts of the Spirit: A Study of Calvin's Comments on 1 Corinthians 12:8–10, 28; Romans 12:6–8; and Ephesians 4:11." In *Exploring the Heritage of John Calvin. Essays in Honor of John Bratt.* Edited by D. E. Holwerda. Grand Rapids: Baker, 1976.

Synan, V., ed. *Aspects of Pentecostal-Charismatic Origins.* Plainfield, NJ: Logos, 1975.

_____. *Charismatic Bridges.* Ann Arbor: Word of Life, 1974.

_____. "Discerning the Charismatic Renewal." *Theology Today* 39 (2, 1982): 187–93.

_____. *The Holiness-Pentecostal Movement in the United States*. Grand Rapids: Eerdmans, 1971.

_____. *In the Latter Days: The Outpouring of the Holy Spirit in the Twentieth Century*. Ann Arbor: Servant, 1984.

_____. "Reconciling the Charismatics." *Christianity Today* 20 (April 9, 1976): 46.

Taylor, J. V. *The Go-between God: The Holy Spirit and the Christian Mission*. London: SCM, 1972.

Thomas Aquinas. *Summa Theologiae*. London: Blackfriars, 1976. Vol. 7: *Father, Son and Holy Ghost*. Edited by T. C. O'Brien.

Thomas, R. L. "Tongues . . . will cease (1 Cor. 13)." *JETS* 17 (1974): 81–89.

Toit, B. A. du. "Die ontvangs van die Heilige Gees in Samaria. 'n Eksegetiese studie van Handelinge 8:14–17." D.Th. diss., University of South Africa, Pretoria, 1977.

Torrey, R. A. *The Holy Spirit, Who He Is and What He Does*. Westwood, NJ: Revell, 1927.

Tugwell, S. *Did You Receive the Spirit?* New York: Paulist, 1972.

_____. "Is there a 'Pentecostal Experience'? A Reply to Fr. Francis A. Sullivan, SJ." *Theological Renewal* 7 (Oct./Nov., 1977): 8–11.

_____. "Faith and Experience I: The Problems of Catholic Pentecostalism." *New Blackfriars* 59 (699, Aug., 1978): 359–69.

_____. "Faith and Experience II. Charisms and Ecclesiology." *New Blackfriars* 59 (700, Sept., 1978): 417–30.

_____. "Reflections on the Pentecostal Doctrine of 'Baptism in the Holy Spirit' I." *HeyJ* 13 (3, 1972): 268–81.

_____. "Reflections on the Pentecostal Doctrine of 'Baptism in the Holy Spirit' II." *HeyJ* 13 (4, 1972): 402–14.

_____. "So Who's a Pentecostal Now?" *New Blackfriars* 57 (1976): 415–20.

_____. "The Speech-Giving Spirit." In *New Heaven? New Earth? An Encounter with Pentecostalism*, by S. Tugwell, P. Hocken, G. Every, and J. O. Mills. Springfield, IL: Templegate, 1977.

Tugwell, S., Hocken, P., Every, G., and Mills, J. O. *New Heaven? New Earth? An Encounter with Pentecostalism*. Springfield, IL: Templegate, 1977.

Turner, G. A. "Evaluation of John R. W. Stott's and Frederick D. Bruner's Interpretations of the Baptism and Fullness of the Holy Spirit." *Wesleyan Theological Journal* 8 (1973): 45–51.

Tuttle, R. "The Charismatic Movement, its Historical Base and Wesleyan Framework." In *Guidelines: The United Methodist Church and the Charismatic Movement*. Nashville: Discipleship Resources, 1976.

_____. *Help Is on the Way: Overcoming Barriers to Spirit-Assisted Prayer*. Nashville: The Upper Room, 1983.

_____. *Wind and Flame: A Study of the Holy Spirit*. Nashville: United Methodist Publishing House [Graded Press], 1978.

Veenhof, J. "Charismata–Supernatural or Natural?" In *The Spirit-Empowering Presence*. Unpublished proceedings of a conference July 16–19, 1984, Institute for Christian Studies, Toronto.

_____. "The Charismatic Movement and its Impact upon us." *RES Theological Forum* 11 (1, 1983): 1–8, 22–26.

_____. *De Parakleet. Enige beschouwingen over de Parakleetbelofte in het Evangelie van Johannes en haar theologische betekenis*. Kampen: Kok, n.d. (after 1974).

_____. "Der Paraklet." In *Theologie des Geistes*. Edited by O. A. Dilschneider. Gütersloh: Gerd Mohn, 1980.

_____. "Pontifex Maximus." *Gereformeerd theologisch Tijdschrift* 78 (1978): 4–15.

Verryn, T. D. "Historical Perspectives on the Emphasis on the Holy Spirit." In *The Spirit in Biblical Perspective*. Edited by W. S. Vorster. Pretoria: University of South Africa, 1980.

Vorster, W. S., ed. *The Spirit in Biblical Perspective. Proceedings of the Fourth Symposium of the Institute for Theological Research (UNISA) held at the University of South Africa in Pretoria on the 10th and 11th September 1980*. Pretoria: University of South Africa, 1980.

Wacker, G. "Taking another look at the *Vision of the Disinherited*." Review article of the book by R. M. Anderson. *RelSRev* 8 (1, 1982): 15–22.

Wagner, C. P. "A Third Wave? Signs Point to a Rediscovery of the Spirit's Power by Christians Outside the Pentecostal and Charismatic Movements: An Interview with C. Peter Wagner." *Pastoral Renewal* 8 (1, 1983): 1–5.

Wallis, A. *The Radical Christian. "The Axe Is laid to the Root of the Tree."* Eastbourne, England: Kingsway, 1981.

_____. "Stay in or Come out? The Church in the House." *Renewal* 52 (Aug./Sept., 1974): 14–16.

Ward, H. S. "The Anti-Pentecostal Argument." In *Aspects of Pentecostal-Charismatic Origins*. Edited by V. Synan. Plainfield, NJ: Logos, 1975.

Ware, K. T. "Orthodoxy and the Charismatic Movement." *Eastern Churches Review* 5 (2, 1973): 182–86.

Warfield, B. B. *Counterfeit Miracles*. London: Banner of Truth, 1972. Reprint of 1918 edition.

Wassenaar, C. S. J. "Die trek-en stootfaktore wat 'n rol speel by die aansluiting van lidmate by die Hatfield Baptiste Kerk." M.A. thesis (Sociology), University of Pretoria, 1981.

Watson, D. C. K. *One in the Spirit*. London: Hodder and Stoughton, 1973.

_____. "Stay in or Come out? New Life from Inside." *Renewal* 52 August/September, 1974:10–13.

Wead, R. D. *Catholic Charismatics: Are They for Real?* Carol Stream, IL: Creation House, 1973. Original title: *Father McCarthy Smokes a Pipe and Speaks in Tongues*. Wisdom House, 1972.

Wesley, J., and Wesley, C. *Selected Prayers, Hymns, Journal Notes, Sermons, Letters and Treatises*. Edited by F. Whaling. Section III "A Plain Account of Christian Perfection." London: SPCK, 1981.

Wild, R. A. *The Post-Charismatic Experience. The New Wave of the Spirit*. Locust Valley, NY: Living Flame, 1984.

Williams, C. G. "Glossolalia as a Religious Phenomenon: Tongues at Corinth and Pentecost." *Religion* 5 (1975): 17–33.

_____. *Tongues of the Spirit. A Study of Pentecostal Glossolalia and Related Phenomena*. Cardiff: University of Wales Press, 1981.

Williams, G. H., and Waldvogel (Blumhofer), E. "A History of Speaking in Tongues and Related Gifts." In *The Charismatic Movement*. Edited by M. P. Hamilton. Grand Rapids: Eerdmans, 1975.

Williams, J. R. "The Charismatic Movement and Reformed Theology." Unpublished article.

_____. "The Coming of the Holy Spirit." *Theology, News and Notes* (March, 1974): 14–16.

_____. *The Era of the Spirit*. Plainfield, NJ: Logos, 1971.

_____. *The Gift of the Holy Spirit Today: The Greatest Reality of the Twentieth Century*. Plainfield, NJ: Logos, 1980.

_____. *The Pentecostal Reality*. Plainfield, NJ: Logos, 1972.

_____. "Pentecostal Theology: A Neo-Pentecostal Viewpoint." In *Perspectives on the New Pentecostalism*. Edited by R. P. Spittler. Grand Rapids: Baker, 1976.

_____. "Profile of the Charismatic Movement." *Christianity Today* 19 (Feb. 28, 1975): 9–13.

Wimber, J. *A Brief Sketch of Signs and Wonders through the Church Age*. Placentia, CA: Vineyard Christian Fellowship, n.d.

Wogen, N. L., ed. *Jesus, Where Are You Taking Us? Messages from the First International Lutheran Conference on the Holy Spirit*. Carol Stream, IL: Creation House, 1973.

Zablocki, B. D. *The Joyful Community. An Account of the Bruderhof, A Communal Movement now in its Third Generation*. Chicago: University of Chicago Press, 1971.

Ziemer, C. "In und neben der Kirche: charismatische Bewegung in den Kirchen der DDR." *Die Zeichen der Zeit* 6 (1979): 218–26.

Primary Sources of a Corporate and Institutional Origin

The Baptism in the Holy Spirit. Report of the Theological Commission to the 169th Regular Session of the Reformed Church in America June 1975. Oklahoma City: PCC, 1975.

"The Charismatic Movement in the Lutheran Church in America. A Pastoral Perspective." Appendix B. In *The Holy Spirit in the Life of the Church, from Biblical Times to the Present*. Edited by P. D. Opsahl. Minneapolis: Augsburg, 1974.

"Erneuerung der Kirche aus dem Geist Gottes. Zum gegenwärtigen charismatischen Aufbruch in der katholische Kirche der Bundesrepublik Deutschland und zu seiner Auswirkungen im Leben der Gemeinden. Im Mai 1981 von der Deutschen Bischofskonferenz zustimmend zur Kenntnis genommen." In *Erneuerung in Kirche und Gesellschaft* 10 (1981): 2–31.

"Gospel and Spirit: A Joint Statement." Appendix in *Those Controversial Gifts: Prophecy, Dreams, Visions, Tongues, Interpretation, Healing*. Edited by G. Mallone. Downers Grove, IL: Inter-Varsity, 1983.

Guidelines: The United Methodist Church and the Charismatic Movement. Nashville: Discipleship Resources, 1976.

The Life in the Spirit Seminars Team Manual. Catholic Edition. Ann Arbor: Servant, 1978.

The Life in the Spirit Seminars Team Manual. Rev. Edition. Ann Arbor: Servant, 1979.

The Lutheran Church and the Charismatic Movement: Guidelines for Congregations and Pastors: A Report of the Commission on Theology and Church Relations of the Lutheran Church-Missouri Synod April 1977. Appendix B in *The Holy Spirit in the Life of the Church, from Biblical Times to the Present*. Edited by P. D. Opsahl. Minneapolis: Augsburg, 1974.

"Malines Document I: Theological and Pastoral Orientations on the Catholic Charismatic Renewal." 1974. In *Presence Power Praise: Documents on the Charismatic Renewal*. Vol 3. Edited by K. McDonnell. Collegeville, MN: Liturgical Press, 1980.

"Malines Document II: Ecumenism and Charismatic Renewal. Theological and Pastoral Orientations." 1978. In *Presence Power Praise: Documents on the Charismatic Renewal*. Vol 3. Edited by K. McDonnell. Collegeville, MN: Liturgical Press, 1980.

"Malines Document III: Charismatic Renewal and Social Action: A Dialogue." 1979. In *Presence Power Praise: Documents on the Charismatic Renewal*. Vol 3. Edited by K. McDonnell. Collegeville, MN: Liturgical Press, 1980.

"The Person and Work of the Holy Spirit, with special Reference to 'The Baptism of the Holy Spirit.'" Presbyterian Church U.S. 1971 General Assembly. Oklahoma City: Presbyterian Charismatic Communion, n.d.

Present Truth. Special Issue: Justification by Faith and the Charismatic Movement. Articles: "Justification by Faith and the Baptism of the Spirit": 9–15; "Protestant Revivalism, Pentecostalism and the Drift back to Rome": 21–29. Authors not mentioned. Edited by R. D. Brinsmead. Fallbrook, CA, 1972.

Report of the Special Committee on the Work of the Holy Spirit to the 182nd General Assembly United Presbyterian Church in the U.S.A. New York: Office of the General Assembly, 1970.

Riglyne ten opsigte van die charismatiese beweging en die charismatiese gawes. Produced by the Algemene Kommissie Leer en Aktuele Sake Ned. Geref. Kerk. Pretoria: NGKB, 1979.

Toward a Pentecostal/Charismatic Theology: "Baptism in the Holy Spirit." Society for Pentecostal Studies's Fourteenth Annual Meeting, November 15–17, 1984, at Gordon-Conwell Theological Seminary.

INDEX OF NAMES